THE DARK THEATRE

The Dark Theatre returns to the bankrupted warehouse in Hope (Sufferance) Wharf in London's Docklands where Alan Read worked through the 1980s to identify a four-decade interregnum of 'cultural cruelty' wreaked by financialisation, austerity and communicative capitalism. Between the OPEC Oil Embargo and the first screening of *The Family* in 1974, to the United Nations report on UK poverty and the fire at Grenfell Tower in 2017, this volume becomes a book about loss.

In the harsh light of such loss is there an alternative to the market that profits from peddling 'well-being' and pushes prescriptions for 'self-help', any role for the arts that is not an apologia for injustice? What if culture were not the solution but the problem when it comes to the mitigation of grief? Creativity not the remedy but the symptom of a structural malaise called inequality? Read suggests performance is no longer a political panacea for the precarious subject but a loss adjustor measuring damages suffered, compensations due, wrongs that demand to be put right. These field notes from a fire sale are a call for angry arts of advocacy representing those abandoned as the detritus of cultural authority, second-order victims whose crime is to have appealed for help from those looking on, audiences of sorts.

The Dark Theatre is an indispensable text for activist communities wondering what theatre might have to do with their futures, students and scholars across Theatre and Performance Studies, Urban Studies, Cultural Studies, Political Economy and Social Ecology.

Alan Read is a writer and Professor of Theatre at King's College London.

THE DARK THEATRE

A Book About Loss

Alan Read

LONDON AND NEW YORK

First published 2020
by Routledge
2 Park Square, Milton Park, Abingdon, Oxon OX14 4RN

and by Routledge
52 Vanderbilt Avenue, New York, NY 10017

Routledge is an imprint of the Taylor & Francis Group, an informa business

© 2020 Alan Read

The right of Alan Read to be identified as author of this work has been asserted by him in accordance with sections 77 and 78 of the Copyright, Designs and Patents Act 1988.

All rights reserved. No part of this book may be reprinted or reproduced or utilised in any form or by any electronic, mechanical, or other means, now known or hereafter invented, including photocopying and recording, or in any information storage or retrieval system, without permission in writing from the publishers.

Trademark notice: Product or corporate names may be trademarks or registered trademarks, and are used only for identification and explanation without intent to infringe.

British Library Cataloguing-in-Publication Data
A catalogue record for this book is available from the British Library

Library of Congress Cataloging-in-Publication Data
A catalog record has been requested for this book

ISBN: 978-0-367-43637-7 (hbk)
ISBN: 978-0-367-43640-7 (pbk)
ISBN: 978-1-003-00477-6 (ebk)

Typeset in Bembo
by Wearset Ltd, Boldon, Tyne and Wear

For
Beryl Robinson
&
our daughters
Florence & Hermione

CONTENTS

PART I
The loss adjustor: collateral damage in the capitalocene   **1**

1   The Dark Theatre: bankruptcy and the logics of expulsion   9

2   The eruption of the audience and the dictatorship of the performatariat   60

3   All the home's a stage: social reproduction and everyday life   109

      Interlude: dreadful trade: the vertigo of attractions   152

PART II
Living currency: scenes from the last human venue   **159**

4   Irreparable state: compensations of performance   171

5   Arrested life: ecology of the new enclosures   198

6   Cultural cruelty: extraordinary rendition and acoustic shock   227

7   Poor history: field notes from a fire sale   265

      Outstanding debts   301
      The Milliner's shop   306
      Bibliography   311
      Index   321

SUBTITLED CONTENTS

PART I
The loss adjustor: collateral damage in the capitalocene　　1

1　The Dark Theatre: bankruptcy and the logics of expulsion　　9
　The lie of the land 19
　Unexceptional politics 22
　Ethnography of the everyday 26
　Cheap natures 35
　Avant garde agency 37
　Filing for bankruptcy 40
　Compound interest 43
　Accounting for action 52

2　The eruption of the audience and the dictatorship of the performatariat　　60
　The royal remains 70
　Interregnum and inequality 74
　Dictatorship of the proletariat and limited legitimacy 77
　Real utopia 81
　Performatariat and performance 83
　Populism and the people 87
　The social and surveillance 90
　Black Friday 97

3　All the home's a stage: social reproduction and everyday life　　109
　Infamy of the insignificant 112

Mimicry of man 115
Theatre's coming home 118
Inside-out 122
Outside-in 129
Private view 142

Interlude: dreadful trade: the vertigo of attractions　　152

PART II
Living currency: scenes from the last human venue　　**159**
Wall Street crash 160
Living currency 164

4　Irreparable state: compensations of performance　　171
Phantasms: Purgatorio *and* Paradiso　173
Simulacra and stereotypes: Go Down Moses　177
Impulses: Orpheus and Eurydice　184

5　Arrested life: ecology of the new enclosures　　198
Informal assembly 202
Phyto-performance 208
The English Garden Effect 214
Critical commons 219

6　Cultural cruelty: extraordinary rendition and acoustic shock　　227
The worker at play 229
The virtuosi 234
Summing up 239
Unexceptional victim 244
Disappearance, loss, damage, compensation 248
Cultural cruelty 254
Demonic territory 258

7　Poor history: field notes from a fire sale　　265
Field notes from a fire sale 268
Pyro-politics 271
Poor history 274
The fire this time 278
Public Inquiry 280
Authorities and activists 283
Anti-social housing 287
The loss adjustor returns 289

x Subtitled contents

Outstanding debts 301
The Milliner's shop 306
Bibliography 311
Index 321

PART I
The loss adjustor
Collateral damage in the capitalocene

Loss does not travel well, if it travels at all. Loss is a 'singular type of disappearance' the 'irreversible disappearance of some irreplaceable thing', its singularity necessarily makes loss specific to something, someone, somewhere.[1] When I descend into the six-storey, galleried, subterranean auditorium to witness something called *An Occupation of Loss* in 2016, a performance work by Taryn Simon, I encounter a score of professional mourners, from Albania, Venezuela, Greece and China, whose laments rend the air.[2] But not for me. For someone, somewhere, I am not quite sure who. They are being paid now, by the miraculous producers Artangel, and they were paid then and there, by those who needed mourning and were able to pay for it. Judging by their watches and their shoes, some are mourners of very high esteem, there is no need for patronage here. In the absence of pity, critical thought can thrive.

A man in an overcoat with a hat stands in the flickering penumbra of an Ottawa house-fire lit only by the flames and the circling lights of the first responders. It is 1991. We don't know the name nor occupation of this man but discover later he is Noah Render, an insurance adjuster. Where I am watching this film by Atom Egoyan we would call this figure, 'the loss adjustor', the one responsible for judging damages and compensation due.[3] It is unlikely that we would consider this role to be anything more than an accounting of loss, an inventory of those things irrecoverable, recoverable and indeterminate in ashes. He may well take responsibility for the fire sale that follows, the knock-down recovery of any assets that will mitigate insurance losses. But in this film the actor Elias Koteas plays a part, hardly innocently called Render, in such a way as to insinuate himself into the emotional lives of those recently traumatised, to strip them of the only thing they have left, their dignity. He repeats the company slogan as a mantra through the film: 'You may not know it yet, but you're in shock'. In this insurance business the modus operandi appears to be seduction of the precariously grieving, and abuse of their trust. In the flicker of this film cynical reason can flourish.

2 The loss adjustor

In the grainy photograph from some time in 1917 a woman acquainted with style, confidently carrying off a broad belt and buckle, stands in front of a milliner's shop in an East London street. She is the first woman in this neighbourhood to own her own tailoring business and she is about to lose it. Her husband has been gravely injured in the Great War and will return from his posting with the King's Own Royal Lancaster Regiment on 22 October 1917 to be nursed and die two years later.[4] My grandmother will seek compensation for her loss from the War Office but the handwritten correspondence with the officials of the National Fund, running to several pages, will refuse her claim. She is asking for £350 in damages for the injuries that have ended her husband's life and will necessitate the closure of her business. By the following year there is a new trader at 702 High Road Leyton.

My grandfather, a devout Catholic from a large, local working-class family, has visited and nursed my grandmother's first husband, helping her write the letters whose pleas for support are ignored by the authorities. In these papers my grandfather has described my grandmother on the brink of the demise of her livelihood as 'without capital and without stock'.[5] They subsequently marry and move to Essex where, when my father dies, before I am born, my grandmother opens a small haberdashery shop to 'keep my mother busy' in her grief. My mother is her daughter. Two years after opening and thriving amongst the cotton reels in the early 1960s, my grandmother is persuaded to allow the prank television programme, *Candid Camera* to film a stunt in her shop involving unsuspecting customers. The shop loses its trade and closes the following year. No one got the fake-performance joke, and I haven't since. It would be harsh to quote Oscar Wilde on the odds of losing not one but two means of living, but theatre has a habit of saying something careless when it matters.

Loss is ubiquitous to performance. There is no getting away from it. Nobody appears to have preserved the part of Aristotle's *Poetics* dedicated to Comedy, it is the losses of Tragedy that have survived as far as critical thought is concerned. Walter Benjamin dedicated his post-doctoral study to '*Trauerspiel*', *The Origin of German Tragic Drama* in the 16th and 17th centuries was precisely the movement of the mourning play. The entire discipline of performance study since its unruly inception in the 1960s has been built on the shaking foundations of loss. These tremors have sometimes taken the form of a debate about the live and the mediatised, that which loses itself at odds with that which endures. In its most limpid, and widely quoted formulation from 1993, Peggy Phelan put it like this: 'Performance's life is only in the present. Performance cannot be saved, recorded, documented or otherwise participate in the circulation *of* representations of representations: once it does so it becomes something other than performance'.[6] In other words: total loss, a right off. Nobody cites theatre theory, but almost everyone with some familiarity with the field knows this epithet.[7] Yes, it has been contested and qualified, yet it remains, a searing catalogue of loss. But should it? The melancholy of theatrical discipline from Aristotle to Phelan via Benjamin might suggest loss is ubiquitous to performance, as though handling the damaged goods of 'been and gone' images is the necessary evil that comes with the job title of philospher, critic or cultural historian. But when set against the losses remembered above, unfelt losses, ambivalent losses, felt losses, is there not a deficit to be accounted for, some other less superfluous evil than aesthetic loss to consider?

That deficit is the balance sheet of this book. On the ledger there are blue and red entries as always. On the red side, those losses that have occurred. On the blue side, adjustments made by those who recognise such losses and offer up something of their own practice of loss-making performance to begin to compensate for what has gone before. This ledger is an accounting of what I will call the 'capitalocene', simply the long durée of a capitalist mode of production that has prevailed in Western Europe since the late fifteenth century.[8] And this ledger is only necessary, in my view, because of the *continuing* existence of such an economic system, without it there would be no need for this accounting of the losses predicated by profits. To be clear, I certainly don't think this system is 'eternal' and its very historical contingency, barely half a millennium and counting, undergirds the optimism of this writing.[9]

Theatre and its performances are peculiarly well-suited to the optimism of such compensations, acting through affects as they tend to do, they are commonly concerned with rendering present such past and future feelings. This is not to say for a moment, as indeed Peggy Phelan did in her upbeat subtitle to the book we have just sampled, *Unmarked*, that anything as instrumental as a 'politics of performance' can be achieved. But it is to recognise that in the active disjuncture between losses felt and compensatory actions taken, there arises a possibility for something else to happen. And it is the faltering attempt at such somethings, such essaying of means by which we might 'begin again', that the potential of performance is realised. In losing a comrade whose life-force was one of resolute optimism the glimmer of such dissenting ways might become apparent again. As Mark Fisher insisted against all odds: 'The tiniest event can tear a hole in the grey curtain of reaction which has marked the horizons of possibility under capitalist realism. From a situation in which nothing can happen, suddenly anything is possible again'.[10] *The Dark Theatre* represents one hopeful accounting, or partial register, of such events, an open-ended repair book of 'rends' in the cultural fabric that call for work to be done in resistance to the confident prognoses of the closed book of capital that announces no such work is needed nor necessary. The liquidations common to the capitalocene will be expected here to flow in all, not just one, direction.

Given loss describes something that has by definition disappeared and therefore is not replaceable it is not a question of restoring what was, that is long gone, but rather asking, so what now, what to do in the interests of justice? The reason I could not feel for Taryn Simon's professional mourners, other than enjoying them as virtuosi musicians and vocalists in a performance space (which has nothing to do with mourning per se) is that I knew not for what, or who, they mourned. My ignorance of their subjects of attention is of course the point. The obstacles to their being granted P-3 visas to perform in the US, and Tier 5 visas to allow 'Creative and Sporting' entry into the UK, are meticulously recorded and reproduced in a lavish programme distributed by Taryn Simon to make explicit what this piece is really about. And it is not in my view about mourning. That would be impossible, if not silly. The 'what to do' that *The Occupation of Loss* draws our attention to is, it turns out, something to do with the systemic State hostility to the outsider, in this instance the one who seeks entry to a 'foreign field' in order to lament the loss of those they left behind. Lucky are they who are accorded such recognition of lives lived. To attain such status of freedom to travel and perform, each mourner is required to establish that they are 'culturally unique'.

The cultural theorist Judith Butler would get Taryn Simon. She reminds us that there are grievable and much less grievable lives, and grievability is strictly policed by a world-order of geo-political human accounting. The headline in *The Times* newspaper the day I am writing these words reads: 'Sunbather nearly hit by falling body is Oxford graduate'.[11] I will not rename the well-educated graduate as he has already been identified as having his leisure disrupted by a figure that has fallen from the skies, from the undercarriage-well of a plane landing from Nairobi. An impression of the 'stowaway' is pictured in the newspaper column, a death mask compressed in the concrete garden path. And we already know something of his outline, as the au pair at the Clapham neighbours has told reporters: 'I was doing gardening and I saw something in the sky – it looked like a drone'. Though I can see the rough outline and form of the figure, I cannot name the deceased because all we know is this is a human who has taken their dreadful life into their hands, secreted a blanket and some food in the wheel arch of the Kenya Airways Boeing 787, and hung on up to 22,000 feet when hypoxia would have started to kick in at minus 60 degrees Celsius, to within a mile or two of their promised landing at Heathrow. Scotland Yard police said it was 'working to identify the stowaway' though it is unlikely *The Times* will come back to us with the name when they do. The victim who was once special for someone, is no longer 'culturally unique', they have become part of a dreadful trend. This is the 100th human to fall from a long-haul flight in this way over the UK since records of this sordid kind began. Loss is sometimes brought home to us in ways that suggest, whether we like it or not, loss might *have* to travel. There is no alternative.

Loss can only be perceived as irreplaceable 'from the viewpoint of an interested person'.[12] In the instance of the human being who fell to earth someone in Nairobi waits in vain. Closer to home, and therefore more imaginable, I am obviously a contender to be such an 'interested person' for my own grandmother. I am ashamed to admit I feel differently, less sympathetic to her husband, as pictured outside that same milliner's shop, bow-tied, fob-chained, in a dapper wide-brimmed hat, before the war had started. It is relatively easy to be interested in relatives. It would appear to be far more nuanced to be interested in strangers and their fates. Not least of all those lamented by professional mourners. That figure in the garden is not afforded such ceremonial attention (the 'traumatised' sunbather becomes the headline obscuring the man with no name who fell). The recognition of necessary association with strangers is something that performance specialises in. It is unlikely after all before you went into the theatre and took your seat that you knew King Lear that well, but, notwithstanding his boorish behaviour, you might feel for him by the end of the play given the way two of his daughters treat him.

In the case of my grandmother, as one of the ones vested with remembering her, my writing here enters an economy of forgetting, as a *resistance* to the one who forgets, and in so forgetting 'loses the loss' (for good or ill). Memorialisation of the same Great War that bankrupted my grandmother, on its 100th anniversary in 2014–2018, provided opportunities for remembering, and no more so than for the cultural industries for whom memorialisation is a lavishly practiced, government-funded art.[13] But, as Joe Kennedy and others have contested in nuanced readings of World War II 'nostalgia' and its political mobilisation from the platitudes of a poppy-past, the magnitude of this remembering in memorial multiples, began for some to elide rather than identify critical differences between say, the politics, economics and nationalist power plays of the Great War, and that fight against Fascism of World War II.[14] It was as though for all the memorialisers' best and most subtle artistic endeavours the necessity to remember the 'fallen' required those spectating to align themselves with principles of patriotism, nation and heroism that are as conflicted as they are problematic. The vastness of the military action itself began to be met by the vastness of the cultural response, whether a sea of ceramic blooms or a field of figurines, though in all cases the claim would be made that such scale was made up of multiple miniatures that adequately spoke to the detail of the disaster. The repeated cliché of 'very moving' to perfectly principled acts of this kind did not it seemed to me begin to respond to the kind of language that the War Office used to dismiss my grandmother's small claim, its deep and apparently continuing cruelty, if evidenced by the well-publicised, parlously inadequate treatment of today's homeless army veterans despite all these reminders. I wondered how many other interested parties felt such things beyond the outpouring for the past over present politics?

As the interested one I am responsible in small measure for my grandmother's loss. I carry it with me here, to the last pages of this book, as part of that responsibility, amongst many other losses that *The Dark Theatre* will encounter and for which I assume some responsibility, if only in the act of writing against the grain. In the midst of this book there are multiple forms of what I have chosen to call 'cultural cruelty' in response to other losses where those who might have expected the fourth estate to write on their behalf at a time of crisis, find themselves jeopardised again in publications that should know better. It is as though it is not sufficient for life to be insufferable, but for some of those responsible for writing its histories to feel it necessary to double down on its nastiness. Of the two injustices, the political betrayal and the cultural cruelty, it is the latter that takes on a peculiarly violent force in the age of 'the social'. Those of us just shy to its sharpest brutalities are long immured to State violence, the terms are historically synonymous, but cultural cruelty is a special dividend that has accrued from the sequestration of the peculiar legitimacy granted artists' work, by those who have invented a new variety of administrative power to profit from what they call 'creativity'.

The loss I carry for my grandmother, is of a different order and significance to the loss of a theatre I describe in the first chapter of this book. Although I 'lost' that theatre, a myriad others lost that theatre too. Many would rightly claim their loss was more acute than mine. I only worked at that theatre for eight years from my mid-20s to my mid-30s, my close colleague David Slater worked there for 15 years, and members of the neighbourhood who started working at the theatre when they were one or two years old, in mothers' arms, lost the theatre when they were in their teenage years.[15] One of those 'lost ones', Darren Kenny, picked me up by chance in his taxi in Peckham Rye on the late evening I was writing this, and half way through the journey west, after our talking about the challenges of hailing cabs south of the river in the 1980s said: 'Don't I know you?'. He switched on his light and smiled in the rear-view mirror: '35 years ago you worked with David, didn't you, we made *Back Streets of Bermondsey* in the Theatre Workshop together'. Peering into the front seat I remembered Darren had brought his dog on stage in the show, but the name escaped me. 'Bootsy'. Way before the avant garde started messing with animals and their theoretical challenges to humanist performance there were auspicious precedents being set, and critically considered, in London's docklands. Darren thought Bootsy had been 'distracted' and 'distracting', but then Darren had always boasted a vast hinterland of play, politics and pleasure in that neighbourhood, and now spent the long journey in precisely the opposite direction to 'that home' celebrating 'those days'. Some others whose life landscapes had been more circumscribed had known nothing else than the presence of this theatre that was lost. Though I lost my means of living when I left that theatre, I did not lose my life. How might one account for the differential between such states of loss, even when the object of loss is as superfluous as a theatre?

I will try to do just that in the book that follows. It is called *The Dark Theatre* not because it is about theatre in 'dark times' though I certainly share Saidiya Hartman's appeal to those with stories to tell, the writing of the impossible: 'How can a narrative of defeat enable a place for the living or envision an alternative future?'[16] And it is not called *The Dark Theatre* because it is about either chiaroscuro conditions of performance nor invisible theatrical phenomena, there are perfectly good books available on those murky states already.[17] It is called *The Dark Theatre* because, simply put, this theatre was forced to close. Its electricity was disconnected when we did not, could not, pay the bills, and as the colloquial phrase in English goes, the theatre 'became dark'. The title of this book is as distant from metaphor as one could imagine. The theatre was bankrupted in a different way to the way my grandmother's small shops were bankrupted, but it was bankrupted none the less. I know that because amongst many others I had an interest in it. Not so much a financial one, though I was paid the princely sum of £7,300 a year (£150 a week before tax) to work there, but rather I had an emotional investment like others that reminds me every so often what has been lost. It is not that I now think about it that often, it is just that when I do, and when I did over the last two years in order to write the words that follow, the reasons for my interest in this particular theatrical loss become more present. In displaying this loss in the form of writing I am going to insist on not obscuring the demands of that present with nostalgia for some invented past, but as unflinchingly as I can recognise the conflicted memories these thoughts of loss represent, and think about their resonance today, for me yes, but perhaps for others too. Here ways in which history might become a disadvantage, 'poor history' as I call it by the end of the book, will become, once retold for the present, some kind of critical advantage, or at least opportunity, for further thought and action.

I am not in this book making a vain-glorious claim on behalf of cultural acts that they can *do* anything about such loss, but as Adi Ophir says: 'Whoever understands the movement of loss can control it, at least partially'.[18] I take particular courage in this work from the most obvious anxiety of the capitalocene (if such a monstrosity could be said to have feelings). If there is one thing the long wave of capitalism abhors it is those for whom losses endure, or at least those who recall their losses in ways incommensurate with the market's demands. This economic system called capitalism thrives as long as I am willing, whether able or not, to privatise certain griefs, such as the one my grandmother suffered, and expiate these in the quest for new profits, new opportunities, new natures to be capitalised upon. Such things were once called progress, move on, nothing to see here. Closure, if only of a modest milliner's shop-door, is the preferred mode.

My resistance to such finessing of my family history into economic systems that reap profits for others, forms a small part of this much longer book in which others' losses form the 'community of loss' within which I can begin to feel at appropriate unease, that is confident of an injustice shared if not resolved. This is what you could call 'loss by association'. And this is how Saidiya Hartman calls it: 'Loss gives rise to longing, and in these circumstances, it would not be far-fetched to consider stories as a form of compensation or even as reparations, perhaps the only kind we will ever receive'.[19] Loss by association is something that performance offers as standard, sometimes even, falling back on the showing of such stories in a genre once called drama. But performance is a treasury of modes amongst which narratives, dramatic or otherwise, form only a small compensatory part. This suppleness of theatre should not be forgotten given the acquisitive logic of capitalist markets that will look at, envy, and want to sell something back to those who have suffered losses by way of amelioration for its deeds, in the form of funerals, therapy, drugs, for instance. Even tickets for 'shows' that peddle sentiment and nostalgia have been traded on such bear markets. What happened, the losses suffered, will have been everything to do with that necessity for business at all costs, but, now, because of that brutal fact, it is time to say that all this is frankly none of their business. None of it is. Those losses for good and ill, are for *us* to be getting on with, in our own chosen company, amongst others in whom we trust. I have never been interested in show-business and I am not about to start.

Notes

1 See Ophir, Adi (2005). *The Order of Evils: Toward an Ontology of Morals*. New York: Zone, p. 89.
2 Taryn Simon, *An Occupation of Loss*, Islington Green/Essex Road, London, 17–28 April 2018. Produced by Artangel.

3 *The Adjuster*. Dir. Atom Egoyan, 1991. Premiered at New York Film Festival.
4 This brief history of Charles Aloysius Powell (regimental Number 12326) and my grandmother Florence Powell is recorded in the British Army WWI Service Records (National Archives of the UK) and was brought to my attention by the remarkable Rainhill Civic Society whose members Brian Renshall and Judy Lowe were most helpful.
5 Ibid. Powell Ref. 49604
6 See Phelan, Peggy (1993). *Unmarked: The Politics of Performance*. London: Routledge, p. 146.
7 Performance Studies was the least-cited academic discipline in a national survey as reported by *Times Higher Education* on 18 April 2018.
8 See Kunkel, Benjamin. (2017). 'The Capitalocene', in *London Review of Books*, Vol. 39, no. 5, 2 March 2017, pp. 22–28.
9 See Wark, McKenzie (2019). *Capital is Dead. Is this Something Worse?*. London: Verso, p. 22, for a subtle, lively, if faulty optic on this question of capital's enduring habit.
10 See Fisher, Mark (2009). *Capitalist Realism*, (p. 81) quoted in Simon Hammond, 'K-Punk at Large', *New Left Review*, No. 118, July/August 2019, p. 53.
11 Shukman, Harry and Flanagan, Jane. (2019). *The Times*, London, 3 July 2019, p. 15. In the *Daily Mail* version of this story the house price of the graduate's home in Clapham has been included for good measure in case the reader is considering upscaling into this desirable death path.
12 Ophir, Adi, op. cit. p. 90.
13 The remarkable efforts and industry of the 14–18 NOW:WWI Centenary Art Commissions, lead-curated by the indefatigable Jenny Waldman, were prominent in this respect and engaged 35 million participants according to their web-site: www.1418now.org.uk (accessed on 30 August 2019).
14 See Joe Kennedy on the 'block-by-block reconstruction of British history as unimpeachably upstanding' in *Authentocrats: Culture, Politics and the New Seriousness*, Repeater: 2018.
15 From its inception Rotherhithe Theatre Workshop was sustained by countless members of the Rotherhithe neighbourhood and supported by amongst others, David Slater, Teresa Watkins, Fiona Graham, and successive years of Dartington College of Arts third year degree students, theatre, choreography and writing faculty, and visiting artists.
16 Hartman, Saidiya. (2008). 'Venus in Two Acts', *Small Axe*, Number 26 (Volume 12, No. 2), June 2008, pp. 1–14, (p. 14).
17 See Martin Welton and Adam Alston. Eds. (2017) *Theatre in the Dark: Shadow, Gloom and Blackout in Contemporary Theatre*. London: Bloomsbury, and Andrew Sofer (2013). *Dark Matter: Invisibility in Drama, Theater and Performance*. Michigan: University of Michigan Press. *The Dark Theatre* in fact shares rather more with an apparently counter-intuitive condition of 'the suffering of images' described by Joe Kelleher in his work *The Illuminated Theatre* (2015). London: Routledge.
18 Adi Ophir op. cit. p. 101.
19 Hartman, Saidiya. (2008). 'Venus in Two Acts', *Small Axe*, Number 26 (Volume 12, No. 2), June 2008, pp. 1–14, (p. 4).

1

THE DARK THEATRE

Bankruptcy and the logics of expulsion

It was close to a quarter-century ago that I wrote a book called *Theatre & Everyday Life* (1993) which did what it said on the cover making critical associations between performance and the quotidian that had been misplaced in accounts of dramatic work that voraciously parasited such relations without acknowledging their mutual influence.[1] In the first chapter of that book, called 'Lay Theatre', I recounted a long story about working at a riverside warehouse in South East London during the 1980s and saw out the chapter in a less than affirmative tone, acknowledging a litany of loss:

> Supporting a theatre in such an area for thirteen years eventually gave way to closure. Keeping a theatre open is more or less difficult. Closing a theatre is a provocation to say something else. Where there is interruption in what has been a continuity, questions are asked as to how and why such a situation could have arisen. For 'being there' becomes pattern and habit and is the point at which everyday life begins to incorporate a theatre into itself as though it were somehow natural and given. But this habitual world threatens the fragility of a theatre which demands recognition and favours few can afford.[2]

Despite a pervasive melancholy that marked the loss of privileges few whose lives were already so conflicted could grant a theatre, the book took off from this spirit of disappointment encountering discursive digressions on everyday life, nature and culture, that touched newly emerging thinking on the quotidian, ecology and cultural materialism. The work became quite widely circulated and judging by critical and informal responses was read by those who sought, or at least wished for, a means by which the ubiquitous ephemerality of performance, the lack of the archive and the inadequacy of theatre documentation, were recognised as merely pale palimpsests of the material, palpable and historically contingent forms of loss that underwrote the witness of theatre acts. In the almost complete absence of longitudinal studies of theatrical practice, *Theatre & Everyday Life* perhaps ironically, appeared to represent in its eight-year span, a veritable long durée when compared with the minutiae of individualised performance studies, the radical particularity that served the isolated artistry of the 'one person show', but could not begin to offer the kind of overdue general theory that might reacquaint theatre with its politics. Almost by accident the book stood as a testament to continuity, resilience and bloody-minded optimism, when in cold fact it documented a fleeting encounter with decline, disintegration and loss.

I was recently asked whether I would like to make revisions to *Theatre & Everyday Life* for a new edition in the light of the 25 intervening years during which time the title of the book had not simply come true, but had become ubiquitous across the arts and media where my long-ago identification of 'the eruption of the audience' was now commonplace in everything cultural and meretricious from 'relational aesthetics' to 'social works', from 'fly-on-the-wall' to 'docu-soaps'. But given the work was still in print and widely available I resisted the easier route of repetition and reproduction and set about writing *this* book, that encounters the substance and sentiment of that original project while launching off on some new, more pertinent enquiries for performance and politics in the early twenty-first century, in a place and time where loss-making sets the scene in ways I could not have begun to imagine in 1993.

Before I make presumptions as to any familiarity with the source project I will then briefly characterise where I was coming from those years ago by way of worked and lived experience. During the decade of the 1980s that preceded the writing of *Theatre & Everyday Life* I was responsible for a neighbourhood theatre in a near-derelict, riverside warehouse in Rotherhithe, in the docklands area of South East London in the UK. I have previously described this work as 'directing' a neighbourhood theatre, but for the many democratically-minded participants involved in the project that would instantly raise a quizzical eyebrow, given how deeply unstable the entire project was, quite beyond any 'direction' whatever one's orderly dramaturgical aspirations might have hoped for. I was working closely after all not just with the irrepressible, innovative and ideologically demanding theatre-maker David Slater (who had arrived in Rotherhithe in the mid-1970s and has since those days maintained his close working links with South East London through his inclusive work with the ground-breaking company Entelechy),[3] nor only with a shifting entourage of neighbourhood institutions, agencies and individuals networking broad swathes of the immediate locality, but also, and importantly successive years of students on year-long placements from their arts college base, deep in the West Country rural-realm of Dartington, living in the immediate locality of the warehouse in 'hard to let' council flats (apartments, though that sounds too grand a word for the often damp and dilapidated accommodation on offer), an arrangement that would be inconceivable in the modular-proofed, risk-free systems of today's higher education sector in the UK.[4] Here what was at work, predominantly through the favoured medium of theatre, but much else besides that could not be categorised in quite that way, was a loose alliance of several 100 proximate participants living in local authority housing, of all ages and cultural backgrounds, resisting the forced eviction of their families away from their homes on the river, to inland estates, 'camps' might not be too harsh a word, built beneath the shadow of a new wave of safely-sprinklered towers with glowing corporate mastheads such as HSBC, RBS and Barclays.

The unelected development quango, the London Docklands Development Corporation was operating without democratic restraint, enticing residents away from the profitable real-estate gains of the water which could be bundled up free of contamination by the 'poor', to Kwik Fit accommodation with postmodern filigree in the shadow of these towers. From the Tower of London eastwards, taking in more than 20 miles of prime riverfront, the LDDC was parcelling up swathes of London's historic dockland communities remorselessly incorporating everything that could be capitalised for development, first through the easy-pickings of Wapping and Limehouse close to the established City of London, moving downriver to more challenging urban margins including the Isle of Dogs, West India Quay, Heron Quays and Canary Wharf.[5] The names now exude a lost 'commitment' to Empire and the natures that drove colonial expansion, buried, or you could say inundated, given water was often orchestrated for its design value, by vast monuments to Mammon. Canary Wharf alone accounted for a $10 billion single-development in this zone, offering 12 million square-feet of bankable office space to hyper-accelerated lease holders. Long before the pyramid-glass Shard dragged attention towards London Bridge, the 800 foot-high One Canada Square with its single masonic winking red-eye high in the sky, was standing head and shoulders above anything else in the city at the time.

The 'water' that decorated these developments was never referred to as water by the duplicitous LDDC and their handmaidens of economic delivery the estate agents, or in that US nicety the 'realtor' class, but as 'a' or preferably, *the* 'river view'. Against such euphemisms of expulsion the residents with whom we worked, many whose families' histories in the area stretched back for decades and often into a previous century that had witnessed the flourishing of these outward-looking, now derelict docks, nurtured their own repertoire of resistances, or more often plain obstruction, to the coercions of capital over a turbulent decade deploying theatrical means, street ceremonies, playground protests, occupations and sit-ins. The first chapters of *Theatre & Everyday Life* articulated this history and gave space and oxygen to these endeavours which had not been written about then and like so many subterranean cultural commitments still, remain largely unwritten about now.[6] That said they formed part of a complex of contemporary obstacles to capital's influx with ACME artists' work spaces and housing dating from the 1970s in the area offering an early but problematic sign of 'change'.[7] Such autonomous, artist-led projects were followed by the more sustainable local commitment of the 1983 publication of a 'People's Plan for the Royal Docks', the foundation of the Joint Docklands Action Group and most notably, Lorraine Leeson and Peter Dunn's exemplary Docklands Community Poster Project, all emerging simultaneously within a couple of square miles of this blighted landscape.[8] Over eight years, exactly parallel to my own experience of theatre-making in the area, Leeson, Dunn and their team, working closely with a diverse collaborative network of local participants, designed, constructed and mounted a series of 12 × 18 foot photomurals of remarkable historical detail and graphic intensity on billboards throughout the contested zone.[9] This urban tableaux, 'Changing Picture of Docklands', perhaps inevitably, had to be launched onto the river itself in the years 1984–1986 with the orchestration of a 'People's Armada', a flotilla of boats steered by their lightermen to take our protest cause to the riverside-facing windows of the debating chamber in the Houses of Parliament where construction industry lobby groups were securing the preferential rates for their knock-down fire sale of dockland's historic assets, where they were busy turning a lower case commercial non-entity 'docklands' into an upper case banking behemoth: Docklands.

In re-reading *Theatre & Everyday Life* in the light of these intervening years, and with specific regard to our own work within this broad alliance of arts activism, it is apparent and embarrassing that I paid scant regard to the detail of the financial forces afflicting this once 'proud' neighbourhood, despite the obvious fact they were staring me and others in the face from their lofty heights, and all too busy showering their collateral damage on those below. That blind spot to the financial force of capital betrayed my own naivety during the 1980s and the book would have had to be put on an intravenous drip of economic theory to have resuscitated it from its nascently romantic, largely voluntaristic speculations. The work had an insistently Franco-German influence to it, somewhere between the Bachelardian/Benjaminian borderlands that it occupied, residing, or often 'drifting', as it did between the phenomenological essayism of *The Poetics of Space* by Gaston Bachelard and the melancholic messianism of *The Arcades Project* of Walter Benjamin.[10] But I was not alone in this propensity to poetics over public policy given the ubiquity within urban theory of the preference for the evanescent over the economically literate, following the rationalist dystopianism of Jane Jacobs' *The Death and Life of Great American Cities* and the shift in its wake towards the more anarchist currency of the situationists, the poetic prevalence of psycho-geographers and in their slipstream, the phenomenological subjectivities of *Soft City* by Jonathan Raban, published in 1971.[11]

The area we occupied though that contested 1980s decade was a tightly circumscribed and rapidly reducing zone at the behest of this capital, a ghetto really given its continued existence appeared to be solely now at the mercy of the largesse of those tasked with capitalising on its proximity to the post Big-Bang financial city. If you are familiar with John Mckenzie's prescient film of 1979, *The Long Good Friday*, you will be aware of the quintessential, modestly exaggerated rendering of this gangland terrain. It is not so much Bob Hoskins' Thatcherite developer Harold Shand that carries the film, though his performance is riveting, as the docklands' backdrops, shot by cinematographer Phil Méheux, that capture the effortless film noir of this urban dereliction at the cusp of steroid-driven 'recovery'. What was euphemistically called an 'Enterprise Zone' had been created by the Conservative led government within which planning controls had gone missing with the consequence of a rash of dubious pastel-shaded postmodern architectural facades competing for clients' attentions. With interest rates rising through the 1980s these developments had the habit of bankrupting their developers before the keys could be exchanged, returning zones of uninhabitable bricolage to rubble as quickly as they had risen from the once-cherished public housing that had been the hallmark of an area with deep socialist traditions rooted in the river trades with their solid union affiliations.

It is routine (for some) to blame Margaret Thatcher, the Conservative leader and British Prime Minister of the time, for much of the stark inequalities in this era in the UK, but in 1981 her creation of the Urban Development Corporations, the quintessential neoliberal programme of ideologically driven regeneration 'at all costs', with free-market interventions in this area trumping any and all locally democratic decision-making organisations, could be taken as a paradigmatic project in the acceleration towards a new post-OPEC oil crisis economic contract to which there could indeed be 'no alternative'. Planning regulations were ripped up, there was a tax holiday for incoming companies until the decade-distant year of 1992 and the 100% offset of building costs against company tax attracted Credit Suisse, First Boston, Morgan Stanley and Travelstead Group into the mix with their taste for extravagant Beaux Arts edifices that had no relation to the area's rich and far more utilitarian urban docklands heritage. As Jon Bird put it close to the time, in one of the few critical assessments of the architectural development of the locale:

> Add to this economic incentive the presence of the river, and the context was created for a struggle over representations in which the complex historical and mythological connotations of the Thames and the City are played out in the conflict between dominant and subordinate cultures and economies.[12]

This 'struggle for representation' astutely describes the work we were doing at Rotherhithe Theatre Workshop, south east of Jamaica Road about half a mile from London Bridge, down Tooley Street, cradled in the bend of the river just beyond the ornamentations of Tower Bridge, hard on the river edge, where stood a 30 × 70 foot, two-storey dilapidated warehouse, our theatre. My own council accommodation, state-subsidised public housing in Marden Square to one side of Southwark Park, opposite the sprawling premises of the Peek Frean's factory (30 years later retro-fitted as 'distressed' artists' work spaces), was over this decade more or less, with a craned neck from the fetid balcony at least, within sight of the theatre and all those I worked with, who were my neighbours, friends and foes alike.[13]

When I talk about camps shadowed by banks I am sensitive to the opportunistic mobilisation of that dreadful, historically specific word, from the lagers of South Africa in the nineteenth century, through the distribution of barbed wires of the twentieth. But I will insist that the political, quasi-juridical structure that allowed for the eviction of the residents from their riverside homes in our neighbourhood in the 1980s offers material evidence of a political space that can be associated with that more brutal lineage of camps either side of the twentieth century. A 'logics of expulsion' is what connects these practices and to minimise the deep psychological, physical and cultural impact of such expulsions for one group, while insisting on their relevance for another *wholly different* group, appears to me to be a peculiarly class-blind operation that does not need to conflate one distinct experience *to* the other. There is no necessity to establish equivalence between forms of expulsion, in this regard at least we are not dealing with a numbers game, but what is clearly evident are coeval relations at work here with associated if not diametrically aligned roots.

What is a 'logics of expulsion' that might elucidate this ostentatious expression as anything but an opportunistic endeavour to mobilise class sympathies for others I have no rightful claim to, to weaponise what Joe Kennedy might call 'authentocratic' merit on behalf of my own special performance pleading?[14] Well, according to Saskia Sassen a 'logics of expulsion' describes the sharp growth in the number of people, enterprises and places expelled from the core social and economic orders of our time.[15] If my own work over three decades since that decade in Docklands and the writing of *Theatre & Everyday Life* has been about 'radical inclusion',[16] forms of expansion of the theatre collective beyond professionalism and humanism through performance, then the idea of radical expulsion, its inevitable antinomy with its own force of loss, takes us beyond familiar ideas of growing inequality and captures something of the brutality and complexity of the pathologies of today's global capitalism, what I have called in Part I of this book, the 'capitalocene'. Amongst all the losses mourned in this book I am sorry not to be able to account for the 'loss' of *this* capital, as McKenzie Wark ingeniously does in his recent work *Capital is Dead*.[17] Indeed if what 'we' are experiencing 'is something worse' than what went before then my prognosis in this and the next chapter is that it is the *expansion* rather than the retreat of capital that we might identify as the true vector of our era.

A logics of expulsion (as proposed by Saskia Sassen) allows me to connect two principle experiences of the capitalocene that were obvious within the immediate neighbourhood of the theatre that I worked at during the 1980s:

1. The expelling of low-income workers and the unemployed ex-dock workers from government social housing under the cover of 'development', and the concomitant loss of the immediate welfare of their neighbourhood that followed swiftly upon the loss of their means of living, with the closure and subsequent containerisation of deep-water ports pushed well away from the real-estate gains of the capital. I will characterise this expulsion as loss of home.
2. The simultaneous investment by the banks, that had flooded the very area of the theatre, in loans to advanced extraction industries that had the power to transform natural environments much further afield, way beyond but umbilically linked to these once globalised now loss-making ports, into 'dead land and dead water' that threatened biospheres far away. I will characterise this expulsion as loss of world.

The two processes were examples of the kinds of expulsion Sassen has identified, which when thought together become a 'logics' of loss, the one depending on the other for what it can do.

I use the ugly neologism capitalocene for two reasons to periodise these logics. The first not wholly irrelevant to a writer is that the word's ugliness begins to mimic, in miniature measure, the ugliness of what it purports to describe, and that is no bad thing in an age of euphemism. But second, the ugly, epochal transformations that interest me in this chapter are rooted in diverse and often older histories and genealogies than are commonly recognised, emerging in the Late Medieval and Early Modern periods in Europe, closer to the long historical view of capitalism rehearsed by Emmanuel Wallerstein, Giovanni Arrighi and later Jason Moore.[18]

In Wallerstein's version of this long durée, capitalism is first and foremost a historical system with both an existing and present potential for gratuitous disempowerment, but always and importantly a *past* reality of systemic violences.[19] In this narrative, 'capital', that is accumulated wealth, is a form of accumulation over time that requires specific historical relations to be established by the holder of capital in order that such accumulation can continue without undue hindrance. Capitalism then is the word for the system when such continuity of relations is secured. It is this self-regulating aspect of capitalism that has accelerated towards the commodification of everything that can be turned through others' labours to an opportunity for surplus value and profit. And, for the purposes of a book called *The Dark Theatre* it is in Wallerstein's view precisely 'bankruptcy' that has been as he describes it, 'the harsh cleansing fluid of the capitalist system'.[20] So, it would appear we are here dealing with theatrical examples of irrigation to a system whose continuation in part depends on such systemic losses described by the word bankruptcy. Arboriculturalists might perceive storm-clearings of forests as an equivalent and necessary process of renewal, but natural systems should not be confused with cultural and economic choices wedded to the ideology of surplus profits. These are not anomalous occasions within capitalist economies but structurally necessary ones for a system that is, as Wallerstein is at pains to point out, a very long way from a natural system active in the conduct of its own regeneration. Rather as Wallerstein chooses to describe it, capitalism is not just a 'not-natural' system, it is 'a patently absurd one'.[21] It is also a violent one, with its own wholly concomitant cultural cruelties that now inevitably follow loss by way of a side order.

Given how often in this book I will refer to this capitalist system as self-evidently absurd, and therefore something my socialist politics both practiced and thought is wholly at odds with, it might be helpful (at some length) to quote Wallerstein on what he perceives historical capitalism, actually, to be:

> Historical capitalism is that concrete, time-bounded, space-bounded integrated locus of productive activities with which the endless accumulation of capital has been the economic objective or 'law' that has governed or prevailed in fundamental economic activity. It is that social system in which those who have operated by such rules have had such great impact on the

whole as to create conditions wherein the others have been forced to conform to the pattern or to suffer the consequences.[22]

I see nothing systemic or structural in the 'information' industries operating through vectoral communications to lay this analysis to rest just yet. Various recent descriptions of such processes range from Margaret Thatcher's neoliberal rally cry (in fact a version of Herbert Spencer's classical nineteenth-century liberal position), 'there is no alternative', to Mark Fisher's recent prognosis (via Frederic Jameson and Slavoj Žižek) that it is 'easier to imagine the end of the world than the end of capitalism'. Both comments do much more than announce a submission to capital, they evidence symptoms of the recent naturalising of capitalism (the first complimentary the second critical) that one would presume any writing about performance and politics would at least need to encounter if not contest.[23] It would be easier to wish it away, but the histories of the theatre practices this book takes as its subject matter suggest there is something more at stake here than wishful thinking.

My starting point for that contestation here and *then*, is precisely the docklands landscape of the early 1980s, a place and time that for many, including Saskia Sassen, obviously represents a vital period of change in both North and South, capitalist and communist economies alike. The first feature of this shift as identified by Sassen, is the material development of growing areas of the world into extreme zones for economic operations that would otherwise have been quite unthinkable or relatable to those communities who found themselves the unlikely objects of the developers' attentions. On the one hand these forces are represented through the global outsourcing of manufacturing, servicing and clerical work and the shift of the docks from the East of London to containerisation in the deep-water estuary stretches of Tilbury, a shift that mimics in small measure the displacement of other once well-established inner-city dockland facilities to the globally networked, downriver deep-water-pools that suited the logistics revolution where containerisation became king.[24] Simultaneously with this drive there is the active worldwide making of global cities, such as the immediate neighbourhood of the theatre, as strategic spaces for advanced economic functions, including financial-cities such as Canary Wharf built from scratch on the site of the brutal renovation of 'old cities', old neighbourhoods such as that of South East London in which the theatre had played its resistant part for several years prior to these incisions in its broadly, if not unproblematic, 'collective' make-up.

These sites for finance are nothing new, they have existed as long as humans have been debtors, some time before they began to barter their way out of such debt, but what is new here, and I would suggest *led* and modelled by places such as the precise location I am describing in South East London in the 1980s, is the capacity to develop enormously complex instruments that allow this version of the capitalist enterprise to securitise, historically speaking, a vast and growing range of entities and processes. Given finance here is selling something banks do not have, not money in other words which banks have a lot of, finance needs to invade, that is securitise, non-financial sectors to generate its new profits. Hence the rise of the 'derivative' so decisively analysed in the cultural sphere in the work of the choreographer and capital theorist, the late Randy Martin. The logics here become ones of extraction and destruction and these are not anomalous affairs as characterised by Martin, they are the systemic deepening of capitalist relations through corporeal, bodily encounters.[25] And by their very nature those encounters are therefore the purview of something we happen to call performance.

Although I knew nothing of Randy Martin's work when writing *Theatre & Everyday Life* my own book was swiftly followed in 1994 by Martin's own first monograph, *Socialist Ensembles: Theater and State in Cuba and Nicaragua*.[26] While the geographies could not have been more different, the 'epistemologies of the South' that Martin was dealing with in a book that insistently foregrounded the role of theatre did much, as in my own writing, to recognise the key principle of what Martin called 'human association', and its special capacity to develop 'the social' through performance.[27] It might be somewhat far-fetched to now call up Boaventura de Sousa Santos's more recent conception of 'Epistemologies of the South' and think this urgent act of unravelling the entrenched biases of post Enlightenment Western knowledge production of the first worlds of the North would have anything to do with something as trivial as *South* London, as distinct say to those other more pressing Souths that are rightly the focus and moral imperative of his argument.[28] But passage after passage of this work chimes with the kinds of inherent 'know-how' that incessantly informed our work in critical relation to normative understandings of practice and theory. Here de Sousa Santos characterises what many residents in our neighbourhood already 'knew':

> The recognition of the struggle and of its protagonists is an act of pre-knowledge, an intellectual and political pragmatic impulse implying the need to scrutinise the validity of the knowledge circulating in the struggle and generated by the struggle itself. Paradoxically, in this sense, recognition precedes cognition.[29]

In Randy Martin's work of the same period there is an associated sense of vital inclusivity that invites me now in hindsight to make this connection. Indeed Martin's own 'field works' in Cuba and Nicaragua were being undertaken in exactly the same years I was committed to the local ethnographies of performance in that small bend in the river in South East London between 1983 and 1991, and we shared an interest in the generative processes of social activity embodied in production and reception as our chosen critical modes of work in those quite distant 'fields'. Where Martin identifies the influence and transformative effects of 'global markets' on civil society in Cuba and Nicaragua, I was watching on in no less wonder at their malicious effects from the decimated Royal Docks to the makeover of the once self-declared autonomous zone of the 'independent' Isle of Dogs, capital ports that after all gave rise to early prototypes of these very markets. Pushing Doreen Massey's arguments for the 'coeval' nature of asymmetric economic development here further than Massey would have deemed opportune, it might at least be noted that these apparently globally discrete developments shared a certain logic which it would be unwise to ignore however apparently distant their geographical locations.[30] The historic betrayal of the *South* of London that the privatisation of Docklands, capitalised from the functionary docklands they replaced, deserves some critical thinking as to how its own epistemologies were traduced in the roll-out of gentrification. From where we worked, it *felt* that all other parts of London, including the more artisanal artists' occupations of the East End, were operating to quite different discursive regimes than the ones brutalising the southern reaches of the river.[31] It is for this amongst other reasons that I wish to insist on specific, historically materialist differentials of urban 'gentrification' before claiming any universal features that might accrue towards a general theory of local disempowerment.[32]

There are many differences between my writing and Randy Martin's, not least of all the capacious geographical imaginary with which he deals compared to my own localism, but there could be no clearer departure from a shared interest in theatre analysis than the radical turn towards economic theory that Randy Martin took in 2002 in his ground-breaking and frankly visionary work *Financialization of Daily Life*.[33] Having learnt the lesson of theatre and performance for the kinds of civil and social arguments Martin wanted to make for his early studies, he now 'rolls out' the significance of the threat of debt to all manner of corporeal and quotidian encounters. For Martin finance has rightly and presciently moved left, right and centre to his social analysis as well as his choreographic critique of how such social relations are always maintained performatively. He was talking about consumer credit and debt long before others in the cultural studies field had begun to recognise the significance of the financialisation of everyday life, and his analysis brought attention for the first time (and well before the sub-prime crisis) to the peculiar dance of the derivative, the desecuritisation of consumer debt and the bundling of bills into bonds that he argued 'spread ownership around in vexing ways'.[34] The routinisation of risk and the normalisation of debt in the Anglo-American psyche and domestic sphere began to set the conditions for 'precarious life' that has become prevalent amongst post-industrial communities, and latterly ubiquitous to the cultural theory of the last two decades of Maurizio Lazzarato, David Graeber and Isabel Lorrey, and especially prominent in the better known but less economically forensic work of Judith Butler.[35] In this broad front the processes of the future became something that cannot necessarily be predicted with any confidence given the continuous state of emergency in the markets, but those processes that were after all the future expressed as a 'cultural fact' could be gauged mathematically, as a measure of abiding risk, a risk that was in Randy Martin's work uniquely theorised as an equation of individual accounting of, and for, *bodies* put under threat.[36] In Part II of this book the introduction of 'living currency' will provide a measure through which to explore exactly how bodies become forms of surplus life in a myriad theatrical examples of precarious performance.

For Randy Martin most interestingly for my argument about the logics of expulsion here, the acceleration of securitisation was the millennial version of the eighteenth century 'Enclosure Acts' in England, but with an ominous immobilising difference: 'Whereas peasants had to be physically removed from common lands to dispossess them of property, now dispossession breeds commons without anyone having to be moved anywhere. Possession has been rendered liquid so that it can be revalued daily'.[37] In my reading of Martin, in this and other respects, I recognise the sagacity of the guide he offers with regard to what I will call 'liquid loss', refashioning the social sciences beyond divisions between culture, economics and politics, and recovering the forces of financialisation as not just the arena of their relations, but the *embodiment* of their affects and effects. A measure of the liquidity of life itself. If the 'logics of expulsion' go some way to explaining the movements of those in that Docklands community (nicely summed up by a patronising headline in the *Guardian* about one of our long-term workshop projects with the German/US choreographer Viola Faber, 'Dockers Dancing!') then Randy Martin's 'social logic of the derivative' characterises our commodification in all such environments of speculation and securitisation, a metrics of daily life that figures a fundamental shift from 'past securities' to 'managing risk' that ensure we stay exactly where finance systems would want us to be, while holding out some 'hope' in a future that we have somehow become solely and individually responsible for however incapacitated by precarious life. As Byung-Chul Han, a theorist who Martin would have enjoyed and argued with, has more recently put it: 'The neoliberal imperative of self-optimisation serves only to promote perfect functioning within the system [...] everything is made comparable and measurable and subjected to the logic of the market'.[38]

So, with Randy Martin and Saskia Sassen's work in mind, what I am concentrating on in this chapter is a general theory of expulsion, a logics of loss, that arises from a single, parochial example close to (my) home in the 1980s, that I will follow with a short judicial coda from the present, somewhat closer to my current working place in the legal quarter of London, that might secure the plausibility of the claims I set out with regarding the ubiquity of expulsion as a dynamic of such coeval yet related environments. A political economy of small performances you could say, that begins with the facts at local, ground-level during the 1980s deregulation 'boom', freed from familiar vocabularies that have undervalued class analysis at the necessary temporary behest of identity politics, and takes us through some perhaps novel geo-political, legal, economic and cultural differentiations that might be of assistance in our shared work between performance and politics as laid out in the following pages of this book.

The lie of the land

The local housing expulsions of the 1980s along the Rotherhithe riverside stretching into the distance down Rotherhithe Street from number 107 where our theatre stood, were obvious and catastrophic for those forced away from what they assumed to be their birth-right, amounting to a simultaneous double movement of 'landgrab' and 'water-containment' that led to a wave of displacements and enforced incarcerations in zoned areas of bland interiority.[39] Let us take the more obvious partner in that land/water twin-set first. Without a clear understanding of 'land' itself little can be made of a theory that seeks to analyse its determining role in this local human experience, what 'expulsion' from that land implies for those excluded from it? As Todd S. Mei in his work on *Land and the Given Economy* draws our attention to, the nature of land and its pivot role in human existence, was long-ago figured by Tolstoy as *the* fundamental human relation.[40] Glossing the loss of land theory in Marx, he seeks to return land to its due place alongside Marxian emphases on labour and capital: 'land is a distinct factor of economic production in relation to two other factors – labour and capital – and by this distinctness it claims a special place within economic theory'.[41] Despite the work of Daniel Ricardo in the early nineteenth century on land's unique capacity to generate 'ground rent' and the unequal incremental value of land, the question of the 'meaning of land' itself often lay dormant in political enquiry as though its obvious material presence required less hermeneutic work to reveal it. Land subsequently has therefore fallen into inattention, in plain sight, not least of all in much theatre and performance study that is fascinated by space, nuanced in its critique of place, dedicated to its urban (and sometimes rural) manifestations, concerned for its potential for artist-led gentrification, but remedial in its recognition of the land law that dictates what can and cannot happen from one site to another. Indeed when the land becomes effectively 'lawless' as to some degree it did in the docklands regeneration era as brutally mirrored by that film *The Long Good Friday*, one cannot but notice the loss of liberties that such planning regulation had once legitimated and protected. It is the ontologically unique status and influence of land that draws our attention to it here. We are after all a species that is by definition 'landed', despite those of us who estuary-swim wishing we had retained something of our amphibian natures. The centrality and what Todd Mei calls 'givenness' of land to dwelling was made quite apparent in the phenomenological emphases of *Theatre & Everyday Life*, but its part in 'making' and 'production' that Mei articulates as equally significant factors of land use received little attention in that early work, while the reduction of land to 'labour' and 'capital' received no attention at all.

It is impossible writing these words today to avoid that question of land, home, property and inheritance, in a city such as London scarred by the imperative to offer soup kitchens and food banks for the homeless. And its claims on our attention are ubiquitous in the theatre 'proper' where, during the editing of this chapter I happened to see Anton Chekhov's rarely produced 'first play' being performed by the fine Dublin-based company Dead Centre. That this staging happened to take place at the Battersea Arts Centre, where this book will end in seven chapters' time, and that I was encouraged to be at the performance by two colleagues whose work appears and reappears as an influence, Joe Kelleher and Nicholas Ridout, adds a small symmetry to the proceedings. Suffice to say here that in the self-reflexive, meta-theatrical scenes of the staging of an impossible play as imagined by the company, land, and the property secured on it, forms as one would expect in any Chekhov a nascent, yet principle, part. Waving a gun at the audience to ensure we understand the Chekhovian principle that it will, if it appears in the first act, have to go off by the last, the director of Dead Centre who is staging his own version of the work given its parlous history tells us: 'property of course is one of Chekhov's main themes' and goes on to set the scene for us as the characters assemble on a naturalistic set that does not look quite right:

> OK. So. The play is set in Russia. 1878. This is the country estate of Anna Petrovna, widow to General Voinitsev. She inherited this big house from her late husband and is now struggling to keep up the payments. So, you see we already get the theme of property in the stage-setting, even before anyone speaks.[42]

The director is speaking this straight into our ears through a pick up, receiver and headphones that we have somewhat supinely agreed to wear for the occasion at his request. We are in other words being alerted in this sub-voce subtext to the ubiquitous undertow of land and property in dramatic works of this moment and kind, as though as to remind us of the landed politics of what we are about to observe, and perhaps have been observing for generations, without necessarily quite noticing the terms of the contract.

The acquisition of land (as this short Russian excursion has reminded us) is of course not a lone-wolf event as Saskia Sassen has made clear in her detailed empirical studies.[43] It requires, and in turn stimulates, the making of a vast global market *for* land. Land by its nature through its acquisition capitalises itself precisely through the way it is laboured into surplus value, ironically often as demonstrated in Docklands by precisely *not working* the land (if one equates working with an agricultural model of care and effort common to the region where I am editing this book in Truinas, as implied by the French *Terroir*) as it rises in price through an apparently magical process of patient profiteering. As Sassen describes it, such laborious forces also entail the development of a rampant specialised servicing infrastructure to enable accelerated sales and acquisitions, secure property or leasing rights, develop appropriate legal instruments, and in the case of the Docklands community I am talking about, push for the making of new laws to accommodate such expansionist purposes in other sovereign countries with whom the newly arriving leaseholders who have been largely gifted this land, predominantly multi-corporation banks, will do their unfettered deals.

The novel types of contract and forms of ownership signified by Sassen, I would suggest here, were precisely prototyped in places like the Docklands area of London in the 1980s, and when these modellings could not be resisted, were exported globally. That would be the only 'universalising' tendency of neoliberal gentrification I would want to allow for here, cognisant of the acute asymmetric forms such urban development takes. For instance, the water that had once provided the means to profit the historic docklands (as distinct to the retro-fitted financial city of the capitalised Docklands) now provided through the 1990s the submersible means for newly developing fibre-optic cables to deliver these deals to the unsuspecting, but according to the entrepreneurs who knew better, 'waiting world'. These channels of instant communication and transaction were exported globally precisely by means of the very water that, somewhat unusually, lay so close to the land from which the sea-trade routes departed. The same could not be said of landlocked cities that found their own, wholly distinct ways, to gentrify and 'upscale' themselves using quite different communications channels

When the Tesco supermarket chain in the mid-1980s alighted on a massive keystone development at the border between Rotherhithe, Deptford and Bermondsey, now a Bermuda triangle of inflated sales into which speculative investors have disappeared for three decades, their chosen motif was, not coincidentally, a spectacularisation of these waterways themselves, reimagined in the form of animatronic tableaux of the high-seas occupied by irascible pirates. As commercial branding went, the pirate, 'the enemy of all' after all,[44] appeared a peculiar aide memoir to the likelihood of being ripped-off in the aisles, but the supermarket landscape was nevertheless littered with pirate ships, eye-patched figures, and all manner of parroted paraphernalia as though the buccaneering franchise was going out of business and needed subsidy to be brought back into appearance. The 'Black Atlantic' that had provided the slave trade with its aquatic geography was, in the precincts of Tesco, reimagined as a place of nautical play, of desert island sanctuaries (often housing the oasis of a Coke or Pepsi dispenser) and risk-free shipwrecking that the philosopher Hans Blumenberg would have been alert to given his lifetime commitment to writing sea-states into land-lubber view. As Blumenberg put it in his work *Shipwreck with Spectator* the sea persists in the human imaginary as an arch metaphor in which operate just three existential states: to drown, to be saved, or to witness. In the case of Tesco we witnessed the drowning out of any aspiration the local neighbourhood might have had to be saved from this commercial calumny, the rapid loss of the independent, the idiosyncratic or the idealised small-industry that had once typified these very streets of now-razed and synthetically-flooded waterscapes.[45]

Unexceptional politics

Each of these shifts of expulsion, including those businesses that worked to a different economic rhythm than multi-corporations enticed into the area by generous tax breaks, brought new and dangerous challenges for those summarily displaced. As tower blocks with river views were forcibly cleared, retro-fitted with cladding of a higher health and safety order than was the case for those further West, at an investment level that the residents of the newly 'refurbished' (*sic*) Grenfell Tower close to my more recent home in West London could only dream of, those expelled from their long-term communities found themselves bunched within inland corridors of dilapidated high-rises and mid-war low-rise housing that were barely fit for purpose. As Giorgio Agamben has reminded us (drawing on a rich tradition of exceptionalism from Thomas Hobbes to Carl Schmitt) all camps are born *not* out of ordinary law but out of 'the state of exception', of which this lawless land-acquisition of Docklands in the 1980s on behalf of capital and the new financial city could be taken as one extreme urban example, which set the models for many such acquisitions that followed. As Agamben describes it: 'The camp is the space that opens up when the state of exception starts to become the rule'.[46] The camp is paradoxical in this respect as it is a piece of territory that is placed *outside* the normal juridical order, but not simply designated as an external space. Rather what it captures is not just what happens *within* its confines, though that can be awful enough, but also what is happening *without*, where the conditions for humans to be deprived of their rights and prerogatives are fostered to the point that acts against their interests no longer appear illegal, to those inside or out. Camps historically fall back on a certain internal consensus as to what is and is not acceptable, enforced by a policing regime with little or no relation to the norms that would commonly prescribe action within the realm of ordinary law. The rash of private security firms that took rich pickings from this very Docklands zone during the 1980s are one uniformed and ear-pieced wireless measure of just such control.

This extreme state describes very well the kinds of rampant dislocation and disturbance that became business-as-usual through the 1980s Docklands land wars. But it nevertheless does register a somewhat hyperbolic tone for what were after all, though serious threats to security, para-legal exclusions that did not commonly lead to death. There *is* though, it must be said, substantial evidence of the mental health consequences of these rapid changes and deep and abiding distress amongst those treated with such anti-democratic disdain. So what if, in the spirit of Randy Martin's work on the financialisation and embodiment of everyday life, we were here to invert the presumption of 'the state of exception' that Agamben offers us and rather consider ways in which this movement of displacement and decampment is precisely one everyday example of what became *unexceptional* politics in this Docklands realm?

This unexceptional character of everyday politics and oppression has recently been articulated by Emily Apter in the following way:

> Overflowing the bounds of realpolitik or informal politics, what I call *unexceptional politics* could be thought of as the material and immaterial stuff of politics that encompasses everything from government gridlock and dysfunction to political cunning […] from politicking to Occupy or Maidan, with their neo-anarchist strategies of occupation, assembly riot, strike, obstination […] interference and creative leveraging.[47]

I am attracted to this partial theory in this context. It helps me think through the *actual* modes of operative resistance common to those Docklands' years for its recognition, as I have argued at length elsewhere, that our activist energies might well be reserved for the possibility that, despite all signs to the contrary, 'we really don't know what politics is' and in so 'not-knowing', might think twice about calling out its placeholder names in lieu of practising some kind of politics in the worlds within which we, actually do, work.[48] This 'calling out', what others might unhelpfully call virtue-signalling, is what I call 'pseudo-politics' that has corrupted performance seeking the political at every turn. I am very much with the much-missed K-Punk blogger Mark Fisher in this respect when, in *Capitalist Realism* he says: 'Nothing is inherently political; politicisation requires a political agent which can transform the taken-for-granted into the up-for-grabs'.[49] Theatre has long been, in its unexceptional, anti-didactic sense, less 'in-yer-face', and more 'up-for-grabs' amongst those who might make best use of its political subtleties.

A small example of 'the unexceptional' in the political realm, of impasse and obstinacy that turned the normative taken-for-granted towards the up-for-grabs, will suffice in the local context I am discussing. A group of young people who had long worked within the Rotherhithe Theatre Workshop project were, in the early 1980s, somewhat bemused and not at all happy that their local underground station, Surrey Docks, opposite their homes in the high-rise block Canada House, was about to be renamed Surrey Quays by the unholy alliance of the London Docklands Development Corporation, their clients Tesco Supermarkets (again) and the ever-pliant Transport for London.[50] With the development of that piratised hypermarket at the edge of Deptford on reclaimed land previously occupied by the Surrey Docks network of inland river pools and waterways, the original name of the area (for the developers at least) had an unfortunate affinity to the Cockney Rhyming Slang phrase used to describe the venereal disease Gonorrhoea. It was not uncommon to hear the phrase, such and such (discretion being the key here) 'has a touch of the Surreys', a lyrical, typically truncated phrase, that owed its derivation to the rhyming of Surrey Docks with Pox. For the realtors' hell bent on their purification of this once shabby area, Surrey *Quays* would nicely displace any such memory of promiscuity (a history of name-changing for political purpose that Brian Friel skewered so beautifully in his work on Irish local myth and narrative, at the behest of colonial British rule, in *Translations*[51]).

This group of young people intuitively understood such name-changing was a 'bad thing', the foretaste of economic displacement for those lacking the accoutrements of gentrification and agreed to meet at the underground station on the morning of its ceremonial opening by the then Tory government Minister for Transport, a man called Cecil Parkinson, who was well known and disliked for quite particular reasons that went some way deeper than party politics. Parkinson was the closest ally of the then Prime Minister Margaret Thatcher and just months earlier in 1982 as Chairman of the Tory Party during the Malvinas/Falklands War had acted in close consort with the PM and as a public 'comms' face of the military dispute. Despite being such close allies Thatcher had only recently become aware of his predicament having covered up his 'responsibility' (as Conservatives referred to such matters) for the pregnancy of his parliamentary office secretary, Sarah Keays, in an extra-marital affair that had lasted under the press-radar for a number of years.[52] The affair (and news of Sarah Keays' pregnancy) was broken to the press during the Tory Party Conference in 1983 and Parkinson was forced to resign, not just from his ministerial position but any likelihood of leading the party he was being groomed to assume was in his gift beyond Thatcher's interminable reign. The episode was later immortalised pseudonymously by Alan Hollinghurst in his novel *The Line of Beauty*, which is a nice twist as it recognises the significance of urban myth in the telling of this narrative. Here is our own version of that partial truth that we used to share through the 1980s at Rotherhithe Theatre Workshop.

On the morning of the renamed station opening the young people grouped together in a tight knot close to where the black, top-of-the-range, Ministerial car of Parkinson drew up. Parkinson started to make his way towards the ribbon-cutting ceremony at the incongruously modest foyer of the pompously retitled station, but before he could get there a melodious chant to a well-known football hymn that had long rung out across the Kop-end at Anfield in Liverpool, was swelling from the protesting crowd: 'Surrey Quays, Surrey Quays, Surrey Quaaaays; Surrey Quays, Surrey Quays, Surrey Quaa-aays; Surrey Keays, Sarah Keays, Sarah Keeeeays; Oh Sarah Keays, Saraaaah Keaaaays!' At once flippant and devastating, ignominious and prescient in its debunking of his apparent power to call things as he wished (including this area that had long gone under the name Surrey Docks), it was not just a matter of a political figure of such reactionary credentials being pushed back by young people's well intentioned words (he was despatched to his car immediately by his security minders and driven away at speed before getting the chance to cut the ribbon) but how in a single eliding lyric this 'unexceptional' community chorus (with no assistance from the go-to TV choirmaster Gareth Malone) had found a way to denigrate the architect of an expeditionary war, fought on the other side of the world, while in affectionate terrace-inspired crowd sourcing, supporting the mother of his child who he was never, despite his daughter's serious epileptic symptoms, to see again.

This episode has entered a long history of debates about local name-changing worthy of Brian Friel's politics of nomenclature in that long-running play *Translations*, that reflect their significance for the area. It is clear for instance that the widespread internet conjecture that 'civil servants' wanted to skewer the unpopular Parkinson with the suggestion of renaming the station Surrey Quays themselves, is some way wide of the mark, given the shopping centre was already progressing in its development under that neutralised-nautical title.[53] But what is clear from these online exchanges, which re-emerged when TFL were lobbied by the local community in 2008 to return the name from Surrey Quays to Surrey Docks, is the unanimous understanding that the name came from the diktats of a 'shopping centre' and replacing as it did deep local relevance with commercial considerations was roundly considered by residents as an all-too-common but serious slight to local history by global business interests.

Of course a theoretical side-effect of any such reorientation of what stands for our political vocabulary (as evidenced in this communal *mise en scene* of protest) is the concomitant recognition here that 'the Political' in this neighbourhood could only ever be conceived as a placeholder term to describe 'the multiplicity of forces, structures, problems, and orientations constitutive of modes of existence and being-in-community' that this anecdote would appear to elucidate.[54] What working alongside those protests, performances and practices in Docklands precisely brought to my attention everyday over more than eight years during the 1980s, was the way in which an apparently non-political vocabulary of words and gestures can be endowed with political significance, the apparent loss of a historically verifiable reality being usurped by a form of political realism suited to the structured realities of the protestor's own preferred forms of address. In this case a nimbly repurposed football chant with a twist of nomenclature that precisely reversed the presumption of name-changing those in power would consider their own prerogative (and certainly not others').

Ethnography of the everyday

So it is apparent from those pages written 25 years ago, that I did consider these wholly unexceptional *experiences* of disturbance at some length in *Theatre & Everyday Life* having taken Jonathan Raban's affect-laden *Soft City* as a field-guide. And it is clear I was more interested in phenomenological and corporeal experiences of such symptoms of the capitalocene, subjectivities of capitalism you could say, as distinct to any kind of economically informed critical account of the structural causes of such pathologies. I am not sure I mis-sold my portfolio however as there was printed, in quite distinctive font on the cover of the book in the elegant design of Simon Josebury, a subtitle that read: 'An Ethics of Performance'. Indeed prior to publication I recall having to fight hard with the commissioning editors for the pluralised form of 'ethics' to avoid any misapprehension that this was a work of moralising cant. And in keeping with this spirit of post-Empire pluralism the Introduction of *Theatre & Everyday Life* opens with a fierce and at the time unpopular critique of the presumptions and colonial calumnies of an exotic ethnography, common among performance studies specialists in the US at the time led by Richard Schechner via the anthropologist Victor Turner, boosted by the relative 'fly at all costs' planet-be-damned liquidity of the University travel-expenses regime that I was presuming the word ethics (from ethos, or placemaking) would contest:

> The ritual enquires of theatre anthropology have enriched the possibilities of what is considered part of the theatre field, but as field work, have left to some degree, the domestic to the sociologist and the statistician. The nature of the domestic is chameleon in the sense that the theatre maker is often not of the place of performance, knows little about it in a geographical or historical sense and less about its emotional qualities. This 'lack' is an ethical concern with very specific cultural consequences. Ethos after all derives from the sense of 'being at home' and to deny this propensity for the theatre maker would not appear to me to be an encouraging start for a theatre philosophy. The local and particular are as demanding of consideration now as the cosmopolitan. They are closest to the everyday, are less easy to extrapolate from their context, and less easy to bring 'home' to be studied.[55]

Given I wrote this a full quarter of a century before Extinction Rebellion came into being this commitment to a critical localism would seem to be telling. It also, it has to be emphasised, had little effect on the expense-account University and its fetishism of global mobility in pursuit of 'international recruitment' that has scarred the 'internationalised' university sector since, with its off-shore campuses irrigated at the expense of others bankrolled by some of the world's most dubious human-rights-lite regimes.

The narrative of *Theatre & Everyday Life*, a study of what it was like to recognise 'being here' as distinct to 'being there' and its potential for performance, runs something like this. On my arrival in the dockland's neighbourhood in 1983 it had been immediately obvious that the theatre director Peter Brook's overly idealised, borderline imperial, inherently expansionist conception of the theatre as an 'Empty Space', as laid out in the first of the Granada Northern Lectures of that title and later published as a set of four best-selling essays, would have to go.[56] Not least of all because its presumptions and politics seemed so cruelly to mimic in cultural form the pressing dilemma of those in the neighbourhood resisting expulsion from land others precisely considered an empty space.[57] Our first critique of this modernist theatrical orthodoxy contested Peter Brook's purist fantasy of the 'empty space' awaiting its theatre, a tabula rasa for professionals to enter and exit at will. We (by which I mean my close colleague David Slater, and all those who worked with us at Rotherhithe Theatre Workshop over those years in Docklands) counter intuitively perceived theatre to have been superseded in that populated place by the quotidian performances of everyday life, those that remain for good and ill and make any encounter between performance and 'its' space so problematic and persuasive.

The small histories of Surrey Docks above should have made quite explicit why that might have been the situation in a locality crisscrossed with fierce microaffiliations and historical betrayals. In each case study in *Theatre & Everyday Life* the fetishised myth of the isolated artist is dislodged from the centre of the scene to allow what I called 'understudies', those as-yet unwritten and un-regarded by hegemonic cultural forms to take their due part. At the very time we were protesting and performing in this agonistic way, the French philosopher Jacques Rancière was writing on 'the part of those who have no part' (*avoir-part*) during the 1980s, while we were *enacting* this substitution.[58] Rancière and I subsequently, some years later, gave consecutive keynotes for Martin Spanberg's 2004 iteration of the Frankfurt Sommerakademie where concepts of 'the artist formally known as audience' and 'the emancipated spectator' were first circulated, debated and adopted.[59] But *Theatre & Everyday Life* did not just precede and in places forecast such political philosophy, it also accompanied, and in many ways predicted a swathe of work in environmentally responsive cultural theory that followed in its immediate wake, from Bruno Latour, Graham Harman, Isabelle Stengers, Mark Fisher and Jason Moore, in conceptual arenas such as social networks, object ontologies, cultural hauntology and ecological dimensions of the capitalocene.[60] My book was not of course the cause of any such front of radical inclusion and cosmopolitanism, but it certainly was not irrelevant to these writings which, as cultural theory often does, inevitably occupied far more visible political and social policy arenas than the dubiously 'aestheticised' marginalia of performance studies, the *'really* merely cultural' to double down on a well-known phrase coined by Judith Butler, could routinely claim for itself.[61]

Theatre & Everyday Life conceptualised a 'lay theatre' that resisted both the paternal welfarism of community arts rhetoric and the separatist presumptions of a professionalised realm. The principle conceptual category of the work, perhaps its *only* workable concept, Lay Theatre, articulated diagnostic and heuristic tools for those seeking to forge relations between cultural interventions, critical citizenship and what the political scientist Lea Ypi might call now 'avant garde political agency'.[62] It offered the first sustained encounter in the theatre studies field with conceptualisations of the 'amateur' and 'failure', critiquing previously hegemonic notions of 'professionalism' and 'virtuosity', and was unusual at the time for its braiding of detailed materialist theatre histories within fully rounded ecological frames of reference.

The first part of *Theatre & Everyday Life* thus, given its aims, *had* to bring into question the Paris-based director Peter Brook's received presumption, the modernist avant garde idealism of the 'empty space' of theatre. It was the least we could do to push back against such received and untroubled wisdom, however isolated we became from the mainstream in so doing. Intemperately stated criticisms, close to what some inaccurately described as an 'ad hominem attack', taking on, as these balanced rational arguments did, a 'master' of the contemporary European stage, were only heightened by the dubious lack of scrutiny that master's work had been receiving for some years, a form of soft patronage that the UK theatre affords those established white male figures in decline from previously authoritative positions that they in all honesty never sought. The knighted English actor, Sir Laurence Olivier had suffered the same fate some years earlier. The equally knightable playwright Sir David Hare was soon to follow. In the latter case as evidenced by the deeply disappointing production of *I'm Not Running* at the National Theatre. Given the play was ostensibly about the travails of a female politician it was mounted in 2018 to broad bemusement from a younger generation of women writers whose work found no place on their 'National stage'.[63] The deeply problematic production miserably evidenced an inexorable decline in Hare's once original dramaturgy which had been, in its early collaborative form in 1971 under the umbrella of Portable Theatre (with Howard Brenton, Snoo Wilson *et al.*), responsible for the scathing *Lay-By*, that as seen in Edinburgh had partly been responsible for my interest in theatre in the first place.[64]

In the subsequent three long chapters of *Theatre & Everyday Life*, Lay Theatre, Regarding Theatre and Everyday Life (echoed in the first three chapters of this sequel), I asked us to look again at a *populated* place in which, with due regard for Prince, 'the artist formerly known as audience' has always already been at work.[65] These ghostings of the theatre machine are, I wanted to suggest, what give performance its palpable and problematic politics, and I have seen no evidence to suggest any change on that score since. Theatre is always exclusive in this historic respect, an act of aesthetic expulsion preceding a political debt to those it has exiled – performance as apologia in stark fact, good reason for its often melancholic mode of mourning-play. The cultural logics of expulsion as evidenced in this Docklands decade over a period of intense financialisation, thus mimic the material exclusions of those rendered precarious in the neighbourhood by rapacious debt. Lay Theatre was not conceptualised at the time to address this question of such debt to expulsion, but in retrospect following the last decade of theorisation of the debtor-creditor relation, does invite us to think again about its political potential. As Maurizio Lazzarato has more recently put it: 'The negative that debt institutes informs the historical conditions from which struggle turns away to invent new forms of subjectivation and new possibilities of life'.[66] I suspect should Randy Martin still be with us this would be the Tri-via crossroads at which our work would now meet.

The second part of *Theatre & Everyday Life*, subtitled 'Nature Theatre Culture', positioned performance as the mediating arbiter between conceptions of nature and culture, ferrying the understandings of one, to and fro, through the (sometimes proscenium) frame of the other for analysis and activation.[67] Written from within the heart of that declining docklands neighbourhood that had once profited from the exploitation of 'cheap natures' of Empire, here the capitalocene is recognised for its profoundly ecological dimension. While the work was avowedly local in its reach, taking account of our continuous cultural resistance in the form of performance and images to the tsunami of capital inflows to the area, the very far-reaching influences of these banks and multi-corporations, in and across landscapes very far away was, of course, always actually the point. Any analysis that forgot this continuous stretching of the local to the global (as *Theatre & Everyday Life* largely did) was destined to a fatal partiality.

The performances and theatre we made with those embattled residents of the neighbourhood over that blighted 1980s Thatcherite decade, performances that numbered in their hundreds ranging across all genres from choreographic, experimental, scripted, educational, theatrical, pantomimic, site-specific, we eschewed all such labels ('social theatre' and 'community theatre' were especially unpopular considered as they were trite betrayals of the complexity of what we called 'the really-real'), would routinely make these associative links and force-fields of power appear in ways that theatre is peculiarly suited to. Many of these performances are detailed in *Theatre & Everyday Life* and can be readily sought out there, but one is especially relevant to the present enquiry as a single, relatively simple year-long ethnographic account, the first of a number in this book that I have given the name 'field notes' to hint at their immersive, participant-observation tone and reach.[68]

For some years following the decline of the docks themselves by far the most prominent employer in the area, a ten-acre site owned by the biscuit manufacturer Peek Frean (or Frean's as it later possessively became), had dominated all aspects of local lore and life.[69] It was not just by far and away the go-to place for women in the area to seek part and full-time employment, but it permeated the locality with its distinctive aromas that marked the seasonal changes of biscuit production. My local authority housing in Marden Square on Drummond Road looked out directly over the high eastern wall of the factory and the brocaded curtains in the flat were drenched in its sweet succour smells. If it was June it would be the raisin-fruit sweetness of the Christmas puddings that were being made to be shelved and matured by the end of the year, if it was Bourbon (first introduced to the world by Peek Frean in 1910) it would be Thursdays when that biscuit run was at its height in the week.

Very early in my time in Rotherhithe I had therefore, necessarily though not quite by choice, been assailed, Louis Althusser should he have had a more olfactory Proustian persuasion might have said *interpellated*, by the call of this manufacturing logic with its strictly marked calendar and its all-embracing labour values.[70] I was an early enfeebled example of the body produced by capitalism, increasingly nauseous as this continual aromatic assault came upon me year after year. I had long known, given the play and I were exact contemporaries, that John Osborne's angry young man Jimmy Porter had somewhat incongruously built his paean to a lost faith in post-war Britain from the platform of a market sweet-stall 'candy counter' in *Look Back in Anger*. But here the testing of values appeared much less individual and far more to do with communities and bodies of shifting power that could, if opened up, tell us something about longer durée movements of employment and expulsion in the neighbourhood.

It is not that we did not recognise these economic forces, the 'body productive' would be the phrase used in theory today, but back in 1985, we simply 'spent a year' working at the factory in a perhaps misguided daily (and sometimes, when we were insomniac, nightly) attempt to absorb what the rhythm-machine of the factory was doing to those who worked on its continuous line. The factory had after all never been diverted from its true biscuit-path, since its founding in 1857. Indeed during the First and Second World Wars it continued to produce biscuits, prisoner of war parcels and canned puddings for the troops without a day's interruption except for those mornings required to clear up after intermittent bomb damage from the night before.[71]

The company had been founded by a Mr Peek, a partner in a London firm of tea merchants looking to diversify from their quintessential business of Empire and East India trade routes into something more soft-centred. The links between this industry and Empire are unlikely to stop there given this late nineteenth-century heritage, and indeed when Mr Peek teamed up with Mr George Frean, an established maker of ship's biscuits from the English West Country that one would imagine might have provided sustenance to the slave industry from Bristol, the dubious commercial compact was complete. The invention of what were called 'docker-holes' that stopped biscuits from inflating to enormous size under pressure, allowed for financial expansion and the purchase of the ten-acre site between Keetons and Drummond Road in 1866, just a short walk from Hope (Sufferance) Wharf, the later location of our warehouse theatre, a scale of operation that seemed stupendously out of scale for such a small object of culinary attention at the time. The nineteenth-century Franco-Prussian war provided the massive new factory with its first huge orders, between 10–11 million Navy biscuits for the armies involved, and the factory started on the all-day and all-night production that it was still pursuing when we arrived to look around and take up occupation in 1985 on hearing of the threat to the factory's survival in the area.

In the first of a number of 'fire sales' that this book takes as paradigmatic of the financialisation of everyday life and the fate of those put into its debt, the burning down of the old Dockhead Peek Frean factory that preceded the relocation to Drummond Road site on the night of 23 April 1873, was not only one of London's biggest fires since the Great Fire of 1666 (also ignited of course in a 'baker's house'), but was also responsible for the speeding up of the new factory in Bermondsey to the manufacturing levels that secured its long-term profitability. Eye witnesses to that massive conflagration, including the then Prince of Wales, watched as flour, eggs and sugar cascaded from the burning windows and on hitting the scorching street below were instantly baked into a single, street-wide biscuit of more than a 100 metres in length. Given the poverty levels of the time, not dissimilar to those recorded in Mayhew's London maps of the 1840s, it might not be wholly apocryphal that those without food came in their hundreds to chip away at this vast delicacy, removing it in slabs to eke out their dwindling provisions.

This curious 'history' was always present and correct at the Peek Frean's factory taking up space on the shelves of a network of display cases in the foyer which visitors were invited to attend to while waiting for interviews, tours and samples. But there was for those of us who spent serious backstage time there a more modest but nevertheless systematic history of corporeal labour at work in this site. It was these bio-mechanics of production that really interested us given choreography, writing and theatre imagery were our own means of production. On my first day I was shown into a middle manager's office where George was sitting in his black suit at his desk with a Custard Cream biscuit hanging from what appeared to be a thread but was, when invited to inspect it, which I was by way of warning, a long human hair. George was introducing me to the first law of Peek Frean's, the necessity for hygiene at all times and most urgently the need to ensure one's hair was tied back and net-covered well away from the passing produce on the line. In the months ahead, now in residence you could say, standing at that production line with those women who quality-checked the passing biscuits, I never again saw the abomination that I was shown on that day. That's why Peek Frean's could make the apparently generous offer that anyone finding a body part in their biscuits would be eligible to free company produce of their choice for life.

As 'scene after scene' of this kind flowed through the year we began, with the close collaboration of the women on the production line and in consort with the students from Dartington whose accommodation surrounded this well-aerated industrial behemoth, to build what was then the novel concept of a site-specific theatrical event to take us into a night shift with the staff. Starting with the in-house garage mechanic, Greg, we imagined a work that could sweep though the factory site, setting out from its vehicles plant, making play of its inherent narrative contours while honouring its mysterious atmospherics of production. I had shown Greg an image, *Gas* (1940) by the American painter Edward Hopper, of a forecourt attendant attending to a petrol pump, over-lit by the winged Pegasus of the Mobil sign.[72] And we conceived the first of 32 rhymed scenes in which the narrative of a night shift in the factory started to be played out in factory time (it was all factory time as the production line never stopped) until it closed down days after our last performance on site. The performance we made over that year was called *Multiple Angel*, the affectionate family nickname for Charlie Chaplin, whose machinations in his prescient work *Modern Times* was one of our influences as to how bodies became choreographed into industrial processes.[73] And the first scene of my script for *Multiple Angel*, identical in length and stanza-form to all the others, went like this:

> We who have worked on the night shift
> Know that the light will fall fast
> For behind us lie ruins that reach to the sky
> And buildings that shadows have cast
> Across the sun and its satellites, planets and stars
> The firmament heavens above
> The place of archangels,
> The site of the saints
> The poets and prophets of love.
> This slow moving cannister, casket of ore
> A beacon that tells us of impending war
> Will one day come falling in silent reproach
> On all that has gone by, whether by car or by coach
> And not stopped or slowed at the sign of the steed
> Who thought that their travel was best done at speed.
> How much more we would know
> If for once we were lifted
> Above this flat place into which we have drifted
> In the arms of St Christopher
> On the back of a horse
> Beyond the trajectory of this cannister's course
> And out into the yonder, the distance, the blue
> To the stars called Audi, Mercedes and VW.[74]

This half-baked history of biscuit production in Bermondsey might now appear somewhat tangential to the overtly political concerns of our collective work, and certainly at romantic odds with the sharper financial critique of this book, if it were not for our discovery of an apparently ephemeral document that had been produced at Peek Frean's in the 1970s to accompany the £3.5 million reconstruction of their Bermondsey factory (just a few years before we spent time in residence there exploring their production processes). In that glossy brochure, produced at some expense and evidently designed to persuade those who might have thought biscuit production was a marginal part of the post-OPEC oil-crisis economy, the Marketing and Sales Director (effectively a modest way of saying what would now be called without pause, the CEO) a descendant of one of the company founders, M. S. Carr, lays out in exquisite David Brent, managerialist *Office* toned detail, what is expected of the Peek Frean workforce:

> Our objective is to produce more brand leaders and many more volume-selling biscuits so that the very word 'biscuit' is synonymous with Peek Frean. Ambitious? – Yes, but through the complete reorganisation and expansion of all the departments at Peek Frean that contribute to the selling effort, and by introducing new relationships and new attitudes among all the personnel concerned, we are poised now for a major breakthrough.

It is as though Mr Carr has been reading Byung-Chul Han fully four decades before he got around to writing his own version of neoliberal critique: 'Today, we do not deem ourselves subjugated subjects, but rather projects: always refashioning and reinventing ourselves'.[75] Mr Carr pauses in his oxygenated prose at this point before delivering what is evidently his coup de grace:

> The word 'BISCMANSHIP' epitomizes this new concept in selling biscuits. It means much more planning ... an intensified searching for new ideas ... free discussion at all levels ... new channels of communication ... working together as a coordinated team ... and above all killing off all prejudices and misunderstandings that may have arisen from the previous remoteness of 'Head Office'.

In a coda worthy of any neoliberal manual of corporeal and psychic appropriation to the marketing cause, Mr Carr finishes with a flourish that would have graced the satire of Malcolm McDowell's coffee salesman in Lindsay Anderson's great diagnostic film of the UK's economics of Empire, *O Lucky Man!*:

> Through the reorganization of the Peek Frean departments actively concerned with selling we have forged a chain in which every individual functions – whether product research, brand control or field selling – is interlinked. Each link represents a vital function and the whole chain provides that powerful machine that will give Peek Frean dominance in the Biscuit Market.[76]

By the end of this paean to 'Biscmanship' Mr Carr is capitalising Biscuit at every turn, convinced as to the merits of the workforce that will administer this grab for total power amongst all available comestibles. Now knowing and admiring the UK based performance work of Touretteshero (Jess Thom) as I do, there is an uncanny symmetry between this artist's brilliant channelling of the word *biscuit* that erupts to spectacular effect in her lyrical language, and its deployment as a placeholder here 'signifying all'.[77] The second half of the brochure is dedicated to a series of profile shots and biographies of those management flunkies expected to deliver this revolution, a Brylcreemed cadré of 17 white, besuited (though biscuited comes to mind given what I have said above) middle-aged men, whose demography and age is quite at odds with a predominantly mixed-race female workforce notable for its inclusivity. A closer look at their job titles does reveal however something of the inherent radicalism of this lighter-than-air factory despite its gender challenges: E. J. Warden (Manager) is tasked with 'keeping abreast of all systems which might benefit the organisation' including, very early for the time, computers; T. L. Colborne is described as an 'Experimental Manager' and is focused on 'process' and the 'full use of technological advances and improved ingredients', while A. G. Nevill, who was invalided out of the army following a grenade injury is as the 'Experimental Baker' responsible for innovation from plant trials through to manufacture.

Indeed Peek Frean's was from its early days a leader in pensions, an early adopter of medical, dental and optical services for their employees, and sported a Dramatic Society founded in 1908, taking theatre up somewhat earlier and more seriously than every UK university where performance-specific curricula were, following the historic anti-theatrical prejudice of Oxbridge, effectively excommunicated, until Bristol University broke the embargo in 1947. In this spirit we found a cache of 1906 nitrate-heavy film stock abandoned in cannisters in the factory basement, and with the help of Christine Edzard's remarkable local company Sands Films located in a spectacular double-block warehouse next door to the Theatre Workshop, recovered the deteriorating frames for broadcast on the terrestrial UK Channel 4. If this sounds familiar to the conceptual art-lover, it was an early example of the 'factory gates' genre later made artistically recognisable by the German artist Harun Farocki, in the Tate-owned installation *Workers Leaving the Factory in 11 Decades* (2006). Meanwhile *we* simply thought of it as fascinating black and white documentation of what it was to leave work in tumultuous, hatted and capped numbers, inconceivable in post-industrial Britain today. For those working with us in Rotherhithe it was a searing record of loss, what Walter Benjamin would describe, like all historical documents, as a document of barbarism.[78] The factory was closed within days of our third and last performance of *Multiple Angel*, after 130 years of another kind of continuous production on site, spilling countless long committed workers into the dole queues. Three full decades later the Drummond Road site has, at the time of writing, just been announced by the developers Grosvenor Estates, as the centrepiece for the £500 million 'Bermondsey Masterplan', a mixed use of public spaces, amenities and private development, all of which will be built with sensitivity to the 'historic' nature of the site and its significance for a local population for whom it was the key and for some, only, employer following the running down of the docks.

Of course our performance work, our 'ethnographies of the everyday' you could call them, took us much further afield than the gates of a local factory, we were open and available to all everywhere, except when we decided not to be, either on the grounds that a potential participant held racist or homophobic views, not uncommon for communities struggling with severe poverty and fear of the economic influence of 'outsiders', or rather more modestly but no less significantly, those in the press, media or mainstream theatre whose presumptions about this 'kind' of long-term committed work were just so boring and irrelevant to the innate critical creativity of those with whom we worked. We occupied hairdressers' premises, not just because there was a willing and relatively immobilised potential cast of third-age participants there amongst those women having their hair permed (over one- and two-hour stretches of enforced sitting under futuristic plastic-pod hair-driers), but because those women shared historical and affective narratives of the picaresque 'stories of their hair' with such verve and generosity. And young teenage women with children, on seeing this work, who wanted to participate, found ways in which to convert the limited but nevertheless attractive annual budget of the theatre (paid for by Dartington College of Arts, safely 300 miles away West and wholly out of touch with the necessities of infrastructural social spending) towards an investment in washing machines and tumble dryers that after diverting the council's subsidised water supply could operate as a kind of pop-up laundry in the basement of the theatre, thus freeing them from laundry duties in the launderette down Jamaica Road and facilitating their day-long presence in the workshop to pursue the theatre that they wished to pursue with that great innovator and theatre-making friend of theirs, David Slater, and his numerous allies.

Cheap natures

My own commitment at this time amongst these people who had taken it upon themselves to make things happen (theatre) and resist other things happening (exclusion) then equally concerned protection of those residents' well-being *and* protection from the loss of their land for development by rapacious outside interests with no interest in them. But this work *also* necessarily concerned thinking-through questions of the environment and its shaping through what was most starkly obvious in the area, the workings of the capitalocene. The docks themselves with evocative names like Cinnamon Wharf, drawn from the British Empire's trade in spices, explicitly pointed to the ever-present *environmental* milieu of our work. Of course, given there was no anthropocene then, or no talk of it at least, although we were clearly at the docklands' heart of one of the industrial motors *of* that anthropocene, there was no capitalocene either, quite yet, or again, no one describing it in quite that way. My view from where I stood amongst those docks over those years alongside others, was that capitalism was less an economic system, less a social system and more a way of 'organising nature', with an emphatically lower-case 'n'. Not a capitalised and removed 'Nature' that is an abstract 'out there', but a nature, or natures, *within* each and all of us as we worked a land that was called Rotherhithe with its own natural history. The origin of the name of the place itself told a story before our arrival that Raymond Williams would have cherished for his work on the mutability of landscape, *The Country and the City*, should he have come across it. Reder was a 'place' after all, where 'heier', cattle, were once landed. The country *in* the city. Reder heier, or Rotherhithe as it came to be known in the 1700s around the time the Herengracht canal in Amsterdam, with its sweeping curve of four-storey banking houses, was being developed. Our crisis, the one we were living through was not one of capital *and* nature, but, as Jason Moore put it, of modernity *through* nature. Nature was never just there of course, not least of all in these docks where the incongruous city farm reminded us of commercial constructions of the 'natural realm', it was always and everywhere historical. It was capital's aim to ensure nature worked harder and harder in each of it cycles, at the teeming edge of which were dockland landscapes of this very nature, engineered by the Dutch, British and North American industrial revolutions, broadly speaking over the last 300 years since those 'domestic' banks started being built on the Gouden Bocht, the 'Golden Bend' of Herengracht in the 1640s.

Now those banks were all around us, lacing the contours of the Thames, finding their own way of facing out towards their heart of darkness, the water of this colonial trade. From where I stood this hardly looked like the grave-yard of capital. The search here, as Jason Moore has pointed out in his formative work on *Capitalism and the Web of Life*, is a seeking out not just of nature but successively 'cheaper and cheaper natures' to feed the motor of Empire.[79] It is something identifiable and substantial called 'cheap nature' that is the torque of capitalism. Historical capitalism thus implies and necessitates, beyond the working definition offered by Emmanuel Wallerstein earlier, historical *nature*, and historical nature since the sixteenth century implies and necessitates historical capitalism. The category of the anthropocene as a mode of explanation for these dynamics, the kind of humanist frame that should it have been available, which it wasn't, would have appealed to me at the time of writing *Theatre & Everyday Life*, and makes for a far easier story than the one I am telling here as it does not challenge the naturalised inequalities, alienation and violence inscribed in modernity's strategic relations of power and production. It does not ask us to think about these relations at all by way of its liberal patina. An abstract humanity is at work throughout the writing if not the practice of the anthropocene, all the key material concerns of Performance Studies for instance, those of intersectionality especially, are wiped clean in the interests of the *anthropos* as a largely abstract collective human actor. That elision, that loss of the precision-violence of capitalism, irrespective of well-meaning alliances, therefore, simply will not do, however attractive the catch-all phrase.

It is, anyway, materially obvious with climate change, waste proliferation and attendant environmental crises that while capital itself might be experiencing some kind of long death-moan, capitalism is still busy exhausting its ecological regime. And that is a narrative that owes a very special debt to the land being acquired from under our feet by those banks in the 1980s. What Jason Moore describes as that process of getting extra-human natures, and humans too, to work for very low outlays of money and energy, is the history writ large in the Docklands community of capitalism's great commodity frontiers and capitalism's long waves of accumulation. The appropriation of frontier lands, of which the violating camps I evoked earlier, those that stretch from Calais to Raqqa, become the outsourced border zones for 'resource wars' fought elsewhere, have been the indispensable condition for each great wave of capital accumulation represented by those towering banks, from Dutch hegemony in the seventeenth century, through the English industrial revolution and attendant British Empire of the late eighteenth and nineteenth centuries, to the rise of neoliberalism in the 1970s and 1980s in the post cheap-oil crisis of the US and European North. But as Jason Moore and others are right to point out, this 'cheap nature' strategy has been failing for at least a century now and with the fig-leaf of financialisation, and the capitalisation of reproduction beginning post-2008 to reveal their own multiple contradictions, it is quite apparent as I write this book that the capitalocene far from ending is entering another 'systemic spasm' that will have further serious consequences and make the current camps we are discussing, lacing the fringes of Western Europe, appear modest by comparison.

Avant garde agency

Notwithstanding the deployment of esoteric language to explain these forces, words like anthropocene and capitalocene for instance, as a performance specialist I can at the very least notice quite readily the *mise en scene* of that Docklands time and place. A *mise en scène* of unexceptional politics meeting immovable objects that certainly alerted me to the necessity of conjoining cultural and environmental thinking and action at every turn. These scenic arrangements took the form of a sequence of interventions in the civic life of the neighbourhood in direct resistance to the antidemocratic initiatives of the planning quango the London Docklands Development Corporation, who, requiring no planning consent beyond their own unilateral decision-making, and with generous sweeteners from the government in the form of those generous tax breaks, ran riot across the landscape here, while very far away from Lagos to Ogoniland, the extraction industries their corporate clients supported, reeked a more brutal havoc on bespoiled and devastated populations elsewhere.[80] The loss of world indeed.

Our theatre work was built on models of course, we were responsible for students and neighbours alike who had a strong sense of their own structural appetite for change and intrinsically understood education's critical relation to any such change. Resisting the platitude of Peter Brook's 'Empty Space' was not simply an altruistic defence against those who fiercely protected their neighbourhood against all new comers, the neighbourhood after all was already known for its occasional lazy race-hate speech and all-too-common estate-based identity divisions. The empty space was surely populated, but that population was as often a bellicose, belligerent and bigoted dissensus, as it was anything like an avant garde liberal consensus. No, given her well-aired views on these matters in her compendious book *Artificial Hells*, Claire Bishop would not waste too long on niceties with us now if we had bought into the soft welfarism of that discredited patrician wing of community arts social management at the expense of agonism and innovation.[81]

Rather the resistance to the 'empty space' required us to recover not just those communitarian practices that preceded us, but also those *avant garde* political agencies that had come before in the form of artists' interventions that had a peculiarly close attachment to, and derived from the non-professionals (as far as art practice went), the lay-community, who had in fact brought them into being with no help from 'emerging' artists' subventions. There were hundreds of these that we recovered as part of our work, this South East corner of London had always been a remarkably fertile territory for abandoned practices of this nature, and their disappearance from the scene was only another expulsion, another logics of loss to consider amongst equally pressing commitments to the recovery of histories that would remind us of the territory's insistent protection of social justice when threatened by industrial force.

To put concrete detail to those 'hundreds of examples', take for instance US visual artist Mary Kelly's collaboration with Margaret Harrison and Kay Hunt on the 1973–1975 multi-media project *Women and Work* that at the time of writing in 2018, not before time, has been recovered and shown at Tate Modern in the Blavatnik Building/Switch House, under those artists' names. First exhibited at the local South London Gallery in 1975 this sociologically comprehensive and meticulously accumulated collection of punch-cards, black and white portrait photographs and interview films, displayed a rhetorical minimalism to aesthetically deliver what those women in Peek Frean's knew all too well given the Equal Pay Act of 1970 had failed to adjust such matters in their favour, the continuing discrepancy between their corporeal labours and those men who occupied the totality of the management positions above them. We knew a great deal of this 'Document on the Division of Labour in Industry' years ago, in around 1984, about a decade after it was carried out in the 1970s, because we knew those women who had been the subjects of this work, who would come to the theatre warehouse some years older and wiser and told us that they had spent time working with Mary Kelly on this project at that Bermondsey Metal Box factory. It has to be said though they were never sure quite what the outcomes of the project had been nor, as was often with our hard-to-please allies, were they very impressed by the lack of instrumentalism of that art practice. In the intervening years they had registered what is most commonly noted but elided by the paean to 'political theatre' that those craving social worth for their art maintain, that the project had not improved their conditions of work beyond the satisfaction of working together on the project which, as a resident said with the economy of critical thought common for the neighbourhood, was what they did everyday anyway. Art appeared not to 'add value' in quite the manner expected of it, which meant in any other manner than to generate further 'wealth' for an already nascent art market, years before Jay Jopling bought out the 1970s former paper warehouse that he had Casper Mueller Kneer Architects transform on the rapidly 'improving' Bermondsey Street into his third London based 'White Cube' gallery in 2011 (in his trade mark concrete-sheer).[82]

Or with avant garde agency in mind, we might return to that work at the Peek Frean's biscuit factory discussed earlier, that took up a prominent ten-acre site in the neighbourhood and over the years had provided employment for almost all the mothers of the kids who used to come and work with us at the theatre workshop.

What does it mean when one sees one's own work, both within the factory and 'on' the factory, and amongst those who work *at* the factory précised by Harun Farocki and incorporated into an installation now owned and showing continuously at Tate Modern in London, just a matter of metres, but a world away from the Southwark neighbourhoods I have been describing? We will come back to Tate Modern and their litiginous viewing platform in Chapter 3, but it might be noted here that in a legal battle to preserve the right to attract tourists to their Herzog de Meuron designed brick pyramid in London in Fall 2018, the Director of Tate Modern, Frances Morris, had to make an unusual appeal to the High Court Judge, Mr Justice Mann, that the 'view' the viewing platform offered of South London was part of Tate's commitment to its South London neighbourhood. Such a debt, if you will allow me to call it by its name, might be better redeemed, given what has to be cleared to allow an institution of this kind space to build in an unfettered way, by reconnecting works such as Mary Kelly's and Harun Farocki's to the lives of those in the local communities precisely in South London from which these were created. It is peculiar that the righteous, and right, international disquiet about the reparation of cultural artefacts that routinely circle around museums (most notably obviously the Parthenon Sculptures, otherwise known by the colonial deniers as the Elgin Marbles, at the British Museum) does not extend to these local initiatives of those in this less 'true South', whose labours have been adopted and some might say appropriated by big-ticket artists who, with different degrees of care for those they have 'curated', barely look back on what they have left behind beyond their work. This kind of 'cultural cruelty' will set the pace in Part II of this book.

Taking these two brief case studies as exemplars of many others, avant garde political agency as far as I understood it during our own work, was concerned not with these *representations* per se, but the testing of viable forms of *resistance* and the propositions for political, social and cultural transformations that these works initiated, in the workplace.[83] If there were representations they were 'real representations' that were required in such volatile contexts. Throughout this work ours (by which I mean all those involved not just those who instigated the work) was always, rather unfashionably given the foibles of postmodernism heavily backed by cultural theorists at the time, a normative perspective, not just an explanatory one, normative standards being those that pertained to an ideal standard or model, an ethically responsive, radically inclusive counterforce to hegemonic forces of artistic conservatism. These normative concerns could not of course be proved or disproved, rather they were there to be weighed and judged. That was our work amongst others, weighing and judging normative principles, ethical attitudes, reasons for doing things as well as not doing those things. For instance it was patently impossible for us to *prove* that the local council should provide adequate housing for those expelled from their homes, the workforces pictured by Mary Kelly in her work, or as in Harun Farocki, leaving their work, those on the production line involved in our theatrical events, and those in their threatened homes seeking to maintain their livelihoods. Rather what was significant for us was to surface and make apparent the opinion that they *should be* provided for. Sometimes but not always such surfacing took the form we call performance. But such theatre, however avant garde, only ever had fleeting association with politics, especially desired political outcomes.

When the eminent Brazilian theatre-maker (and soon to be politician and legislator) Augusto Boal visited for a week in 1985 to work with the neighbourhood of seriously regular participants who amongst a much larger group of blow-ins numbered in core membership about 50 people of all ages, the community constantly challenged Augusto to trade in his high-flown rhetoric of change for some substantial yet much more modest gains *in* the neighbourhood, in one case, chillingly now, seeking support to expose the hopelessly inadequate lifts, fire regulations and exits in one of the highest blocks in the borough, at 27 storeys now looking back, well above Grenfell Tower heights. Boal was peculiarly unable to respond to these invitations having apparently become enamoured with his own aesthetic regimes of 'Joker' and 'Forum Theatre', and I have to say the guru status he never sought, something which our neighbourhood participants had very little time for having had next to no training in the cultural deference that afflicts the British in the face of an 'international reputation'.

Our real and abiding interest over this decade then was in how moral principles might make the journey to become political obligations amongst those in a nascent neoliberal domain, justified and propped up I have to say by a spineless postmodern relativism rife within the academy and artists' milieu alike who presumed no such thing mattered. We were asking here what conceptions of political agency might support normative innovations and political transformations? Performance, in the circumstances I have described, provided the activist mode for the trying out of such diagnostic and heuristic experiments in agency. Avant garde political agency, as Lea Ypi has recently theorised it, included the heuristic role of conflict for developing a normative account able to improve on its rivals both with regard to problem diagnosis and its capacity to guide political transformation given *existing* political structures.[84] We were no anarchists, that was unlikely in a working-class, or post-working-class community, that recognised the protection existing political structures already gave to many of those most unjustly treated by statist politics, but our actions were always heuristic in the sense that they could not be optimal but had to settle with being 'good enough'.

Filing for bankruptcy

This 'minor journeying', 'ethnographic localism' you could call it, recovering archaeologies of avant garde agency and communitarian creative practices continued for me until the early 1990s when the theatre was forcibly closed from beneath us. To the immediate left of the short flight of entry stairs to the theatre there stood proud on the wall a single light switch with two settings: On/Off. We had neither had the inclination nor the resources to fit a permanent rig to the ceiling of the warehouse theatre for the decade-duration of our stay, despite continuous encouragement to do so from those wedded to an illuminated form of theatricality that might mimic those newly arrived theatres upriver with names like the National Theatre. And while a long-suffering technician arrived from the West Country to fix some temporary scaff' to mount some lamps, I cannot recall it being used for anything other than a sort of legitimating 'eye candy' in the spirit of gig-lighting that was meant to look good rather than make other things look good. Like everything in the place over the years the rig was plundered in due course for those who needed garden illumination to light their new 'patios' and BBQs (care of the LDDC) and we returned inevitably to the one wall-mounted fixture that never let us down. So, without simplifying matters too much, between 1977 and 1991 the light switch was on. Then it was off. Dark Theatre. A matter of loss. Small history I suppose, just one of a plethora of theatre bankruptcies then and now. 'Close the door behind you' was the only kind of closure offered by the local authority in those pre-trauma days.

In 1983, the year I arrived at the warehouse, just downstream from Tower Bridge, if my memory has not deceived me, and there is precious little evidence of the curious accounting for this theatre over its lifetime, the annual rent on the two-storey building measuring 25 × 10 metres, was around £875. By the time I left in 1991, the annual rent was in the region of £25,000. An increase of something like 2,800%. In that first year we were able to count on the neighbourhood, the supporting college and on one unforgivably indulgent occasion the LDDC itself, to raise the annual rent, but within a decade the hike to that astronomic level of commitment had, like all other community initiatives around us ranging from the Time and Talents Centre to the long-standing Finnish and Norwegian seaman's missions, become a financial pressure too far.

Given all our work was being conducted for free with some who could not afford school uniform nor lunches never mind cultural taxation, it was inevitable that we would have to close. No one had any property that could otherwise have been used as collateral or guarantee against loss so we were essentially bankrupt and in default of our lease once the financing college had decided to pull its long-standing and generous funding (and more valuable still given their immense energy, intellect and talent, the years of students who came with it).[85] It was not perhaps surprising that it was the banks themselves who had eventually swept away our resistance with their tide of credit to another city just beyond us, the increasingly hawkish developers, and wanted us out in order to sell on the modest theatre to convert it into four, rather less modest 'luxury apartments'.

Everything I have discussed so far grew out of disappointment, most obviously expressed amongst the young people of the neighbourhood themselves who on losing a precious and long-running escape from the mundanity of their everyday lives, took it upon themselves to lever up the Canadian Maple sprung dance floor (that had been laid in the early days of the theatre workshop by a far more positive and playful local council) and torch the west-end gables of the now-deserted upper storey where double warehouse doors fell from above into the rubbish skips below, setting fire to the accumulated theatrical detritus from our years of operation that

42 The loss adjustor

we had cleared from the workshop on closing just weeks before. That disappointment was also summed up by a short note (italicised in the revealing excerpt below) to the foot of the authoritatively constructed local history web-site written with the exemplary care of the local historian Andie Byrnes. In a meticulous record dating back to the 1850s from its origins as an 'open coal wharf and depot', in the exact riverside site of Rotherhithe Theatre Workshop, the years of theatre-making I am celebrating in this chapter do not even appear to have taken place. None of it, though a very great deal besides *has* taken place which makes good sense given the appropriate marginalia that cultural practice scribbles at the edge of the much larger and significant industrial forces of this location through longer histories. Mr Byrnes writes:

> The building now known as the granary was used for storage during the sufferance wharf phase, and only later became a granary, serving the nearby Thames Tunnel Mills. In 1974 part of the property was acquired by the Industrial Buildings Preservation Trust and was converted [...] to premises for crafts workers, including silversmiths, potters and knitters. It is worth noting that this was done over a decade before the regeneration of the area by the London Development Corporation. [...] Hope Wharf was transferred into the hands of Southwark Council in 1977 and closed a few years later in a 'rundown' condition [...]. *It's really rather sad that this particular brave experiment failed.* [my emphasis.] In 1997 the properties that made up Hope Wharf were converted to apartments.[86]

The 'brave experiment' that the author writes about here appears to include the attempt at an infusion of craft-based practice in the Wharf buildings, but makes no mention at all of the 15 years that Rotherhithe Theatre Workshop deceived to flatter, insisting that it had made some sort of contribution to the life of the neighbourhood during this tumultuous time, and generating speculation in pedagogic circles that it offered something of a model for other kinds of cultural commitment over unusually long periods of activity. Indeed this whole effort and enterprise appears in this authoritative account simply to have contributed to its eventual entropic 'run down state'. But it was not as though I had not seen our elision from history coming. Ghosting has existed very much longer than current business etiquette manuals on office harassment would imply. I had read Michel de Certeau on *The Writing of History* and was confident the physical if not psychic traces of our efforts would be gone within years if not months, avalanched as these precarious remnants were by the pressing concerns of 'progress' in what W. H. Auden would have called this 'small untidy spot'.[87] I wrote about that disappointment of loss at the start of this chapter, but the passage in its original form in *Theatre & Everyday Life* continued:

> There was always something there, but the remains of a theatre are less coherent than buildings suggest, and it is these fragments which are testament to

what happened and why a theatre rarely sinks without trace. That a building remains, means little in a time when the combustibility of theatre has been so reduced. Like other transformations in the neighbourhood a theatre can become a cinema, a bingo hall, and a carpet warehouse within a generation.[88]

But the combustibility of this particular building had not it seems been so reduced. It appears to have readily taken the paraffin and rags that did for its upper part shortly after closure. And it is in the after-burn of this miserable act of defiance that such disappointment of closure might be most acutely felt. So, perhaps in a wilful act of resistance to such melancholy of loss, in keeping with my exhortation to continue to treat the disappointment, the closure of the dark theatre, as an opportunity to 'say something else', our riverside home was called Hope (Sufferance) Wharf after all. I took some time recently to follow-up at one remove the more recent history of the Docklands landscape I have been criss-crossing over the last pages. It offers me the second example of a fire sale in which damaged goods (in this case a cindered theatre) are struck down at cost and sold on to mitigate financial distress, in this instance for Southwark Council, who on losing our annual rental were faced with the reality of an oversized space they could not disperse to clients so angry were those who had occupied the 'theatre' for 15 years. If 107 Rotherhithe Street had on our arrival been ghosted by its previous history as a place of precarious labour, industrial injury and death were routine in a wharf building of this kind, on our departure it became 'off-limits' to all those who had participated in its subsequent revival as an apparatus of the political imaginary.

Compound interest

To seek out this fire sale, a bonfire of the vanities you could call it given the *dramatis personae* I am about to introduce in a short concluding coda to this chapter, I spent some time in another no less 'local' neighbourhood, but a rather different one, the historic legal-quarter in and around the Strand and Fleet Street in central London. During 2017 I spent most of February, March and April (the entirety of a short research leave from university teaching duties) at the Royal Courts of Justice observing a trial between Mark Holyoake, (in)famous for in 2010 allegedly bringing an Icelandic-waters fisheries business, British Seafood, to its knees, and two very well-known real-estate developers in the UK, Nick (Nicholas) and Chris (Christian) Candy, commonly in and beyond the press referred to as the 'Brothers Bling' for their obvious pleasure in sartorial standards some way in excess of those commonly sported in British estate agency. They were fighting over the control of a piece of prime real-estate on the fringe of Belgravia in central London, Grosvenor Gardens House. The site was described in points one to three of his final judgement by The Hon Mr Justice Nugee in the following way:

> Grosvenor Gardens House ('GGH') is a Grade II listed mansion block designed by the distinguished Victorian architect Thomas Cundy III and

completed in around 1868. It is situated in the Grosvenor Gardens Conservation Area in the City of Westminster, on the eastern edge of Belgravia, just around the corner from Victoria station. [...] When an opportunity arose to buy the freehold, Mr Mark Holyoake (the First Claimant in this action), who had some experience of developing property in the area, was attracted to the idea of buying it with a view to converting it back into high-class residential use, and on 18 July 2011 caused Hotblack Holdings Ltd (the Second Claimant, 'Hotblack'), a Jersey company ultimately owned by him, to contract to buy the freehold for £42m.[89]

The problem was that Mark Holyoake did not have £42 million and like many far smaller fish before him he could not complete on the deal on the desired date. He was about to be fried and he knew it. At this point he went to his old school friend Nick Candy, and Nick's brother Chris, seeking £12 million, funds which were readily made available on perhaps economically proportionate but nevertheless strikingly good rates for the Candy's, should anything delay their prompt repayment over a strictly demarcated time-frame for completion. Such accelerated payments are not unusual in real-estate development given the potential rewards for swift completions on properties involving 'change of use' clauses.

So, 25 years on from the small economic and social histories I have opened this book with, during the Spring months of 2017, I spent some quality time observing these not-unrelated daily proceedings of a civil case in the Royal Courts of Justice in London. Local news, for once again I was 'close to home' with my ethnographic enquiry, as Court 30 in the Rolls Building backs directly onto the King's College London Maughan Library where I sometimes write when I am in need the kind of securities that a building which was once warehouse to 500 years of paperworked English law can offer. While this is almost macrobiotic research, field notes from the familiar, nothing of interest is further than 200 metres away, I hope this does not make these concerns parochial, nor without relevance to the wider concerns of this chapter with bankruptcy signalled in its title. I would suggest indeed that precisely what I am looking at in this tiny area of the world called central London, disproportionately effects everything I can conjure up in writing elsewhere regarding something I have characterised as the capitalocene that appears so lofty and distant when named in that neologistic way.

What I was witness to in Court 30 was a case that, according to the summary of the Clerks, involved alleged acts of extortion, physical threats, defamation, fraud and industrial-strength tax evasion, the last of which appears to be beyond the remit of the case and therefore, though strictly excluded from direct discussion, a ghoulish presence in the rarefied air of Court 30 throughout the proceedings. All common practice for those in the businesses that were spawned in that property-rush that drove us from Rotherhithe, the one in the Docklands that today has spread like a rash of gated enclaves parasiting off the taste of another new elite of the super-wealthy. There is something peculiarly attractive about the Candy Brothers, (Holly Valance does not step out with Nick for nothing), their immense and rapacious work ethic, contemporaneous 'email' evidence is always cross-examined and timed so one knows that a huge volume of business is being done by these people in hours that most of us described by Occupy as 'the 99%' are fast asleep, if we have a place to sleep; their demanding aesthetic standards on behalf of their clients who they have educated to move beyond ubiquitous bling to appreciate the modernist lines of a Richard Rogers' residential masterpiece at One Hyde Park (at the top of which was delivered the world's most expensive apartment of its time), their Italian boots and tailored suits, and what the judge calls their 'love of Anglo Saxon language' that they coyly refrain from repeating in court in case it offends those of us sitting there pretending not to be shocked at the workings of this financial 'system', now laid absolutely bare as a sea of systemic abuse, for us all to witness. Mr Justice Nugee more than once quite openly describes the prevailing degree of 'dishonesty' hanging over this case, a miasma of mendacity, following multiple claims and counter claims of 'lying' under oath, as though that were wholly natural to this particular business domain, and as so prejudicial to right justice that he will have to weigh his own interpretation as to who on earth he can believe in this sorry charade.[90]

But what was I really doing in that court each day? Well I suppose I was interested in examining the thing I can only suggest is as close to Friedrich Nietzsche's 'will to power', his idea of 'millionfold growth', as I am likely to be given public access to at the outset of this twenty-first century, that precise accelerated development towards financialisation that the history of this chapter has described. After this absorbing spectacle, which went under the name of a Tort proceeding, there will be very few billionaires of this kind who will risk allowing disagreements over money to get as far as this kind of exposing legislation. The pre-trial settlement business will be the norm from now on in. What I witnessed was a marathon one-off, and it speaks to the systemic fraud that the litigants here mistook for business-as-usual. It should not go without mention that Mr Justice Nugee in note number 526 of a massive judgement, some months later, dismissed all claims against the defendants, the Candy Brothers (and their company CPC), with the following, drier than dry summary: 'I have now considered all Mr Holyoake's and Hotblack's claims and found none of them established. It follows that I dismiss the claim'. But by then the exposure of the court room had already generated considerable press coverage and provided insights to the property-world that would be impossible to garner from a business textbook, Harvard MBA or indeed the copious bibliography of debt theory that has emerged in cultural critique over the last two decades.

By way of insight to what really happened then it might not be inappropriate to recover in anecdotal terms some of the key relations on show within the courtroom itself, the *mise en scène* of the capitalocene after all. Indeed the law, that is the very thing lawyers are trained to interpret but surprisingly often goes missing in the *sturm und drang* of court room action, had gone absent without leave for many of those days over three months and one was left with this semblance of personal relations as the true matter in hand. In this spirit I was asked, on a slow news day, for the 'dramatic highlights' of the court case by my new colleague James Lumley, city correspondent for the reputable industry journal *Estate's Gazette*, who sat next to me most days in court explaining the finer details of Corporate and Tort Law to me in the infrequent breaks in the proceedings. This is how *Estates Gazette* profiled my thoughts on their popular web-site (accompanied of course by the ubiquitous podcast with me identified as the presenting author just in case I thought I could escape the attentions of the Candys' lawyers). I have added in square brackets one or two afterthoughts now on re-reading these field notes exactly two years later:

Holyoake vs Candy & Candy
Alan Read's Dramatic Highlights in Reverse Order:

5. Paternal Love
'Following a sequence of bitter exchanges in which the broken trust between Nick Candy and Mark Holyoake was laid bare, Nick turns to Mark and says in a moment worthy of Martin Scorsese in his prime that he is a "good father". Mark nods by way of recognition of temporary suspension of hostilities and regaining of mutual respect. "Family" would appear to be a key signifier in this court as in many others (from Naples to Chicago) where perceptions of loyalty are at stake'. [I had originally told those in the court when asked what I was doing there that I was writing about the friendship between the protagonists of this case, and specifically in the theoretical context of Jacques Derrida's understanding of friendship when placed alongside Carl Schmitt's conception of politics as a matter of relations between 'friends' and 'enemies'. From the outset it was obvious no one believed this theoretically over-endowed cover though it did increasingly interest me as the case continued and exchanges as personal as this became the norm. See below, No. 2.]

4. The Polygraph
'Mark Holyoake would not appear to be more asset rich than cash rich, according to the Candys, but that doesn't stop him grandstanding to the public gallery: "You take the lie detector test Chris and I will give £1m to charity!", he shouted. This was one of very few moments where there was direct address to those sitting outside the cordon of the two legal teams and it drew attention to the world of legal procedure and its limits (not least of all as polygraphs aren't admissible evidence in UK courts)'.[91] [The continuous deceit, lying and calumny that characterised these court proceedings, including my own duplicitous role as an under-cover writer, a form of endurance dishonesty, was the single most obvious taxonomy of real-estate business available to the impartial onlooker. Where witnesses on both sides were perceived as notably trustworthy (which they clearly were when they were) Lord Justice Nugee took it upon himself in judgement to comment on this as though in this particular corporate arena, truth had become the first victim of the law.]

3. Michelin Stars

'Granita was once known as the North London site for a deal that changed UK political history. [UK Labour politicians Tony Blair and Gordon Brown brokered their notorious political pact there in May 1994 after the sudden and unexpected death of Labour Party leader John Smith.] But the network of high-end restaurants, bars and clubs in which these contested deals were done stretched from Guernsey to Monaco via Lake Geneva where it appeared between the tables that everyone knew everyone else's business. What was obvious from these exchanges was, contrary to the neoliberal mantra of meritocracy, a new "old boy's network" was precisely what was underway throughout daily court business and indeed appeared to have prompted the whole reason for being there in the first place. I thought it positively feudal'. [*Guardian* newspaper 'Wealth Correspondent', the nominatively-determined Rupert Neate, asked me one day what I thought of most interest in the case and I recommended that rather than ask a low end café-dweller such as myself, he do the necessary work joining up the stars of the Michelin-rated restaurants, where each of the assignations between the 'leading men' had taken place, to draw the map of a loan that owed its peculiar form of currency to global cuisine of the highest possible order.]

2. Private Box

'The Gents' toilets on level five of the Rolls Building were modest in size with one closet and a pair of stand ups but had to accommodate in close proximity the personnel of two parties who were ambivalent at best about each other and downright hostile at worst. The *Evening Standard* [London evening free newspaper] story of the head-butting, grievous bodily harm trial that had arisen from action that took place in the Rolls Building toilets below on level one the previous year [and recently covered in the press], reminded me of the relative decorum that was being maintained amid those hostilities at this rarefied level. It was the kind of "personable" that you might, if you were certificating Pixar videos, call "MILD THREAT". Nick Candy generously, and genuinely asked me on the final day: "Do you have any leaflets for your play?" which if I was paranoid I might have interpreted as something other than a simple offer to circulate them for me through the concierge of One Hyde Park. But was that not the point of the whole case anyway? Interpretation and reinterpretation of words. I will be dropping some leaflets off to One Hyde Park quite soon'. [From the first day of the trial I had been identified by the Candys' reputation managers from Bell Pottinger as 'that Theatre Professor from King's College' which had suggested to their team that I was in the courtroom each day working on a script for a forthcoming play about the ever-debonair Nick and his alter-ego the ever-brooding Chris. Despite my continual denials that this was what I was doing (mostly in the toilets), they either never understood the distinction between theatre theory and practice, they would not be the first to confuse those relations, or, preferred to think of themselves characterised on stage at some future date irrespective of my, obviously, dim-view of their conduct (despite all claims against them on this occasion being set aside allowing presumably for a happy ending). Their willingness to subject themselves to such widespread international scrutiny through damning press reports of their once private lives had obviously set the scene for their sanguine acceptance that they would see themselves played by two less good-looking actors on a West End stage in costumes that just wouldn't meet their demanding couture standards.]

1. Alleged Threat
'The evidence of Mrs Holyoake was put into question under cross-examination by counsel before she took the witness stand. But the continually repeated refrain of "alleged" by the [Candys'] defence QC to describe the threat she had understood to have been levelled at her unborn child was assertively resisted by Mrs Holyoake on the grounds of simple respect for her feelings. In a gender skewered courtroom in which over a 51-day trial (other than hard-working court personnel and, I suspect, some invisible female cleaners) there were just two women who *spoke*, an expert banking witness and Mrs Holyoake. Amongst two vast legal teams and a case judiciary that was wholly male, this seems to be a worthwhile resistance by Mrs Holyoake to (gender) business as normal'. [I spoke about this exchange with Mark Holyoake on the day after it happened sharing with him my own deep sense of unease as to the nature of the cross-examination his wife had endured. He was grateful for the recognition that this just did not seem appropriate inside or outside a court of law. I was struck by a gnawing feeling that despite having arrived in this place some months before determined to damn everything about the rapacious business people involved, there was something in the care of their personal communications with me and with each other, that was, astonishing as it seemed given the comparison I was now making in my mind, increasingly alien in the University sector I frequented, now driven by marketisation and securitisation. I realised with shame that I was spending my university-subsidised research leave sitting in this place not because it represented an obvious hell (which it did) but because it told me something very stark about a campus heaven I thought I knew and couldn't necessarily count on for much longer. The courtroom operated to contracts of legal transparency, retribution and justice (perhaps, though we had to wait months for a judgment) that had gone missing some years ago from higher education managements divorced from any degree of regulatory oversight.]

These serious concerns that *Estates Gazette* saw fit to publish (a confidence in their un-libellous nature that gives me strength here) should not be trivialised because they have been hyped-up in the headline, nor undermined by me making facetious links between the scandal of University financialisation and criminality, for they do after all describe a pathological undertow to the very culture of the capitalocene as described so far in this chapter. What is more through this case I *was* also given the unusual opportunity to track the secret life of a loan that having begun between two friends at £12 million had gone so spectacularly rogue over the last five years that one friend was now seeking a redress of £130 million in the courts only to discover that in so doing each and all of the claimants in the case on both sides have been described by the cross-examining councils as 'pathological liars'. Again it is not the shock of the new that this represents for us sitting there as the predictable bad new days rearranged in another yet more heightened form of baroque embezzlement. Not embezzlement of each other, who really cares for this extreme version of the capitalist culture-class, I certainly don't (or didn't until I met the residents of Neo Bankside who I will return to later), but of those beyond them, described in court as the 'rats and mice', those lowly investors who buy in below the protected 'mezzanine level' of transaction, those who *do* pay for the roads, schools and hospitals with their taxes, but who will never recover their money amongst this very limited company, come what may. When this was put to Chris Candy by the cross-examining council there was unfettered laughter in the court from the Candy supporters who considered such a proposition as ludicrous. 'Other people pay taxes' I heard someone say from the back of the courtroom, before Judge Nugee shot them a look that appeared to be channelling his partner Emily Thornberry's Corbynesque (after the Labour leader of the time) distaste for those exceptions who consider themselves beyond the social rule.

The trial was in fact concerned with a handful of quite prosaic, yet unedifying technical issues in law: economic and physical duress, undue influence, fraudulent misrepresentation, unlawful conspiracy, unlawful interference and blackmail. But its more salient relevance to this book is its staging of the life of a financial loan for all to see. The proceedings here conjured up Maurizio Lazzarato's theory of 'indebted man' (*sic*) but now brought into harsh focus:

> Debt creation, that is the creation and development of the power relation between creditors and debtors, has been conceived and programmed as the strategic heart of neoliberal politics. If debt is indeed central to understanding and thus combating neoliberalism, it is because neoliberalism has, since its emergence, been founded on a logic of debt.[92]

This logic of debt is indeed the very same logic that inscribed the dynamics of expulsion and loss described earlier in this chapter.

In keeping with Lazzarato's diagnosis, the baroque loan-trail evidenced in this case runs between two friends in London, between their office in Belgravia and Knightsbridge and their offices in Guernsey and their penthouse in Monaco. It runs between their Ibiza villa and their super-yachts called Candyscape I and Candyscape II floating in their foreign, tax-free harbours. It runs from a disused Heli-Pad of dubious significance in Battersea (that defence for Mark Holyoake can see from his South London apartment window) to the toxic grid-ceremonial of the Grand Prix circuit. It runs from the debt collectors' moneymen unleash on each other from Russia, Saudi Arabia and Uzbekistan (all familiar to Mischa Glenny's unflinching reportage in *McMafia*) and the rather more prosaic ex-head of security at Westfield Stratford, the Dickensian-sounding Mr Knuckley, who despite continuous probing nobody appeared to know or wanted to take responsibility for. It runs between the alleged threats one makes to the other, regarding the safety of his wife's unborn child. It runs from the failed IVF of the wife of one of the defendants who claims he 'would never say such things about the unborn', and it runs to those who invest in these apartments at £6,000 a square foot for whom the Candy premium represents a staggering 300% over any other residential building that struggles to realise £2,000 a square foot in exactly the same location. And, inasmuch as any of this relates to what has gone before in this book so far, the exterminist nature of these developments of course drives the continuous expectation, that with a city on heat as London always is, despite all short-range Brexit signs to the contrary, there is 'nothing to see here', business-as-usual, no reason to look beyond these transactions to identify those in camps of a rather different kind elsewhere, who at the time of writing are the inevitable victims of such loans, defaults, investments and threats – indeed those with whom I am principally concerned in this book, the victims at a rather less-well represented and very uncertain crime scene.

But if the 'dramatic highlights' and the 'peripatetic loan' are not quite the central focus of what I wanted to discuss with regards to this trial, what was described in court as this 'Alice in Candyland' case, what is? The point I am raising here is somewhat more parochial, more local, in keeping with my commitment to brokering a general economy for performance from the particularity of evidence at the outset of this book. Without warning or apparent note, during cross-examination of the co-defendants, the 'Brothers Bling', Candy & Candy, much to my astonishment, the dark theatre returned. Unheimlich. I knew on our forced departure in 1991, that 107 Rotherhithe Street (the address of our Theatre Workshop on the river) had been developed by property speculators, everything with a 'river view' was, but sitting in Court 30 of the Rolls Building off Fleet Street, surrounded by financial journalists, personal security and their ubiquitous entourage of reputation managers (from Bell Pottinger just before their own 'reputation' was shredded following political manipulation in South Africa), I realised that the very building we had spent those years working in, resisting the developers, had experienced what Nietzsche described as 'millionfold growth', the kind of exponential growth that that short, terse note in the Rotherhithe blog written by Andy Bryers could hardly hint at that six short years after our removal: 'In 1997 the properties that made up Hope Wharf were converted to apartments'.[93] That line came back to me with a vengeance, with compound interest you could say.

Now refashioned as luxury residences for 'high net worth individuals', our poor dark theatre no longer had light switches but state of the art high-end human sensors and fingerprint recognition in a matt-aluminium plate on the door. Legitimate Presence/Illegitimate Presence appeared to be the only two options available on calling round. As a code it seemed to sum up the new private compound culture, the surveillance sensibility of a neighbourhood once walked and once enjoyed for its unusually familiar open-door policy. Council for the claimant, Mark Holyoake, was asking what value one might place on such 'technologies of the self' in some arcane side-bar to the main legal arguments? And I realised that the very example they were using to discuss these technologies marked out the theatre that I had worked with 30 years before, the one we had been evicted from and the one that following innumerable refits and up-scalings had been bought by business *confrères* of Candy and Candy and transformed into a luxury condominium block with fingerprint sensitive security. As I sat in Court 30 the dark theatre was now fully illuminated again for me, it was in the spotlight, it was collateral evidence in a legally contested scene involving alleged extortion, threats, fraud and tax evasion. X marked the spot in a cultural crime scene where a certain class had to be eviscerated, and that spot had suddenly become all too apparent for this observer. Nick Candy smiled and said: 'Your Honour, we don't work with shady people'. The public gallery laughed again. After three months in this place with these people I had begun to lose my sense of humour.

As Giorgio Agamben has pointed out this is no laughing matter. Having refused to accept invitations from States (including the US) where bio-metric data determines access through borders, Agamben notes for the first time in the history of humanity, 'identity' is no longer now a function of the social persona and its recognition by others, but rather a function of biological data which could bear no relation to it. He is presumably not a fan of touch-sensitive security. In this process we have literally lost touch with our own means of identification. The new entry system to that luxury block of apartments, that was once a dark theatre with free access for all, now shows us something crucial for our future about the impersonal, the potential of the impersonal in an increasingly personalised world. An increasingly personalised world that has never perhaps, felt more impersonal, where our supposedly defining human-hands have provided, in such touch-sensitive privatisations of once public places, the very means to dehumanise us. This 'digital data', designed to exclude all those who once were welcome, for the one or two hedge managers who now are, epitomises and marks our age as avowedly as the digital data-base that accumulates, collates and centralises it, and it is this realm of communicative individualism, or surveillance capitalism, that will become the shadow of theatre in the next chapter.

So, taking my starting point from *this* dark theatre and its aftermath, its fallout on my life you could say (and many other people's lives), the coming chapters in this book will now proceed to reflect upon a quarter-century interregnum of uber-accelerated economics, a state of financialised exception in which the irregularities of the global markets in 2008 will soon appear a mere ornament. These chapters will consider the following questions: While the capitalocene describes the continuous conditions of production of 'cheap nature', historically orchestrated from these very docks, what might activism look like in such a scenario? How are the epistemic implications of structural injustice to be addressed through performance? What kind of critical philosophy or cultural politics might be adequate to such acts and how might such strategies offer innovative, immanent, diagnostic and heuristic potentials for performance thought and practice? Beyond the ubiquitous radical particularity of performance theory is there any such thing as a general economy of theatre, and if so, who wants or benefits from it?[94]

The sober proposition I am offering in this chapter (the switch marked Off) is that we should start by recognising what precisely it means to be making, talking and critically addressing performance in the capitalocene as characterised in detail in this chapter, inside and outside the courtroom, whose brutal character demands that we understand that forms of knowledge and intelligence we might respect and admire are often at the origin of long transaction chains that can end in never-simple expulsions of race, identity and class. My affirmative insistence (the switch marked On) is that now is the time for rethinking avant garde political agency, the commitment to fostering the *mise en scène* of justice through performance, a commitment given the circumstances I have outlined, that has never been more necessary. So, what is there left to say, or worth saying in the time that remains, when a theatre closes, when it goes dark, and then is illuminated again, as something else, fearful yet familiar, Off/On?

Accounting for action

I suppose, to close this chapter, what I am doing in thinking about each of the discrete *mise en scene* above, is revealing an aversion to abstract speculation. Throughout the several years of work I have described here, and one reason for taking the time to take you back with me through this writing to something I do not commonly discuss so disappointing its denouement when set against the celebratory evocations of participatory public forms of theatricality by those less blunted by loss, is the prominence I wish to give to *figures*, often rather mundane unexceptional figures, but also economic figures, a general economy of performance that stimulates thinking of one kind and action of another. Here everything and anything in the world, even that capacious compound interest of 'millionfold growth', can be thought provoking, deserving of contemplation and wonder yes – not simply an ultimately replaceable representative of a genus of an 'idea', a source of inexhaustible singularity and multiplicity, but most pressingly an invitation to *action*.

Accounting then for action. But action to what purpose? Thinking and practising in the interests of radical inclusion I hope, against the logics of radical expulsion, I hope. The dynamics here mark a contestation between those logics that force people and non-persons out (competitive capitalism) and those that bring people and non-people in (what I call socialism). In this work it is not sufficient to *note* those who are expelled in the spirit of an outmoded ethnography of surveillance, but to cross into the spaces of the expelled, to capture the moment and work amidst that site of expulsion lest we forget the pervasive disempowerment of loss. That is the work I would like the following chapters to delineate if not deliver. Philosophically and analytically beneath the specifics of each of the domains I have placed alongside each other here lie emergent systemic trends. Despite their enormously diverse variety from the empowerment of the global banking system, as evidenced by the London Docklands Development Corporation, to the enfeeblement of its local democracy, these dynamics are ones of liberated profit-seeking and indifference to environment. Whether such movements look different in London, Barcelona, Berlin, Copenhagen, Riga, Paris, Brussels, the locations of the chapters to come, as they clearly do, might for once not be the only point. Such forces are different because of the precise, historically differentiated way they share something coeval, connected yet as-yet unaligned. And, as such, if destructive forces cut across my own oh-so parochial, local London boundaries, I can only imagine what I would discover should I be more emboldened to travel much closer *to* home, and really to open my eyes at what is most taken-for-granted at my own back door rather than feign inclusivity by roaming to sites for whom informed indigenous others must surely be the (financially supported) expert witnesses now. It is not as though my West London neighbourhood is not deserving of scrutiny as regards racist exclusions and evictions. At the moment the air outside that door is filled with the after-burn of not just toxins (appalling as that is) but also a corporate atrocity at Grenfell Tower that will unfortunately, but necessarily, close out this book. Given its title, *The Dark Theatre*, to avoid the implications of that mausoleum to hope simply because I happen to pass it every day, would be to add further crime to crime scene.

In such an atmosphere of gloaming, critical rigour becomes imperative given that these forces are subterranean and our interpretive methods in search of the social are simply not up-to-date nor up to scratch in a performance field still in thrall to the radical particularity of the non-conformist example. The more I rail against the platitudes of Political Theatre, Immersive Theatre or Community Theatre, terms that I have castigated for three decades since starting work in Rotherhithe, the more I announce my dependency on something that I take it might be called a politics of performance. Here a land-grab in the small corner of the world that was my decade amongst so many others in Docklands, is one small concrete instance of a much larger and elusive type of grab. The capitalocene as I am characterising it through these ethnographies is thus marked by the expulsions that I have outlined, but also is characterised by the erasure of corporeal incorporation, the sublimation to the markets of our very identities, the kinds of losses that my 'Field notes from a fire sale' will describe, including my own incorporation of course given how well theatrical audiences suit the dynamics of appropriation of our noble resistance. Thus the question of who quite might be responsible for those plots of land sold to something called multi-corporations, was always beyond us if we did not understand the global *incorporation* of everything that lay before us. Amongst these sophistications it is shocking to observe the elementary brutalities that accompany such expulsions of the systemic. It is these brutalities that form the cultural cruelties consequent upon loss that make up the further studies that follow in Part II of this book, those 'Field notes from a fire sale' that follow like day follows night this accounting in the ashes. It is the diagnosis of such predatory formations, and resistance to them, that will require a performance politics worth its name and practices of performance that meet those rightly demanding ambitions. And it is that task that *The Dark Theatre* seeks to play.

So what is at work here is a question of membership and constitutive participation. I think this is what was realised at the outset of writing this book, in 2017 in the UK, when for the first time in three decades an overtly *socialist* manifesto was offered to an electorate numb with neoliberal, austerity-cant, with platitudes such as 'strong and stable'. 'Strong and stable my arse' as the obvious rejoinder went from civil and uncivil socialist canvasser alike as we walked with each other from door to door in our constituency, seeking to elevate the Labour candidate Rupa Huq's wafer thin majority from a precarious 350 (to a robust if not landslide 13,000 as it turned out). It was the recognition by a newly energised younger electorate of a larger 'life space' than had for long been thought possible. The disappointment of these hopes in the subsequent UK Brexit election of 2019 merely heightens rather than diminishes their claim to my attention here, makes more urgent the seeking for association over atomisation, the significance of the solidarity of the labour union over 'self-help'. The micro-spaces I have been attending to over the 30 years since writing *Theatre & Everyday Life*, might offer some figures yet for working in this historically saturated life space, not an empty space but a life-world teeming with experience and expectation. Yet each space, as we witnessed so horribly, close to where I live in this West London constituency, just weeks after I set about writing these words in summer 2017, gives notice of a capacity for destruction that if it is not faced will violate us, and violate others, beyond us, much less able to survive corporate nihilism's savage attentions.

A logics of expulsion, logically, would conclude with the expelled. But where are the expelled? The spaces of the expelled require us to think and act with critical care, to conceptualise them yes, but to realise them and to enter alongside them, to join them. It is our imperative to make such spaces, shared situations of collaborative endeavour to which we have legal as well as ethical and theatrical commitments. By identifying, naming, and entering such spaces of the expelled, in writing here but also and always in practice elsewhere, there is the opportunity to recognise the populations of each when they make representations to us, to enter the collective of consideration that we consider our own. The expelled who are the collateral damage of a logics of expulsion become *subjects* of our discussion and our attention as we work with them, together again in vital associations of loss. I am grateful for your joining me through reading this writing in the further legitimation of these expelled, who amongst other things become worth thinking seriously about again, and consequently acting alongside, something that I insist theatre still has some small relevance to, despite all obvious signs to the contrary.[95]

Notes

1 See Read, Alan. (1993). *Theatre & Everyday Life: An Ethics of Performance*. London: Routledge.
2 Ibid. pp. 24–25.

3 See http://entelechyarts.org (accessed on 1 March 2019).
4 For the background to this project see 'Lay Theatre' in Alan Read (1993). *Theatre & Everyday Life*. London: Routledge, pp. 23–57 and endnote 1. p. 238 for key participants to whom I remain grateful for the work that made the place as they wished it to be imagined, if not realised.
5 See Jon Bird's brief but excellent summary of this urban development in 'Dystopia on the Thames' in *Mapping the Futures: Local Cultures, Global Change*, London: Routledge, p. 120, 1993, and 'The Art of Change in Docklands' by Lorraine Leeson and Peter Dunn, in the same volume, p. 136. As with other records of this decade long fight of attrition Rotherhithe Theatre Worksop is not referenced here.
6 It should not be forgotten, though 'student' work often is, that there exists a substantial 15-year archive of dissertations written by exceptional Dartington students whose work contributed so much to this project over the late 1970s and 1980s. Those documents provide a remarkable primary resource for anyone wishing to pursue longitudinal studies of theatre in a single, specific location prey to 'gentrification'. The question, given the troubled institutional history of Dartington College of Arts since removal to Falmouth University, is: where are these archival treasures now?
7 See Harvie, Jen. (2013). *Fair Play: Art, Performance and Neoliberalism*. Houndmills: Palgrave for a detailed and thorough account (especially pp. 62–107) of why the term 'problematic' might be an appropriate cautionary note here.
8 I am grateful to Dominic Johnson who generously shared with me his copy of William Raban's illuminating film *72–82*, commissioned by Acme Studios which tells part of this story. London: Lux, 2015.
9 'The Art of Change in Docklands' by Lorraine Leeson and Peter Dunn in *Mapping the Futures: Local Cultures, Global Change*, London: Routledge, p. 136, and archived here: www.arte-ofchange.com/content/docklands-community-poster-project-1981–8 (accessed on 1 March 2019).
10 Bachelard, Gaston. (1992). *The Poetics of Space*. Trans. Maria Jolas. New York: Beacon Press. Benjamin, Walter (1992). *The Arcades Project*. Trans. Howard Elland and Kevin McLaughlin. Cambridge: Harvard University Press.
11 See Jacobs, Jane. (1961). *The Death and Life of Great American Cities*. New York: Vintage Books. Raban. Jonathan. (1971). *Soft City*. London: Picador.
12 See Bird, Jon, op. cit. p. 124.
13 When I say 'distressed' I don't necessarily mean the artists are 'distressed' (though given the prognoses of this book for their continuing work there would be good reason to be) but rather that the patina of the nineteenth-century workspace was important to the developers and their branding of the area as historically linked to 'sweet labours'.
14 See Kennedy, Joe. (2018). *Authentocrats: Culture, Politics and the New Seriousness*. London: Repeater Books.
15 See Sassen, Saskia. (2014). *Expulsions: Brutality and Complexity in the Global Economy*. Cambridge: Harvard University Press. This exceptional work has shaped the narrative dynamics of this chapter.
16 See Read, Alan. (2007). *Theatre, Intimacy & Engagement: The Last Human Venue*. Basingstoke: Palgrave.
17 Wark, McKenzie. (2019). *Capital is Dead. Is This Something Worse?* London: Verso.
18 Wallerstein, Immanuel. (1983/2011). *Historical Capitalism*. London: Verso. Arrighi, Giovanni. (2010). *The Long Twentieth Century: Money, Power and the Origins of Our Times*. London: Verso. Moore, Jason (2015). *Capitalism in the Web of Life*. London: Verso.
19 See Wallerstein, Immanuel. *Historical Capitalism*, op. cit. p. 7.
20 Ibid. p. 18.
21 Ibid. p. 40.
22 Ibid. p. 18.
23 Fisher, Mark. (2009). *Capitalist Realism: Is There no Alternative?* London: Zero Books.
24 See Boyle, Shane. (2016). 'Container Aesthetics: The Infrastructural Politics of Shunt's Boy Who Climbed Out of his Face' in *Theatre Journal*, Vol. 68. No. 1, March 2016, pp. 57–77.

25 Martin, Randy. (2002). *Financialisation of Daily Life*. Philadelphia: Temple University Press, and *Knowledge Ltd: Toward a Social Logic of the Derivative* (2015). Philadelphia: Temple University Press.
26 See Martin, Randy. (1994). *Socialist Ensembles: Theater and State in Cuba and Nicaragua*. Minneapolis: University of Minnesota Press.
27 Ibid. p. x.
28 De Sousa Santos, Bonaventura. (2018). *The End of the Cognitive Empire: The Coming of Age of Epistemologies of the South*. Durham: Duke University Press.
29 Ibid. p. 3.
30 The idea of the coeval runs throughout Doreen Massey's work with one example her fine catalogue essay: 'Some Times of Space', in *Olafur Eliasson: The Weather Project*. Ed. Susan May. London: Tate Publishing, 2003: www.f-i-e-l-d.co.uk/writings-violence_files/Some_times_of_space.pdf (accessed on 1 March 2019).
31 These gentrifications take quite distinct cultural, geographic and historical forms as insisted upon by David Savren in response to Susan Bennett's IFTR Keynote in Shanghai, Shanghai Theatre Academy, 8–12 July 2019.
32 Susan Bennett, IFTR Keynote, Shanghai, 2019: https://seoulstages.wordpress.com/2019/07/31/conference-notes-from-shanghai-part2-iftr2019/ (accessed on 30 August 2019).
33 Randy Martin, *Financialisation of Daily Life*. Philadelphia: Temple University Press, 2002.
34 Ibid. p. 20.
35 Lazzarato, Maurizio. (2015). *The Making of Indebted Man: An Essay on the Neoliberal Condition*. Trans. Joshua David Gordon. Cambridge: MIT Press. Graeber, David. (2014). *Debt: The First 5000 Years*. New York: Melville House. Butler, Judith (2015b). *Precariousness and Grievability: When is Life Grievable*. London: Verso: www.versobooks.com/blogs/2339-judith-butler-precariousness-and-grievability-when-is-life-grievable (accessed on 1 March 2019), Lorrey, Isabel. (2015). *State of Insecurity, Government of the Precarious*. Trans: Aileen Derieg. London: Verso.
36 See Appadurai, Arjun (2013). *The Future as a Cultural Fact: Essays on the Global Condition*. London: Verso.
37 Martin, Randy, op. cit. p. 141.
38 Han, Byung-Chul. (2017). *Psycho-Politics: Neoliberalism and New Technologies of Power*. Trans. Erik Butler. London: Verso, p. 29.
39 I am grateful to Queen Mary London University *Quorum* organised by Tatjana Kijaniza who curated a seminar in January 2019 that was of great value to this work not least of all the suggestion by Dr Ella Parry-Davies there that I might consider more carefully the significance of water as well as land given the docklands location of my analysis. Those present, engaged and critically supportive of this work included Martin Welton, John London, Martin Young, Dominic Johnson, Heidi Liedke, Michael McKinnie, Giulia Palladini, Martin O'Brien and Lianna Mark.
40 See Mei, Todd S. (2017). *Land and the Given Economy*. Evanston: Northwestern University Press.
41 Ibid. p. 5.
42 See Dead Centre. (2016). *Chekhov's First Play*. London: Oberon Books. p. 13.
43 See Sassen, Saskia, op. cit. for a detailed discussion of these themes.
44 See Heller Roazen, Daniel. (2009). *The Enemy of All: Piracy and the Law of Nations*. New York: Zone Books.
45 See Blumenberg, Hans. (1996). *Shipwreck with Spectator: Paradigm of a Metaphor for Existence*. Trans. Steven Rendall. Cambridge: MIT Press.
46 See Agamben, Giorgio. (2000). 'What is a Camp?' in *Means Without Ends*, Minnesota: University of Minneapolis Press, p. 39.
47 See Apter, Emily. (2018). 'Introduction: Unexceptional Politics', in *Unexceptional Politics*, London: Verso, 2018, p. 1.
48 Ibid. p. 1.

49 See Fisher, Mark. (2009). *Capitalist Realism*. London: Zero Books.
50 This group was led by the indefatigable duo, John Grennan and Steph Bryce whose radical intelligence and innately affirmative spirit illuminated Rotherhithe Theatre Workshop through their late teenage years in the 1980s. They were supported in turn by guardian angels amongst whom Dot and Alan Pedel and Jo Brundish were ever-present.
51 Friel, Brian. (1995). *Translations*. London: Faber.
52 See https://medium.com/@abarbararich/1983-the-line-of-beauty-and-keays-v-parkinson-79bd012beaf2 for an account of the relationship that opens with its literary representation in *The Line of Beauty* by Alan Hollingshurst (2004).
53 A blog record of the attempt to return the name to Surrey Docks can be found here: http://londonconnections.blogspot.com/2008/03/surrey-quays-could-go-back-to-being.html
54 See Apter, Emily, op. cit. p. 11.
55 Read, Alan. (1993). *Theatre & Everyday Life*, pp. 8–9. I remember the feminist scholar and performance historian Sue-Ellen Case, my tutor for a return summer semester at the University of Washington in Seattle in 1988 during which time I was completing my PhD, encouraging me quite forcefully to reconsider using the terms 'ethos', and 'ethics' in my already over-long thesis. I think her sensitive critical words amounted to: 'Drop them before they sink you!'. In the late 1980s, prior to the widespread translation of Emmanuel Lévinas into English, ethics was a term which was still redolent with moralising mission. Anyway I resisted Sue-Ellen with an opportunistic claim to be following Michel Foucault's 'ethical turn' in his later work, and stuck with ethics in all its problematic normativity.
56 See Brook, Peter. (1968). *The Empty Space*. London: Penguin.
57 I am grateful to an anonymous reader of the manuscript who encouraged me to make these parallels between culture and context much more explicit.
58 See Rancière, Jacques, www.scribd.com/document/34219878/Jacques-Ranciere-Ten-Theses-on-Politics (accessed on 1 March 2019).
59 Martin Spanberg returned to this encounter at De Balie in Amsterdam in 2015, on this occasion with a camera recording the occasion: https://vimeo.com/123248562 (accessed on 1 March 2019).
60 See Harman, Graham. (2018). *Object-Oriented Ontology*. London: Penguin. Stengers, Isabelle (2010). *Cosmopolitics*. Trans. Robert Bononno. Minneapolis: University of Minnesota Press. Latour, Bruno. (1993). *We Have Never Been Modern*. Trans. Catherine Porter. Cambridge: Harvard University Press. Moore, Jason, op. cit. Fisher, Mark, op. cit.
61 One minor motive for offering this recapitulation of *Theatre & Everyday Life* in the form of a new volume called *The Dark Theatre* is to see what leeway there is to retroactively insert one's contribution to cultural debates after they have occurred without apparent awareness of the theatre and performance scholarship with which they might hold fruitful relations. Given in the UK in 2018 Theatre and Performance scholarship was statistically outed by *Times Higher Education* as the least-cited field in the humanities, relevance remains an unlikely pipe dream.
62 Ypi, Lea. (2014). *Global Justice and Avant Garde Political Agency*. Oxford: Oxford University Press.
63 The 2018 controversy of lack of women writers represented in NT repertory continued into 2019: www.bbc.co.uk/news/entertainment-arts-47747855 (accessed on 24 August 2019).
64 Reference here the excellent online *Unfinished Histories* archive: www.unfinishedhistories.com/history/companies/portable-theatre/ (accessed 1 March 2019).
65 See Read, Alan. (1993). *Theatre & Everyday Life*, pp. 23–149.
66 Lazzarato, Maurizio (2012) *The Making of Indebted Man. An Essay on the Neo-Liberal Condition*. Trans. Joshua David Gordon. Los Angeles: Semiotext(e), p. 163.
67 See Read, Alan. (1993). *Theatre & Everyday Life*, pp. 151–236.

68 Ibid. pp. 1–57.
69 For my original brief account of this work see *Theatre & Everyday Life*, pp. 46–47.
70 See Althusser, Louis. (2001). *Lenin and Philosophy and Other Essays*. Trans. Ben Brewster. New York: Monthly Review Press.
71 See Guéry, François and Deleule, Didier. (2014). *The Productive Body*. Trans. Philip Barnard and Stephen Shapiro, London: Zero Books (first published in 1972).
72 Edward Hopper, *Gas*, 1940, Museum of Modern Art, New York: www.moma.org/collection/works/80000
73 See *Modern Times*, 1936, written and directed by Charlie Chaplin.
74 For *Multiple Angel* and other associated texts see www.alanread.net.
75 Byung-Chul, Han, op. cit. p. 1.
76 M. S. Carr in *Biscmanship and You*, 1970s (n.d.) brochure produced by the Peek Frean company, Keetons Road, London, London, SE16.
77 See www.touretteshero.com for a record of this brilliant work.
78 See *Workers Leaving The Factory in 11 Decades*, Harun Farocki, 2006, Tate Modern: www.tate.org.uk/art/artworks/farocki-workers-leaving-the-factory-in-11-decades-t14332 (accessed on 24 August 2019).
79 See Moore, Jason, op. cit. *Capitalism and the Web of Life*.
80 See the commitment and work of Platform over three decades: https://platformlondon.org/about-us/ (accessed on 1 March 2019).
81 See Bishop, Claire. (2013). *Artificial Hells: Participatory Art and the Politics of Spectatorship*. London: Verso.
82 See Ann Jones: https://mostlyfilm.com/2012/03/21/newish-art-galleries-the-ever-expanding-white-cube/ (accessed on 1 March 2019).
83 See Ypi, Lea (2014). *Global Justice and Avant Garde Political Agency*, op. cit.
84 See Ypi, Lea, ibid.
85 Amongst these students were Deborah Levy, Bush Hartshorn, Yolande Snaith, Kevin Finnan, Desperate Optimists, Forster & Heighes, Michael Hulls, Michael Mayhew (miraculously returning from apparent college expulsion), Sadie Hennessy, Fred McVittie, Andrea Phillips, Andrew Siddall, Sarah Archdeacon and about 200 others, all whose work made a difference then and now.
86 http://russiadock.blogspot.com/2015/02/hope-sufferance-wharf-and-granary.html (accessed on 25 October 2018).
87 de Certeau, Michel. (1992). *The Writing of History*. Trans. Tom Conley, New York: Columbia University Press, especially the first two methodological chapters, and W. H. Auden *Musée des Beaux Artes*, 1938.
88 See Read, Alan. (1993). *Theatre & Everyday Life*, 1993, pp. 24–25.
89 See p. 1 of The Hon Mr Justice Nugee's fascinating judgement of the case No: HC-2015–003369 can be read in its entirety here: www.judiciary.uk/wp-content/uploads/2017/12/holyoake-v-candy-20171221.pdf (accessed on 24 August 2019).
90 www.judiciary.uk/wp-content/uploads/2017/12/holyoake-v-candy-20171221.pdf
91 The *Jeremy Kyle Show* polygraph controversy can be accessed here: www.bbc.co.uk/news/entertainment-arts-48756290 (accessed on 24 August 2019).
92 See Lazzarato, Maurizio. (2012). *The Making of the Indebted Man*, Los Angeles: Semiotext(e).
93 The theme of 'millionfold growth' in the 'jungle work' of Friedrich Nietzsche, was prompted by my being invited by Despina Panagiotopoulou to the critically generative symposium *The Jungle Factory* (13 March 2017) funded by the College of Social Sciences, Arts and Humanities and held at the Attenborough Arts Centre, University of Leicester, UK. www.eventbrite.com/e/jungle-factory-symposium-2017-tickets-28947053416#. I am grateful for this support for my work during the early days of conceiving and writing up *The Dark Theatre*.
94 These were the questions posed by 'The Jungle Factory' conference to which we were asked to respond. I have adjusted them here for my own purposes but am grateful for the prompt they offered to the thinking in this chapter.

95 In reading a closely-argued 63 page chapter that makes up Part 1 of *Theatre, Intimacy & Engagement*: 'On the Social Life of Theatre: Towards a Science of Appearance' (2008) Janelle Reinelt (the commissioning editor of that volume for which I will always be grateful) appears to have detected a sentiment in my writing with which she is 'profoundly out of tune' and shared this disquiet in a public lecture at Warwick University in 2015: 'What I came to Say': Raymond Williams, the Sociology of Culture and the Politics of (Performance) Scholarship (2015). This is how Reinelt puts it:

> There is a rising tide of opinion in recent theatre and performance scholarship that politics and theatre should be uncoupled; along the way identity politics should be discarded and theatre studies should turn increasingly inward to examine the apparatus of performance/theatre itself. […] The arts we are told in some quarters, can no longer play a meaningful role in amelioration or critical intervention, and thus political ambition for theatre is derided as obsolete or even harmful, complicit with neo-liberalism's capture of the spectacle and the subject. The arguments sometimes begin with gentle mockery of the intention to 'do good', as if the naivety of imagining that performances could mean something or change anything was a ridiculous and outdated idea. These disparagements can come from some of the most intelligent and respected performance scholars in the UK, such as Nicholas Ridout, Joe Kelleher and Alan Read.

Given this was Janelle Reinelt's 'valedictory lecture' to the discipline she served with such distinction I would not wish her to be left with a false impression (that in turn might leave the field with an even falser one). I think I do make it quite clear in a brief passage in *Theatre, Intimacy & Engagement* what I think, and that is because of the things I have done and am continuously committed to doing: 'I do not for a moment abjure the political, nor do I concur with the theatrical equivalent of those lily-white cricketing fantasists who once proclaimed at the height of apartheid in South Africa: "Take the politics out of sport". But I do take issue with the false claims made on behalf of theatre and politics, performance and the political and, with others, take exception to any presumption as to where any such political efficacy lies'. *The Dark Theatre* makes this commitment to politics not just explicit but the *a priori* of all performance and in that sense offers nothing different to my first writing in *Theatre & Everyday Life* three decades ago.

2
THE ERUPTION OF THE AUDIENCE AND THE DICTATORSHIP OF THE PERFORMATARIAT

In March 1993 the publication of *Theatre & Everyday Life* was marked by a launch at 43 Harrington Gardens (the Kensington base of Boston University), in a row of London's most beautiful nineteenth-century houses designed by George & Peto. The music played in a terrace of five-storey Dutch-gabled masterpieces, just doors down from the house previously owned by W. S. Gilbert of 'Gilbert and Sullivan' light-opera infamy whose populist works, following the roaring success of *Trial by Jury* in 1874, propelled them to society fame and wealth, and almost continuous opprobrium from the culture-class today. The drawing-room party was lubricated by some decent riojas and simple tapas that my partner and I had brought back from our local *bodega* in Barcelona in the absence of a publisher's drinks budget. It was ever thus. The reception was attended by a teeming group of friends and colleagues who had, given there were no mobiles nor social media at the time, wondered where I had disappeared to a couple of years before on the sudden closure of Rotherhithe Theatre Workshop where I had been working through the 1980s.

I was in London enjoying this convivial bourgeois setting, on strict day-release from my job in Barcelona where, since 1991, I had been teaching English to young, production-line workers, in their teenage years at the Roca lavatory factory. This precarious work followed the closure of the Docklands theatre which, one worse, had gone from precarious to bankrupt, and had economically sustained me through the previous two years of writing the book, just published, that was now sitting before me in small piles amongst the drained bottles. For a writer the Catalan conditions were auspicious as classes started at 6.00 am in the northern suburb of Muntaner on the blue-line subway and continued until the beginning of the factory working-day at 8.00 am. With a few 100 pesetas in my pocket I would decamp back into the city at *Plaça* Catalunya, walk south ten minutes on the Ramblas to take up my seat at 10.00 am in Gaudi's Palau Guell on Nou de la Rambla opposite *Plaça* Reial, after downing a couple of bitter, brandy-cut Cortado's in the bar opposite, frequented by some members of the local, vital, and continuously jukebox feeding Trans community. Marlene Dietrich singing *Sag Mir Wo Die Blumen Sind* was on the café loop.

At the time the Barcelona Theatre Institute held the lease on the building for its precious archive, and remarkably made this treasure-trove accessible to me each day of the working week without cost. I would sit entirely alone in the library (save the always attendant and helpful librarian) in a chair-passing-as-throne, designed and hand-hewn by Gaudi, an unusual bibliographic arrangement that did not endure for long after I had left Barcelona in 1994 to work at the Institute of Contemporary Arts on the Mall in London a stone's throw from a much poorer architectural order of palace. The theatre library was soon shifted from its prime-location at the edge of the Barceloneta port, at the far south end of la Ramblas, giving way to the inevitable post-Olympics restoration project of Gaudi's masterpiece, to become another example of what Barbara Kirshenblatt-Gimblett would later call, with regards to the Los Angeles Festival amongst other sites, 'destination culture'.[1]

All that previously was so sympathetically about 'playful process' in this vibrant city through the 1980s, the decade during which time Rotherhithe Theatre Workshop in London had fought for its life, had, since the Olympic preparation building-wave in 1991, taken on a rather more threatening profit-led endgame sensibility. The expulsion of the library was one small marker of much worse to come. I was beginning to experience what you could call 'development *déjà vu*', but this recollection was anything but false memory syndrome. In this brief meantime in its ostentatious Gaudiesque history, I was after everything the archive had on *corre-foc* (fire-running dragons), *castellos* (human-tower-building clubs) and *sardanas* (the rather prim but always technically refined public-square dances) for my work on theatre and everyday life and the collective forms of companionship and compassion that Catalan cultures seemed to offer. I was interested here in 'cultures' in the plural, thinking more inclusively about this province by way of distinction to the apparently homogeneous white working-class neighbourhood that I had just left behind after a decade in Docklands. All of these public forms were examples of what I later came to call *fakelore* (as distinct to the more prosaic folklore), street-acts restored relatively recently as each of these ceremonial practices had been. They had been recovered from some mythical independence-minded mist by the Catalan Adjuntamente seeking to preserve the city's political links to its long, pre-Franco, Catalan past, an act of conservative heritage that hinted at a darker side to the performance of politics that my voluntaristic enthusiasms about theatricality at the time, wholly formed in London's Docklands, were still loath to admit. I was here having to face up to the perversion of the plural in the interests of a capitalised, Olympic Culture, that I later realised had given rise to a class of its own, with a special susceptibility to cruelty. For the purposes of this book I have rather ominously called this the 'culture-class'. On the night of that book launch, just such local disdain for the light-operetta recitative-inclined neighbour, W. S. Gilbert, that once occupied the next-door-but-two mansion, was palpable.

Having read some celebratory excerpts from the book to the assembled company at the launch (that included future literary luminaries such as Deborah Levy the novelist who had once been a student at Rotherhithe Theatre Workshop) I injudiciously went off-script in the heat of the moment thanking everyone for coming and promising that we would return to this ornate venue to celebrate my planned follow-up book, *The Eruption of the Audience* on the same date in March 1995, two years later. The self-imposed deadline seemed an age away. Overwhelmed by the portents of the occasion, I think I might have somewhat unfortunately described this pairing, the book being launched and the one about to be written, as a diptych and I must admit I already had the matching covers by the photographer Markéta Luskačová in view. It seemed perfectly obvious to me that having written about 'the artist formerly known as audience' at length in a chapter of *Theatre & Everyday Life* optimistically titled, Lay Theatre, it could only be a matter of time before the coming-to-be of my prognosis on the 'eruption of the audience' and their inevitable expansion of influence into all zones previously protected as a securely curated landscape for those in the self-preserving cultural professions. That is, the culture-class I was so concerned to contest in the promised book, about to come into this small-corner world.

Well, in the extended quarter-century delay that has opened up since the unfulfilled promise of that follow-up work, if not other quite different books that I did manage to write on performance and architecture, animals and intimacy, race and psychiatry, environment and law, at least one part of my projection has been realised to a previously unimaginable degree.[2] For all its cultural circumscription it is a revolution that bares comparison with other mass-mobilisations in the name of 'the people' and it has been driven by a fearless majority (when we are not expressing our myriad anxieties), an apparent democratisation of performance exponentially beyond anything I might have imagined for the Lay Theatre, that I would like to characterise, analyse and give name to in the coming pages. The title of this chapter says it quite clearly: if the eruption of the audience was what I thought I would be writing about next, it was 'the dictatorship of the performatariat' that we finished up with.

The dictatorship of the performatariat in which an apparent 'freedom' for cultural expression is exposed as merely an interlude, or as I would have it here, an interregnum, is best described as a condition of 'psycho-politics' where a faux or imagined liberation is the precondition for further subjugation.[3] It is the defining character of such an interregnum that those supposed freedoms for liberated theatricality that arrived with the 'emancipated spectator' I celebrated in *Theatre & Everyday Life*, now take the form of a pseudo-participation in analogue and digital media regimes once presumed to be somewhere wholly beyond us, but dressed to imply they now welcome our new intrusions. It is the capitalocene as characterised in the previous chapter that in its latest manifestation that some rather unimaginatively call neoliberalism provides the apparatus to exploit such apparent freedoms to, and of, expression. Here 'emotion, play and communication', as Byung-Chul Han puts it, are infinitely exploitable. Indeed through social media we become an 'auto-exploiting' species, labouring at our various enterprises but no longer, as Marx would have said against the oppressions of capital, rather engaging in an inner struggle with our own sense of self, sold back to us as the opportunity for unlimited self-production. Auto-performance is the hallmark of this broken revolution.

It was not always this way; one might recall a time in Western Europe when backed by labour unions the 'exploited' were once able to find forms of solidarity and combine to resist those who were busy with the exploiting. This is how Han glosses this historical moment and its current perversion as recently evidenced in Fall 2019 by people described as 'working-class commuters' piling into Extinction Rebellion protesters at East London's Canning Town Station:

> Such is the logic on which Marx's idea of a 'dictatorship of the proletariat is based'. However, this vision presupposes that relations of repression and domination hold. Now, under the neoliberal regime of auto-exploitation, people are turning their aggression against themselves. This auto aggressivity means that the exploited are not inclined to revolution so much as depression.[4]

While the techno-theorist Bernard Stiegler would appear to have ignored the game-changing paradigm shift of social media in his televisually based work (which I will address at some length in the second part of this chapter), I too want to recover a recent analogue history through which the eruption of the audience was first made manifest.[5] In the UK alone, though US, Chinese and international media have mimicked and sometimes driven these developments, since the closure of the dark theatre in 1991 and its own positively primitive forms of participatory politics and performance, we have witnessed multiple televisual prototypes of such faux cultural participation. Most obviously these experiments in voluntary self-exposure were first weaponised (in the UK at least) by the tide of telephone and then 'online' voting that prepared the 'comms' ground for the competitive conditions of cod-communitarian inclusion of *The X Factor* and *Britain's Got Talent*. These cultural slights were fast followed by the bully-business freakonomics of *The Apprentice*, incarceration fly-on-the-wall fables of *Big Brother* and the mockumentary of *The Office*, the 'structured reality' revolution of *The Only Way is Essex* and *Made in Chelsea*, the common cooking culture of *The Great British Bake Off* and *Come Dine With Me*, the home renovation dramas and property-porn of *Grand Designs* and *Location Location Location*, the borderline pathologies, polygraphs and suicidees of 'The Shows' Jeremy Kyle and Jerry Springer, the perfect storm cross-over coupled-up Robinsonian date-show appeal of *Love Island*, and perhaps the most obvious yet illuminating example, *The Audience*, in which members of communities were collectively asked to address a 'life changing' dilemma faced by 'one of their own' having had no apparent experience of the challenge in question. Despite their apparent lack of expertise 'the audience' was never without advice for the hapless subject squirming with indecision in their innocent hands.

There are some critically informed theoretical ways to begin to reflect upon any such apparent distinction between my earlier voluntaristic conception of participatory performance through the 'lay theatre' in Rotherhithe, South East London, and this rather more erratic, ecstatic and eclectic eruption of a global audience that began by dictating its own terms of screen-operation, and perhaps inevitably, with the emergence of surveillance capitalism, finished up being contractually dictated *to* at every turn of the channel. On the one hand reaching for Frederic Jameson in *Postmodernism: The Cultural Logic of Late Capitalism*, the repeated 'failure of the future' that any politically naïve hopes for the efficacy of a lay theatre might necessarily circumvent, now heralds a cultural milieu in which pastiche and revivalism, whether that be a sentimentalised recovery of a taste for fine-dining or architectural revivalism, become the new, very old, refurbished norm.[6] Here practices at the verge of their abandonment are retooled for new television markets that might be willing to buy into them again if prompted enough. But it has to be admitted, that when Jameson wrote this influential work of cultural theory, there was a very different stake, perhaps even faith, in political progress than one might discern today in Western Europe and North America. Although the extended riff on his original idea was published by Verso in 1991, seven years before that in 1984 just after I started working in docklands, Jameson had published the two key essays that acted as the fulcrum to the project in *New Left Review* and the *New German Critique*, and had summarised his position on the postmodern, a 'condition' that he largely drew from his understanding of architectural Populism.[7]

At the time we at Rotherhithe Theatre Workshop were being buried by exactly that architectural Populism in the form of *Beaux Artes* filigree, but back at our riverside warehouse we *were* resisting the balmy attractions of postmodern relativism, running daily events in support of the 1984–1985 nationwide UK miners' strike amongst many other political causes figured in the first chapter of this book. There can be no doubt that at that time of writing his major work, for Jameson at least, there was, still, a robust and pluralistic socialist imaginary open to us (at least in Docklands during those embattled days) that is a very far cry from the union retreat that has swept back socialism since, in the intervening years. Indeed when the publishers of *Theatre & Everyday Life* offered me a hard-copy book-jacket draft blurb for clearance with the celebratory phrase 'this outstanding work of postmodern theory [...]' I wondered whether anyone had read the book and replaced it with the more accurate '[...] this overdue *challenge* to postmodern theory [...]', for that was undoubtedly what it was, with a normative ethics and the force of a socialist politics in its sails.

While the Docklands represented Margaret Thatcher's 'water front', and the Malvinas/Falklands War her 'maritime battle', her 'land assault' was best exemplified by that miners' strike, her 'taking on' the National Union of Mineworkers at Orgreave and at pits ribboning across the historic mining communities of north and middle England during 1984 and 1985, that could least afford their existential industrial loss. We recognised the landed nature of the miners' strike was *our* struggle for docklands terrain (long before hash-tag solidarities that started 'I am ...') and the 'Women Against Pit Closures', many of whom were partners of the threatened miners themselves, made regular fund-raising visits to our warehouse theatre. On one notable occasion we were joined for a benefit concert led by the multi-instrumental Brighton-based band Attacco Decente, playing one of their very first gigs with arcane hammered dulcimers and tongue drums, and whose anthem was the onanistic crowd-pleaser, 'Touch Yourself'. This of course went down very well with the riotous gathering who had long been supported by 'Lesbians and Gays Support the Miners' and their *Pits and Perverts* events. This assorted company revelled in their sleepover in the warehouse, not least of all because of how much money we had raised from amongst a strapped dockland's neighbourhood, showing solidarity with an aligned cause. These kinds of threatened, yet pervasive, social alliances at the time Fredric Jameson was writing on 'the cultural logic of late capitalism', were very much harder to imagine a quarter of a century later, in postmodernism's wake.

Or on the other hand, in seeking the shift from the enthusiasms of 'lay theatre' to the emotive analogue eruptions of the audience catalogued above, one might note the obvious surprise and shock with which Fredric Jameson encounters the corrosive effects of capitalism on the imagination in his bracing 1980s work. With respect to the greater depth and complexity of Jameson's work it might be generative to characterise the present, by which I mean the second decade of the twenty-first century, as Mark Fisher does in response to Jameson, not as one of an apparent '*beyond* modernity', so much as one of a psycho-political state of 'capitalist realism' closer to the project of Byung-Chul Han I have already drawn upon: 'What we are dealing with now is not the incorporation of materials that previously seemed to possess subversive potentials, but instead their precorporation: the pre-emptive formatting and shaping of desires, aspirations, and hopes by capitalist culture'.[8] It should be admitted in the light of this critique not one of the television programmes I have profiled above represents any serious alternative to the mainstream, there is no serious alternative to the MSM at this juncture. What I have been sketching are simply stylistic ornamentations to that mainstream discourse, given airtime for as long as their recuperating producers see fit before sweeping off towards new under-represented constituencies in need of public exposure and emotional embezzlement. Here any kind of really-real revealed for all, can only, as in Simon Reynolds' take on Hip Hop, signify a reality 'constituted by late capitalist economic instability […]'.[9]

In complimenting the critique of the postmodern condition that Jameson has characterised as the 'cultural logic of late capitalism', Mark Fisher offers a perhaps less portentous, but nevertheless topical and nuanced reading of popular cultural tropes as warped evidence of not just this 'economic instability', but in the spirit of Randy Martin, the psychic and embodied warfare this represented.[10] In his *K-Punk* posts, recently gathered in a compendium of that name dedicated to his irascible thought by Darren Ambrose, Mark Fisher dedicates serious time and space to an early acid critique of the TV series *Benefit Busters*, that he likened to a 'grim parody' of a reality TV talent show, and in characteristically mordant style nailed the hidden force of what was really going on in the shallows: 'One can hardly underestimate the role that reality TV plays in generating […] lottery thinking […]. The persistent message is that any situation can be rectified by the application of dedicated self-improvement'.[11] It should be emphasised it is not all 'reality TV' that gets to Fisher, *The Hospital* and *Our Drug War* are given credit for revealing forces of class disempowerments at work in deprivation, and *Benefits Street* is recognised for delivering something on its bland, but perhaps unusual promise to 'be about community'. Fisher identifies form rather than content as the true challenge of these works, where documentary elements become entwined in what Gilles Deleuze, writing about cinema, called an 'image block', mixing game-shows, makeover programmes and entertainment forms in a bastard genre, while on the stratification of social-ranking Fisher is quick to skewer the class deficit there always is between those on one side of the camera, shooting these lives, and those being subjected to this scrutiny.[12] Here voiceovers are routinely outsourced to those with recognisably 'working-class' voices, such as Tony Hirst a recent exile from *Coronation Street*, who fronts for the Oxbridge graduates who have mobilised their good fortune and 'fought' their way into television production on the far side of the clapper board. The obsession with 'twists' introduced to once engaging formats such as *Big Brother* become for their celebrity iterations a 'self-parodic situation where the only constant is perpetual instability'.[13] This sounds very much like the culturally specific state Fisher started out with in his early analyses, now imbued into everyone on a panoptic set that mimics our everyday domestic privacies-made-public.

If, as Mark Fisher figures it, capitalism is a 'kind of dark potentiality which haunted all previous social systems', an abomination that Feudal societies in their own historic turn once tried but failed to ward off, then capitalism surely, given the examples above and the lessons of Theodor Adorno in *The Culture Industry*,[14] arrives bringing with it a 'massive desacralisation of culture' in its wake.[15] Here an infinitely plastic capitalism metabolises and absorbs everything which comes into its contact, not least of all the cultural conventions being restaged for new profits in these exemplars of supposed democratic inclusiveness. Fisher (after Nietzsche) recognises a 'dangerous mood of irony' here in which a 'detached spectatorialism, replaces engagement and involvement'.[16] This is a timely reminder that what we are watching is not quite Jameson's characterisation of Pollyanna Postmodernism as a 'purely fungible present', where spaces and psyches can be processed and remade at will, but a desiccated, managerialised multiple-choice option available from a strictly curated menu of recovered microeconomic modes: consumption (*Come Dine With Me*), construction (*Grand Designs*), community (*The Audience*) and care (*Ambulance*). Here we are offered something close to a 'dictatorship of choice' and terms of engagement that will inform this rather more sober take on the libidinal pleasures of the lay-community than I could conjure up in *Theatre & Everyday Life*.

What can perhaps be agreed, as the novelist A. L. Kennedy has presciently noted, is what links almost all of these emergent democracies of representation is the degree to which their subject matter are, at their very moment of circulation and recognition, most acutely under threat of abandonment, excision or extinction by high capitalist instability.[17] In this respect, I would suggest, reality television scheduling mimics natural history programming in which increasingly threatened species are given more and more air time in revelatory sequences of close-up naturalism that mark the precise moment of that animal's disappearance from our lives.

Picking up this broad idea and trying it out on my own examples is illuminating and maybe not so wide of the mark. As austerity bites from 2010 onwards in the UK, and secure employment is put under the duress of the precarious gig-economy, *The Apprentice* would appear to suggest that there is always a cab waiting to whisk you away after being summarily fired, to make your last job pitch to millions before setting up in a rival field to 'Lord' Sugar or Donald Trump. As the communitarian impulse to 'live together' is superseded by the isolationism of social media, *Big Brother* and its communal instinct reveals itself by insisting on expelling one of its number at the behest of those who bother to phone in. As the guests settle down to *Come Dine With Me*, the statistical likelihood of groups eating at a dinner table and sharing conversation without the interruption of social media has never been so low. While couples might see their way criss-crossing the 'undervalued' regions of Britain through the planning nightmares of *Grand Designs* to build their dream home the investment in public housing (as evidenced by the Joseph Rowntree Trust in the UK) has never been more etiolated, and when one of those well-publicised doer-uppers crashes through the rotten ceiling of the soon to be razed architectural lost-cause, the first responders that arrive filmed by the *Ambulance* film crew are part of a labour-force cut to the bone by local authority austerity cuts that followed the 2008 financial crash. And last, but ecologically certainly not least, the environmental disrepair that will inundate low-lying lands, well before the projections of Busted's eponymous hit 'Year 3000', will have done for *Love Island* long before the next bunch of contestants has an opportunity to burnish their tans and future-proof 'I'm a Celebrity' reputations by the Casa Amor pool in the high-noon days of global-warming. It will be *Sunken Love Island* by then.

But the eruption of the audience I am identifying here was underway long before my well-known, and often much-loved/derided (delete according to taste), examples above. In Ray Bradbury's 1953 novel *Fahrenheit 451* the book-burning 'fireman' Montag is married to a woman called Mildred who we first meet in a 'TV parlour' reading a script that would appear to foreshadow the 'reality TV' genre four decades before its eruption. As Mildred explains to her husband: 'Well, this is a play, comes on the wall-to-wall circuit in ten minutes. They mailed me my part this morning. I sent in some box tops'.[18] It would appear in this dystopian vision of literature-free society that cereal packets can be redeemed for another kind of cultural inclusion that will necessarily replace the imaginations of reading. 'They write the script with one part missing. It's a new idea. The home-maker, that's me, is the missing part'. Here the responsibility for social reproduction in the absence of poetry has fallen to those women who have secured the right breakfast flakes.

> When it comes time for the missing lines, they all look at me out of the three walls and I say the lines. Here for instance the man says, 'What do you think of this whole idea. Helen?' And he looks at me sitting centre stage, see? And I say, I say – […].

While the conflicted Montag is earning his money burning books on behalf of the State, Mildred is aspiring to the time when they can lavish $2,000 on what she calls a 'fourth wall': 'It's really fun. It'll be even more fun when we can afford to have the fourth wall installed'. By then this room that Montag seems perfectly happy with in its current arrangement would cease to be anything like theirs at all 'but all kinds of exotic people's rooms'. All this despite the fact they are already in debt to the 'third wall' that had only been purchased and fitted two months before, and within a few pages their lives have taken a sudden and irrevocable turn in defence of the poetry of the great outdoors of escape over the prosaic pantomime of domestic incarceration.

It is now largely forgotten that two decades following *Fahrenheit 451*, just before the sociological 'demise' of the working-class in the wake of post-class intersectionalism of the 1980s and 1990s in the UK, there was another honourable precursor to each and all of the post *Big Brother* arrangements of this newly democratised incursionary force, perhaps one truer to Bradbury's visionary domestic scene. The name of the television series gave the game away: *The Family*. The 'fly-on-the-wall', perhaps 'fourth wall' recovery of the lay indiscretions of *The Family* did what it said on the film-can and followed a 'working-class' household in the South of England, the six-strong Wilkins family from the dormitory town of Reading, over a period of 3 months on the BBC in 1974, culminating in the wedding of one of the daughters that was pursued by paparazzi in an ominous foreshadowing of what was to follow in the 'shaming fields' of social media.

Produced by Paul Watson and directed by Franc Roddam, *The Family* mimicked a US series from the year before, predictably called *An American Family*, but to those of us unaware where America was at the time arrived in UK living rooms as an unrecognisable hybrid that floated somewhere between the documentary passions of the homeless in Ken Loach's *Cathy Come Home* (1966) and the staged fictions of Nell Dunn's *Poor Cow* (1967), again directed by Ken, but then more formally calling himself Kenneth Loach. In our Catholic family I recall the former being celebrated for its campaigning originality while the latter was simply off-limits to this ten-year-old on the vague grounds that it involved 'adult content' (that I suspect had something to do with my widowed mother's surprise at seeing her matinée idol Terence Stamp getting 12 years in the slammer for robbery). By the time their successor *The Family* hit the screen its apparent umbilical relationship to story-line strands in the long-running UK TV soap *Coronation Street* made it perfectly acceptable viewing. And its languid rhythmic pulse, punctuated by the eruptions of anxiety of the 'working-class everyday' of this family's daily perturbations were, it must be stressed, quite distinctly at odds with the cut-and-paste cynicism of the exposé ridden episodes of *Candid Camera* in the early 1960s that, as I recall in the opening to this book, had brought my grandmother's small haberdashery business to its knees. In these exercises in embarrassment-induction, the unsuspecting audience had only been invited to the party on the strict understanding that they continue to experience the ridicule that marked the previous two decades of televised shame for the commons, embarrassments that continued in the canned laughter put-downs of *You've Been Framed* and the publicly induced pratfalls of Dom Jolie's *Trigger Happy TV*.

Mark Fisher identifies *The Family*, or at least its US version, as the 'roots of this televisual culture', by which he means the apparently inclusive idiom I have been tracking through this chapter, not least of all because of its neat symmetry with the cynicisms of the Watergate scandal with which he wants to draw some telling political resonances.[19] He aligns this trend alongside, but not wholly contiguous with, the 'fifteen-minute' celebrity-status prognostications of Andy Warhol, who, in a peculiarity of history, had been a correspondent with Lance Loud, one of the subjects of *An American Family*.[20] It is hard to imagine anything remotely equivalent happening to members of the suburban-Reading, Wilkins' family, in the UK edition of the same show, but that does not mean *The Family* did not have its own avant garde effects. Gillian Wearing the British-based artist and film maker has acknowledged the influence of *The Family* in her work, not least of all in her film *Self Made* which was shot in collaboration with the Method acting 'guru' Sam Rumbelow, and featured seven aspirants drawn from hundreds of submissions seeking to play 'themselves' or a 'fictional character' in a film advertised by Wearing.[21] In this respect Gillian Wearing comes late in the day to a terrain of quotidian co-option of non-professional practices that, as *Theatre & Everyday Life* demonstrated, had already marked the history of twentieth century European arts work from the 'ready-mades' of Duchamp (lifted in turn from Baroness Elsa von Freytag-Loringhoven[22]) through Surrealism, Situationism, Mass Observation, and almost all early twenty-first century live art practices.[23] Mark Fisher has written about this cinematic project at length drawing some acute historical distinctions between what was then and now: 'Wearing's work certainly has less in common with the brashness of twenty-first century reality TV than it does with the convergence of drama, psychotherapy and social experiment that came together in the 1970s and continued on into the 1980s'.[24]

Exactly four decades after that first airing of *The Family* on British television, Channel Four inadvertently marked an inauspicious anniversary for the 'interregnum of the inclusive' on 6 January 2014, with its opening-series episode of that much maligned new 'documentary' *Benefits Street*, so calamitous yet critically caustic an exemplar of this lay genre that merely being named in its number by the reactionary press amounted to the public-shaming of those who 'chose' to participate. Given they had little choice on the arrival of the film crews, it could be said these reluctant anti-heroes were now not just the innocent victims of a corrupt benefits system but working for next-to-nothing at the behest of a nationally televised exposé. *Benefits Street* and its profile of Winson Green life in Birmingham, on the now notorious James Turner Street, actually offered no more outlandish a portrait of contemporary life in the UK than many documentarists would consider something called 'factual programming'. While Deborah Orr in a thoughtful piece for the *Guardian* questioned the merits of casting 'non-professional people to provide popular television', the words horse and bolted come to mind given the ubiquity of this eruption of the audience into all manner of television output in the four decades previous. Orr's rallying conclusion is especially revealing and unusual as it makes again the case for participatory practices that at Rotherhithe Theatre Workshop had been thriving some years previously:

> Longstanding progressive arguments – for intensive early intervention for families who aren't coping; for education that help children to discover their talents and nurture their life-skills, not just to be employable; for work that is secure and well-paid; for homes that are socially subsidised without the need to have a child to get one; *for community arts outreach* – these are arguments whose force and urgency are backed by *Benefits Street*, not threatened by it. The left should stop wringing its hands, and start making those arguments. [my emphasis.][25]

But what Orr misses in this analysis is the undoubted recognition in neoliberalism that what was once the willing submission to the power of hegemony as described in the early psycho-politics of Antonio Gramsci, has now accelerated to become the 'willing' self-exploitation of those same peoples' own 'right to be seen' (on a screen). Here in a process that Byung-Chul Han calls 'transparency' there is nothing as idiotic as the violence of a previous political emptying-out of a person's interiority, but rather as Han puts it, such processes occur as forms of 'voluntary self-exposure'.[26]

The royal remains

So with this significant auto-exploiting reflex in mind, having sketched out this short history of cultural and theoretical precursors to 'the eruption of the audience' and the broad chronology of a four-decade interregnum bracketed by *The Family* (1974) and *Benefits Street* (2014), it is perhaps timely to explain the name I have given to this historical formation. For the purposes of this chapter I want to recognise these entryist subjects to the groves of cultural representation, treated so generously now by a once frosty media, as 'the performatariat'. The performatariat is not unlike its appearance-shy predecessor the proletariat but started out with greater ambitions away from revolution in the local street, to revolution on the global screen. What was once quaintly called the communicative individualism of the 'social media highway', a period of polymorphous plenty in which power appeared to reside with the digital end-user, has in the last decade and a half between 2004 and 2019 (at the time of writing) given way to the dictatorship *of* the performatariat by the vectoral management of surveillance capitalism. We will return to this oppressive category of life later but suffice to note here its theorists are many and with the exception of the early, ground-breaking work of Meghan Morris and the later interventions of McKenzie Wark, apparently mostly men, from Michel Foucault via Jean Baudrillard to Frederick Kittler and Seb Franklin. But following Shoshana Zuboff's more recent publications the category has taken on an especially persuasive dimension for the arguments of this chapter for as Zuboff insists:

'Surveillance capitalism unilaterally claims human experience as free raw material for translation into behavioural data'.[27] This new form of capitalist accumulation may not necessarily only be wedded to the digital, as it is in Zuboff's narrative, but begins for me with this analogue televisual revolution of those who previously lacked public appearance but, proudly led by the Wilkins family, walk out blinking into the light to be rendered by social and cultural commentary for their 'living currency'.[28]

The simplistic figure of such an 'external threat' cannot begin to account for the ubiquitous movement of our transition from 'subjects' in search of subjecthood to 'projects' in interregna of self-fashioning. The performatariat in its first phase of televisual public exposure traded in a 'meantime' power, often shorter than the 15 minutes offered up so generously earlier in the analogue age by Andy Warhol. Like the proletariat before it, the performatariat in its maturity should be recognised as a cultural formation, perhaps even a class with an acute self-consciousness, whose significance comes most sharply into focus at a historically marked moment of interregnum where shifts between one established order give way to another, where Antonio Gramsci in his *Prison Notebooks* observed 'morbid symptoms' would prevail as the old cannot die and the new struggles to be born.[29] It is precisely that capital cannot and will not die that is the characteristic of this age of interregnum exposés.

It is not that this modern interregnum marks anything as obvious as the span between two kings and their disposition and restoration (as would have historically been the case in European interregna). Rather to pick up an idea from Erik Santner's work *The Royal Remains*, his response to the study by Ernst Kantorowicz of the medieval conception of the 'King's Two Bodies', I would suggest that it is 'the royal remains' that now shape the very thing I am calling the performatariat. Here a process of inverse glorification *reverses* what in Inigo Jones' time, in the sovereign state of the early seventeenth century, would have been the direction of acclamation, from people to monarchy. It is 'the people' in their ceremonial finery as the performatariat now, four centuries later, who begin to dominate, if not dictate to, the media and entertainment agenda. It is the perception that acclamation is now their due. There is nothing too base, or debasing, that cannot be turned into headline gold in this milieu of idiotic inclusivity.

Theatre was never far removed from this attention-seeking milieu of course. Performance is hardly immune from the urge to show off. The international success of *Les Misérables* both the nineteenth-century novel (a best-seller in its own time) and the musical play that has dominated the late twentieth and early twenty-first century world stage, has been critical in the passage I am describing, that is the shift from royal to popular sovereignty in the form of a performatariat, who play the part of a previously gagged and suppressed powerless Public. Where royal sovereignty operated through a conjunction of political-theological dynamics, *popular sovereignty*, the invention of the performatariat in my argument, is secured through a bio-political operation like all other neoliberal conceits of democracy. It is not just a public's health and life that becomes the issue of governance now, but the sublime substance of a performatariat who become the bearers of the 'royal remains' that used to enthral us (before the then PM, Tony Blair, invented Princess Diana as the 'Peoples' Princess' while she was still in the morgue in a Paris suburb).

When we move from inside the court to outside in the street (or now on the screen), the modern afterlife of the King's body from Inigo Jones' era becomes apparent in the form of a sovereign form of 'performing *as* Public'. The afterlife of the 'Royal' remains, is not just made manifest through a fawning British submission to the enduring afterlife of monarchical power and privilege, it *is* that afterlife. And it lives it out in spectacles of the poor, of the subjected, where the weak can be endorsed by our presence as empathetic spectators delivering hard-earned garage flowers to Diana's gate, shedding our tears for a loss we feel as acutely as our own kith and kin.[30] In this sense Cosette, the emaciated brush girl with the surprisingly good hair, figured in the promotion of *Les Misérables* (not the subtle complex character as written by Victor Hugo), becomes the role-model for all those wannabees who seek exposure at all personal cost on the *Jeremy Kyle Show* (RIP). And, somewhat contrarily, my proposition would be that our newly-minted, sovereign 'Public' has been sustained, as far as this multi-award-winning musical stage-version goes at least, by those very spectators, those 70 million people in 42 countries who have been enjoying the wretchedness of the poor as manifested in that one, very well known, theatrical representation called *Les Misérables*. It is the theatrical spectacle that the dictatorship of the performatariat demanded and got, 'Theatre McTheatre Face' you could call it after a myriad other populist re-namings of once serious things. And this despite early signs to the contrary that 'The Glums' might just be too miserable for popular appeal. This juggernaut of injustice shows no signs of disappearing any time soon, from its berth in the appropriately named Queen's Theatre on Shaftesbury Avenue at least.[31]

I am certainly not immune to these contaminations of monarchical succession. My very place of work, King's College London (founded by *King* George III after all), includes the East Wing of William Chambers' magnificent Somerset House where I established the Performance Foundation which was opened by the current sovereign *Queen* Elizabeth II in 2012.[32] Here Somerset House, replaced Denmark House, a *royal* palace, and was built in 1789 on Inigo Jones' infill, masonry preserved from the early seventeenth century that Jones was partly responsible for designing, his foundation you might say. On this site now stands the founding centre in Britain for just the bio-political operations I am describing rather abstractly, where an idea of such investiture of the people, as a Public, was invented and inscribed for the first time in Europe, where humans became invested with authorities of a symbolic nature towards a newly invented thing called a Public. These were the first 'purpose built' public offices in the UK and, since 1789, the year when Jones' columns were finally consigned to become layered infill for Chambers' Somerset House foundations, that publicity machine, has been busy creating manageable publics through stamp duties, salt charges, licensing offices, tax operations and the administration of public records. Surplus life conjured up administered in these very rooms from 1789 onwards.

Performance is interested in such processes of *investiture* of the performatariat in as much as such protocols are 'business-as-usual' for theatre, further disturbances in the space of representation and appearance. It is such representational disturbances palpable in the resonance of images that are our material milieu and our expertise if we have one as theatre theorists. And of course, politically speaking, these representations connect with our capacity to *feel represented* in the social field, as the performatariat for instance, to experience the representations as 'viable facilitations of our vitality' as Eric Santner puts it. So we tend not to treat our performance research outcomes as somehow divorced irreparably from our own conduct, outside the theatre, from which we sustain our field. Impact is standard for us in that respect, it goes without saying. The problem for us well-gelled hygienists is that when there was public investment in the conception of the 'King's Two Bodies', for instance during the Stuart seventeenth century in England, it was the sublime *flesh* of the monarch that underwrote and supported the operations of governance built upon it. The significance of the Royal Standard in battle, or indeed the enduring prosthesis of the monarch's Crown, were simply fetishes of this creeping and creepy royal flesh, and as such were to be guarded as a standard bearer would with one's own, all too fleshy, life. The question of what might, in a post-monarchical society, secure the operation of the new bearer of sovereignty, is, in my view critical, and precisely alerts us to the significance that the performatariat is playing for good and ill.

To be clear the thing that was being fatally eroded at the height of the performatariat, post 2008, is a confidence and presumption in the neoliberal state as the normative economic setting to which there was apparently 'no alternative', the thing that was being born was a revolutionary access to the means of public dissemination to such new-found scepticism. Of course as post-war Iraq has demonstrated all too vividly for those of us who marched with our young children against the Allied invasion in 1993, and then looked on sceptically at the post-war 'reconstruction' from afar, but also as in *all* such 'de-thronings' such as that of Saddam Hussein, the people who in the absence of the newly-departed sovereign become a performing public, a performatariat, are now both blessed and cursed with a 'surplus of immanence'. We are 'all' the little brush girl now. Je suis Cosette! The negative post-monarchical energy has only one place to go, and it is into *them*, the performatariat in their newly spectacular Republic of Play. And that 'them' always appears to hold out hope for 'us'. As Eric Santner says: 'The new bearers of the principle of sovereignty are in some sense stuck with an excess of flesh that their own bodies cannot fully close in upon and must be managed in new ways'.[33] I don't mean that this inhalation and induction of sovereign surplus, is a cause of contemporary obesity, though that might be worth exploring for its relationship to those royal remains, I am rather suggesting that we are all, in our (my) retarded relationship to Royalty, saturated with the effects of such sovereignty without, in this sceptered septic isle, ever having quite quit the habit of the queen (or king). Especially when that habit is manifested in the glorification of an empty signifier such as 'the Public', whether that be the massed voting viewers of *The X Factor*, the public vote as part of the *Eurovision Song Contest*, or the lynch-mob seeking paedophiles here and there on the back of an afternoon of dialling across the shock-jock stations with the intention of preaching 'right' from the pulpit to the public at large.

Interregnum and inequality

In thinking beyond the naïve claims of 'lay theatre' with recourse to this historical recovery of the sovereignty of the emancipated spectator, we then have three categorical terms at play in this chapter: performatariat, interregnum and dictatorship, two of which in will require some careful handling in the coming pages, and one, the D word, that is so far removed from critical comprehension it might sensibly be avoided but whose recent barbarous history need not necessarily exclude it from our considerations.[34]

Let's return to the nature of interregnum first for the state through which something comes about will in good measure dictate the form of any such 'coming about'. If *The Family* in 1974 marks the onset of the interregnum I have described as 'the dictatorship of the performatariat' is there any foreseeable end to this age of televised 'morbid symptoms'? After all the appearance of *Benefits Street* four decades later on Channel Four in the UK, on 6 January 2014, can only be considered an opportune coincidence of an apotheosis of austerity aesthetics, hardly a measure of deeper social structures. Or can it? I would like to be specific here about the time of this 'interregnum' given any historical moment could only be characterised as a period by evidencing a recognisable coming-into being and coming-out of ending.[35] Such bookending would in its traditional monarchical form, as we have just tracked, be marked by the deposition of sovereignty, the expulsion of the theatre, followed by the restoration of the king. It is not that we await any such ending in some sovereign, or indeed messianic moment here, but rather that we have (in the UK at least) already witnessed such a condition of interregnum closed-out by two not-unrelated events. The first of these is a symptom, not a cause, that is the corporate manslaughter of community, and I will return to the fire at Grenfell Tower as one such crime scene to close this book. The second is the diagnosis of a set of conditions that had long set the scene for Grenfell Tower to happen. Its deceptively modest title: '*Statement on Visit to the United Kingdom, by Professor Philip Alston, United Nations Special Rapporteur on Extreme Poverty and Human Rights, London, 16 November 2018*' could not have prepared its readership for what was about to be offered back by way of a pre-Brexit European gift from the rapporteurs of the United Nations, more commonly identified with reporting on theatres of war in rubble-strewn no-go-zones.

The speed with which Phillip Alston's comprehensive UN report was rubbished by the serving UK Conservative government is wholly indicative of the serious threat that government ministers knew it represented to their parliamentary futures (given it chimed so closely with the well-received Labour Manifesto pledges of the 2017 UK General Election that delivered such a stunning riposte to Teresa May's presumptuous 'strong and stable' illogic). In close proximity to the Windrush scandal and the oxymoronically entitled Home Office's 'hostile environment' policies that preceded it, the response (or lack of it in the case of the then prime minister's detached discomfort) to the Grenfell Tower fire, the continued ambivalence to the caustic effects of austerity, the increasing use of food banks by those falling below the subsistence wage but key-workers too, the mismanagement of the welfare benefits system and the botched introduction of Universal Credit as evidenced by the award-winning film *I, Daniel Blake*, and the debacle of Brexit negotiations which threatened to further impoverish precisely those betrayed northern communities amongst whom a significant minority and sometimes majority had seen leaving Europe as the sole means to, as the special adviser Svengali Dominic Cummings insidiously coined it, 'take back control'. This taking back control had less to do with any urban myth of widespread racist attitudes within communities at least (statistically this has been proved to be some way far from the actual mark which comes as no surprise to anyone who has spent a moment in the culturally diverse, inclusive and convivial cosmopolitan landscape of Doncaster which voted 69% to leave the EU[36]), but rather a looser sense of regaining control in the dog-years of austerity flatlining of wages, significant unemployment massaged by the insecurities of a newly burgeoning gig-economy, desire to escape the diktats of a European banking elite that had not only despatched Greece to the cleaners, but had accompanied the UK government's own slavish commitment to saving the skins of the bankrupting financial system and its banks in the sub-prime tsunami of 2008.

These pathologies of the State were recognised by the searing UN report in which like a latter-day Australian inversion of Daniel Defoe who had conducted his best-selling 'Tour Thro' the 'Whole Island of Great Britain' in 1724, the UN special rapporteur Philip Alston had travelled the length and breadth of the UK during 2017, almost exactly three centuries later, identifying twenty-first century poverty and abuses of human rights in this sceptic isle. Defoe opens his account as follows: 'here is the present state of the country describ'd, the improvement, as well in culture, as in commerce, the increase of people, and employment for them'.[37] The counter-arguments in Alston's travels, that were swift to identify the haves and have-nots of Grenfell Tower and wider Kensington, were already evident in the first two damning sentences of the explosively concise 24 page report:

> The UK is the world's fifth largest economy, it contains many areas of immense wealth, its capital is a leading centre of global finance, its entrepreneurs are innovative and agile, and despite the current political turmoil [Alston is referring to Brexit negotiations here] it has a system of government that rightly remains the envy of much of the world. It thus seems patently unjust and contrary to British values that so many people are living in poverty.[38]

Laying aside what on earth 'British values' might once have been or might be, Alston proceeds to itemise, through a sequence of devastating categories, the serious and borderline-illegal, politically-motivated betrayal of those least able to help themselves since 2010: 'The results? 14 million people, a fifth of the population live in poverty, four million of these are more than 50% below the poverty line, and 1.5 million are destitute, unable to afford basic essentials'.[39] The government's predictable knee-jerk rejection of these findings is complicated by the evidential sources from the UK's own recognised agencies that statistically back-up the report's harshest condemnations of a failing system: The Centre for Economic Performance and the London School of Economics, The Institute for Government, The Joseph Rowntree Foundation, the Welfare Conditionality Project, all in turn provide the leg-work for Alston's report in its successive headings. The coruscating submission covers just about every infrastructural 'innovation' of post-World War II Britain: Universal Credit, the Digital Welfare State, Automated Benefits, the dismantling of the broader Social Safety Net, Legal Aid, Local Authority Cuts, the figuring of Employment as a catch-all cure to poverty amongst those least likely to benefit including women, children, those with disabilities, pensioners, asylum seekers and migrants, and rural isolation. The great auteur of austerity, the filmmaker Ken Loach, could not have made it up. The razed-earth record of *I, Daniel Blake* (2016) and *Sorry We Missed You* (2019) will stand as a cinematic diptych of shame for those in UK governance through the second decade of the twenty-first century.

We will come back to this damning indictment of post-austerity UK later, but it would be as well to note here that peculiar contradiction that the UN report's identification of the 'Digital Welfare State' offers us. By the end of the interregnum, during which time those successors to the Wilkins' family in Reading have established themselves as the everyday heroes/pariahs (delete according to taste) of a new televisual medium, the government is sharpening its digital expectations of exactly these kinds of *Benefits Street* subjects in what they called a 'total transformation' of the government of these very people. As the UN report summarises this little commented-upon policy revolution: 'The 2017 Government Transformation Strategy was presented as "the most ambitious programme of change of any government anywhere in the world"'.[40] Governance here is described as moving towards 'digital by default', a roll-out of automation, data science and artificial intelligence that must have come as something of a surprise to those 53% of low-income broadband internet exiles documented as still being without the resources, access, skills or motivation to use online systems from home. In a cruel irony for those 99% not covered by the munificence of the nearby Apple Guru bar, with digital assistance being outsourced to libraries and civil society organisations, the savage austerity cuts to local service budgets since 2010 have led to the dismantling of the public library services at the very moment they were most in demand by those threatened by Universal Credit procedural changes. As the UN report puts it: 'In Newcastle alone, the first city where "full service" Universal Credit was rolled out in May 2016, the City Library has digitally assisted nearly 2000 customers between August 2017 and September 2018'.[41] Given evidence suggests more than one-third of Universal Credit claims fail during the application process and never even reach the payment stage, whatever the government's wild justifications with regard to the simplification of previous processes Universal Credit offers, as Alexander Zeldin's *Faith, Hope and Charity* at the National Theatre in London in 2019 made all too clear, if you are already dropping below a very uncertain poverty line in twenty-first-century Britain, you are simply excluded from those societal measures that post-war governments have 'traditionally' intended to support your well-being.

Dictatorship of the proletariat and limited legitimacy

There is no serious cultural attention being paid to the shapes, forms or modes of resistance in the UK that might adequately respond to such damning conditions of inequality as evidenced in this UN report. While the planet and the city burns the performatariat is co-opted as the play-space for any such democratic expression by way of the ultimate diversion. Outside these new enclosures, self-help and healing are the only alternative for those expelled from the *Big Brother* studio house. Such self-fashioning formations of the 'neoliberal condition' have, as Mark Fisher made limpidly clear in *Capitalist Realism*, made the question of alternative modes of social organisation almost impossible to think, never mind ask out-loud, or, fantastically, seek for *each other* as distinct to 'ourselves'. So, given my insistence at the end of the last chapter that hope might prevail, what could a transitionary phase of politics (beyond the soft signs of cultural expression) actually look like should one be courageous (foolish) enough to speculate about such a thing? As the seafarers knew in the absence of a 'good story', new adventures are simply inconceivable. The following interval of imagination in this chapter, might therefore be considered a temporary fable, to test out one transitionary arrangement that has the advantage of being what almost no one reading this could possibly ever want. It is not that as I write these words in 2019 the 'prorogued Parliament' of the UK is not giving me food for thought with regards to such regimes of anti-democratic will.

By way of introducing the question of dictatorship, the most problematic term of my titular-trio alongside the in-between of the interregnum and the rise of a class I have called the performatariat, it might be helpful for a moment to concentrate on the specific question of whatever happened to the 'people' and their historic quest for representation prior to their most recent media outing. Indeed, before I make further outlandish claims about this movement I call 'the dictatorship of the performatariat' I had better establish whatever happened to the dictatorship of the *proletariat* that even more fleetingly preceded it, and whose disappearance might tell us something hard to hear about the ministrations of a liberal culture-class whose twenty-first century avowal of engagement, inclusivity and access might balk at the necessity for a dictatorship (an interregnum after all of by definition limited legitimacy) to bring about their own stated aims and objectives.[42]

For Karl Marx writing in the 1800s a contradiction has arisen in which the conditions of ownership have come into conflict with those seeking to change the relations of production, the proletariat's struggle against the bourgeoisie that is intended to bring about, in Marx's prognosis, a communist social order. Our own actual experience of such forces has been one of mutated forms of crisis, immaterial modes of production such as neoliberalism and the financialisation of everyday life as considered in the opening pages of this book. These capitalist mutations, what Han calls psycho-politics, are driven by auto-exploiting labourers corrupting their own enterprise: 'People are now master and slave in one. Even class struggle has transformed into an *inner struggle against oneself*'.[43] There is no recognisable 'multitude' here as hoped for by Antonio Negri, but rather the solitude of the self-fashioning entrepreneur of their social media identity. In this sense amongst others the 'proletariat' would appear (in Han's theory at least) to have disappeared from the current political horizon. But what if we look again to trace the proletarian's historical formations? They are not quite so easily dismissed as a passing chimerica of loss.[44]

Here I would like to think about the proletariat in a more performative mode, inasmuch as it performed itself, indeed, as it was originally imagined by Marx himself, in *Critique of the Gotha Programme* (1875), published in the *Neue Zeit* in 1891.[45] The early prognoses were auspicious. Karl Korsch in his 1923 work *Marxism and Philosophy* considered the *Critique*, despite its marginal, epistolatory form, 'the most complete, lucid and forceful expression of the bases and consequences of [Marx's] economic and social theory'.[46] It was in fact, in its origins, a further episode in a long reckoning between Marx and Ferdinand Lassalle, a loquacious figure within the German workers' movement of the 1860s, whose penchant for theatrical, Greek-inspired dramas, had led to Marx critically savaging one of his early plays, *Franz von Sickingen*.[47] Despite its modest immediate effects the *Critique* stands as an exemplary 'dialectical-materialist' text, a remarkable close-reading of 'The Programme' as imagined by Lassalle in which the programme's vagaries are excoriated (though the *Critique* ironically did nothing to adjust the programme adopted by the Gotha Conference in 1875 at which it was targeted.) This is no mere negation in Marx's critique, but as in the articulation of 'the dictatorship of the proletariat', what Karl Korsch calls a sequence of 'positive' developments that will lead to desired ends through the relations between a present and a future society. The dictatorship of the proletariat was the shape of that 'between'.

But where and how did the formulation of the dictatorship of the proletariat first arise? One of the shortest and most enigmatic passages concerning such presents and futures within the Critique is also one of its most famous:

> The question then arises: What transformation will the state undergo in communist society? In other words, what social functions will remain in existence there that are analogous to present state functions? This question can only be answered scientifically, and one does not get a flea-hop nearer to the problem by a thousand-fold combination of the word 'people' with the word 'state'.
>
> Between capitalist and communist society there lies the period of the revolutionary transformation of the one into the other. Corresponding to this is also a political transition period in which the state can be nothing but *the revolutionary dictatorship of the proletariat*.

Now the program does not deal with this nor with the future state of communist society.[48]

The *outcome*, or after-effects of the critique of the programme Marx is writing about, remains for us largely to imagine, and as part of that fantasy the possible form, dynamics and effects of the dictatorship of the proletariat are up-for-grabs despite what the Marx-Engels-Lenin Institute said in their Preface to the 1932 edition of *Critique of the Gotha Programme*: 'the idea of the proletarian dictatorship runs like a red thread through all the teachings of Marx and Engels, through all their works'.[49] If such a transitionary phase is largely to be imagined in the subtext to Marx's actual writings, then let me continue that fabular exercise here with due regard for what precisely Marx understood by *dictatorship* itself.

The concept of dictatorship was always conceived by Marx, and subsequently Lenin and Rosa Luxemburg within the strict limits of a *transitionary* mode, heralding the collapse of capitalism and the communist freedoms that would follow, one whose authorisation was secured nevertheless by some kind of reference to 'a people'. As the political scientist Lea Ypi recalled, at King's College London in a public seminar on the necessary difficulty of recalling such 'dictatorships' from their abuses by intervening histories of the twentieth century, for Rosa Luxemburg this would amount to a 'manner of applying democracy' not its cessation, and for Lenin the dictatorship of the proletariat would set the conditions for the first time for the 'democracy of the majority'.[50] For Lea Ypi exploring the neglected contemporary valences this controversial historical subject might offer us appeared to be a way of thinking-through an alternative to commonly advanced political theories or modes of action. Anarchist or Liberal accounts of governance are separated by a sea of continuous incomprehension and as such I would invite us alongside Lea Ypi rather to focus on a Marxist theory of *legitimacy*, situated somewhere between ideal and non-ideal modes of theorising. I was attracted to that proposition at least and suggest here such active rethinking of this taboo domain might account more plausibly for the kinds of utopian potential of the performance theory mentioned earlier, of José Muñoz and Jill Dolan, now coupled with an adequate theory of justice. It would appear to me that without contesting ground such as the dictatorship of the proletariat for its contemporary relevance any aspiration towards something called a politics of performance will struggle to assume its critical significance.

It should not go without saying after all, with Lea Ypi and I am sure many of those reading this, that in rethinking the topical force of dictatorship in this way, I too would like to assume that there is something wrong with capitalism, and something wrong with exploitation, and that both signify and induce states, or conditions, of corruption of the senses and the unjust that I would wish to limit, not advance, with my own choices and actions. Such limitation will then necessarily impel us to consider what might actually, I mean really, happen in the immediate aftermath of such unjust social arrangements. Just announcing the 'end' of these arrangements does not begin to address any such necessity.

The opening chapter to this book, with its focus on Saskia Sassen's concept of a 'logics of expulsion', tracked one precise historical theatrical example of such injustice and endeavoured to resist their most pernicious effects for those least able to protect themselves from errant power. Nevertheless, despite its potential theoretical leverage, you might well ask why one would want in any reaffirmation of the necessity for right action against already violating forces to recover words and practices such as 'dictatorship' that speaks to us now from the twentieth century, most obviously through the tyrannous regimes of Hitler, Stalin and Mao. Indeed Engels described Social Democratic 'big wigs' and their fears of the *Critique* as the 'wholesome terror' of these very words that announced the 'dictatorship of the proletariat'. Of course, in Marx's defence, as though defence were needed from me when he has David Harvey onside, for Marx at least this intervening period of history means nothing. Marx did not have the benefit of future-proofing to back him up when he identified the two-millennia old *Roman* concept of dictatorship as his touchstone for this state of interregnum as outlined in his *Critique of the Gotha Programme*. Again, you might well wish to resist any such Roman model yourself, given its own brutalities, but to get to where *Marx* was wanting us to think (and given what I have said so far in this book regarding capitalism that might not be a wholly irrelevant interest) requires us to think with the Romans for a while. Indeed to read Marx at all an understanding of the significance of the Roman Republic, not least of all under Augustus the subject of his lightning-fast doctoral thesis (completed within six months during the winter of 1840–1841) makes for essential reading.[51]

The Roman conception of dictatorship, as explored by Marx the student, described the supreme office composed to guide the Republic under conditions of unrest. Dictatorship was always conceived as a speedy and strictly temporary intervention in which the Consuls would nominate a dictator whose terms of office would be brief, with the precise restriction on their powers that they could abrogate laws but not create new ones, and whose officers would retire within a six-month span. Thus dictatorship for the Romans, if no one else, was perceived as a *freedom-restoring* institution seeing out the threats of crisis from outside and only legitimated *by* such extreme crisis from the inside. Surprisingly, as Lea Ypi points out, looking back across the twentieth century the reputation of dictatorship did *not* suffer in the 1800 years following the Romans with Machiavelli and Rousseau amongst others extolling its *temporary* virtues. Dictatorships were synonymous with teleological ends, always in view and scheduled as the prerequisite for the dictatorship in the first place. This temporary condition, a protection against coercive powers withdrawing to a single interest group, was in Roman politics to be inaugurated in the midst of collapsing systems where the populous was not prepared for self-government. So, when Marx talks about the 'dictatorship of the proletariat' and does so as a placeholder in the absence of any more concrete evidence of the character of the Communist state beyond any such interregnum, it is with this freedom-restoring dynamic in mind, offset from the outset with the vestiges of the necessity of its own *limited legitimacy*. Don't worry, it's not for ever.

Real utopia

Lea Ypi asks how such limited legitimacy might be distinguished from liberal and anarchist models of action? The kinds of political mechanism we might wish to critically consider, channel or challenge in any discussion of contemporary performance and its politics perhaps? A liberal position would foster a justification of the State at the point where certain criteria commensurate with liberalism are fulfilled. An anarchist model cannot allow for the State in the first place, it can never be fully legitimate, or indeed legitimate at all, and will always fall short of the demands of anarchist expectations of freedom. For Marx and Engels of course the State would, in time and in turn, wither away transforming from an organ of coercion of society, to an organ subordinate to society.

The dictatorship caught between these various calculations might, in my reading, be considered by some a necessary transition cost towards any such future, real, not hypothetical, utopia, with the construction of any such utopia depending on the specific contexts of the *transition* in question. The material nature of any place that well known 'utopianists' in theatre study, such as Jill Dolan (in *Utopia in Performance* of 2005) and the much missed José Muñoz (in *Cruising Utopia* of 2009), would stake a claim to, might incur material costs of which such transitional arrangements might sit starkly on the debit side of the ledger (according to the orthodoxy of historical dictatorships) or, as here might be reimagined for how such in-between times might offer precisely those conditions that allow for the articulation of those morbid symptoms of the capitalocene and the necessary activism to act upon them, and move beyond them. Such transitionary costs are not commonly calculated by those unlike Dolan and Munoz for whom utopia is a one-way destination of the imagination devoid of losses. Utopias as Thomas Moore opined do not come easy, and not without cost, as their successive failures have always reminded us.

Chantal Mouffe and Ernesto Laclau amongst a broad front of European Left political theorists from the 1980s onwards, have always circumvented the messy necessity of encountering these transitional arrangements of, for example, dictatorship, by working towards defining a 'left politics' in which the old ideals of communism as a teleological endgame (what Bruno Bosteels calls the 'actuality' of communism) and concomitantly 'the end of politics' that would ensue in communism's wake, were, effectively to be abandoned. But with any such abandonment, helpfully for those wishing to avoid historical embarrassments, comes the abandonment of thinking *quite how to get there*. In practice. What Mouffe did offer however in the absence of a route-plan, at the very moment liberal consensus-politics in the UK assumed the Blairite/Anthony Giddens spectre of the 'third way', was a timely thinking-through of 'agonism', in her brief but prescient book *For a Left Populism*, which sought to galvanise the kind of dissensus that Jacques Rancière had long been espousing. In other words not a map so much as a mash-up soundtrack for the jostling journey ahead. As Mouffe put it: 'to reaffirm the *partisan* nature of politics in order to create the conditions of an "agonistic" debate about possible alternatives'.[52] It is this call to a partisan politics that informs my conception of a partisan *critique of* performance in this book, that begins to approach the demands of Mouffe's enthusiastically expressed but vague prognostications as to the role that 'culture' might play in any such resistance to the rise of the political right.

In a post-crash, post-2008 rejoinder to the widespread questioning of what she calls the neoliberal condition and its austerity politics, Mouffe seeks a left Populism and the construction of something she describes as a 'frontier' between 'the people' and 'the oligarchy' in search of a deeper democracy. In this sense this frontier and its populist moment announces for Mouffe at least a return *of* the political after years of what by some, not least of all the influential performance scholar Janelle Reinelt, has been perceived as a period of post-politics.[53] And in my book it is precisely the dictatorship of the performatariat that most persuasively offers both symptom and diagnosis for how any such anxiety about post-politics might best be argued with, and allayed, with some more detailed thinking-through of what lies *between* where we are and where we would like to be, and the models for such interregna of the imagination as much as the infrastructure of its practiced arrangements. You are at liberty to intercede with your own transitionary arrangements but in order seriously to imagine the future the absence of such thinking is testament to historical cowardice. Indeed if 'we' don't think such things through, others will think things through for us, as the largely 'performative' play for prorogation by the Boris Johnson government led by Dominic Cummings showed a somewhat startled UK, comfortable in its parliamentary assumptions, in early September 2019.[54]

What Mouffe encourages is a 'left-populist strategy', as she describes it, aimed at the 'construction of a "people" in pursuit of democratic resistance to the breaking neoliberal order'.[55] Mouffe's contention is of course that this is a continuation within what she calls a pluralist liberal democracy rather than a fundamental break *from* any such liberal democracy. While I have grave reservations about the likely efficacy of any such continuity, given the entrenched power and structural violence that this institutional history describes, I do not quibble as a theatrical specialist with Mouffe's prescription for getting there: 'It is through representation that collective political subjects are created they do not exist beforehand'.[56] This is why a partisan polemic towards what stands *for* performance (if not partisan performance itself) is in these circumstances in my view so urgent. And the recognition of what I have called the dictatorship of the performatariat as critical to the staging of that scene seems at the very least an urgent corrective to theatre studies' preference for what Paul Rae calls 'peak performance', clichéd returns to all that is agreed to be good and worthy of accounting-for on today's stages, apparently untroubled by the online static that is inundating what amounts to attention in that meat space.[57]

Performatariat and performance

The slippage between political representation here and 'representation' tout court, that is performative appearance, would appear to be moot. Mouffe is talking about institutions of representation in this phrase, but I am talking about the dictatorship of the performatariat and how one might make more collective sense of its claims to our already burdened attention? As the performatariat transitions from the ones doing the dictating, to the ones assuming the dictation during the four-decade interregnum I have identified, one can trace the cyclical incorporation of those who might have thought themselves dancing-clear of the logics of expulsion analysed in the last chapter. Perhaps it should be no surprise that such apparent freedoms are so many chimera. The construction of this book pursues a sequence of just such theatrical endeavours in the following chapters, where styles, rhythms and phantasms of representation are tried out in various forms of theatrical manners. Each stages some kind of 'crime scene' of aesthetic rearrangement that, as in Antonioni's film *Blow Up*, are backgrounded in the bushes, while the performatariat now occupy the foreground with their attention-seeking static. In this pixelated undergrowth any claim to have found 'the People' cannot be some kind of empirical referent but consistent with a quarter-century of writing about performance since the publication of *Theatre & Everyday Life*, I would agree with Mouffe, will always require a discursive construct to be enacted through some kind of appearance making practices beyond theoretical identification: '[The People] does not exist previously to its performative articulation and cannot be apprehended through sociological categories'.[58]

Within this sober and sobering historic context the performatariat, the cultural category amongst my challenging trio of terms under construction here, is significant for my arguments in this book not because the performatariat itself receives undue attention as the chapters proceed, there is not that much to say about it beyond what I say here, as it has traded in making itself self-evident, but rather for the *measure* the performatariat offers against which theatre and performance will do their work for now and the foreseeable future in such demanding social circumstances. It provides the persistent and insistent foreground, the static and the echo of each and all of the live art acts that this book takes as its focus in the wake of the bankrupted warehouse in Docklands, the dark theatre. And it sets the pace and tone of an 'apparent' democratisation against which any claims for genuinely collective acts of cultural intervention would understandably have to be subsequently set and tested. That will be one of the purposes and measure of the analyses of the theatrical practices that follow in the coming chapters. It is not remotely adequate any more, I would suggest, to make isolated claims for performance without this ever-present social media qualifier (until such a time as that social media squall blows over for the next high-return thing that in turn will render the digital vectoralists the equivalent of the VHS Video tape anachronists of the early 2000s).

The performatariat (happily, given it is such an inadequate neologism) then does not need me here to continuously reference it because it has become ubiquitous to the conditions of anyone daring to tackle the long-form of a book such as this one, during the peculiar dictatorship of the current cultural conditions of online short-form reference and accountability. But not insisting on its naming on the following pages does not for a moment imply it has disappeared from its ever-present influence. To get a sense of this phenomenal context, a kind of gestalt in which the most obvious cultural shaper of our experience of theatre, that is social media, is commonly precluded from the perspectives of performance, one might turn to Walter Benjamin who wrote in the aphoristic notebooks of his *One Way Street* in 1928 of the relation between foreground and distance in which the habitual patterns of life tend to obscure the backdrop for the foreground that preoccupies us. A visit to a school corridor left long-ago alerts one to this concealing conundrum in that it appears uncanny, not only have we grown but, returning as an adult, setting eyes again for the first time on the scene, reconnects foreground and distance in productive and unsettling ways that would have been impossible during the habitual desire paths of childhood.[59] So, I will continue to set the scene of the performatariat in this chapter to direct your eye towards the live arts of performance I am interested in you encountering with me, now, perversely, despite their valiant calls to our digitally distracted attention, relegated to the *background* hopefully never losing sight of the relation between such distanced acts and the immediate, much closer imperatives of the buzz of the performatariat that engineers our imaginations to this, not that, here and not there. Each chapter that follows will thus allow for the 'whole pageant' that in William Carlos Williams' ekphrastic poem on Pieter Breugel's lost painting *Landscape With Falling Icaraus*, distracts our gaze, but with some closer observation admits to the event of something 'off'.[60]

This common mode of displacement, by no means peculiar to performance or eventhood, has a continuous *verfremdungseffekt* about it, distantiating us from ourselves towards others while never allowing more than communicative individualism to maintain for that meanwhile. I do not consider theatre to be an exception to this continuity, it after all has its own atomising mechanics that I have discussed at length in a book called *Theatre, Intimacy & Engagement*. I am not here interested in setting up synthetic live-vs.-media conflicts, polarities that characterised the well-circulated debates in performance studies in the US and UK between Philip Auslander and Peggy Phelan in the 1990s, but rather will insist on keeping Walter Benjamin's displacement exercise in mind, reconnecting more or less distant acts of performance in the background to follow, with the continuous messaging of the performatariat that pre-empt, foreground and often simply envelope by a process of ever retreating leakage all such engagements, certainly within the Western European landscapes that are the immediate grounds for this book.[61]

I am to this extent simply rehearsing and then adjusting the necessity of reversal wrought by the quarter-century old arguments originally laid out in *Theatre & Everyday Life*, which when published in 1993 came as something of a provocation for those who wanted to make premature and, I thought, inadequate alliances between the 'arts' in the interests of mutual gain. I took this to be a very bad idea, irrespective of the tempting profits for theatre, on the grounds that performance's special attributes would likely be lost in any such mass-mobilisation in the name of something called culture, or even Culture as you sometimes see it written by those most anxious about its wholesome relevance to others' well-being while covering for its painful political inadequacies. You know the kind of thing, when an institution such as a University earnestly offers its employees and dependents 'Cultural Activities' to distract them from the self-understanding that their standard conditions of service and serial mismanagement by those paid City salaries to 'manage' are the challenge to their mental health and the actual cause of their precariousness.[62] I did however in my arguments in that book, that 'televisual' images were quite different, phenomenologically and otherwise from theatrical acts, make one small caveat there, with an eye on the horizon beyond 1993: 'Unless the communications media are to take a radical departure from their current authorised practices and state-licensed operations this situation appears to determine the near future of anything approaching a non-conformist medium'.[63] Well, it is obvious from the global reach of the performatariat that that 'radical departure' has been realised if not yet very nearly burnt-out in a black hole of reverse celebrity and notoriety tracked by media dystopians such as Charlie Brooker in his Netflix series *Dark Mirror*. At the point at which in 2019, following a polygraph test on the *Jeremy Kyle Show* that 'proved' (*sic*) he was lying about his fidelity to his partner, Steve Dymond committed suicide, the switch on this particular brand of precarious personality-porn was flicked off in the UK (until the next afternoon ratings-chaser emerged from the swamp marked 'commissioning').[64]

When I voiced my scepticism about the radical potential of the 'televisual' in *Theatre & Everyday Life* in 1993, in Britain we 'struggled' by in another kind of merciless media-lite dystopia, graced by about five regular channels with the BBC and ITV utterly dominant in what stood for the 'market' of the time. My North American friend John Pryor (later an eco-entrepreneur, if that is not an oxymoron, and sometime Mayor of Telluride, which clearly is) had arrived in London as advance party for the cable-company Anixter in 1983 on the understanding that 'we' could do with 100s more channels, a fantasy that I assured him would be of absolutely no interest for those of us happily reared in the 1960s on two, BBC and ITV, that anyway required us to adjust the aerial on the roof to stabilise the picture. I should have been more cognisant of where this 20-something was housed by his company, in a swish apartment off Kensington High Street, to gauge their estimation of his likelihood of success. While John was laying his first 1,000 kilometres of cable under my sceptical analogue watch, we fed coins into call boxes, reversed charges when we could not afford to, shared 'party lines' with neighbours, paid for things with perforated cheques over counters staffed by humans who knew our names, sent letters with stamps delivered by 'post-people' and tussled with the toner on early-onset fax machines the size of a television, which in turn were the depth of a coffee table. Four decades later Anixter are selling video-surveillance systems back into the UK market with alacrity and there are 998 more channels listed on my server than I had once deemed wholly necessary to human life.[65] And John? Well according to the internet that I suspect I can only access because of his former company, he has subsequently dedicated two decades of work to renewable energy, clean tech, sustainable aquaculture, green building and affordable housing, so our self-sacrifice to his cable charms has not been without a side dividend for the planet (while Anixter go on heating it up with their voracious server-roll-out).

It is perhaps ironic though indicative of an explicit distinction I want to reiterate between theatre and other arts and media (that I am sustaining here from that key argumentative passage in *Theatre & Everyday Life*), that throughout the rise of this mediatised performatariat I am tracking, there was a continuous and well-meaning attention to the dynamics of apparently associated 'everyday lives' through what latterly became known as Verbatim Theatre. The 20-year repertoire of Kilburn's treasured Tricycle Theatre in North West London through the 1990s and early 2000s under the enlightened artistic directorship of Nicholas Kent was one of the more obvious manifestations of an international movement with *The Colour of Justice*, *Deepcut* and *The Riots* (amongst many others) offering fine examples of the verbatim form. But Verbatim, capitalised to denote a recognisable and widely archived theatrical tradition with its own expertise, operates quite different rhetorics of inclusion and exclusion from the media movement I am describing as the performatariat, differences which clarify for us the lineaments of the performatariat itself.[66] While Verbatim, at least of the kind I am describing in this brief sketch, casts professional performers in roles directed by professional directors and supported by professional stages, the appearance of the 'everyday' in its narrative, acts coincidentally to the action in hand, edited in such a way as to ensure focus is on the pre-decided 'meaning' of the scenario for a public's attention in the peculiar form of an audience.

The media phenomena I am focusing on here before returning to the meat-space challenges of theatre in the rest of the book, became so ubiquitous that eventually the inevitable happened and the ultimate meta-referential commission came in the form of 'nationally representative' television viewers providing their own critical take on a strictly-apportioned 28 hours of weekly television scheduling. The widespread success of Channel Four's *Gogglebox* in which families and couples sitting on sofas around the UK watch televised families and couples sitting on sofas around the same islands watching the same televised excerpts and commenting on them has sold into China, US and the Ukraine markets, is one measure of the proliferation of what Michel de Certeau and Nam June Paik, long-ago, articulated as a pluralistic form of 'making do' with the surprising uses to which the magnetism of media might be put against the one-way-street of passive consumption studies.[67] In this case it is the 'craft' of the television critic that has been democratised to within an inch of its life as reflective practice, and it is that craft that distinguishes this group from the performatariat as its own self-reflexive sub-group, the commentariat, often commenting precisely *on* the very performatariat I have identified, in a perfect storm of cod-democratised culture that a previous impoverished proletariat could only have dreamed of by candle-light in the absence of a 60″ flat-screen.[68]

This partial and somewhat arbitrary catalogue of the performatariat's recent media appearances could be repeated for any country in the world with a regular mainstream TV tradition. All that was needed was a populist appetite for the truism that that media has been definitively co-opted, inundated you could say, by the eruption of the audience. By definition the performatariat could *not* include professionalised members of the social group that defines their exclusion, the culture-class, that amongst many others included those virtuosic singers that graced *The Voice* under the tuned-ear of that chair-swinging quartet of judges just shy of their own best days, or indeed the kitchen confidentialists that brought their culinary exceptionalism to the table in *Master Chef*. It is not therefore the media itself that is the issue, it would not be fair to shoot the analogue messenger during this interregnum, it is rather the co-option of those previously outside the curated worlds of production, entering the hallowed groves of representation, that is notable. Of course, given the strict governance of the terms of such involvement by those media-oligarchs, little has changed since 40,000 years ago in subterranean Chauvet when the first spectator stepped forward in the cave and blew red-plant pigment onto their hand, to become the means of production, and then, so pleased with themselves as they must have been with their digital image, insisted on repeating that fingered gesture all over the wall to become the first digital media-monopolist.[69] The broken finger of that first digital-dictator identifies them as the early media sister (the size of the digit would indicate it was either woman or child) of Rupert Murdoch and Mark Zuckerberg.

Populism and the people

I had presumed in 1993 when I prematurely announced that follow-up book to *Theatre & Everyday Life* it would, as with my concept of the Lay Theatre that had threaded through that work, offer a subversive celebration of all that resisted the inevitable sway of the virtuosity of the 'artist', the 'mastery' of the professional, and amplify a necessary and long-overdue howl against the exclusion of the love of the practising-amateur by those who should have known better.[70] But this was, of course, rather innocent I have to admit from the perspective of 2018 as I write this chapter, and some years before the rising tides of what popularly and rather vaguely came to be called 'Populism' across Europe (reported on the day I write this in the *Guardian* as marked by populist parties having more than tripled their support over the quarter-century in question to one in four of all eligible voters).[71] Such populist forces across Europe were fast followed by Trumpian rhetoric in his first term as President in the US, but before these trends were made manifest there seemed little threat in such a voluntaristic paean to the 'will of the people' as I had been in thrall to in *Theatre & Everyday Life*, in their ceaseless search for recognition by a media and publishing world strictly policed, as they had always been, by gate-keepers from that culture-class, schooled in the Oxbridge tradition of benign exclusion and democratic indifference. But as I sit here now, writing this in London, with that copy of the *Guardian* to one side of my lap top, and my iPhone muted to the other, there are the conspicuous forces at work amongst others that impact upon everything I had thought the Lay Theatre could become.

As the major enquiry into what the *Guardian* calls 'European Populism' led by researcher Matthijs Rooduijn and reported on by Paul Lewis, Sean Clarke and Caelainn Barr, through the Autumn of 2018 lays out, a 25% swing of support to populist parties represents an 18% increase since 1998, with, disconcertingly, far-right forms of Populism gaining vastly more traction than those on the left. A corrupt, 'self-serving elite' is contested in the *Guardian*'s model of Populism by an 'overlooked ordinary people' in an analysis that bears significant parallels with the cultural sphere I am sketching out here from the inception of *The Family* in March 1974. Over the same period, as the 'eruption of the audience' in all forms of cultural representation has attracted viewing figures in the tens of millions to terrestrial television that advertisers thought had disappeared with the high-water mark of the 1977 *Morecambe and Wise Christmas Special* in the UK, democratic norms regarding media, judiciary and human rights have been rolled back with right-wing populists in Hungary, Poland and Italy making significant gains against the long-overdue post-war liberatory movements of minorities and the marginalised.

It should not go without saying that neither the rise of Donald Trump (oft quoted as previously a media construction of *The Apprentice*) nor the hard-line Tory immigrant-baiting rump of Boris Johnson's Hard Brexit (with its flagrantly flawed bus-side claims as to the likely dividends for the National Health Service of leaving the EU) would have had any likely purchase without these sweeping populist gains. And while those gains did not cause the rise of the performatariat, they did not either hinder its own march. Five of the world's seven largest 'democracies', including the United States, India, Brazil and Philippines found themselves through this rise with populists in power when at the outset of those sweeping gains for the performatariat, back in 1998, only Switzerland and Slovakia had notable populists in government. Whether one reaches for post 2008 recession and austerity restraint, post Iraq, Syrian and Yemeni migration, or the globalisation of trade as obvious contributing factors to this populist up-swell, it is the 'eruption of the audience' as represented through social media that for my purposes most deftly captures these logics of authoritarian exclusion while *apparently* practising a politics of participation. As predicted by the maverick iconoclast Christof Schlingensief in his contaminating work *Auslander Raus!* on the public-square apron in the shadow of the Vienna Opera House in 2000 (a performance installation that directly channelled the performatariat form and politics of *Big Brother*'s exclusionary violence, rewritten to target the right-wing Austrian Freedom Party), micro-fascism under the guise of parliamentary-corporatism has now returned as a junior coalition party in Austria for the fourth time since their founding by a former Nazi in 1956.[72]

It is easy enough to quote the usual suspects here, Alpine politics have long channelled isolationist rural myths to advance right-wing exclusionism. But the populist trends picked up by the *Guardian* researchers had of course to include the irritatingly cold fact (for the Nordic Noir lovers at least) that Scandinavia has seen its own emergence of nation-first, anti-immigration populists during this same period, including the neo-Nazi originated Sweden Democrats securing 17.6% of a vote that just 20 years ago had barely registered at 0.4%. Coalitions in Norway and

Finland have, somewhat unthinkably, had also to account for the presence of the right-wing Progress Party and the Blue Reform Party respectively by 2018.

None of this is a surprise to me living and working for part of each year in the isolated rural Drôme area of the South of France, chosen for its extraordinary beauty and swimming rivers, but more soberly, in my valley of Truinas at least, for its honourable resistance traditions to Fascism during World War II. It is always and everywhere apparent that this small paradise is nevertheless still precariously close to the right-wing stronghold to the south in the city of Orange and the notoriously exclusionary suburbs of Carpentras, but also, curiously given its Festive culture, the Papal prefecture of Avignon where, at the time of writing, Marine le Pen has a growing fan-base that one must imagine find the annual theatre politics and its noble unionised heritage hard to take. Simultaneously, France being France of course, with its complex 'terroir' traditions, there has in the mid-2010s been an unlikely surge of support for Jean-Luc Mélechon and his Left-populist eco-socialist movement La France Insoumise. And, further afield yet, at the bank-beating 'heart' of Europe, any trip in a taxi between conference sessions in Hamburg or Berlin will remind the traveller as to the distinct unease amongst German taxi drivers at least when it comes to Angela Merkel's initially relatively generous immigration arrangements for refugees during the 2010s, that so shamed those resisting any such hospitality within the UK government of the day. The far-right 'Alternative fur Deutschland' was directly the consequence of Merkel's stated preference for 'bailing out' the Greek economy after the 'crash', irrespective of the fatuousness of any such life-line given the banks' complicit relations with Greece's economic woes. The political detail here will, almost certainly before publication of this book, be replaced by a new generation of names to conjure with. Angela Merkel is already on her way through the exit as I write, and the UK is too fluid a basket-case during the long and winding road of Brexit to keep track of its political personnel changes in the slow form of paper-published writing. But it is the broad *populist* forces that parallel and oxygenate the performatariat that I want to establish here. They are less likely to subside than the here-today gone-tomorrow social platform personalities any time soon.

As Chantal Mouffe describes neoliberalism it is the term best suited 'to refer to this relatively new [now four-decade-long] hegemonic formation which, far from being limited to the economic domain, also connotes a whole conception of society and of the individual grounded on a philosophy of possessive individualism'.[73] Commonly, with the upsurge in identity politics, class formations that were familiar to us most stubbornly in Docklands, what once might even have formed something called a proletariat, have been to large degree underattended to, indeed there was a class essentialism that might have perceived the locality of the dark theatre as 'white working-class'. Despite what I said earlier about my appetite for plural cultures in Barcelona following the *apparently* white working-class experiences of Rotherhithe, nothing could have been further from the complex truth in describing our ethnically diverse neighbourhood. In fact on second and more careful thought, beyond such apparent mono-culturalism, what became obvious was precisely the pluralistic identities of those present to our work in Docklands, and most significantly those too anxious to leave their public housing for fear of the incipient and overt racism of the area despite its internationalist origins as a 'world port'.

The 'populist moment', as Chantal Mouffe calls this alarming right-surge 'tide', after all dialectically contains its affirmative opposite, or so 'we' might hope. The neoliberal hegemonic formation that has coalesced over the last three decades since the departure from Keynesian economics in Western Europe following the 1973 oil 'crisis' and, in a much more local sense, our not disconnected expulsion from the bankrupted dark theatre in South East London, bears within itself the nascent models for a left Populism of potential equal and opposite force to the alarming litany outlined so far. The unbridled market that we saw flourish around us in Docklands described in detail in the last chapter, constituted by local authority deregulation, the privatisation of land, and the subsequent governmental fiscal-austerity imposed upon those who most suffered from these losses to profit, were simultaneously bolstered by the 'Big-Bang' of the financial city and the 'free markets' and 'free trade' that empowered the shift to the containerised ports down river. We were all too familiar with the lineaments of the neoliberal turn and its corporeal and psychic encounters with our own 'less well-being' (though no one mentioned that NL word in its voracious height in the 1980s).

The social and surveillance

So, given this brief European tour of the cultural performatariat and the populist strongholds that have given that spurious notion of anti-elitism succour for good and ill, right and left, there can be no greater mark of a generational shift with all previous presumptions as to the identity of that audience that was meant to be doing that 'erupting' brought into doubt than the period that has separated *Theatre & Everyday Life* from this book, *The Dark Theatre*, its much delayed follow-up. But to my right on my desk, beyond the hard-copy relic of the *Guardian* newspaper that I have been referring to so far, is a somewhat different reminder of the forces that have widened the gap between then and now, smaller than the *Guardian* but no less portentous in its populist messaging. I am writing these words on Wednesday 21 November 2018, the day of the *Guardian* launch of its in-depth survey or Populism, and as it happens the former *Daily Mirror* editor, vegan sausage-roll hater and Arsenal supporter, Piers Morgan (yes, that dates it) has taken it upon himself to grace the debate on his *Good Morning Britain* television 'flagship', another kind of launch, but one that I suspect was followed by rather more than the waited upon the *Guardian* to fall on their mat. On his *GMB* wake-up show Morgan has vented his dislike for the way that the UK pop band Little Mix dress, or 'don't dress'. The National Art Library in London where I am writing this is a strictly policed acoustic zone for all the right reasons, but it is obvious without sound that what Steve Coogan might call the 'Twittersphere' is echoing with indignation and counter-claim regarding this intervention. The exchanges are heightened but typical of any other day in this place so merit some closer analysis than they possibly deserve.

Given the symmetry of dates I will simply track part of this one day's fortunes in the life of the commentariat and their peculiar popular front with the performatariat. To be clear, as honed professional performers, up to their eyes in the credits accrued to media and pop performers, neither Piers Morgan nor Little Mix are the performatariat and nor is it likely they will become part of that hallowed company until their passing moment of fame (in 2018 at least) is folded back into their anonymous older age. The performatariat vastly outnumbers either right now and includes all those who *stage* their responses to these developments on the Twitter feed and myriad other 'social' platforms. They are not just writing back here as letter writers to *The Times* have done for centuries in indignation (not always from Tunbridge Wells), they are rhetorically staging their responses in languages, images, GIFs, punctuated graphic layouts and emojis worthy of any dramatic score. Here the 'artist formerly known as audience' has returned the favour to active spectatorship, becoming the audience *as* artist.

The social media iteration I happen to be transcribing kicks off on the morning of Thanksgiving Eve 2018 (but by looking down at your mobile device now, or scanning your digital optic implant, you could take any day since on 'the social' as an exemplar of exactly the same force-fields of cut-and-thrust). Indeed the degree of anachronism you might feel in reading this account from the lofty perspective of historical hindsight simply marks one measure of this fugitive, insistently ephemeral, feral form. Piers Morgan responds to a Little Mix album launch and 'strip campaign' in which they are covered in 'haters' words' in broad felt pen uppercase, countering arguments about their supposed empowerment from his co-presenter Susannah Reid with 'claims of cynical exploitation' by marking their bodies with the language that is directed at them. (Later Morgan, with some justification, claims this cause-celébre inking is a plagiarised image from Dixie Chicks own *Entertainment* front cover of some years before.) Jesy Nelson (ex *X Factor*, see below for narrative significance) from Little Mix is subsequently reported by the media as branding Piers Morgan 'a silly TWAT over nudity complaints on BBC Radio 1' which provokes in turn the following 'come on' from Morgan: 'If you're brave enough @LittleMix – come on @GMB tomorrow and say when (*sic*) you've just been saying about me on Radio One to my face. Then we can debate your cynical exploitation of nudity to sell records'. The response to this offering garners 2,557 comments, 1,430 retweets and is liked by 11,700 within 24 hours after posting. Successive tweets carrying associated hashtags suggest that the sudden reappearance of Little Mix in Morgan's peculiarly erratic hierarchy for attention (that trends towards Arsenal, Donald Trump and a long-running spat with *The Apprentice* host Alan Sugar) is something to do with his recent meetings with Simon Cowell who had once, in the more lucrative days of *The X Factor*, represented them through his Syco management arm. Others such as an account named 'Up the Reds' makes links to Morgan's time as a national newspaper editor calling him a 'perennial ad for contraception' and pointing to something that is plain inaccurate, but often libellously alleged and, rightly, routinely denied by Morgan, namely 'when he hacked dead girl's phones […] to sell newspapers'. In fact Morgan was already quite well known enough without this common calumny having presided over the debacle of the publication of fake images of Iraqi soldiers being 'tortured' by members of the Queen's Lancashire Regiment on the front cover of the *Mirror* newspaper. That said during the long-running Leveson Enquiry Lord Leveson described Morgan's claims to have come to the party after phone hacking had already taken place, as 'utterly unpersuasive'.[74]

Somewhat incongruously Ariana's mum Joan Grande wades into the fray with a question: 'Honestly what is wrong with you @piersmorgan? Didn't your mother ever teach you, if you don't have anything nice to say, don't say it!' which is in turn backed up by Little Mix, who are immediately followed by the more famous daughter Ariana backing up her mum *and* Little Mix. Ariana 'claps back' at Piers and Ariana Grande then 'drags' Piers with a tweet that will one day be preserved for its historical compression of the genre:

> also @piersmorgan, I look forward to the day you realise there are other ways to go about making yourself relevant than to criticise young, beautiful, successful women for everything they do. I think that'll be a beautiful thing for you and your career or what's left of it (Black heart).

The emoji of the black heart is not even available on the antiquated 2018 MacBook 11 inch I am typing this laboriously on with all the fingers of both hands rather than the single digit required of the world of the 280-character rapid-fire exchange, with barely a typo between them that I'm struggling to keep up with here in real-time. Indeed it is most unusual for Morgan to slip up as he does in his 'c'mon' tweet where he substitutes 'when' for 'what'. Morgan has to be precise as he pushes back on others (thereby giving them a nano-second of typological fame amongst his *circa* seven million followers) by routinely correcting their grammar and spelling like a demonic school teacher vainly trying to improve the formal composition of their peculiarly lyrical hate (for him). Morgan's catchphrase 'you're not your' possibly did more for the grammatical standards of the UK in the 20-teens than anything since the 1944 Education Act.

Paul @nextthankyou tweets: 'ariana and little mix "ending" piers morgan is probably one of the best things that happened in 2018'. Which beyond asking what kind of 2018 Paul can possibly have had if this is the best thing that has happened for him until now in late November, is liked more than 1,000 times, which suggests Paul is indeed having a much better Twitter year than I can muster with my average of one or two likes per hand-crafted posting. As Edward Said reminded us in his formatively modest essay of 1982, 'Opponents, Audiences, Constituencies and Community',[75] it is good to know your place as an academic swimming unnoticed in a very big pond we might call the public sphere, in this case amongst the gargantuan reach and range of all this online responsiveness.

Paul himself operating out of @nextthankyou, is channelling in that strap an Ariana motif, riffing as it does on the 'Thank U, Next' lyric that Ariana has just made famous with the launch of her song a couple of long Twitter weeks before.[76]

Piers Morgan, perhaps sensing 'Thank U, Next', is passing him too quickly along a line to the door marked chilly comes back some hours later:

> When everyone finally stops screaming at me about this @LittleMix @ArianaGrande furore, they will suddenly realise I'm right. There's no need for young female pop stars, with millions of young female fans, to use nudity to sell records, it's tacky and sends the wrong message.

This return to the fray is commented on by 1,637, retweeted by 1,157 and liked by 11,000 within an hour. That evening in the UK then brings a slight lull, but early the next day there are more reasoned responses on the go. Max @SpillerOfTea (a handle that constantly shifts depending on Max's current mood, and will be something quite different, if anything, by now) chimes in with a message full of Thanksgiving cheer, classically, for this poster, opening with the abbreviation for a Public Service Announcement that might also for the medically minded evoke the Prostate Specific Antigen test:

> PSA for misogynistic wankers:
>
> Female pop stars can wear as many
> or as few clothes as they see fit, and it's
> no one's fucking business but their own.
>
> Fuck off and control something else,
> like your ability to have your penis
> in a vagina for more than 30 secs
> without spaffing up.

I have laid this out more or less as it is in the tweet to ensure that Max, Spiller of Tea whose tweets specialise in a baroque form of Rabelaisian rhetoric is recognised for something he does remarkably well on behalf of equality, his commitment to LGBTQI+ and notably Trans rights is steadfast and prolific, he does not allow his work to subside into euphemism leaning rather to industrial level scatology in defence of a robust conception of human rights. This has four retweets and 38 likes within 12 minutes of posting and is presumably being read over lunch by hundreds more in the UK as I write this paragraph-response to it. When I check the precise meaning of 'spaffing up' I am offered a definition by Webster's online dictionary: 'the present participle of to spaff-up'.[77] So this is perhaps some sort of play on full employment or hasn't quite made it to this year's 'word of the year'? A short ten minutes later Max, Spiller of Tea, is tweeting again though his mind seems to have drifted to more pressing demands: 'Which one of you cunts has hidden my cream jumper?' which is liked within a second by six, while five people including those identifying as male, female and indeterminate have commented: 'It's in the wash', 'points at cat', 'Sorry, my bad', 'I keep telling you it's where you left it' and 'It's in the car'. All helpful suggestions I would have thought. And so Thanksgiving spirals away from Piers and Little Mix towards Max's lost jumper that just seems all the funnier for being 'cream'. But only on my Twitter feed of course in quite that order and mass. No one else has my feed, it is numerically impossible for that alignment of the performatariat stars to have taken place anywhere else. Bespoke banter. I am left to imagine, for not too long given I am writing this at the same time, all those other narrative trajectories of @theorygurl's Cis takedowns, Owen Jones' Labour defences, Gary Lineker's Peoples' Vote, Trump's own Trumpism, and Ricky Gervais' animal rights, that haunt this stream of performatariat consciousness (and that is just in this Brexit blighted archipelago of insignificance that by the time they 'get it done' will require detailed alternatives to be added in just about every other geo-political locale that this book reaches with their own wholly distinctive *dramatis personae*).

But by now I am close to being inundated by the very thing I have suggested earlier I would keep in right proportion. I have spent the last hour (and three pages) cross-checking the rise of Populism in a daily newspaper with a concomitant 'five minutes of fame' (and a further three pages) logging the eruption of the audience on my Twitter feed. In the meantime my lap top where this text is (was) being written has darkened off entering energy-saving mode. Looking away now from my newspaper and my mobile, despite what these observations on and off line might suggest, and back to that other larger, less annotated, page-like screen, I am reminded this book is no longer called *The Eruption of the Audience*, but now rather ominously, *The Dark Theatre*, and that apparent turn for the worse, or at least gloomier forecast from volcanic excess to bankrupt evacuation of loss, might inaccurately hint at a mood swing that the author has gone through in these intervening years since that rioja fuelled book-launch night in the early 1990s, as though I might have 'gone off the people' *tout court* the minute 'they' started behaving badly, or at least, started 'appearing' more readily to disagree with me.

What *has* prevailed in this meantime is a much sharper sense of how the voluntarism of my conception of a 'lay theatre' and 'eruption of the audience', even the revolutionary dictatorship of the performatariat, has in its own turn given way so rapidly within a decade to the morbid symptoms of surveillance capitalism. The 'Aware Home' hive-like smart-house engineering of the early 2000s was predicated on the assumption, as Shoshana Zuboff points out, 'that the rights to that new knowledge' broadcast out of the domestic sphere by the online linked machinery within, 'and the power to use it to improve one's life would belong exclusively to the people who live in the house'.[78] It does not take Zuboff's love of Gaston Bachelard's affection for 'home' in *The Poetics of Space*, to recognise the likely destination of any faith in that personal information being kept personal for very long. After an apparently slow start of a couple of years, in which Tim Berners-Lee's altruism on founding the worldwide web without profit, such generosity had soon given way to Google (later Alphabet), Cambridge Analytica and Apple corporations' rampant data-harvesting and marketisation of spheres both in and outside the home (Maps/Street View), political persuasion and interference (Trump election campaign) and within our own bodies (Fit-Bit/iPhone).[79]

Given these unilateral claims to privacy and knowledge were once (for two millennia since Aeschylus's first 'extant' drama *The Persians*) considered the province of a shared concern for their representation in a medium called theatre, it is not as though the force-field represented by surveillance capitalism does not strike to the heart of a book of this nature. It really is nothing that new. Indeed by substituting Zuboff's term 'surveillance capitalism' with my own of 'theatre', the parallel becomes notable: '[Theatre] unilaterally claims human experience as free raw material for translation into behavioural data'.[80] I think in our field we call that thing, the generation and reception of laughter and tears in or outside an auditorium, amongst other things, plays and performances. Jon McKenzie long-ago (indeed before the acceleration of surveillance capitalism itself) already identified for us the manner in which performance had always been implicated in a marketised culture to 'perform or else!'[81] so it should not come as a surprise that the very means by which we might become increasingly depersonalised by the corporate *uses* of technology (like the US gun lobby resisting limits to sales of automatic weapons) never technology itself, are always already imbricated within modes of performance that we have long celebrated when they take the forms we call 'culture', or 'aesthetics' or even 'theatre'.[82] Here what we thought was our own internet agency has become a matter of our becoming subject to its rendering of our knowledges and our experiences, we have become *its* surplus and at a speed and reach that theatre might look upon, admire or resent depending on our appetite for the algorithmic.[83]

The processes I am describing here, a 'coup' from above as Zuboff puts it, are not just an overthrowing of a peoples' new-found sovereignty of expression, but precisely the forestalling and corruption of the dictatorship of the performatariat, the premature bringing to an end of what might have been thought a brief golden age of democratic representation in which 'netizens' could have once welcomed the emancipatory promise of their chosen social platform. Within a few years of our dark theatre being declared bankrupt, in this new digital scenario it is 'dark data' that provides 'the moral, technical, commercial, and legal rationale for powerful systems of machine intelligence that can capture and analyse behaviours and conditions never intended for public life'.[84] Technology communities cast this dark data as the intolerable 'unknown unknown' that might disrupt their expansionism towards an infinite network of digital things, and in a peculiar way shadows the 1878 observation of sociologist and criminologist Gabriel Tarde: 'In this pell-mell of improvised politicians, no one knows who is speaking; nobody is responsible for what he says. Each is there as in the theatre, unknown among the unknown, requiring sensational impressions and transports [...]'.[85] The dark theatre, bankrupted as it was, in its own way threatened the very existential well-being of a thing called the National Theatre barely half a mile up river whose presumptions of 'National' relevance surely began with our own disappearance from their doorstep. We were their neighbours after all, paying the taxes that maintained their repertoire in our 'national' name, and it would not take a knowledge of Hegel's master–slave relation to understand this necessary reciprocity of existence in anything but a wholly anti-democratic society.

The emergence into the screen-light of the performatariat parallels the beginnings of its necessary co-option by the media it thought its own. As Zuboff says of the necessary 'illuminatis' of surveillance capitalism, 'There can be no shadow, no darkness. The unknown is intolerable'.[86] In such a continuously illuminated state the truly solitary is forbidden and in as much as that is shared by several millennia of theatre rhetoric concerning the ubiquity of the crowd, one might say we got what we deserved from the latest round of rendering of our lives for the sake of live arts. Zuboff gives barely three pages in her door-stop book *Surveillance Capitalism* to artists and their activism (wholly in keeping with almost all big-thinkers for whom the cultural sphere is always operationalised to back-up another pre-existing argument, rather than foreground its own terms of practiced, affective, reference).[87] And, unlike publications such as those of Nancy Adajania and Ariella Azoulay that dig deep into the cultural sphere in pursuit of their civic politics, the sentiments expressed are vague at best: 'Our artists, like our young people, are canaries in the coal mine'. The work to record articulate and analyse that canary's song, never mind the chiaroscuro of that mine, the starting point for any sensible aesthetic theory, is indicative of the summarising logic of metaphorisation here.[88] While Zuboff has much larger fish to fry this is a pity, and though obviously not a fatal blow for a project of such daring, is something of a disappointment for a book that in its title calls for 'The fight for a human future at the new frontier of power'. One wonders without detailed critical address of those interventions *themselves* (amongst which I would include a prominent place for theatre, for reasons this book made clear in Chapter 1 and will continue to promote in Part II) it is hard to imagine what could merit such a voluntaristic subtitle to a work which dwells in such copious detail on a dystopian, digital disasterism.

It is a mark of my enduring optimism in the full-throated life-force of this conflictual exchange, what Miranda Joseph might in turn call my own incipient 'romanticism', that collectives, crowds, communities, publics, parties (amongst which 'the People' figures as a problematic but enduring census) persevere as mobilising figures in my own argument in this chapter, and in the pages that come.[89] It might be something to do with this romantic optimism that I have taken so much guilty-pleasure in writing this follow-up book to *Theatre & Everyday Life*, and that I consider it critical to have done so to register some of the seismic digital and social media shifts that have avalanched the UK and Western European cultural scene that I have begun to sketch in here against the tide of surveillance capitalism. I would not want to go as far as Ernst Bloch or Jill Dolan and call this 'hope' but getting on with *doing* whatever that hopeful sign implies seems the very least one could do in the meantime of the performatariat's noble sacrifice of their anonymity to be rendered for their feelings, facts and family histories.[90] That is the performatariat 'sent over the top' before us, and for us, Joseph Cerniglia, Mike Thalassitis, Caroline Flack, and those who will follow in giving their lives to the cause.[91]

There is after all apparently nothing that the performatariat cannot perform until such a time as their contract is suspended for overstepping the broadcast guidelines. At the far end of the performatariat reserved for those retirees from conspicuous life, a right-wing devout Christian politician such as Ann Widecombe is willing to deny the mean-spirited Conservative decorum of her previous political identity with the chance to be ignominiously wind-milled around the floor of *Strictly Come Dancing* like a human mop, while Greg Louganis the distinguished Olympic diver coaches a motley collection of celebrities to enter the water straight in *Splash!* It is as though Eddie the Eagle and all Olympic ingénues that followed in their technically abject non-performances have been enticed (by lucrative offers or an extended Warholian promise of fame for a standard series length) to form the equivalent of a historical riot of the ridiculous in the ruins of an increasingly entropic enclave of elitist expertise.

Black Friday

But what if one were to look again and consider the potential for the latent energies of this apparent riot as a *party* (in both senses of that word, playful and organisational) of some practiced sort through which our unexceptional avant garde finds its voice. What I used to call the 'lay theatre' perhaps? I will come back to the idea of Culture's collateral damage in Part II of this book but here we should not just elevate the weak 'side effects' of the riotous party I am describing, but also recognise here its shrapnel-like ricocheting effect amongst the populist dynamics of these interregnum days. Such collateral damages have very little to do with the magnitude of fictions of cultural catastrophism as outlined by Shoshana Zuboff with her reference to the canaried coal mine, but are more like the indelible markings of a city street scene where pock-marked buildings remind us of our predecessors' true precarities at other times of militarism, far more injurious than these skirmishes in the culture wars. In London, now, these markings are as likely to have been caused by a spat over something *bought* as something genuinely fought.

Take 'Black Friday' for instance, a consumptive, cadaverous coda to the dark theatre if ever there was one. In the UK with no Thanksgiving to give, despite the reparations Empire might invite or 'force from us', the Friday that falls after the Thanksgiving-Eve-Wednesday and Thanksgiving-Thursday which has set the scene so far in this chapter for my discussion of Populism and the performatariat, gives way on the subsequent Friday to a small-scale skirmish that would embarrass our US counterparts in the dark arts. As Jodi Dean laconically puts it: 'Our most prevalent image of crowds is that of Black Friday shoppers surging through the doors of Walmart'.[92] Given the work Dean wants 'crowds' to do on behalf of social revolution, it is some admission that their most prevalent and immediate imaginary is the cascading masses with their 'personal wants' pell-melling through 'big-box stores'. Collective desire has gone missing amongst a realised fantasy of other brands, or 'goods', but more than that, as Jodi Dean helpfully points out for our purposes here: 'Black Friday shoppers know the role they play'.[93] The desperation of the 'punch, kick and grab' that Dean identifies as being 'played out' for the watching media is, without being pious, far less prevalent in the UK, where queueing still has a phantasmic hold on the vast majority of those who wait (possibly in respect to our grandparents' narratives of the supposed endless good-humour of the war-time ration line). Perhaps we disappoint in our passive realisation of these consumption events and Dean hastens to link our own crowd manifestations with what she has the good grace and nous to call 'football'. But on the 'Black Friday' morn, heading back towards the V&A National Art Library to complete this chapter, a scene of some interest catches my eye at the far end of Kensington High Street that might offer a more coherent transatlantic bridge towards Black Friday parallels. The fact that this scene happens barely yards from the George & Peto building in SW7 where the 'eruption of the audience' was first announced at that book launch in 1993 that I began this chapter with, does little conceptually for it, save to mark the powerful 'lay lines' (as in relations between lay communities and professionals) in this corner of historical West London, where community is and has always been a matter of a diverse rich-mix (or at least since the orchards were swept away from the edges of Hyde Park for the Great Exhibition of 1851 and the construction of Albertopolis that followed).

The crowd that Dean is after identifying forms in a place and it 'depends on the boundedness of a setting to concentrate its intensity'.[94] In the case of the Kensington store front that I pass it is obvious that the crowd can be 'there' but *not* over there. It is the event of the 'SALE' that permits the gathering that would otherwise be moved on for the observance of public order and safety. The characteristics of crowds that Dean wants to pull out from the mass are all there: 'charge, atmosphere, pressure, expectation, excitement', what Dean calls the 'positive expression of the negation of individuality' might even, given there is half an hour to go before the aisle race starts, be at work as well on this side street at least.[95] Here there is a strange conjunction of desires at work. The big-item BLACK FRIDAY SALE with its outlandish store-front fonts, would appear to have fostered a peculiar kind of collective presence in anticipation of the doors opening at 9 am. How one might begin to disentangle such bourgeois belief in the elixir of flat-screen acquisition, from this more collective sense of the atomised-before-entry, is difficult to navigate.

The first thing to notice here is far from distracted scanning of the inveterate consumer, as the shoppers wait in line many are channelling the very media and narratives that this chapter has encountered as the platform for the performatariat and its ever-present, equal and opposite commentariat. They are assiduously mopping up on the day's previous online narratives, from Piers Morgan *et al.* as the murmur of outrage has given way to new and improved anxieties and angers. Here in these early morning screen-lit faces one can gauge some ways in which Jodi Dean's harsh but accurate portrait of the ubiquity of identity politics is now playing out:

> Identity as an operator for a politics is now itself fully saturated. Symptoms of this saturation include the reduction of the space of change to the individual, the circulation of the momentary outrage in the affective networks of communicative capitalism, the practices of calling out and shaming that

undermine solidarity, and the contradictory and destructive attachment to national and ethnic specificity. They include, as well, the complex mutual policing of who can claim what identity under what conditions and what authorises such a claim.[96]

But perhaps because of, rather than despite all this I want to hold out for what this street scene, worthy of Bertolt Brecht, *circa* 1930, might tell us about the complex relations here between conceptions of community and the capital that such scenes exist within (in my case in London) but also the capital (as in economic force) that obviously drives such scenes.[97] The fleeting equality that temporarily brings together this street scene that Brecht would undoubtedly have scrutinised and analytically poeticised for the edification and education of his professional off-road actors under 'electric suns', is in fact closer to the bourgeois' flattening equality of the kind that Marx critiques just adjacent to that fantasy of the dictatorship of the proletariat in *The Critique of the Gotha Programme*.

I have an ally here in observing these scenes for their affirmative as much as their dystopian dimension in Miranda Joseph who despite the avalanching critiques of community that come with the twenty-first century that she knows only too well, and in certain cases has sympathies with, nevertheless bravely wants to account for 'the persistence and pervasiveness of community'.[98] Situating community within its 'social processes' for Joseph, 'communal subjectivity is constituted *not by identity* but rather through practices of production and consumption […] both the rhetorical invocation of community and the social relationships that are discursively articulated as community are imbricated in capitalism' [my emphasis].[99]

I take it amongst many 'social processes' Black Friday might not be a bad day nor place to observe the dynamics of such things in their least likely, nor obviously, fortuitous arrangement. As Lenin said after all, politics is in the end 'concentrated economics'.[100]

While *potentially* resistant to capitalism, though now never presumed to be so, it must be recognised how community itself is always in economies such as where 'Black Fridays' exist constituted in a tension *with* any such capitalism. For Miranda Joseph the first defence should be a shake-down of the incipient voluntarism that comes with conceptions of community, the way that 'Fetishising community only makes us blind to the ways we might intervene in the enactment of domination and exploitation'.[101] In seeking these alignments and distinctions Miranda Joseph then precisely departs from 'streets in general' where such things might be said to cohere or exist in states of continuous suspension, and rather retreats to the aesthetic realm, launching into an extended case study of the San Francisco Mission District, and the gay/lesbian theatre company Rhinoceros from 1984 (around the time I arrived at Rotherhithe Theatre Workshop, a project with remarkably sympathetic ties to Rhinoceros in Joseph's description), and the development of her research-proper into questions of community from 1990 (again coincidentally, or not given the Reagan-Thatcher neoliberal economic front, around the time that our own theatre was being driven from the neighbourhood in which it had played its part over 15 years of rapid social change and exclusion). Miranda Joseph, with great honesty, addresses the problem of aesthetic value in their work with Rhinoceros, something that we would have recognised every day in our own theatre-making in Docklands through the 1980s: 'During the period of my research, the organization understood itself to be in crisis. It was in dire straits financially [...] it was generally understood to be producing poor quality work'.[102] Joseph details in candid prose the problems of exclusionary practices in the company, again exclusions that we were all too familiar with through our years of work in Docklands with such high-principled community claims. Joseph is here talking about the marginalised potential for Queer politics and practices in the repertoire, but the more general structural and systemic fault line is clear in their everyday management proceedings, as indeed it was in ours: 'As the meeting unfolded [...] I noted the implicitly exclusionary deployments of community [...]'.[103]

But what is there to be said beyond the aesthetic example, back at the Black Friday *economic* scene that I wanted to unravel, the queue that I would liked to have joined if I could have found its snaking end? Miranda Joseph helps us by building upon her theatrical, case study critique how, in classical liberal theory, the public is a sphere of 'abstract citizenship' in which private interests – communal or individual particularities – 'are left behind in construction of a larger political community'.[104] The public sphere meanwhile is not of course indifferent or neutral but rather marked by the particular interests of a dominant group, those who demonstrate difference will be excluded or marginalised from participation in any such hegemonic sphere. The multifarious accommodations of pluralistic identities that the communicative individualism represented by that sale-queue scanning its screens, gestures towards the kinds of micro-guarantees against exclusion that mobile technology could be said to have offered each and all of those with the capital wherewithal to access such streams of self-affirmation. There is nothing whatsoever new in this as McKenzie Wark reminds us:

> While mediation is characteristic of all modern polities, it is not all that new. It is not the case that 'this conjuncture of street and media constitutes a very contemporary version of the public sphere ...' [as Judith Butler claims and Wark is critiquing]. Unless by contemporary one means a century and a half of 'twitter revolutions'. Already by the 1840s, telegraphy starts to shape a *virtual geography* of the event.[105]

Miranda Joseph helps us in the finessing of this Black Friday queue for rather than settle for the 'whatever' of community that Giorgio Agamben might after Jean-Luc Nancy, rather characteristically and neutrally surrender to (and there is something of that 'whatever' hanging over this scene as some late Autumn drizzle drizzles on us), she suggests we should think of the *passions* of community and its forces of activism. In this queue on this day, Joseph's clarion call for commitment to causes might have found their perverse dark side. As she says: 'I propose that progressive movements would be well served by articulating themselves through a critique of capitalism'.[106] There would appear to be little critique of that particular economic formation at work here though, given the purpose of this scrum as opening time approaches. Contrary to earlier analyses of community which focused on the tendency of community to universalise particularities and social hierarchies, Joseph goes on to insist

> I argue that the work of community is to generate and legitimate necessary particularities and social hierarchies (of gender, race, nation, sexuality), implicitly required, but disavowed by capitalism [...]'.[107]

While this is undoubtedly true with regards to each individual's place within this heaving form for which the word queue is now somewhere short of accurate, there can be no doubt that what is at 8.59 am coming true is Miranda Joseph's rather more prosaic claim that 'community is complicit with capitalism and also that communities are, through capitalism, complicit with each other'.[108]

Let's enter that queue at its half way point (to the chagrin of some behind) and explore what possibilities might stand in this least opportune gathering? This is not quite the 'vectoralist class' that McKenzie Wark characterises in their valediction to capital, but it is an extensive vector of communication which traverses the spaces of the sidewalk.[109] This is certainly no 'romantic' collective on offer here, though collective of a peculiarly familiar modern-kind it is, with none of the face to face contact one might have associated with human orientations that pre-lapsarian pastoral scenes imagined by Rousseau at the May-Pole would once have offered. The 'value' that is at work in the line, a constant adjustment to what is or might now be not, available from within the store-offers is being judged by each and all as those further to the front are walked away from the throng towards the security of the store lobby, with their 'overnight' vouchers in hand, securing them the top-value items at the steepest savings. In the face of that 'value' it would not be immediately obvious what 'values' in Miranda Joseph's term could possibly be ascribed to any such grouping, beyond guess-work based on their algorithmic social media scores, their follows, likes and favourites, their Air b'n'b and Uber ratings. Just because a member of the queue happens to have an apparently continuous feed related to animal welfare, the care of cats, and vitriolic online denouncements of those who have been CCTV'd binning them in wheelies, would not, as playwright Martin McDonagh has shown us so visibly in his dramatic conjunction of feline-care and splinter-group terror in *The Lieutenant of Inishmore*, have anything necessarily to say about their actual, in-the-world altruism when it comes to the welfare of other humans with whom they might clash in this particular queue, or worse, in the race through the lobby to where the Sony's stand boxed and bar-coded.

One might notice for instance a propensity in this queue to unlimited self-reproduction, the always running ever-populated handheld social media streams would suggest anything is possible from 'paedo-vigilantism' to 'radical-veganism'. In any such circumstances as Byung-Chul Han has suggested, the demographic measure of 'a dictatorship of the proletariat' that I have been historically tracing here 'is structurally impossible'.[110] But I am not at all sure that the necessary corollary to that class disappointment is to conclude as Han does that 'Today, the dictatorship of Capital rules over everyone' nor as McKenzie Wark does that 'capitalism has already been rendered historical'.[111] Yes there is a general degree of auto-exploitation at work in this very queue, that is obvious given the hardship those camping in the doorway overnight have endured for the sake of a knock-down wide-screen Hitachi. It is indeed unlikely that there is any definable 'we' at work in this queue given the high stakes positioning in a line which, when 9 am comes, will presumably throw the caution of the collective to the wind. Here as much as any civil-war scene one might imagine the exploited are as likely to turn aggression towards themselves as towards any perceived 'dictator' of their Black Friday blues, if any such fat-controller (to quote the Rev. W. Awdry's Thomas the Tank Engine) is identifiable behind the (store) curtain. For Byung-Chul Han the consequences of this loss of the 'responsible other' is as likely to lead to *expression*, you could say performance, as it is to anything that might once have been called revolution. In this queue the needs that capital itself has generated are the needs that those in the line thought they had invented for themselves. They have just 'liked' it on someone's Facebook after all they must be in some sense considered part of someone's community of preference.

But as Miranda Joseph has taken the trouble to point out: '[...] precisely through being cast as its opposite, community functions in complicity with 'society', enabling capitalism and the liberal state'.[112] There could be no truer arrangement of that dialectical dependency, what Jacques Derrida might have called a supplement to capital's power, that has inadvertently brought this community with nothing in common (other than a bargain) together on this very morning. There is no denouement to this scene, no passing act of kindness, no Damascene conversion where one who realises their aggression gives way to another less-abled who has no means to aggress, no handing over of the goods to those most in need (of a 60″ digital HD screen). But neither is there, in the movement of the line, as a distant, single bell under Gilbert Scott's high roof of St Mary Abbots, rings out to mark the tolling of the hour, the push-and-shove that one might have presumed would be the 'order' of the day.

I wonder at this apparent gesture of what you could call, before Donald Trump, civility? At this point those who hear the bell might also hear the call of an 'opening' (of the store), that all here are now about to be debtors in the eyes of that lord (as well as the store cards many carry), all guilty (*schuldig*) in the eyes of that god-of-credit, which for Nietzsche after all also stood for debt. Indeed, despite the bell-tolling, the passing of the opening hour, there is something like a lethargy of human-progress towards this inescapable door of upgraded-televisual debt, becalmed by the all-enveloping interest in what each person has before them by way of unfinished narrative here, scrolling there, a half finished text here and a tweet to some distant calumny, by Piers Morgan perhaps, or a directional suggestion to Max, Spiller of Tea, still in search of his cream jumper, there. In their own fashion each participant in this line on this Black Friday observes their own devotionals with a bowed head. That is, devotional in its original sense, of that which is submissive or obedient to some other order.

The dictatorship of the performatariat is well underway again, but now revealing itself amidst this bell-ringing as closer to something like a holy-ghosting, a holier-than-thou deference to each other's privacy of prayer. As Han puts it: 'Smartphones represent *digital* devotion – indeed, they are the *devotional objects of the Digital*, period. As a subjectivation-apparatus the smartphone works like a rosary – which, because of its ready availability, represents a handheld device too'.[113] In this line those under the tolling bell move forward at a stations-of-the-cross pace self-observing, self-monitoring, convincing themselves they are under their own control, with each mobile handset offering the mesh screen of confession that once separated by the cool lay-community (Fleabag) from the hot-clergy (Andrew Scott), personality signifiers that might well be wholly incomprehensible in a short year, but in this fleeting meantime before their own loss to our shifting attention, inundate today's Black Friday social media timeline.

We may not quite be 'in the moment' as some would have us in this snaking line, but that does not mean the multiple 'elsewheres' are not without their own efficacy for the well-being of these present souls. When Alain Corbin in 1998 wrote his magisterial work on the rural acoustic envelope, *Village Bells*, his 400 pages of closely-worded celebration of the sonic community of a myriad believers networked in the French countryside by the tolling sound of the local church peel, those summonsed through the lanes could not have envisaged a call-to-arms of this flat-screen kind.[114] But the histories he tells in those chapters have a certain ring to them that the future-thinker in Ray Bradbury would have been proud of, as harbingers of a future forged from an archival past. As Corbin puts it:

> The unfolding of campanarian disputes, the intensity of the passions they aroused, and the entrenched positions of the contending parties serve to show just how important the thousands of such quarrels over bells are for anyone wishing to follow the ways in which an apprenticeship in politics was realized.[115]

It is just such a peculiar progress of this Black Friday kind, set off against its distant communicative cousin at St Mary Abbots, that is the apparently contradictory impulse, the 'apprenticeship in politics' I would like to sustain from this chapter. That tolling from London's tallest spire, must be ringing from the 'Verger's Bell', added much later from the Whitechapel Foundry in 2007, as bell-ringing of the full-set is strictly limited to Thursday practice, Sunday service, and religious holy days. I'm not sure St Mary Abbots Kensington observes the Black Friday Agreement, this is no full-set, but a passable peel nonetheless. Without denying, ignoring or belittling the complex cultures evidenced in the unholy alliance, lined up on this unholy morn, I would want to retain these ever-present tensions between community and capitalism as the continuous backdrop (for the time-being until those transitionary arrangements are with us) against which other kinds of theatrical action are destined to play out their part, on the part of others who, compared with those present and incorrect here, when push does or, as in this case, does not come to shove, have, really, no part. In other words, and there is no other way to describe us, for I am amongst 'them' now, we are the 'unknown among the unknown' who need to know everybody, without apparently knowing anyone. Let us see whether something as apparently antiquated as theatre has anything whatsoever to offer such contemporary losses of the collective.

Notes

1 See Kirshenblatt-Gimblett, Barbara. (1998). *Destination Culture: Tourism, Museums and Heritage*. Berkeley: University of California Press.
2 See Read, Alan. (1996). *The Fact of Blackness*. Seattle: Bay Press, *Architecturally Speaking* (2000). London: Routledge; 'On Animals', *Performance Research*, Vol 5, No. 2; 2000, *Theatre, Intimacy & Engagement* (2008). Houndmills: Palgrave; *Theatre in the Expanded Field* (2013). London: Bloomsbury; *Theatre & Law* (2016). Houndmills: Palgrave.
3 See Han, Byung-Chul. (2017). *Psycho-Politics: Neoliberalism and New Technologies of Power*, London: Verso.
4 Ibid. p. 6
5 See Stiegler, Bernard. (2010). *Taking Care of Youth and the Generations*. Trans. Stephen Barker. Stanford: Stanford University Press and for a commentary on Stiegler's reliance on televisual phenomena see Han, Byung-Chul. (2017) op. cit. pp. 26–27.
6 See Fisher, Mark. *Capitalist Realism*, op. cit. for a critique of the foregrounding of postmodernism. p. 7.
7 Jameson, Frederic. (1984a). 'Postmodernism: Or The Cultural Logic of Late Capitalism', *New Left Review*, 1/146, July/August 1984. Jameson, Frederic. (1984b). 'The Politics of Theory: Ideological Positions in the Postmodern Debate', *New German Critique*, No. 33, Modernity and Postmodernity, Autumn 1984, pp. 53–65.
8 Han, op. cit. p. 9.
9 See Simon Reynolds quoted in Fisher, Mark. (2018). *K-PUNK*. Ed. Darren Ambrose. London: Repeater p. 10.
10 See Hammond, Simon. (2019). 'K-Punk at Large', *New Left Review*, 118, July–August 2019, pp. 37–67.
11 See Fisher, Mark. (2018). *K-PUNK*. Ed. Darren Ambrose. London: Repeater, p. 212.
12 See Deleuze, Gilles. (1981). *Cinema 1: The Movement Image*. Trans. Hugh Tomlinson. London: Athlone.
13 Fisher, Mark. op. cit. p. 257.
14 Adorno, Theodor W. (2001). *The Culture Industry*. Trans. E. B. Ashton. London: Routledge.
15 See Fisher, Mark, op. cit. pp. 5–6.
16 Ibid. p. 6.
17 See Kennedy, A. L. (2019). *A Point of View: Cookery Shows … and Hungry People*. BBC Radio 4, Sunday 24 February 2019. I am grateful to Beryl Robinson for bringing this to my attention.
18 Bradbury, R. (1953/1993). *Fahrenheit 451*. London: Harper Collins, p. 27. Following quotations from this page.
19 Fisher, Mark, *K-Punk*. op. cit. p. 258
20 Warhol had first used this phrase some years before in a 1968 catalogue for his show at the Moderna Museet, Stockholm, but 'Nine days wonder' dates back to the Early Modern period.
21 For background to Sam Rumbelow see: www.methodacting.co.uk/sam-rumbelow/ (accessed on 10 March 2019).

22 www.artsy.net/article/artsy-editorial-elsa-von-freytag-loringhoven-dada-baroness-invented-readymade (accessed on 24 August 2019).
23 See *Theatre & Everyday Life*, Chapter 3 'Everyday Life'.
24 Fisher, Mark, op. cit. p. 222.
25 See Orr, Deborah, in the *Guardian*: www.theguardian.com/commentisfree/2014/jan/24/benefits-street-caused-controversy-worthwhile-legacy (accessed on 24 August 2019).
26 Han, op. cit. p. 9.
27 Zuboff, Shoshana. (2016). *The Age of Surveillance Capitalism: The Fight for a Human Future at the New Frontier of Power*. London: Profile, p. 8.
28 Klossowski, Pierre. (2017). *Living Currency* (2017), Trans and Ed. Daniel W Smith, London: Bloomsbury.
29 Gramsci, Antonio. (1930) *The Prison Notebooks*, Notebook Number 3, see https://isreview.org/issue/108/morbid-symptoms (accessed on 24 August 2019). I write this at a time in UK political history when the morbid symptoms of 'Brexit Britain' are widely thought to prevail at pathological levels and while that between-time will pass like other apparent 'crises', the performatariat I would wager will have played an unusually prominent part in its un-stately progress as it slips across our distracted horizon of interest.
30 See Kear, Adrian and Steinberg, Deborah Lynn. Eds. (1999). *Mourning Diana: Nation, Culture and the Performance of Grief*. London: Routledge.
31 Statistics for box office global returns for *Les Misérables* can be found here: www.delfontmackintosh.co.uk/news/les-miserables-continues-astounding-success-into-its-34th-year.php (accessed on 24 August 2019).
32 One might ask, where is the 'flesh' of the Monarch now? That might be the kind of question Eric Santner would encourage us to answer. *I* couldn't tell you, because on the 29 February 2012, when I waited in the receiving line for the Queen, I took hold, somewhat warily, of a gloved hand (for Royal hygiene purposes I presume).
33 Santner, Erik. (2011). *The Royal Remains: The People's Two Bodies and the Endgame of Sovereignty*. Chicago: University of Chicago Press, p. xxi.
34 In the spirit of Giorgio Agamben's invitation to profane 'sacred', or from the root of the word sacrare 'separated', words back into operation through play, the recovery of the term dictatorship in this company could be seen as a concerted attempt to ward off the real threat to understanding, the sly-civility of euphemism. See Agamben, Giorgio. (2007) on the 'sacred' in *Profanations*., Trans. Jeff Fort. New York: Zone Books.
35 If this doesn't sound like a late attempt to gain entry to *Private Eye* I am indebted to Nicholas Ridout who, at an animated dinner (accompanied by Joe Kelleher) of *moules et frites* at a Brussels café following a production of *Orpheus and Eurydice*, put this expectation of historical exactitude firmly on the table.
36 Doncaster voted Leave: 106,260 (68.94%), Remain: 46,922 (31.02%) in the UK/EU Referendum. There was a significant spike in police reports of hate speech but that *followed* the Brexit vote which might be considered a form of self-fulfilling prophecy given the dog-whistle campaign of UKIP and even Conservative Party ERG members.
37 For an annotated online resource of Defoe: www.visionofbritain.org.uk/travellers/Defoe/1 (accessed on 24 August 2019).
38 'Statement on Visit to the United Kingdom, by Professor Philip Alston, United Nations Special Rapporteur on Extreme Poverty and Human Rights'. London, 16 November 2018 and available online here: www.ohchr.org/documents/issues/poverty/eom_gb_16nov2018.pdf (accessed on 24 August 2019).
39 Ibid. p. 1.
40 UK Government, 'UK Government Transformation Strategy', 9 February 2017, and available online here: www.gov.uk/government/publications/government-transformation-strategy-2017-to-2020/government-transformation-strategy (accessed on 24 August 2019).
41 UN report. op. cit. p. 9.

42 Erica Whyman and Rufus Norris discuss the prognosis here but do not appear to grasp the obvious antidote: www.thetimes.co.uk/article/theatre-is-snobbish-and-parochial-say-erica-whyman-and-rufus-norris-kgh8nd786 (accessed on 24 August 2019).
43 Han, op. cit. p. 5.
44 Rancière, Jacques. (2012). *Proletarian Nights: The Workers' Dream in Nineteenth-Century France*. Trans. John Drury. London: Verso.
45 Marx's original manuscript was lost.
46 See Korsch, Karl. (1970). *Marxism and Philosophy*. London: New Left Books, p. 129.
47 See Liedman, Sven-Eric. (2018). *A World to Win: The Life and Works of Karl Marx*. London: Verso. Trans. Jeffrey N. Skinner, pp. 564–565.
48 See Karl Marx, Archives, *Critique of the Gotha Programme*, Lea Ypi drew my attention to this resource and I rely upon it here: www.marxists.org/archive/marx/works/1875/gotha/ch04.htm and Marx, Karl (1933) *A Critique of the Gotha Program*, London: Martin Lawrence, pp. 44–45.
49 Marx, Karl. (1933). *A Critique of the Gotha Programme*. London: Martin Lawrence, p. 10.
50 Lea Ypi, King's College London, *Seminar in Contemporary Marxist Theory*, 22 March 2017, chaired by Alex Callinicos, and of foundational importance for these paragraphs.
51 This doctoral period of study and completion is brilliantly covered by Sven-Eric Liedman, op. cit. pp. 68–74.
52 Mouffe, Chantal. (2019). *For a Left Populism*. London: Verso, p. 5. (My italics for the simple reason I am attracted to this proposition and do not believe we should be unnerved by such a thing within the privileged securities of academic writing).
53 Ibid. p. 6. Also see Janelle Reinelt, op. cit. 'What I came to Say' accessed here: www.researchgate.net/publication/283882145_%27What_I_Came_to_Say%27_Raymond_Williams_the_Sociology_of_Culture_and_the_Politics_of_Performance_Scholarship (accessed on 24 August 2019).
54 See Jonathan White's LSE Blog at: https://blogs.lse.ac.uk/politicsandpolicy/performative-prorogation/ (accessed on 3 September 2019).
55 Mouffe, op. cit. p. 36.
56 Ibid. p. 56
57 See Rae, Paul. (2018). *Real Theatre*. Cambridge: Cambridge University Press, and his discussion of 'peak performance', also Rufus Norris and Erica Whyman: www.suttontrust.com/newsarchive/theatre-is-snobbish-and-parochial-say-erica-whyman-and-rufus-norris/ (accessed on 29 August 2019).
58 Read, Alan. (1993). *Theatre & Everyday Life*, op. cit. p. 62. It is transparently obvious that sociological categories are one, very well-tested means of precisely doing this kind of significant work.
59 Benjamin, Walter. (1976). *One Way Street*. Trans. Edmund Jephcott. London: New Left Books.
60 The subject of Auden's poetic insight hanging in the Musée des Beaux Arts is a copy as I discovered when looking for it in the recent (2019) Breugel retrospective at the Kunsthistorische Museum in Vienna.
61 See Phelan, Peggy (1993). 'The Ontology of Performance', in *Unmarked*. London: Routledge, and Auslander, Philip (1999). *Liveness: Performance in a Mediatised Culture*, London: Routledge.
62 During the decisive UCU national strike of March 2018 across the UK it was made apparent that the TV celebrity choirmaster and impresario Gareth Malone was offering 'well-being' sessions for King's College London staff but on the 'wrong side' of the picket lines (if protecting your right to a pension, and therefore one's well-being in later life is sufficient reason to demarcate a right and a wrong side). On speaking to Malone's manager, seeking equivalent support with strike-singing on the 'right' side of the barricades, I was informed that the workshop fee to secure Mr Malone's services would be a minimum of £50,000 for a three-hour session (excluding VAT and travel). I demurred and we asked our nineteenth-century specialist Brian Murray to play the guitar for us

on our renditions of Woody Guthrie instead. We 'won' all the demands we made as conditions of our ending of strike action so our singing cannot have been wholly counter-productive.
63 See Read, Alan. (1993). *Theatre & Everyday Life*, London: Routledge, p. 59.
64 See UK Parliamentary Inquiry into Reality TV: www.parliament.uk/business/committees/committees-a-z/commons-select/digital-culture-media-and-sport-committee/inquiries/parliament-2017/realitytv/ (accessed on 24 August 2019).
65 See Anixter at: www.anixter.com/en_uk/about-us/contact-us/global-locations-contact-info/europe/united-kingdom.html (accessed on 24 August 2019).
66 For an overview of Derek Paget's early framing of the form: www.temporada-alta.com/wp-content/uploads/verbatim_theatre_oral_history_and_documentary_techniques.pdf (accessed on 24 August 2019).
67 See de Certeau, Michel. (1983). *The Practice of Everyday Life*. Trans: Steven Rendall. Berkeley: University of California Press.
68 See Jacques Rancière, op. cit. *Proletarian Nights*.
69 See Read, Alan (2013). *Theatre in the Expanded Field*. London: Bloomsbury, and Mondzain, Marie-José (2007). *Homo Spectator*. Paris: Boyard.
70 See Ridout, Nicholas (2013). *Passionate Amateurs*. Michigan: University of Michigan Press; Nicholson, Helen, Holdsworth, Nadine, Milling, Jane (2018). *The Ecologies of Amateur Theatre*, (2018) Houndmills: Palgrave.
71 See 'Revealed One in Four Europeans Vote Populist', the *Guardian*, Paul Lewis *et al.*, Tuesday 20 November 2018.
72 Paul Poet, *Auslander Raus!: Schlingensief's Container*. (2005). Monitorpop Entertainment. DVD. Peter Sloterdijk discusses the *Auslander Raus!* project from the safety of a hotel bar in Paul Poet's great film of the installation and its effects. His prognosis that it operated as a 'dirt magnet' for extreme forms of public opinion and prejudice nicely sums up the conduct of the current state of affairs in that very place.
73 See Mouffe, Chantal (2019). *For a Left Populism*, London: Verso, p. 12.
74 Mark Sweeney in the *Guardian*, Friday 30 November 2012, www.theguardian.com/media/2012/nov/30/piers-morgan-phone-hacking-leveson-inquiry (accessed on 24 August 2019).
75 See Said, Edward, https://philpapers.org/rec/SAIOAC (accessed on 15 December 2018).
76 See Katherine Lyndsay: www.refinery29.com/en-gb/2018/11/216377/thank-u-next-twitter-joke-ariana-grande-wrong (accessed on 24 August 2019).
77 The word 'spaffing' was later picked up ingloriously in relation to what was perceived as money wasted on sex-abuse cases and enquiries by UK member of parliament, Brexit cheerleader and soon to be Prime Minister Boris Johnson. See: www.theguardian.com/politics/2019/mar/13/boris-johnson-under-fire-over-remarks-about-child-abuse-inquiries (accessed on 24 August 2019).
78 Zuboff, op. cit. p. 6.
79 At the time of writing the UK government through the auspices of the NHS has announced it will trial health monitoring of geriatrics through *Fit-Bit* personal technology, a proposal whose deep dark irony is not lost on the Twitter commentariat itself.
80 Zuboff, op. cit. p. 8, surveillance capitalism here substituted by theatre to check its effect.
81 McKenzie, Jon. (2001). *Perform or Else!: From Discipline to Performance*. London: Routledge.
82 Zuboff, op. cit. p. 15.
83 Of course anyone remotely acquainted with the last three decades of performance history will be only too aware that companies such as Blast Theory, Rimini Protokoll, Gob Squad and Fanshen, have made this their landscape of operation.
84 Zuboff, op. cit. p. 210.
85 Taine, H. A. (1878). *The Revolution*, 'Les origins de la France contemporaine' vol. 1, Trans. John Durand, London: Daldy, Isbister & Co., pp. 30–31. Quoted in the excellent work of: Dean, Jodi (2017) *Crowds and Party*. London: Verso, p. 117.

86 Zuboff, op. cit. p. 241.
87 Ibid. pp. 488–492.
88 Ibid. p. 491.
89 See Joseph, Miranda. (2013). *The Romance of Community*. Minneapolis: University of Minnesota Press.
90 Bloch, Ernst. (1954/2013). *The Principle of Hope*. Trans. Neville Plaice, Stephen Plaice and Paul Knight, Boston: MIT Press, and Dolan, Jill (2005). *Utopia in Performance: Finding Hope at the Theater*. Michigan: University of Michigan Press. Note here the truly hopeful work of Wickstrom, Maurya (2018). *Fiery Temporalities in Theatre and Performance: The Initiation of History*, London: Bloomsbury.
91 Joseph Cerniglia and Mike Thalassitis were two high profile victims of the fallout from participation in 'reality television', Caroline Flack hosted Love Island and 'won' Strictly Come Dancing.
92 See Dean, Jodi. (2018). *Crowds and Party*. London: Verso, p. 118.
93 Ibid. p. 118.
94 Ibid. p. 119.
95 Ibid. p. 120.
96 Ibid. p. 256.
97 For the following discussion see: Joseph, Miranda. (2002). *Against the Romance of Community*. Minneapolis: University of Minnesota Press.
98 Ibid. p. viii.
99 Ibid. pp. viii-ix.
100 See Choonara, Joseph. (2017). *Unravelling Capitalism*. London: Bookmarks Publications, p. 8.
101 Ibid. p. ix.
102 Ibid. p. xi.
103 Ibid. p. xviii.
104 Ibid. p. xxi.
105 See Wark, McKenzie, www.publicseminar.org/2016/06/butler/ (accessed on 24 August 2017).
106 Choonara, op. cit. p. xxxi.
107 Ibid. p. xxxii.
108 Ibid. p. xxxiii.
109 Wark, McKenzie. (2019). *Capital is Dead*. op. cit. p. 55.
110 Han, op. cit. p. 6.
111 Ibid. Han, p. 6; Wark. op. cit. p. 26.
112 Ibid. p. 2.
113 Ibid. p. 12.
114 Corbin, Alain. (1999). *Village Bells: Sound and Meaning in the Nineteenth-Century French Countryside*. Trans. Martin Thom. London: Papermac.
115 Ibid. p. xi.

3
ALL THE HOME'S A STAGE
Social reproduction and everyday life

On a summer's evening in June 1991 the London International Festival of Theatre had in their inimitable way arranged for 12 of us, each day, to sit on bleachers in Bobby Baker's capacious kitchen in North London. Baker was already a well-known multi-media artist, active in the ACME arts scene in the 1970s, in the East London docklands area that provided the landscape for our work at Rotherhithe Theatre Workshop (that had closed a few short weeks before Bobby had invited us round). Though I had not seen it I was aware of a performance she had made called *Drawing on a Mother's Experience* first shown in 1988 that dramatically tracked eight years of her own mothering commitments. In *Kitchen Show* we were effectively picking up the story three years on and invited to observe Bobby Baker's daily life, in an event made up of 12-plus-one exquisite scenes forged from her experience of preparing food for her family, tidying away, escaping the demands of the interior and exercising in the garden (as her cat) caped with a black-plastic bin-bag. Each scenario, echoing a benign nod to Martha Rosler's knife-wielding video work *Semiotics of the Kitchen* of 1975, was latterly marked on her white, lab-coated body with *memento mori* that accumulated over an hour into an unruly uniform of the woman's and mothers' labouring quotidian. Where Rosler's practice had always been webbed into structural questions of New York homelessness and property violence (in keeping with the experiences of those we had worked with in parallel in East London at Rotherhithe Theatre Workshop), Bobby Baker was inviting us to attend to a more psycho-political interior experience of exclusion from the presumption of securities at home. Where Rosler drew her curtains on scenes from the battlefield in *House Beautiful: Bringing the War Home* (1967–1972), rather like the first and second act relation between hotel room and theatre of war in Sarah Kane's later play *Blasted*, when Bobby Baker looks from the kitchen window into her garden it is the *garden itself* that appears simultaneously attractive and awful, the epitome of the unhomely outdoors.

I later drew upon this once private experience of the politics of intimacy and the ethics of engagement three times in *Theatre & Everyday Life* (which was as much as anyone else's theatre I had written about in that volume which registered my immense regard for this apparently quiet thing I had seen). In the first iteration in a chapter on smell, or 'olfaction of the everyday' as I primly put it, I had placed two of my favourite theatre artists together in a discussion of that most ineffable of phenomenological encounters:

> those whose work in theatre derives most deeply from the everyday are intuitively able to confront the everyday's most meaningful odours. The miasma that hung over the turf of [the Wuppertal choreographer] Pina Bausch's *1980* encompassed dancers and audience in a canopy of nostalgia and unease, and from the epic to the domestic, the smells of Bobby Baker's *Kitchen Show* were a reminder that this was a workplace as well as, for the moment, a play space.[1]

I saw a logics of the everyday within this work which I later in the book wrote about as 'modalities of action' and 'formalities of practice' shared by work as diverse as 'Armand Gatti's theatre in factories, Olivier Perrier's performances with farm animals and Bobby Baker's domestic routines'.[2] In the third reflection upon the troubling beauty of *Kitchen Show* I explored the subtle complexity of 'props' borrowed from the everyday 'a pair of shoes in Robert Lepage's *Dragon's Trilogy*, [...] a beach towel in Pina Bausch's *1980*, a pile of plates in Jan Fabre's *The Power of Theatrical Madness*',[3] a trilogy of object ontologies topped by the table mounted swivel cake-stand that Bobby Baker perches upon in her mock grand-finale, accompanied, if my recollection has not failed me, though this is not born out by the filmed documentation, by her daughter playing Beethoven's *Bagatelle in A Minor* (*Fur Elise*) on the piano, turning through the Baker's Dozen 13th-scene of that small and excruciating show.

But while I had been present to, and recognised, Bobby Baker's work for what it appeared to be, theatre that is, it is apparent I had no means to address its wider significance in its moment, by which I mean not just its subtle critique of the repetitions and beautiful banalities of that cruel kitchen, but the undertow concern for mental health that on re-seeing the filmed documentation, more than a quarter of a century later, is so stark in the work.[4] Indeed, with hindsight I realise now that the 'woman at the window', a stock aesthetic, oft-painted figure of nineteenth-century anxiety, that conceivably could have been familiar to the painter Edgar Degas, would have in 1991 'looked on' and down upon an always urban congress, not unlike this apparently well-to-do North London street, with about as much agency as Søren Kierkegaard's anti-hero Constantius, in his cyclical work *Repetition* of 1843, peering down from the Konigstadter Theatre boxes in Berlin unable to influence the irritatingly original dramatic action.[5]

It has to be admitted then that while *Theatre & Everyday Life* gave no attention to 'social reproduction' whatsoever, neither did it begin to address what Karl Marx himself referred to 'one of his best points' (that came to frame 'social reproduction' itself a century later), in his foundational first volume of *Capital*. Here Joseph Choonara summarises that keystone concept in the following way:

> workers produce new value worth one hour of labour time. But the capitalist does not need to pay the workers the value they produce. Instead of paying the workers for their labour, the capitalist is paying the workers for their 'labour power' – for their capacity to labour. The value required to hire labour-power, the wage, is simply the value needed to reproduce the labour-power, to provide the worker with food, clothing, shelter and other needs. In general this is far less than the worker creates.[6]

The differential arising between one and the other measures the 'surplus value' available to the capitalist, which in turn becomes the basis for the profit that drives the capitalocene and is continuously necessary for its renewal against all alternative organisational arrangements for an economy. And there is nothing in the digital and gig economies that fundamentally alters this systemic arrangement. So far so basic, to any such system at least. But as Tithi Bhattacharya asks,[7] following a long history of work from Silvia Federici in the 1970s on housework, reproduction and feminist struggle:

> If workers' labour produces all the wealth in society, who then produces the worker [...]. What kinds of processes enable the worker to arrive at the door of her place of work every day so that she can produce the wealth of society?[8]

Bhattacharya is talking about kitchen work, preparation of food, security to sleep, and beyond, those zones umbilically linked to anything one could call 'home', school education, transport infrastructures and the recreational spaces of everyday life sustained by those who care for them with their own often concealed labours. Here a certain kind of labour, processual as much as productive and predominantly conducted by women, is recognised as reproducing society as a whole (something that appeared to go missing in Marx's otherwise meticulous, though avowedly masculinist, materialism of labour). In this fundamental reorientation of what might count for such labours in the first place, the entire definition of what constitutes 'economy' comes up-for-grabs (hence my interest in this chapter in the *oikonomia* or conduct of the domestic sphere) and urgently returns us to engage necessary but undervalued questions of gender, race and sexuality that are now brought to the fore in an analysis that moves some way beyond Marx's partial focus upon the determinist constructs of capitalist production. Importantly and trenchantly, without losing sight of a working-class, but here reconfigured as a *global* working-class (within which border concepts such as 'gore capitalism' become urgent and thinkable), the presumptuous link between class struggle and production is widened on the back of these feminist theoretical labours, to offer more scrupulous attention to class exploitation but now in the form of material and historical instances of oppression combining abstract analyses (as in Marx) with concrete circumstances.[9]

So, if I say 'theatre's coming home' (in ironic echo of the hollow chants of male England football supporters deluded as to the sport's complex origins) I mean that rather literally, that something about theatre in the European modern period requires *home*, or the habitual everyday repetitions of the *oikos* as experienced in Bobby Baker's kitchen, to allow theatre to do what it does in its own realm of apparently public disjunctive similarities.[10] And, what is more, it is the *repetition* of this return, coming home from theatre on a second, third then fourth occasion, that draws our attention once again to the recurring economy of the everyday and its brutally cyclical forces of social reproduction, the 'infamy of the insignificant' as Jean-Luc Nancy called it in a radio broadcast on the nature of the quotidian.[11] These 'insignificants' would appear to be at odds with the *theatre*, where repetition is, precisely, as Søren Kierkegaard was at pains to point in his work *Repetition*, some years before Peggy Phelan's ontology of performance did a surprisingly similar job, quite impossible to secure despite all recurring signs to the contrary.[12]

Infamy of the insignificant

In the travelogue contained in the first part of *Repetition* written in 1843, Constantine Constantius, whom Kierkegaard describes as a Danish *rentier*, presumably with a freehold elsewhere given his apparently endless means, stages a series of encounters with Berlin. In the process he follows Kierkegaard's own well-documented tracks through the city, including walks through the Tiergarten, attendance at a performance of Johann Nestroy's farce *The Talisman*, and a passage by steamer to Stralsund on the Baltic.[13] Neither autobiography, nor fiction, Constantius's *report* from the field, something like the kind of 'Field notes from a fire sale' I catalogue in Part II of this book, plays itself out in an irresolvable tension between these two genres. This chain is predicated on the lost love of a woman, an actress, who as Gillian Rose points out in an eloquent though opaque essay on *Repetition* in her work *The Broken Middle*, does achieve a repetition of her own, while Constantius repeatedly fails in his own quest for the securities of habitual circularity.[14]

We should not, despite the gender specificities of this part of the chapter, miss the significance of Kierkegaard's unusual method in this revolutionary work, something between an ethnography of the imagination and an immersive Renaissance memory chamber, what he at the time called on the fronts-piece of his publication, 'Experimental Psychology', though we might now more accurately with the hindsight of Edmund Husserl, call this work: phenomenology. For what Constantius's travelogue details, as Marc Katz demonstrates, is the breakup of the emerging bourgeois-urban subject into a sequence of 'serial identities': 'both within the text's frame', Constantius retraces his own steps returning to those places that cause him most disturbance whether public interior such as the theatre or domestic interior such as the rented home, 'and outside of it (while Constantius follows Kierkegaard's Berlin itinerary he himself is framed when he later turns up in the pseudonymously authored *Stages on Life's Way*, in 1845)'.[15]

In a pattern that, at least at first glance, is familiar to Marc Katz through standard contemporary critical models of the 'dispersed self', this repeated bracketing of experience is highlighted as a part of subject formation: 'Since every attempt at self-recuperation is an act of self-mediation, unitary identity is made unstable simply by being an object of retrospection'.[16] When Constantius returns to those sites in Berlin where memory traces have been left, Katz suggests that he stages an uncanny encounter with himself 'as flâneur': 'by establishing a chain of dislocating *selves* whose successive acts of hyper-active self-estrangement, provide the piece with a narrative [...]'.[17] But while we might here recognise the old urban proclivity for the dérive of the privileged 'wanderer' (Constantius would still appear like a latter-day trustafarian to have no economic demands upon him in the form of commitments to paid work, and certainly can afford to return to the theatre ad infinitum to observe its most subtle shifts), the unusual feature of Kierkegaard's report is the way it binds us back into a continuum between a ceremonial auditorium and a domestic interior.

In Berlin of that period as Marc Katz points out, there was a proliferating market for tourist guides, within which the city was beginning to be delineated through an itinerary of consumable sites viewed from panoramic vantage points. The Konigstadter Theatre would have operated as a double of any such site, presenting to the public both a place to be seen 'in vistas' and a place from which to witness dramatic vistas from highpoints in the gods. While Katz suggests that 'Doing a city', that cosmopolitan *cri de coeur* of consumerism, began here, it should be noted that this 'doing' is predicated in Constantius's case, on an unusually detailed narrative of simultaneously 'doing a home', he describes it after all as 'one of the best apartments in Berlin'.[18] Making and unmaking that home of course not *despite* the fact that it is rented but perhaps precisely *because* it stands between the theatre and his 'other' home as a third point of supposed stability, that of course given his distributed and disturbing symptoms begins all too quickly to offer no such thing.

But before the tell-tale signs of 'homesickness' kick in for Constantius, let's go back to the theatre for some of that 'repetition therapy' from which the domestic sphere begins to distance itself and unravel. Constantius's account begins with a performance, a detailed recollection of *The Talisman*, a Johann Nestroy comedy whose central conceit concerns the persecution of a 'red-haired' ingénue called Salomé, he saw performed the year before at the Konigstadter Theatre. Recalling his visit to this canonical work, Constantius compares his theatre box to an 'apartment living room', the private space of bourgeois memory and 'archive of souvenirs' as Marc Katz describes it: 'one sits at the theatre', Constantius writes, 'as comfortably as one does at home'.[19] Indeed, Constantius's dismissive hauteur with regards to those balconists whose 'pathological' laughter associate them with the low-life of theatrical farce, is architecturally framed as a crowd who unable to enter the street scene themselves look down upon it from their distant window above.[20] This braiding of 'theatre house' and 'home' is a most unusual one and marks

Kierkegaard out as the first phenomenologist of their relations, while Constantius's 'report' represents the first fruits of that empirical enquiry. As Constantius recollects being seated, he in effect Katz suggests, takes his place within a fully naturalised bourgeois code of the private and public sphere, so that by acquainting the reader with the theatre's sightlines, he simultaneously asserts his qualifications as 'tourist guide, memoirist, and viewing subject'.[21] As he says so helpfully, for those of us intending to go to the Konigstadter any time soon: 'In the first balcony one can be assured of getting a box to oneself. If not, may I recommend to the reader boxes five and six to the left [...]'.[22] Constantius here assumes the mantel of cultural concierge to his willing readers.

But the 'fully naturalised bourgeois code' that Katz identifies in this spectatorial arrangement, extends even further towards the recesses of his box where a 'nook' conceals 'a single seat that is incomparably comfortable'.[23] This 'seat' will return to haunt Constantius on return home, but here, as there, it is a seat to be sat in *alone*, recessed sufficiently from the audience to ensure the required degree of isolation amongst others, 'solitude in company' as Nicholas Ridout would have it.[24] Constantius is absolutely adamant he is seated here neither as 'aesthete' nor 'critic', 'but if possible as nothing whatever', a ghost in the (theatre) machine no less, and one who is 'satisfied with the fact that one is as comfortably seated as if in one's own living room'.[25] Here Constantius, and Kierkegaard through him, makes clear the expected relation between the *oikonomia*, the economy of the private household and the economy of the public auditoria. They are certainly not the *same*, but they are predicated on a reciprocal set of principles and of costs, psychological and social.

While Constantius 'sits alone in his box' as he puts it, his first experience of performance is of the orchestra in this empty place whose 'music rings throughout the hall, somewhat *unheimlich*'.[26] For a theatre this is a quite curious observation given that one might not expect an auditoria of spectacle to be *heimlich* (homely) in the first place. But it is clear Constantius's economy of the theatre is one predicated on just such a relational model and it is a model that he has carried across the city square from the very apartment he has just left. Although, following the 'staged artifices and potential shocks' of the theatre as delineated by Marc Katz, the arrangement of furniture in this bourgeois *interior*, in Constantius's case across the square from the theatre, might usually be expected to serve to stabilise identity by establishing a domain of familiarity, habit, repetition even. But when Constantius returns home from the theatre, and re-enters his Berlin apartment, he sees that his 'prepared' desk and his velvet chair have been disturbed, or at least they can only provoke 'bitterness' in him. He is bitter because there is nothing he can think of that 'corresponds', as he puts it, with this familiar yet estranged furniture.[27] He has had a failure of performative imagination then, what he took for granted at the theatre as a realm of doublings cannot be secured in this domestic place. He finds that something has quite literally 'taken' place. And he uses this phrase, or its Danish equivalent, quite precisely, for 'taken place' is what he means. When we say something has 'taken place' we might think of an event, the stuff of theatre, the one from whence he has just come. But what if that place has, as with Constantius here, really been *taken*? How could place be *taken*, and what might replace it, there being no vacuum in rented accommodation, any more than nature?

Constantius is beginning to demonstrate a condition, a symptom of disorientation, well before Sigmund Freud was around to analyse it for what it was, and what is more Kierkegaard gives us the lineaments without the prejudice of psychoanalytic reduction. And it is a symptom some way beyond and more severe than Marc Katz's interesting figuring of Constantius as a 'dispersed self', though I am deeply drawn to Katz's reading of these 'passage works' in all other respects, as is obvious from my leaning on his analysis though the streets of Berlin. But here something more detailed is needed as to the precise 'nature' of just such a 'dispersed self' with the name Constantine Constantius as it is critical to any adequate understanding of the human habitat and its administration, psychic and otherwise through the *oikonomia* of social reproduction.

Mimicry of man

On re-entering his apartment after the theatre, 'resemblance has gone awry' for Constantius.[28] This resistant audience member, now seeming civilian, has just returned from the theatre, where a farce has expertly mobilised the art of mimicry as the ultimate anti-utilitarian luxury for those with surplus time and capital to spend (and like almost all male philosophical heroes and anti-heroes, he certainly has the private means to indulge just such thoughtful leisure). Constantius, on return to his dwelling, is confronted with the more 'animal instinct' of mimicry as a mode of self-preservation or self-defence, ironically 'being at home' is more threatening than 'being out at the theatre'. He is the bourgeois abroad while at the Konigstadter, but here it is a matter not of the 'surplus excesses' of performance, but of brute domestic survival. Here the problem of the signification of space for the living organism, for Constantius in this case, becomes an obsession *with space*, and its de-realising effects. In this disturbed and disturbing apartment we are entering what Jacques Lacan later called 'another space besides geometrical space', that is the dark space of groping dreams and hallucinations.[29] This is not so much then a study of the dark theatre as the chiaroscuro of domestic dwelling, or as Minkowski put it, a lack of distinction between milieu and organism: 'Dark space envelopes me on all sides and penetrates much deeper than light space [...]'.[30]

The fundamental question for Constantius here on return home from the theatre, though Kierkegaard never says it, becomes then one of *distinction*, and the associated problem of ascertaining distinctions. Distinctions, that is, between the appearance of the furniture and an aspiration for that furniture to be something else (what is real and imaginary), between the armchair in light and in dark (between wakefulness and sleep), and between his corporeal male-self and his previous memory of being home (between ignorance and knowledge). The primary distinction that might once have been taken-for-granted, the demarcation of an organism from its environment (what Constantius establishes through his fetishistic, and one might venture, masculinist choice of seating in the theatre), begins to break down in this post-theatre domestic scene where his 'masculine autonomy' is under threat. The theatre after all is where such disturbances of order *are* the economy of performance, it is not perhaps surprising that Constantius is suffering these 'after affects' given the obsessive, spectacular, masculine-manner of his theatrical attendance in full evening wear, every night, and often, he boasts about his stamina, twice-a-night.

What Kierkegaard in his study of Constantius's behaviour offers is a reflection on this phenomenon and more than that, an articulation of its male pathology. That pathology is figured as the set of phenomena referred to as a compulsion to 'mimicry' in which these very distinctions that would otherwise secure some semblance of identity within a cast of 'dispersed selves' begin to break down in the service of similitude at all costs. Here the doubling economy of the theatre auditorium has entered the *oikos* of the household with disturbing and distributing effect. Indeed the 'hold' on the house, Constantius's vertical hold that is, his measure of erect masculinity you could say, is beginning to slip. As he hits the floor, giddy with the disturbance of privacy he realises, all the home's a stage. A hard one that has become soft.

By experiencing for us Constantius's movements (he was after all immobilised from the beginning of Kierkegaard's record in his service of his analysis of repetition) Kierkegaard's experimental psychology adopts a classificatory system deriving 'from the phenomena themselves', and not their interpretation. This gives the text its marvellous immediacy and modern, soft-psychoanalytic ambience. Biologically we know that mimicry cannot alone be a defence mechanism for creatures, including humans. Indeed mimicry's defensive capacity in pop zoology is wildly overrated thanks to its easy, essentially humanist, performative veneer of camouflaging. Why would mimicry have any relevance to the defence capability of creatures that exist in the deepest oceans, unable to see, beyond any natural light, as it surely does for it is as prevalent there amongst cephalopods, as anywhere? So, 'a masculine disorder of spatial perception' is all this domestic experience that Constantius is experiencing, can be.

Space here then, as Constantius enters his room, becomes what you might call, after the French Surrealist, Roger Caillois, whose work I have been drawing upon in search of this pathology, 'repetitive space', a 'double dihedron', continuously changing its size and location, the male figure moving towards the furniture, the desk and the velvet armchair, and thus pulling their own dihedron of perception of these artefacts along at the same time.[31] And it is a dihedron of representation, shaped by the same horizontal plane as before (which is represented though, rather than perceived) and cut by a vertical plane just where the disturbed and disturbing objects of furniture appear in the distance from their enveloping gloom. Matters become critical for Constantius with 'represented space' because the living creature, the organism, Constantius in his habitat, is no longer located at the *origin* of the coordinate system as a man might expect in his own bourgeois home, but, on return from the theatre, has simply become one dihedron among many. An experience that peculiarly and unsettlingly mimics that disjuncture just felt amongst foreign masses at the theatre. Dispossessed of its privilege, the male bourgeois creature, it (Constantius in this case) quite literally no longer knows what to do with itself, or *himself* without the protection of this carapace of self-care. Under these conditions one's sense of personality (as an awareness of the distinction between organism and environment and of the connection between the mind and a specific point in space) is quickly and seriously undermined. This condition then I would suggest takes us towards the realm described by Roger Caillois, as 'legendary psychasthenia', temptation by space as the creature loses its distinctive form to camouflage, the disorder that registers precisely in the relationship between personality and space that this study of Constantius's *oikonomia* has revealed.[32]

In this condition, space seems no longer to be a matter of male conquest but rather constitutes a reverse 'will to devour'. Space chases, entraps and digests Constantius in a devastating process that Roger Caillois has called *phago-cytosis*, after the engulfing of virus by immune system cells. An inundation that is clear from Constantius's firsthand reporting of his disturbed state. But then it is space that, ultimately, takes *his* place. That is what has 'taken place' on Constantius's return home, he has become excluded from his interior by the very space he had imagined was his for the making. Man *is* the virus in this regard. In this disorientation from home, the masculine body and mind become dissociated; in this process the subject, Roger Caillois suggests, crosses the boundary of his own skin and stands outside of his senses as a spectre becomes divorced from their mortal counterpart. He tries to see himself, from some point 'in space'. He feels that he is turning into space himself – dark space into which things cannot be put. 'He is similar', says Caillois: 'not similar to anything in particular, but simply similar'.[33] And as though playing out Caillois's pathology, Constantius begins to 'dream up' spaces that spasmodically possess him, amongst which of course the theatre auditorium, to which he compulsively returns to find himself, is the apparently 'public' other of this private interior he can no longer endure. Social reproduction and its necessary playing out in public thus consigns this particular 'man' to the plight of a never-fulfilled urge to mimicry.

Here Constantius is beginning the punishing process well known later to the analyst of the schizophrenic personality: depersonalisation through assimilation into space. In other words precisely the process that *mimicry* brings about, morphologically, in many species other than humans. In a related register of experiences, the ascendancy of the night and dark in the psyche, the fear of darkness, also probably derive from the threat that they pose to this collapsing organism-environment opposition, or at least their distinction. Constantius's response to that 'bitter' furniture is, simply, to go to bed. But nothing at home is that simple. In the darkness the armchair looms large and he hurls it into the corner, distancing himself from its animistic reach. In this interior darkness is *not* the absence of light: it is the *presence* of dark space into which one loses ones 'lit coordinates', one consigns those things, including the armchair, that are too bitter for comprehension. Whereas bright space disappears giving way to the material concreteness of objects (something the lit stage is very good at emphasising in the bourgeois theatre, indeed what Joe Kelleher calls in his book the 'Illuminated Theatre'), darkness is thick, it directly touches a person, enfolds, penetrates and even passes through them. Thus the self is permeable to the dark and not the light.[34]

So the 'reproduction' named in this narrative of social reproduction is a realm of domestic repetition if it is anything. This ontology of domestic mimicry, what we might call 'household performance', is less concerned with Peggy Phelan's longstanding, defining conceit for the performance field of 'repetition without reproduction', nor Rebecca Schneider's counter arguments for the performance that remains. Rather we will concentrate here our attention on that somehow more in-between *refrain* that Kierkegaard has introduced us to, that lingering sense that something *similar* might have happened in such domestic sites before, and in seeking that 'similar' our social and psychic status might be at stake in a continuous cycle of loss that registers the disappearance of such similarities.

Theatre's coming home

It should be acknowledged in the obscured light of this nineteenth century example of home from home that theatre's long 'come home' as Bobby Baker brought to our attention through the 1990s, and more recently since Bobby Baker's exertions an avalanche of 'interior theory' that really owes a debt to Kierkegaard's *Repetition* has made manifest.[35] In pursuit of some of these design histories of this domestic sphere to write this chapter, I was loitering in the Victoria and Albert Museum in London taking some time out from carrel 52 in the National Art Library, the desk where much of this book was written. I was trying to imagine an inversion of Jacques' faulty invocation in *As You Like It*, 'All the world's a stage'.[36] Shakespeare's dubiously appropriative line had come to mind on re-reading the third chapter 'Everyday Life' from *Theatre & Everyday Life*, with the hope that I could bring my interest in the quotidian back indoors, away from the pull of the urban exterior that had oriented that work and for some years, encouraged by male, predominantly white flâneurs from Constantine Constantius via Walter Benjamin to the Situationists, been the preferred habitat of the performance scholar. I found myself on a dark corridor hoping to take a diversionary look at the artist-duo Elmgreen and Dragset's temporary installation, titled *Tomorrow*.[37] With 6,000 square-feet of domestically rendered interior, lovingly hewn out of the carcass of five of the V&A's grandest yet most dilapidated rooms, home to a fictional, 75-year-old failed architect, a lifetime's *bric a brac* and a troubling, immersive, film-like environment worthy of Visconti or Bergman, for an unperformed life that has been meticulously retrofitted to the space in a scripted dramaturgy available to all.

On my way there between library and installation and somewhat disorientated, I came across a painting in the permanent gallery: 'Edgar Degas's Ballet Scene from Meyerbeer's Opera, *Robert le Diable*' of 1876, where now, at this time of rewriting in 2019 it still hangs.[38] First performed in Berlin in the 1840s, perhaps at the Konigstadter Theatre that Kierkegaard and his alter-ego Constantius frequented (the Berlin Opera House where it was scheduled to be performed had burnt down in 1843), Meyerbeer's Opera represented in the image depicts the ghosts of nuns who have offended heaven with their 'impure thoughts'. While the congested, grey-haired male members of the orchestra as depicted in the painting apparently contains a number of Degas's friends, my eye was drawn to the rendering of these ghosts, in this staged space, an auditorium of screen-like permeable arches, that shows something between outside and inside, and set to wondering about their theatrical relations with those spectres over the way, in Elmgreen and Dragset's shadowy domestic interior.[39]

If this 'internal' street in the Victoria & Albert Museum, the width of a city thoroughfare, divided a domestic space from a theatre, an *oikos* from an *auditoria* as recorded in Kierkegaard's field notes, what might have been gained and lost over the last four decades of this street's fetishisation as the site for performance enquiry? A proclivity for the pavement, a sensitivity to the sidewalk, that not unlike the appearance of the performatariat tracked through precisely the same chronology of the previous chapter, may well have presented as a symptom, an indication that those very streets were in the process of rapid privatisation with hostile architecture becoming standard, pushing back the 'threat' of rough sleepers, at the moment those very 'same' streets were becoming freed-up from such destitute diversions for more ornamental aesthetic study.

What I some years ago described as the obsession for the outdoor-urban of the 'space cowboys' in performance study and beyond, might have occluded that other space of the home, once marginalised for its gendered irrelevance to the more important business of that male walker, free to roam to and from the theatre, at night, from those darkened byways.[40] I didn't consider the domestic sphere any kind of retreat from exterior 'threat', the environments that Saskia Sassen, Irit Rogoff and Doreen Massey have written so persuasively about with regards to violent mobilities of displacement, migration and enslavement,[41] but after Jean-François Lyotard presumed the *oikos* (in the Greek tradition) or *domus* (in the Latin) was coeval with these external threats not a place of safety, but rather a potential place for tragedy and the daily realm of that most ineffable psychic state, chronic entropy.[42] While not necessarily joining Mahud Darwish in identifying home as a 'mansion of sorrow' the contemporary home as figured by artists would appear to be a privileged site of trauma, melancholy and yearning, while its theorisation by those such as Claudette Lauzon is always as much about 'unmaking' as making do, the 'unhomely' as distinct to the uncanny, the recognition of 'exterior threat' as distinct to melancholic retroversion of the interiority of ghosting unease.[43]

If *Oikonomia* means 'administration of the house' as Giorgio Agamben puts it (and it might as well be Constantius's apartment or Bobby Baker's house given we have just been there 'administering' their erratic encounters as audiences) then perhaps the slippage between that domestic house and the 'Full House' that is the ideal state of the theatre, here at least between the quadrangle I have set up amidst the permeable landscape of Degas's painting, the domestic grandeur of Elmgreen and Dragset's apartment, Constantius's Berlin rental and Bobby Baker's not-so-modest kitchen, is my internal landscape in this chapter.[44] I also set to wondering who else, then and now, might also have witnessed those 'ghosts' on the Konigstadter stage and their relation to a species of related but not quite the same spectres in those other domestic locations? Perhaps we might follow Jean-François Lyotard's definition of the *oikos* in seeking out the more precise character of these unannounced visitors when he says: 'We have to imagine an apparatus inhabited by a sort of guest, not a ghost but an *ignored guest* who produces some trouble, and people look to the outside in order to find out the external cause of the trouble'.[45] (my emphasis). Or indeed we could return to Nietzsche's understanding of 'home' when he recalled: 'the disorderly, story and conflict-ridden household' that results from memory trying to accommodate 'these strange guests'.[46] We will come to those obvious ghosts and discrete guests as this chapter proceeds.

Taking these domestic encounters into account the degree to which performance might, for some time now, have already and everywhere 'come home', been brought home in some way, as in an architecturally footloose, aesthetically domesticated *takeaway*, hinted at in the sharing of the word 'house' for both *auditoria* and *oikos*, that ceremonial of performance lasting for long enough to be somehow reheated at home, provides me with a way through that corridor-width gap at the V&A, between those Degas ghosts and the haunting miserable-en-scene of Elmgreen and Dragset's *Tomorrow*. But what might we discern from such encounters with the home and how do questions of repetition play into social reproduction in such circumstances?

I would propose here that one might begin to recognise the degree to which the urban interior was already to all intents and purposes a theatre of its own kind, self-evidently yes, but importantly an environment for performance which acts as a spectral 'off stage' scene for the continuing, and still largely hegemonic fourth-wall experience of the bourgeois stage of the nineteenth and twentieth century.[47] This theatrical history of the domestic interior has attracted surprisingly little attention in the literature given its influence on the bourgeois stage-setting tout court. Given the Greek origins of the word *oikos* to describe the stagings of the domestic economy, there is of course no suggestion here that it was not always thus. Rather it is in the modern period precisely concomitant with the rise of naturalism *on the stage* that this 'interior drama' takes on the peculiarly closed, uncanny, ghostlike quality that continues to absorb some of the most interesting artists working today, whose diverse practices have been not only actively rebuilding that fourth wall, as aspired to by Mildred in *Fahrenheit 451* as noted in the last chapter, but whose 'compulsion to repeat' has precisely been played out in the construction of a multitude of screenings, a fifth, sixth, seventh and eighth wall, in defence against the attentions, the aspirational involvement of a newly enfranchised audience hoping for 'free entry' who have taken Jacques Rancière's affirmative title, *The Emancipated Spectator*, rather too literally.[48] To ensure that the house itself, now, is recognised for what it is, not so much a tomb, there can after all be very few domestic interiors in the world where someone has not died at some time, but rather as Rachel Whiteread suggested in the title of her sculpture, *Ghost*, a condensing apparatus for spectres and unannounced if not unwanted guests.[49]

I am repeating the obvious by registering this domesticating direction of performance thinking and practice if you simply recall some recent projects curated by producers in the late twentieth, and early twenty-first century, West European curatorial art scene. Artangel projects for instance, which could be taken as an unscientific, representative sample of recent aesthetic works in which the home in all its disquieting, serial banality, looms large, and often. Michael Landy's life-size construction of his childhood home, *Semi-detached* for the Duveen Galleries at Tate Britain in 2004 for instance, cleaved from its repetitive neighbour, its pebble-dashed double.[50] Here in collaboration with Mike Smith Studio, Landy mimicked to the last dash of pebble, his childhood home, that had sat on the Seven Kings Estate in Ilford from 1901, and effectively mimicked in its own turn identical houses across the UK from the Edwardian period. The cutaway of the house did not invite visitors in, so much as screen scenes from Landy's father's life outwards. In her reading of the installation Imogen Racz talks about the 'forensic detail' of the work as though its accumulated verisimilitude amounts to some kind of crime scene where, as Anthony Vidler once talked about the uncanny of the household, 'X marks the spot'.[51] Indeed John Landy had broken his back in a mining accident in 1977 which had required him to be the subject of this house, house-bound you could say, a frustrated do-it-your-selfer who while wanting to 'improve' his home is reduced to regimes of medication and enforced 'recreation' that was doing little to re-create his broken body. We will return to the question of John Landy's disastrous disability, reading it towards a more promising performance of dorsality, in a moment.

Or, in pursuit of that Artangel catalogue of the domestic sphere, more recently Mike Kelley's peripatetic final work, *Mobile Homestead*, the movement of a facsimile of his childhood clapperboard home on a flat-bed truck through Michigan Avenue in downtown Detroit, reversing the 'white flight' exodus from the city during the collapse of the automobile industries of the 1960s and 1970s, eventually returning to the original site of his upbringing, and the original hearth from which the doppelganger departed. Filmed at the time as a searing record of 'depression economics' and screened in cinemas across the UK following his untimely death in 2012, the 'homestead' was envisaged as a future site for community interventions, but one whose ambiguities were all too obvious to Kelley when it came to the place of his birth: 'one always has to hide one's true desires and beliefs behind a façade of socially acceptable lies'.[52] Kelley's work was itself an oblique yet explicit, landbound version of Gordon Matta-Clark's lake-bound *Untitled (Anarchitecture-House on Barge)* of 1974, in which Matta-Clark had recovered a gelatine print of a house-moving by river and displayed it without apparent comment in all its curious contradictions of the uprooted house and the water-borne unhomely.

And going back to Artangel's early days of domesticity, for three gloriously unnerving months between 25 October 1993 and 11 January 1994, Rachel Whiteread's three-storey inversion of a terraced house on Grove Road in East London, eponymously titled *House*, that followed her previously spectred casting of an entire room in *Ghost* (1990), channelling again Gordon Matta-Clark's long-running Parisian invitation to enter the realm of his distressed architectural inversions by resisting all-comers with an exclusion zone of vast, solid matter in his suburban house piece *Splitting* (1974), and *Conical Intersect* (1975) in the Marais neighbourhood where the Beauborg Pompidou Centre was about to be built. In Whiteread's reading 'the dark star of the domestic' you could say, if each of her fillings-in as after-lives of Bruce Nauman's reverse casts of chairs from the 1960s had not been just so white. This work prompted me when starting as Director of Talks at the Institute of Contemporary Arts in London in 1994, to organise the first of my public seminar series there, *Uncanny Encounters*, in which the curators of Artangel alongside the critical writer Jon Bird and radical geographer Doreen Massey, took on the fearful familiar of this legacy of work at large.[53] But given the Marxist, historically materialist orientation of our key-speakers, it was refreshing to recognise the emphasis here was on a politics *not* of the threat of containment of so much domestic freight, but the 'anxiety of expulsion' as Lauzon puts it, in the turning of the house inside-out to expel all foreign matter.[54] That anxiety of expulsion will now provide the pathology of performance, the social reproduction at work in this theatrical science of the domestic, in a single example that perhaps returns us 'closer to home' than we might welcome.

Inside-out

Die Familie Schneider, by Gregor Schneider, was a project realised in Whitechapel in East London and produced by Artangel close to 15 years ago at the time of writing. I am recorded as having been there on the morning of Wednesday 13 October 2004, or at least booked for there, despite the record in the curators' visitor's book still available to researchers in the headquarters of the curators Artangel, that at the time of going there I do not seem to have paid to be there. And according to that same visitor's book, the next day, Claire Bishop, and Bruce Nauman were also there, and the following day: Cornelia Parker, Mark Wallinger, Chris Offili and Tom Morris were there. Everyone was present and correct, or so we thought.

So, what was *there*? Adjacent, two-storey houses at 14 and 16 Walden Street, in a Victorian terrace of remarkably similar but not indecipherable two-storey houses.

The houses were decorated and distressed to the artist's exact specifications. Down to the tiniest wallpaper tear and ceiling stain, this twin-pair were identical. Only one visitor was admitted at a time, simultaneously, to each house. Nobody under the age of 16 years was allowed in, for good reason as we will soon discover. The address was only available on application and accessible only on the receipt of an embossed invitation to *Die Familie Schneider*, 'At Home'. A pair of keys was provided. Visitors were limited to strictly ten minutes only in each house, before exchanging keys on the pavement, and taking each other's place next door where the ten minutes afforded them was granted again, before exiting at about the same time. For the duration of the show, between Tuesday 28 September 2004 and Thursday 23 December 2004 this happened repeatedly, every day, all day. It was 'house full' throughout, all the home was now a stage.

In the house that I entered the entrance hall was empty but there was a sound from the kitchen. A woman washing up, with her back to you did not acknowledge your presence, but showed through her back that she knew you, not so much a ghost as an 'ignored guest', it was obvious, were there with her. The figure of the washing-up-woman is certainly not new to you, the visitor fortunate to have secured a ticket for this long sold-out event, and so ubiquitous as to be shocking in its own mundanity. We know well from the writing of Sylvia Federici that when we speak of housework, a portmanteau term into which washing dishes might be considered a cyclical part, we are not as she says speaking of a 'job like other jobs, but we are speaking of the most pervasive manipulation, and the subtlest violence that capitalism has ever perpetrated against any section of the working-class'.[55] The woman in front of you, nevertheless, continues knowing you are present yet unwilling or unable to register this save the imperceptible tautening of her shoulder blades that must be a reflex on the arrival of each new visitor (and the potential risk of the unknown or very well-known they bring given they have not been vetted by the producers in any obvious way) every ten minutes through an eight-hour performance day. Here the performer, one imagines at least given the reputation of Artangel and the notoriety of the artist Gregor Schneider must be being paid the going rate for theatre labour rather than menial labour, if there is a difference between the two, but that recognition simply serves to alert us to those who are not being paid anything, for not dissimilar labours. While the wage of the performer recognises the status of this person hereon chained to the sink as a worker, it simultaneously identifies you, the visitor as a leisured-class who can pay to watch women working for you, for periods of time that might be uncomfortably adjacent to definitions of modern slavery or sex work as much as theatre. This is the social contract that Federici describes in which you may or may not like what you do, in this case it is hard to imagine the former, but it becomes the only condition under which life itself becomes possible for those thus engaged, given the historic hiding of wages for this work where labour has become apparently a personal service outside capital.

We also know that this woman has trained long for this twin role, of a performer with dexterity, and as a woman through two decades of nurturing by others equally committed towards a state where the domestic has been naturalised as an essential function of a specified gender role. Federici traces this long history and those who have noticed its pervasiveness and then commented upon it: 'From Lenin through Gramsci to Juliet Mitchell, the entire Leftist tradition has agreed on the marginality of housework to the reproduction of capital and the marginality of the housewife to revolutionary struggle'.[56] The kitchen I am in is just one more Feudal state in this violating terrain and we know that the bedroom upstairs, given this is a domestic space that mimics others in the street and beyond, to which we will soon be free to visit, is just another. For Federici the turning over of this pre-capitalist state started precisely in the kitchen and the bedroom that linked both, not just to the question of gender, but to a global alliance amongst the working-class who labour there.

The sense in which the person in front of me figures as a member or participant in some such 'working-class' is what engages Tithi Bhattacharya in her essay 'How Not to Skip Class'. One starting point in this work reminds us that Marx's understanding of historical materialism required us to acknowledge, before all else, that 'reality is not as it *appears*'.[57] To seek the 'reality' of an economy might then be a matter of seeking the secret that capital has obscured from us, that is the role that human labour plays within any such economy. And this human labour as Bhattacharya understands it, globally that is, is by its nature: 'messy, sensuous, gendered, raced and unruly [...] living human being capable of following orders – as well as of flouting them'.[58] Not white man's labour after all.

Before the woman at the sink turns to us there are perhaps other ways to consider what is happening when one is faced with someone's labouring back beyond materialist matters. One for instance might turn to the question posed originally for us in this chapter as to what happened to Michael Landy's father whose back was broken by the coal industry? Or indeed the poet Osip Mandelstam whose characterisation of the 'contemporary' century is that of the broken-backed animal whose vertebrae signifies the break, the disjuncture of our times.[59] For the phenomenologist and historian of gesture David Wills, a human who turns, who *articulates* the movement of a limb, for instance who turns their back on us, has in this process of articulation admitted something 'technological' to themselves.[60] I would add, in this instance, the woman in this process of turning, has abandoned something of that which was not previously machinic *about* themselves, they recover themselves from their chore and labour as they rest their hands in the sink and turn away from work and towards the possible comforts of company. This turn is a *prosthetic* articulation in that it does not deny the figure is still tethered to their work, nor does it slough off the machinery of that work. In this turning figure, technology does not lie somewhere in advance of, or in front of the body, but lies behind that corporeal presence as though affixed to its back rather like a 'kitchen sink', prosaic version, of the dihedron of furniture that Constantius dragged behind him across his Berlin apartment.

Here the prosthetic articulation is one that bonds the woman to the sink before her that is behind her as she turns to me. Bobby Baker had some years before turned from the sink in which she washes carrots giving up on her verticality as she does so and falls to the ground to release herself horizontally into the garden of cat-like escape. But in the kitchen of *Die Familie Schneider* there is no escape, just as there has never been escape from the infernal life's work, 'Totes Haus Ur' in the German town of Rheydt (1985), constructed previously one diminished hallway within the other by this artist, just a labyrinth of false exits. The act of turning in this instance is not so much a resistance to what is necessary, as a repeated, restored behavioural pause in that line of duty. In this scenario my own corporeal presence represents what David Wills would call the 'dorsal chance':

> the dorsal as the chance of what cannot be foreseen, the surprise or accident that appears, at least, to come from behind, from out of range or outside the field of vision, challenging the technocratic faith or confidence and calling into question its control.[61]

The one who arrives is as capable of caress as threat, but that is not what the logics of this kitchen scene imply, though the trust the one who is always here shows those who arrive is marked by their willingness to remain for an extended interval with their back to those who join them for good or ill. The economy of this interior, its *oecumenia*, appears to become by necessity of this scene a 'sharing of inhabitable space', where there was a threat there seems to be something more of a general welcoming at this workplace.[62] There is no ethical encounter of the kind envisaged by Emmanuel Lévinas, a face to face engagement, but rather a 'face to back' that in turning ambivalently recognises one's presence as alive and not quite with them, but nevertheless present in their home, or at least at home, even if it does not seem to be quite theirs.

This turn is just as evident in what passes for my own forward walk as I approach the woman from behind, the turning out at each of my steps, the limping, realignment of gravity that humans call walking, the walker always turns from their path to walk as I turn each step as I move quietly along the corridor towards the sound of the woman working. And here humans, as David Wills notices, in pacing always turn *towards* their back however minimally, every deviation from forward movement is thus a form of retroversion. Apparent linearity always thus makes reference to what lies behind and this calls for a thinking of what *is* behind, a thinking of the back that Wills calls *Dorsality* after our dorsal fin that has become a vertebral column that in the vertical human allows for turning.

Against presumptions of progress in this domestic scene staged by *Die Familie Schneider* it is as though we are being asked to maintain the *dorsal chance*, of what cannot be foreseen, the surprise or accident that comes from behind, in this instance the ignored guest, in this uncanny house. Now, that is me, arriving in the kitchen, heard but not seen, from beyond the woman's range of vision, not in the acute angle of our walking forward, that is about 45 degrees, not in the obtuse angle that I have written about elsewhere with regards to the Transhumance of sheep in Truinas near my house, that expands our sense of what might be constituted as the troupe, but rather in the reflex angle that begins to either side of the 45 degree angle and circuits our backs as we move forward taking space with us. You cannot see what comes from behind by definition, but you can turn, as those pedestrian dancers showed us long-ago in 1960s New York at Judson Church in playful resistance to the gaze that would commonly be on the dancer's back without apparent opportunity for redress. And that is what the woman at the sink does, slowly but very very surely. Indeed, without apparent fear, but somewhat peculiarly in the circumstances of apparent inequality, strikes me as unadulterated pity. For me, us, visitors who might have thought we knew what lay ahead of us but could not imagine what we are about to find upstairs, and down. Meanwhile, the theatre elsewhere, at the Konigstadter perhaps, is still, not always but perhaps too often for maintaining an adequate suppleness, a matter of a face-off, a frontality that this dorsality troubles through performance.

I wrote some time ago, in critical address of other's work, of my distaste for what is called the 'performance *turn*', a metaphorisation of a certain coming-into-fashion of one's discipline.[63] I pushed back on that metaphoric figure with a symptomatic reading of my mother's daily Grand Mal neurological fits when I was growing up, something we also called a 'turn' but in this case material and necessary, as my mother just before entering such catatonic states would pull the family car she was driving to the side of the road and tell us in the back seat that she was going to have a 'turn', and in so doing turned towards us in the back and away from us a she entered that epileptic crisis of the self. The woman at the sink in turning towards us sends us on our way, or at least me, confronted by her own look I am despatched towards the door and the flight of stairs that I notice is to the side and angle that Hitchcock always preferred in his threatening scenography. The hallway appears smaller than it did on entry and the room you have just left shy of the proportions that one might expect from the outside. Not so small as to be obvious, but small enough to induce a small anxiety that things are closing in. There is nothing as obvious as Roman Polanski's *Repulsion* at work here, it is hard to see that film now with anything but the grotesque perspective of Polanski's own history of sexual violence since, but less physically aggressive and more psychically eerie as Mark Fisher would have it.[64]

The shower has been running for some time that is obvious, but it is only on ascending the stair-case that you make out the under-breath groans of a man masturbating. His shadowy figure shows through the faded plastic curtain standing in the bath huddled under the pathetic water-pressure that American visitors would find incomprehensible, irrespective of the one-on-one action you are being offered for your ticket money in this *miserable-en-scène*. The inclination to pull-back the curtain and reveal the man beating his meat behind is tempered by the sure knowledge that all this would invite would be the frontality that downstairs has deferred until so late in the day you imagine it might never happen. There is no turn here, none is needed as everything is on show through the chiaroscuro of a B&Q cyclorama of cheap plastic drapes. Andrew O'Hagan links this scene in his literary imaginary to a childhood experience in Glasgow in which his repeated passing of a tenement where a woman had been murdered years before brings back memories of hauntings that he wants to align with this southern English nightmare.[65] As such O'Hagan never short of a role in other people's dramas from Julian Assange to Fred West wants to figure himself as the haunter, but to repeat, I can only think here of the invited but ignored guest. We did pay to enter after all. There is nothing as dramatic as ghosts at work in this place, that is its obvious charm and terror. To ghost it is to unnecessarily chill it beyond its already morbidly-muggy room temperature. That is its claustrophobic clemency.

Fleeing this blubber-filled pumped-up aquatic scene the bedroom beckons, its brown floor coverings exuding what can only be described as the sickly-sweet smell of a semen-covered carpet. The house at this point is not only closing in on the sojourner, it is now heated to just above a comfortable domestic degree in mimicry of those interiors you have entered in your life with no control over the thermostat. You want to leave but through the doorway, just visible in the cheap laminated wardrobe mirror, diagonally across the room beyond the double bed, is a black-plastic bin-bag with a pair of small feet protruding from its bottom. They appear to be children's feet but that seems unlikely given everyone's mother has told them never to get into a plastic bag, the health and safety implications are inconceivable. So one is left dwelling upon the miniature scale of the bag and a pair of shoes below. If it is a person of restricted growth inside the bag how are they breathing, their whole body is covered, are they dead, or will they suddenly leap out to provide the dramatic denouement that one might expect from theatre as it was always expected and foreseen? Well, given this is Gregor Schneider there is of course nothing, just the now-discernible breathing of the figure who will obviously carry on breathing that way for as long as you choose to stay doing what your parents might say you should never do, staring, at them.

When you finally drag your eyes away, the stairs to the loft from this point are barred by a baby gate (Gregor Schneider knows from *The Poetics of Space* that Gaston Bachelard situates the higher consciousness in that upper realm of the inhabited house and there is nothing like that psychic luxury in this infernal place), which introduces the troubling thought that if the person in the bag is a proxy child, where is the baby of this manor? So, down the stairs to the basement, which is an obvious, but necessary drop into a domestic hell. Where, despite the fact this is Whitechapel and not the caricatured basements of Austria or Belgium, something dreadful has happened, of course. The abandoned room has once been some kind of container to a life, there is the detritus of a baby's needs there, diapers and a forlorn toy, but only the baby's cries can now be heard, just, through some kind of bricked up aperture in the far wall. Incarcerated End. Running back up the stairs and down the now foreshortened corridor to the front door, the woman from the kitchen is sitting on a mock leather sofa in the living room, desultorily flicking through the glossy pages of an interior design magazine, apparently wholly unperturbed by your sudden exit to the street.

There you meet your double who has been in the other house for their own ten minutes of terror, you swap keys and enter number 16 to the left of the house you have just left, 14 to the right. It is identical inside as it is out, down to the nicks in the dado rail, the tears to the wallpaper and the dilapidation of the furnishings. At first you presume the woman washing the same but not same dishes in the same but not same kitchen, is the same woman. But she cannot be the same given you have just left her motionless in the sitting room next door and she has ignored your exit from her house. But if this is not the same woman then it is a remarkably similar woman. It is only then you realise that she is indeed identical and that as you set about the stairs to the shower room you will find the identical male figure there, still desultorily pulling himself off into the trickling water, and above *him* the same 'black bag' body. They are identical because they are identical. Twins that is. The houses are occupied by two families of identical twins, one in each house, whose movements through a seven-hour day were coordinated precisely in acts of the ultimate social reproduction of an abused everyday life. Mimesis and alterity indeed, with you as the alterity interest. Identical until you realise that the only difference between numbers 16 and 14 on that particular street is that in 16, to the left, there is a cellar door where a bed has been supporting someone or something, while in 14, the door is locked. There, just the sound of a baby crying.

This not-haunted house, rather this 'guest house' where like but not like for Kierkegaard, we are the *guests* in this instance, is the heir to a feeling of unease we have been identifying in the domestic interior from Constantius' 'man catastrophe' in the mid-nineteenth century onwards. This uncanny was already long felt as an outgrowth of the Burkean sublime, a domesticated version of absolute terror to be experienced in the comfort of the home: the contrast between a secure and homely interior and the fearful invasion of an alien presence. Its play was one of doubling, where the other is experienced as a replica of the self. Here was a new kind of class of humans wholly familiar to Kierkegaard, or at last Constantine Constantius: not quite at home in its own home. So, a quintessential kind of bourgeois fear, tracked by Anthony Vidler in his architectural theory of the uncanny. A sensation best experienced in the privacy of the interior after the heightened publicity of the exterior interior that is the theatre.

For Marx writing in precisely the year of Kierkegaard's first visit to Berlin, 'individual estrangement' had become 'class alienation'. As he noted in the *Economic and Philosophical Notebooks* of 1844:

> man is regressing to the cave dwelling [...] the cellar dwelling of the poor man is a hostile element [...] a dwelling which he cannot regard as his on hearth – where he might at last exclaim: 'Here I am at home' – but where instead he finds himself in someone else's house, in the house of a stranger who always watches him and throws him out if he does not pay his rent.[66]

Constantine might be privileged enough to have created himself an escape route from renting in Berlin to freehold ownership in Copenhagen, but this does not seem to have assuaged his anxiety at the shifting character of his temporary home.

But in keeping with what we have discussed earlier with regards to 'dark space' and 'legendary psychesthenia', Anthony Vidler would remind us that the uncanny is not of course only, or primarily even, a property of the space itself, nor can it be provoked by any particular spatial conformation; it is, in its aesthetic dimension, a representation of a *mental state of projection* that precisely elides the boundaries of the real and the unreal in order to provoke a disturbing ambiguity, a slippage between waking and dreading. This is the uncanny encounter that Constantine Constantius experiences between auditorium and *oikos*. There is no uncanny architecture, Anthony Vidler has made that very clear, but architecture that is invested from time to time with uncanny qualities, phenomenologically by those fated to reside within. Such as *this* time amidst *Die Familie Schneider*, ten minutes in 14, ten minutes in 16.

The uncanny as I have figured it here after Anthony Vidler, does, exactly a century after its 'invention' as the concept of Das Unheimlich by Freud in 1919, allow for a rewriting of traditional and modernist aesthetic theory as it has applied to categories such as 'imitation', the 'double', *déjà vu*, and once again, 'repetition'. If theoretical elaboration of the uncanny helps us to interpret the condition of modern estrangement as first experienced by Constantine Constantius in Kierkegaard's *Repetition*, here it is the 'unhomely home' and the 'theatre of alienation' that finds its most poignant expression in what Ernst Bloch once called 'the hollow space of Capitalism'.[67] A space that for Constantius, and one might risk here, Kierkegaard himself, was *neither* that of the bourgeois interior, nor the theatrical auditorium, but the restless *itinerary* of the modern subject, finding and losing their way, in the spectacle of commerce that lay between these two imposters to our attention. In the end, it was, after all, the corridor between those ghosts of the theatre and the interior that unsettled me, as I set about writing this in the Victoria & Albert Museum.

And I wrote *these* words in a shaky hand in the Artangel visitor's book hard upon leaving *Die Familie Schneider* for the Whitechapel street on 13 October 2004:

> These distressed houses bring to mind something Roger Caillois said: '*Not similar to anything, just similar*' – for me *this* was the strongest sense of a seriously sensual experience – many of us were here from Roehampton making sense of this together, so many thanks from us all, especially to those 'in doors' committed to us all day.

You know it was me writing this because at the foot of the entry is my signature (and it is written less legibly than it might have been should it have been written by someone else who had been rendered less nervous by everything that has come to pass indoors). To recall it now, and those who were with me, for each time I meet those students who were 'with me' wherever they are now, they remind me we were there, together, alone, is to feel something of the sorrow that Kierkegaard identified as the fate of recollection. But to repeat this now, in this writing, is to feel something of the happiness that he recalled might be in touching distance, in that act of repetition.

Outside-in

Court 16 and Court 14 in the Rolls Building just off Fleet Street in London are similar, just similar too. They are about as identical as the two houses we have just spent ten minutes inside in Whitechapel. But that illuminated chimera, the 'light of the law', the promise of due process, pours into these proceedings with their own sense of promising performance; whereas those years ago in that Victorian terrace in Walden Street, all had been chiaroscuro, a dark *mise-en-scène* orchestrated by Gregor Schneider in all honesty. Each courtroom has high windows but these are really nothing to compare with the windows being contested in the High Court action Fearn vs. Tate Modern which today is taking place in 16, and tomorrow might as well be in 14. If the domestic sphere has provided us with the matter for this chapter, to close Part I of *The Dark Theatre*, there could be no more apposite space to occupy than this legal domain where the very definition of the bourgeois human right to privacy is up for very public grabs.

It is Autumn 2018 and Neo Bankside residents have decamped from their overlooked glasshouse apartments on the South Bank of the River Thames designed by

Rogers Stirk Harbour & Partners to hear the opening arguments laid out by their defence QC in their litigation against, when it is not an accolade granted the rival British Museum, the UK's 'most popular cultural attraction'.[68] As is the common coincidence of the vagaries of court-seating where unlike at a wedding there is little guide as to who sits where in the public-well, I have found myself on this Monday 5 November morning sitting amidst those Neo Bankside residents. On the far side of the court I can see Frances Morris the Director of Tate Modern, a member of the Herzog & De Meuron build team, John O'Mara, and their legal advisers, and I am initially inclined to wish I was over there rather than here. My inclination and political presumption would be to side with the 'publicly spirited' cultural sphere over the claims of the private property class, not least of all given the cost of what they are wearing in shaming proximity to my own casual attire, but it seems churlish to spurn the hospitality they are showing me in their midst despite the fact, unlike with the Candy Brothers that I discussed in the first chapter of this book, I have come clean on exactly what I am doing there. And they are very happy to have me. Indeed they begin to look positively neighbourly compared with the cool emanating from the other side, where at first I thought I might go and place myself in support of their mission, but on looking over sense I might not be as welcome amongst this cultural elite as I might otherwise presume I should be, having committed myself to four decades of educating students as to why they should take Tate and its various, often beautifully incomprehensible works seriously, despite their long-running (recently ended) addiction to sponsorship from the earth-despoiling extraction industries.

I have explained to the Neo Bankside residents around me that I have almost completed a chapter in a book I am writing called *The Dark Theatre* that explores questions of performance in the domestic realm, of social reproduction, repetition and refrain, and covers some homing instincts of display from nineteenth century Berlin to 2004 in a pair of dilapidated houses in Whitechapel, where some kind of cyclical crime appears to have taken place. They look non-plussed probably guessing rightly that the chapter will make for some quite heavy reading, but I remain committed to bringing that narrative up-to-date with a reflection upon the state of privacy laws in Britain today and what those laws might have to do with our understanding of the publicity of community as discussed in Chapter 1 and the individualising influence of social media introduced in Chapter 2. In other words I am mobilising Neo Bankside residents' predicament for the purposes of my argument, and they seem quite relaxed with that utilitarian spirit given they are business people who know what a deal entails. In this high-windowed room called Court 16 there is every chance I will be able to fulfil that promise with the added bonus that those contesting the issue are not a multi-corporation and a public-housing estate (where there would be simply no contest) but cultural wealth vs. private wealth, a far fairer balance of power in this world of High Court fees.

Those I am sitting amongst are predominantly female residents of Neo Bankside, there are two male husbands present, but they are soon to disappear, presumably to wherever the other men are doing whatever it is men do while their wives defend themselves, their families and their livelihoods in a court of law. This is a peculiar form of social reproduction, and one not central to Sylvia Federici's priorities in the 1970s on behalf of the global working classes. But it would nevertheless appear to be labour of a certain sort as a means by which this 'community' reproduce themselves as worthy of the much-vaunted bourgeois right to privacy. By livelihood I really do then mean their 'way of life', their 'living currency' as Pierre Klossowski would coin it, for that is what is being contested here over the coming week of hearings overseen by the appropriately titled Justice Mann. The residents have bought into the Neo Bankside block off-plan, prior to the completion of construction of the glass edifice, aware that Tate Modern are developing an adjacent swathe of land for their long-awaited extension by the Swiss architects Herzog and de Meuron, which by 2008 has gone through several iterations and following the financial crash is about to morph again into the giant brick-clad pyramid that becomes the signature of H&M's attention-seeking extension rising above ten floors. Just below the pinnacle of the building and surrounding the pyramid at its tenth-floor level is a public viewing platform that again, the residents had been made aware of prior to purchase, but on completion and opening to the public in 2018 had outstripped its expected popularity and visitor figures by an exponential margin reaching a total of 600,000 vertigo-free outsiders from 5.5 million visitors to Tate over its first year of operation.

    I am acutely aware of the logistical challenge that the current popularity of contemporary art brings with it, having attended the opening party of the original Tate Modern building on 12 May 2000. On that evening I found myself in a cramped, stop-start all-floors lift, with the personable Director of Tate, Nicholas Serota, who I knew in passing from events at the Whitechapel Gallery where he had previously been director (and I had been a long-time personal friend of the city financier Stephen Keynes, relation of John Maynard Keynes, who was the then Chairman of the Trustees). In that juddering metal box he shared with me his concern that in all the planning Tate had woefully underestimated the potential visitor figures for the building and under-teched the elevator provision by a significant margin. They did not repeat the same error the second time with multiple rapid lifts shooting through the new Switch House pyramid bypassing the irrelevant display floors housing less-popular interventions such as 'participatory performance', disgorging the thousands of visitors whose primary purpose on visiting Tate Modern appeared now to take advantage of one of the very few free views of London that had escaped the privatisation of the viewing platform at the Shard and the extortionate ticket prices to go round in a circle on the London Eye. I was sympathetic to this panoramic cause presuming it to be what it was, simply a coincidental collateral profit from the height and make-up of the building, which taking a pyramidal form, offers an unusually open vista once out on the wind swept walkway high above the Thames to the North side, the Globe and Tower Bridge East, the tourist city West, and the neighbourhood of the long-gone Rotherhithe Theatre Workshop and the dense lattice of fast gentrifying neighbourhoods of Southwark and its spaghetti of railway lines running South. I had no idea, and would have been uncomfortable if I had

had any such preposterous idea, that the viewing platform *itself* would become critical to the identity of Tate Modern in its entirety, or indeed argued over as though it was somehow a rationale for the building's public purpose tout court and without which it would face an existential threat to its mission. Little did I know what was to unfold in that court room over the coming week.

The evidence on this Monday morning appears, given there is unhelpfully never a programme of business in the courtroom, to concern a suite of photographs that have been taken from the direction of the Neo Bankside apartments outwards towards the viewing platform, and the verifiable nature of other photographs shot back in the opposite direction from the platform into the apartments barely 30 metres away. The viewing platform on the day in question has become 'extremely busy' and the public are becoming 'hostile' when told by Tate security guards that they cannot take photographs direct into the apartments opposite to the south side of the pyramid. As though this very act was the sole *raison d'être* of their long-anticipated visit to Tate Modern. It appears Tate have been served legal papers for this forthcoming hearing and are trying to ameliorate the problem of 'voyeuristic overseeing' before it gets out of hand and pre-empts the proceedings. Of the 600,000 visitors to the platform a year it transpires in later evidence that 10% of all visitors took photographs, 4% of which were shot to the 'less-popular' south side of the platform, suggesting that between 12,000 and 24,000 photographs of this view would be in circulation over the year.[69] Meanwhile the owners of Neo Bankside's residencies have started, by way of building a defence portfolio, to take photographs of those taking photographs of them. It is Hitchcock's *Rear Window* on steroids up there. The publicity has apparently started to lead to what council for the residents calls 'abnormal behaviour' for those using a public viewing platform, without quite defining what normal behaviour on such platforms might be, including the recent spate of using telephoto lenses to shoot into the depths of the apartments directly opposite at the Tate's tenth-floor level. Defence for Tate in turn is claiming that while there is obviously evidence of photographing there is no evidence that this intrudes on the private lives of those subjected to this scrutiny. And private lives and their definition in law are significant here as in law it is privacy and its complex definitions that will become the watchword.

I am surprised and somewhat relieved for the sake of sociality to learn that Common Law in England does not and cannot protect a 'general right to privacy' but rather law protects specific rights or specific abuses only. Claimants in law in other words cannot rely on privacy as a freestanding bourgeois right of separation from the rest. By which I mean 'us'. If they want to protect their privacy, as these Neo Bankside residents around me clearly want to do, then they have to identify a pre-existing Tort (that is a precedent case of disagreement between parties with a civil rather than criminal character) and pursue that precedent in court, case by case. For reasons that are not wholly clear to me at this point but are clarified later, the Tate defence team are mounting their case on the principle that in allowing the public to use the viewing platform, Tate are acting in what amounts to a *private* matter. This is the first argument of many I hear in the week that begin to suggest that an institution I had previously thought of as irredeemably public by constitution and nature, given I am amongst many in the UK subsidising it through my payment of taxes, is in fact somewhat closer in its claims to the bourgeois inflected 'private practices' of the Neo Bankside residents who I had damned at the outset for being oh-so-private in the securities of high-end property owning.

It is pointed out that any 'reasonable' person buying a flat in Neo Bankside in 2013–2014 (at the time they first went on sale but before the topping off of the Tate Switch House building) would have known that Tate was building a large, brick-heavy edifice in front of their windows and that a public viewing-platform would be part of that development. A 'freedom from overlooking' and a 'right to a view' are not covered by the law of private use and to give credence to any such claim would, the Tate defence suggests, represent a 'violent move forward' for English law. Given, as Dickens was want to remind us in his legalese novel *Bleak House*, any move in English law is something for the centuries, this assertion rings around the court room like a warning shot to right-conduct. In English existing law, Neo Bankside residents, and the celebrities that might be amongst them and attracting particularly aggressive intrusions on their privacy, could apparently sue for breach of their peace. But such rights are not, according to Tate defence, remotely covered by occasional Instagram images being captured by the public on the hoof as they perambulate the viewing platform in search of the London skyline, even if those images now number 24,000 and upwards a year.

Common Law is shaped by chronology and chronology is all-important to the judiciary in cases of this nature. Council for both parties are expected to represent their clients with continuous and scrupulous regard for any such chronology to ensure that a judgement represents as close to a fair and rational unfolding of events that led to the impasse that brought the parties to the court as a last resort. To launch this chronology it is noted that in 2006 Nicholas Serota's *Tate Director's Report* announces the gallery extension is being planned (but in a quite different form to the one under current debate). The report carries the headline 'Inspiring Spaces' with 'juice bars, shops and terraces' with 'inspiring views', not just for Tate Members like me, but according to the record for the public to enjoy at will. I am not sure whether the 'Tate Head of Coffee' was yet in their £40K post at the time. At this point the key orientation of the offer is North, perhaps not surprisingly, given St Pauls sits centre stage, to the river side of the building towards the heart of the city. Subsequently the revised ten-storey pyramid structure was passed through planning in 2009 with public viewing terraces to the north and the south and, ironically, supported through its passage by the Neo Bankside developers Native Land who were looking to maintain constructive relations with this very close neighbour. Given the influence Southwark Council could have had on the prospects for the private residential block and their zoning of the area with its cultural remit as a Core Activity Zone, it is perhaps not surprising that there was this kind of palpable caution during this early pre-building phase of negotiation. The judge responded to these presentations seeking a clarification that what was being discussed was an 'Art Gallery' *plus* a 'Viewing Platform', and that both in essence constituted what one might call, an art gallery. Martin Creed's neon installation *Work 232* inside Tate Modern, came to mind in this instance. As it shines out: *the whole world + the work = the whole world.* Here, as explained to the judge, the whole gallery plus the viewing platform equalled the whole gallery. In other words, from the start the viewing platform had, according to Tate's Director Frances Morris, been integral to the institution's entire coherence and mission.

On the other side of the road, from the first schematic plans in 2006 for a building that was later to be superseded, it was understood by Tate that the Neo Bankside residences would themselves be buffered by Winter Garden terraces that would act as thermal protection for the apartments that were otherwise composed of sheer glazed walls from the top to the bottom of the building blocks. This screening of the apartments with foliage and a secondary curtain glass wall was later reduced in scale and number, and in some cases the residents incorporated these outdoor spaces into their internal living quarters. While this was technically against the residential leaseholder agreements it appeared in the court room that such niceties were being given a pass as most like-minded people with so much money to spend on inner London high-rise with minimal communal space, a proportional imbalance between private and public worthy of the J. G. Ballard dystopia *High Rise*, would clearly wish to convert their interior footprint to as large an area as conceivable within the legal limits.

Defence for the Tate was questioning this reduction of privacy that the residents appear to have initiated themselves, before nailing my new neighbours in the courtroom with the quite convincing statistic that 600,000 visitors to the viewing platform should not have their viewing rights threatened by these five plaintiffs. To some laughter in court the Tate's QC in pursuit of privacy suggested that they might lower their blinds, they could grow a hedge or even, and this was what had provoked such anger from the outset, consider doing what others do around modernist towers across the UK and install some 'net curtains'. Sir Nicholas Serota had run into some difficulties months before when on announcement of the legal action he had proposed to a national newspaper that net curtains was all that was needed to solve what the High Court would now be considering over several weeks at vast expense. As the proceedings continue there is an apparent omerta about repeating the 'n word' for fear of reviving the bad will it initially caused. The whole thing is taking on the ambience of a genteel drawing-room farce. The QC asks an expert witness whose brief is questions of design to ameliorate the problem why he cannot find mention of net curtains in his statement: 'Is it a dirty word?' to which the witness replies: 'I didn't do it deliberately'.

The problem was that any such net curtains, blinds or other window covering, short of a brick wall or wooden shutters (which were neither permitted nor desired), would become transparent at night with the turning on of any internal light in the effected apartment. Given for the winter months the viewing platform was scheduled to be open every evening until at least 5.30 pm this would mean on return from school the children of the apartment owners would be clearly visible to viewing platform gawpers through the screened windows as they moved around the living space. The residents spoke of the heat and discomfort of the apartments in the summer months and did not want to reduce the already limited ventilation that kept them on the stylish, Gregor Schneider side of muggy. Uniformity of appearance amongst the apartments was apparently all-important to the developers and their management company, who had attached strict design guidelines to the leaseholders which prompted me to think there was little apparent distinction (give or take about £2 million disposable income a year per capita) between living in London's most expensive residential quarters and living in London's most strictly policed local authority housing. The residents spoke of ensuring that they were dressed at all times so as not to be exposed in tourist images posted on the internet, but, when pressed to provide evidence of any such images online, appeared unable to do so without considerable searching. The residents expressed surprise that they had ever become the object of the public's attentions believing when they bought off-plan that those visiting Tate had other interests: 'We thought we would be of no interest to the viewers but we have become the exhibits'.[70] This line of thinking had for some time already dominated commentary in the art world, especially on Twitter, where the symmetry between the domestic 'performances' being viewed by the public from the platform, were very early on associated with those installations in the Tate Collection itself which were playing with not dissimilar domestic rhetorics. It emerges that a 48 hour continuous film shot from one of the effected apartments towards the viewing platform is being offered to the judge for some home-viewing over the weekend: 'It's like watching paint dry' says the defending QC 'We would like your lordship to watch a flavour of it'. The judge replies: 'So you want me to watch paint dry?' The exchanges are beginning at this stage of the proceedings to take on a Warholian flavour of their own.

While this struck some amongst a significant audience following proceedings on social media as an appealing line of enquiry, the symmetry between the everyday and high modernism is always good for comment, what most interested me at this stage of the hearing was the way one of the more outgoing and generously friendly Neo Bankside residents who had welcomed me to their midst, Lindsay Urquart, had reversed the favour on the Tate Director Nicholas Serota and chosen to construct life-size cardboard template models of Serota and his children in their underwear, which were then displayed inside her apartment over a single weekend for all on the viewing platform to see. Here was a sculptural work of modest wit but neither lacking flair nor accuracy, being given a public airing specially for Tate visitors. It would after all, have been difficult for Lindsay Urquart to get *inside* those hallowed walls of Tate with her creation, spaces that have long profited from the energies of precisely those external everyday lives trying to break through the cordon sanitaire maintained by mainstream cultural tsars. The fact that it was a multi-millionaire, or at least someone apparently leading a multi-millionaire's life high in the London sky, making the installation should not divert us for a moment given how wealthy so many of Tate's own installation arrivistes have been since uber-gallerists Larry Gagosian and Jay Jopling entered the scene. I was beginning to wonder whether in capital-fuelled London of the early twenty-first century there was much difference between the favoured conceptual artist and the art-loving aristocrats of apartment living.

I found it curious that this resident seemed genuinely contrite, she called it 'regrettable', that she had done such a thing with papier maché (something only I can judge as I was, understandably given legal longueurs, the sole member of the public who sat in the court room each day of this proceedings) and while it cannot be underestimated that this might well have been due to her fear that it would lose her favour with the judge and the court, it seemed more likely that she was, genuinely sorry that she had exposed this family in this way. If so that appears to be a most peculiarly sympathetic response from one human whose family have been described as 'living in hell' and 'sick to my stomach' under the scrutiny of strangers, towards another whose institution the Tate has chosen to expose that young family (three girls) to that scrutiny while keeping open a much complained about public gallery. These were cut-outs after all, lifelike ones yes, but *papier maché* nonetheless. Unless the Serota family had a peculiarly thin skin and felt the barbs of strangers' eyes on their bodies through the fetish dolls displayed in that window, it is hard to see quite what the resident had to be embarrassed about other than some personal reservations as to her template-cutting skills. And it is unlikely I would guess that the Serotta's do not have a weekend-retreat well away from this London workplace for the weekends when they were making their window appearances anyway. It is wholly indicative of the occasion that the *Daily Mail* newspaper wrote up this particular incident at some length bringing together some of the preferences and *bête noir* of that particular organ: a high regard for wealthy people, a dismal view of contemporary art, celebrities and salacious gossip that attaches to people in their underwear, and of course, their party piece, the value of the 'desirable property' in question.

Writing this last paragraph in quite this way would have been inconceivable to me a few hours earlier on arrival in court that day, but my patience with the language being used by the legal-defence team for Tate, and those giving evidence for Tate, was beginning very rapidly to wear thin. By lunchtime on that first day my allegiances were slowly but surely swinging over to the far (right) side sitting as I was amongst those who appeared to me to be speaking most honestly about their predicament of privacy. I did not exactly like them (yet) but I felt less animosity towards them than I had earlier for simply being rich. I am not sure you could quite say I was ready to go full 'O'Hagan', an author's counter-intuitive reflex of sympathy for wealthy people who don't appear to deserve it (that we will explore in Chapter 7), but I was getting there.[71]

Over the coming days questioning repeatedly returned to the nature of the viewing platform vista and what it was Tate expected from it. The judge was clearly concerned to establish in precise terms quite why Tate was so wedded to maintaining what could have otherwise appeared an arbitrary add-on to their already world-class offer. It was almost as though they did not have trust in their permanent holdings and that unlike the Museum of Modern Art in New York (whose early patrons' wealth secured its sensational collections) with whom they perhaps inevitably feel they are in some kind of competition, could not count on the quality of those works to sustain across the new extension as well as the capacious Turbine Hall and Boiler House of the original development of Bankside power station in the 1990s. It was like a re-run of the notorious Saatchi and Saatchi campaign for the Victoria & Albert Museum which in the 1980s was described as an 'ace caff' with 'quite a nice museum attached'. In this case it was a great viewing platform with 'not a bad gallery' attached. But compared with MOMA, not-bad does not really suffice. It appeared to be critical to the mission that the public platform remained accessible at all times, that it was protected as a 360 degree experience, and unlike its competitors in the panopticon market of the private bank buildings with their restaurants, the Shard, Vertigo 42, St Paul's Cathedral, the London Eye, the Emirates Cable Car, the O2 skywalk and the Sky Garden at 20 Fenchurch Street, according to Tate at least, it must be maintained at all costs. That maintenance presumed that the south side of the terrace adjacent to the litiginous Neo Bankside residences should be considered an integral and defining part of that 'visitor experience'. What had not been accounted for was that the original concept for the building prior to the emergence of the pyramid design in 2008 had been of a quite different architectural make-up, with the whole building clad in glass rather than the subsequent brick rendering the entirety of the building as a vast viewing apparatus in its own right. It was as though in its second iteration the increased privacy of the building, its new discretion, was being compensated for by the supplement of the public viewing platform.

Mr James Arnell was now speaking on behalf of the Neo Bankside residents having pursued and purchased a penthouse flat in Block B, one of the most sought-after accommodations in the building and by definition at the top of the block, most exposed to scrutiny from the Tate viewing platform. I had indeed unwittingly looked into Mr Arnell's accommodation on many occasions when taking air and respite from scrutinising the latest work to grace the Turbine Hall or being enticed to participate in one of its many relational exercises by Tino Sehgal, Kersten Höller or Doris Salcedo. It transpired that Tate and Mr Arnell had previously, and somewhat controversially, for the case in question, come to a negotiated settlement and a 'deal' as to limiting the viewing platform opening hours. In April 2018 Mr Arnell had received a solicitor's letter presented in court reiterating: 'Tate is concerned to be a good neighbour in the Bankside area', and later 'Tate is an active member of the local community', thus evoking two key terms of social association that we considered at length in Chapter 1. Whether either has any real force in such anodyne legal statements is rather up for question and might well usefully be questioned in the context of this discussion of social reproduction and the performance of domestic space.

Mr Arnell after all is buying his apartment from a developer whose lineage can be traced back to a company called 'Native Land' (amongst all possible alternatives). Sylvia Federici was not talking about such companies when she wrote on the 'new enclosures' but her words bare repeating in this context:

> According to the Marxist tradition, the enclosures were the starting point of capitalist society, they were the basic device of 'original accumulation,' [...]

The enclosures, however, are not a one-time process exhausted at the dawn of capitalism. They are a regular reoccurrence on the path of capitalist accumulation and a structural component of class struggle.[72]

On the Native Land web-site there is a stunning portfolio of photographs taken from the very rooms that have been brought into question in this court case, but perhaps not surprisingly despite their value-enhancing proximity, few images of Tate Modern's platform facing off their northernmost view. Without mention of the ever-present overviewing by Tate Members, the development is described in these glowing terms:

> A landmark residential scheme Neo Bankside is one of London's most desirable new addresses. This world-class development, in an unrivalled location beside Tate Modern on the South bank of the River Thames, comprises 217 apartments and penthouses in four 'pavilions', rising in sequence with views towards The City and St Paul's Cathedral. A 50/50 joint venture with Grosvenor alongside a profit participation arrangement with previous site owners Land Securities, this striking development is located at the heart of the 'ribbon of culture' emerging along the South Bank. NEO Bankside completed in September 2012 and has won numerous UK and international property awards.[73]

The puff goes on to detail some of the bare statistics of the development with an interesting social footnote: 'Date: 2006–2012, Status: Construction Complete, Net Area: 250,000 sq ft Residential/8,000 sq ft Commercial/ 11,200 sq ft Retail, GDV: £420m (2014), Joint Venture: Grosvenor, Affordable Housing: 82 Social Rented Units'. Native Land do indeed commit themselves to a proportion of affordable housing not just here but in even higher-end addresses such as Cheyne Walk in Chelsea where they provided 13 units on land that must represent some of the most valuable real-estate in the world. But despite such courtesies to equality in the development game, the reference to a Thameside 'ribbon of culture' and the aspiration to be part of that ribbon strikes a chord given that less than a mile east from Neo Bankside, Rotherhithe Theatre Workshop would have once been potentially part of any such ribbon if it had not been swept away by, well, developers not unlike Native Land.

So my empathy with the travails of Mr Arnell's penthouse purchase might be expected to be at something of a low ebb, but even in listening to his sorry tale I am more sympathetic than I could possibly have imagined. For what follows Mr Arnell's evidence to the hearing are in quick succession witness statements from the head of the security detail at Tate, the only representative to speak on behalf of the Tate architects, John O'Mara, and the Director of Tate Modern itself Frances Morris. As a warm-up for the main show the head of the security team is asked whether he is high up in the organisation which might have been funny given the platform in question, if it was not for the curious coolness of what follows. I am a regular visitor to Tate but there is little in what is described that I recognise, it must somehow refer to an offstage-elite evening-world I know little about despite paying more than £200 annually as a 'valued member'. He is concerned for those colleagues in Tate who are responsible for what he calls 'the visitor experience' but there is a nagging doubt that this experience might have as much to do with the corporate offer to clients of Tate and their expectations than those like myself who happen to drop by for the occasional breather from the beguiling self-reflexive conundrum of Andrea Fraser's *A Gallery Talk* (1989). The Tate head of security understands that Mr Arnell has been seeking some 'relief' from the attentions of these visitors whose own motives for being there might not be quite so distant from the very interests that have brought him to invest in this property in the first place.

Mr O'Mara who follows quick on the heels of this Tate colleague, does not seem to be willing to compromise the strict modernist design credentials of his employers Herzog and de Meuron, resisting repeated attempts at clarification, asking him to suggest ways in which a simple screening device attached to the south side balustrade of the viewing platform might mitigate the effects of those who have taken to photographing Mr Arnell's apartment from that vantage point, without betraying the core principles of the building's design. At first he does not seem to be able to offer *any* kind of suggested alternative to the unacceptable status quo under Tort litigation but when robustly invited by the judge to 'do what architects do' and 'think something up' he blocks again with: 'I could not speculate', as though he is a politician being asked about some personal issue they cannot admit to, for fear of adverse quotations hitting the headlines. The judge remonstrates: 'But *you* are an architect, you come up with architectural ideas, don't you?' John O'Mara blocks again offering his insight that as architects they 'understand the building' which implies that the rest of us don't, and that this is a sensitivity some distance beyond the vulgarity of change to the original, at which point the judge puts it back to him even more forcefully, at the brink of losing his sanguine High Court temper: 'You cannot tell me *as an architect* how to design your way out of this problem?' Not only is it unusual to have the judge entering into the cut-and-thrust of the exchanges, that is obviously commonly left to the advocates, but here it is a judge at the end of his tether with members of the culture-class who unlike the residents do not seem able to talk honestly any more about what they have been invited to come and talk honestly and under oath about. (This will be replicated and magnified in grotesque measure at the Phase 2 opening of the Grenfell Inquiry that we will visit by way of closing this book.) If Tate have been losing my patience somewhat, here Herzog de Meuron one of my favourite architectural practices is losing my confidence even faster. I have long resisted the trite use of the term 'starchitect' to refer to these enormously talented humans, but the conduct on show in Court 16 of the Rolls Building today has made me reconsider my generosity, which is now leaking out towards those I am still sitting amongst who are horrified at the conduct of their 'good' neighbours.

It comes as something of a relief from this architectural stone-walling when the Director of Tate Modern, Frances Morris takes the stand and appears to have come both well-prepared but possibly, given the confidence of her presence in the box, something that fails even the most hardened witnesses, perhaps prepped or even professionally trained for this moment of public exposure. The first clue is that she unerringly keeps her eyes trained on the judge to whom she is effectively speaking as distinct to the probing gaze and searching questions of the Neo Bankside defence lawyer. The first encounter as to preference of title, 'Mrs, Ms, Miss?' does not really fly, but the confirmation that the statement Ms Morris has offered the court is 'closest to justifying the Tate's position in these proceedings' is more promising. Understandably her opening logic that a 'viewing gallery without a panoramic view is redundant' makes sense, but then her argument strays into far more contestable territory suggesting that the platform and its view is 'essential to the vision and values of Tate Modern' in its ability to, as Frances Morris actually puts it, 'address South London'. It is as though the way in this court at least the platform is about to be constructed is as some sort of bridgehead to communication with the local neighbourhood that is perceived as essential to Tate's core mission of being as it has said a 'good neighbour'. The idea that the platform *addresses* this constituency, the one that includes the vestiges of the Rotherhithe Theatre Workshop now gentrified into luxury apartments, is telling both in its derivation from an idea of postal location, but also in its implication of a form of ministry or even dictatorially talking down to others elsewhere. Something for which a raised platform at ten storeys might be quite appropriate.

Frances Morris continues with her rationale of how the platform has become integral to their service. Tate is 'international' but it is also 'local' in its practices and conduct, and Morris claims to speak for all those in the institution when she says: 'I speak for the whole building that would in turn wish to speak for the whole of London in its diversity, and the viewing platform was an essential part of that'. I applaud the mission statement in the first part of that claim but attaching the viewing platform with all its touristic connotations to that promise can only fatally wound its claim to our sympathy. But this is not all: 'Our reason for being is public benefit and a huge part of that is delivered by the viewing platform'. Again I am listening to this carefully but regardless of some of the responsibilities Frances Morris and I share with regard to commitment to communities, I have little clear sense of how a viewing platform, notwithstanding those who might make it to look down on the homes that have been swept away by gentrification for this precise 'cultural zone' where the admittedly Pharoaic pyramid has been built, could possibly, seriously, be described in this way.

The Neo Bankside QC has had enough of this paean to the platform and suggests that Tate have acted in a way that 'rides roughshod over those neighbours'. Frances Morris whips back: 'As well as the neighbours here today there are hundreds of thousands of other neighbours to whom we are responsible'. And I am sure given their government funding and their outreach programmes and genuine relationship to Southwark Schools this is all very accurate and well-meaning. But I am still not at all sure, or at least convinced, as to what the *viewing platform* really has to do with it. The question of harm is not a generic one, but the case could be made that a Neo Bankside child is a child nonetheless and their lives appear to be harmed by the lack of privacy they suffer. Frances Morris, a mother of three herself, does not agree in a phrase that will have wholly innocent, awful echoes when I write this up some months later. 'I don't believe the Tate platform is a harm to children'. Mrs Urquart sitting next to me demurs from this judgement from the witness box, not least of all perhaps because the Director of Tate Modern lives nowhere near the platform and its voyeuristic hordes that have been blighting her children's' lives. Indeed when pressed by the Tate QC on this relative matter of upbringing Mrs Urquart has said: 'My nine year-old daughter was so traumatised [by the overseers] she would not even enter the kitchen'. We are fast approaching an emotional and legal impasse that might have surprised us those years before as we enjoyed the capacious hospitality of Bobby Baker's kitchen.

So, by way of concluding this domestic squabble in the courts, it should be admitted this *Kitchen Show* is somewhat more elevated than Bobby Baker's ground floor version with which we opened this chapter, but somehow despite its levitation debased in its conduct. There appear to be certain traumas shared by different social classes nonetheless. When asked about such effects on her Frances Morris says she cannot answer sensibly as she does not have young children. The QC asks: 'But you do have children?', she replies 'Adult children' to which the frustrated QC says: 'But they were young children once', more as a statement of the obvious than anything approaching factual correction. The judge intervenes again, rather enigmatically this time, pointing out that a child is unlikely to have a law degree and wonders whether they are less conscious of trauma of being watched than adults? At this point Frances Morris is asked whether she would have been willing to have brought her own children up in Claire Fearn's apartment (the leading Neo Bankside litigant) to which Frances Morris replies: 'I brought my young children up in a terraced house on a busy street and would pull the curtains shut. I would have regarded it as a privilege to have brought my children up in Claire Fearn's flat'. But she did not get that chance, and now does not get the chance to endure the unwanted attentions of those who maraud the viewing gallery that looks down and addresses those South London neighbourhoods far below.

The whole hearing is described as a 'monumental disclosure' exercise involving hundreds of thousands of documents in pursuit of a balance of judgement between privacy and publicity. The residents' right to their own view from their apartments given that Tate is an apparently cultural institution with a strong public remit might well in less bourgeois friendly times have trumped other commonly cited rights to a view. But what is stark in these exchanges is that nobody in 2009 when the planning consents were being taken through Southwark's planning committees, could imagine the influence of the rise of social media on what a viewing platform might represent. Indeed, as Bruno Latour might have suggested to the defence lawyers, the very first act in the skeleton argument should have been to look at mobile telephone technology at the outset of this process in 2006, and to look again at its completion in 2012. To do so would be to witness a revolution in camera reach zoom, pixelation, posting and panoramic functions that would have been unthinkable five years before. Given Facebook was only just starting up in 2004, in 2007 the iPhone is launched, the 2009 iPhone only has three megapixels, in 2010 Instagram is born, but by 2016 the 12 megapixel camera is available as standard, it would not take a Latourian technological wizard to expose the real driver of this case, that is the intimate and complex relations between privacy and publicity, modernity and media.[74]

Private view

Fearn vs. Tate Modern offers many avenues for further thought on everyday life and social reproduction. In the summing up of the trial amidst the legal questions of Article 8 of the European Court of Human Rights, we learn about nuisance, privacy, harassment, what is quaintly called in property law 'quiet enjoyment'. The law of emanations in nuisance cases such as this appears to involve infectious diseases, picketing, prostitution, extracting heat, and sky views. The judge reserves his judgement on all such matters, which is not surprising given what a rare case this is involving a leading international cultural organisation and residents with the serious financial means to see this through to Appeal should they so wish. In the days that follow I work back through the notes I have distilled here and realise how centrifugal this case is for the concerns of this first part of *The Dark Theatre*. And how prescient they were in looking out towards Part II of the book where the question of cultural cruelty will return in sharper and more brutal focus.

So to close this chapter I will settle on one branch of such thinking that draws together some concerns already expressed in Part I of *The Dark Theatre* and projects forwards to Part II. Tate Modern is the apotheosis you could say of the relation between modern architecture and what used to be called the mass media, but might now be more specifically defined, as I have earlier, as 'social media'. The iconic modern tropes of Corbusier's architecture, horizontal windows, roof gardens, the glass façade are all here for the viewing from the Tate platform. It is as though nothing much has changed since the construction of the beautiful public high-rise housing blocks of the Unité de Habitation in 1940s Marseille. Inhabitation now includes exhibition, as in that corridor in the V&A I began in with its permeable images of stage and screen, the space is neither inside nor outside, troubling the relation between public and private, with walls that don't quite appear as walls but as images.[75] Le Corbusier's famous definition of the primordial idea of the house has gone missing along the way: 'The house is a shelter, an enclosed space, which affords protection against cold, heat *and outside observation*'.[76] But for Le Corbusier, if not for Mrs Fearn and the other residents of Neo Bankside, *seeing* is precisely what the house is for, the house in the modern period operates as an outward-facing visual device.

In the case of Neo Bankside it appears the residents presumed this was the historic bourgeois right to one-way seeing, the return of the gaze has taken them unawares and they are minded to take that view to law to block its sightlines. But the modernity of the museum demands its own freedoms in this respect, built as it is on the hyper-accelerated principle of a mechanism not just for displaying views of the world (by artists), but ensuring the institution itself is an almighty surveillance apparatus overlooking now, not just those curatorial preferences that museum culture has always invested in, but all others who might become future participants in their programmes to this end. To be outside the modern apartment of the residents is to be seen, to be in the image, but at the same time as the architectural historian Beatriz Colomina reminds us, to be at home is now to be 'more public than the public'.[77] It does not take iPhones and megapixels to acknowledge that we have long lived in this media moment. Roland Barthes put it this way some years ago in *Camera Lucida*: 'The age of photography corresponds precisely to the irruption of the private into the public, or rather, to the creation of a new social value, which is the publicity of the private [...]'.[78] It would appear from the legal process I have been following step by step, with meticulous care given to the long-hand spoken-record I have kept daily in this high-windowed Rolls Court room that, while the 'traditional sense of privacy' as Colomina phrases it is 'not only scarce but under attack' her prognosis as to how to resolve that difficulty might be some way wide of the mark: 'It is better protected legally than with walls'.[79] It should not go without saying that when Justice Mann returns to the High Court with his carefully considered judgement he dismisses the claims of the residents and finds on all counts in favour of Tate Modern. I was (sitting) on the wrong side of legal history, despite its high sartorial standards.

But where Colomina predicts with unnerving accuracy from the vantage point of the pre-social media age of 1994 that the 'right to privacy' has become the right to remain 'out of the picture' she formidably links this recognition with not just the pictorial image, that would be logical enough given media theory of the time, but also the right to remain out of the 'credit report' and the 'disclosed medical record', precisely those features of surveillance capitalism that we were exploring in the last chapter of this book. For Colomina the whole identity of modernity requires us to think of this shifting relation between the *publicity of the private*, and there might be no better recent example of that than the Tate Modern viewing platform episode. In this legal encounter we recognise the role that architecture has played throughout its post-Corbusier modern history as a series of overlapping, coeval and congruent systems of representation. Thus the contemporary museum is not just a device for showing, if it ever was, but is intimately bound to orders of representation which, with the advent of the Tate viewing platform, now appear to include a looking down on others and an impertinent looking into their lives.

This was what art might have once, in the good-old-days, have been expected to mediate on our behalf. There is after all a long and illustrious history of painting that has since the eighteenth century figured the populated interior as its appropriate domestic subject matter. But here the Tate pyramid, perhaps nicely renamed the Blavatnik Building after an oligarch of the Russian extraction industries that powers the air-conditioning, is the overseer of all it surveys. Where subjects might have once thought of themselves as independent from the object of architecture here it reminds us that all such independences are in fact illusions, maintained for as long as they are useful, but to be closed down when the going gets tough. In this sense Tate Modern and its viewing platform is the inevitable heir to the legacy of social media discussed earlier. It forms a key cultural part of the performatariat's desire to be seen and to go on being seen. We are less likely to come down from the tenth-floor and discuss or converse about what we have seen, less likely to share a slow drawing or a painting of what we have witnessed, but we are likely to share with each other a snatched or even stolen image, and if the court case is evidence of anything, circulate at will those images to others irrespective of the intimacy of their contents. This is a freedom that has been fought for at great expense by Tate Modern, and perhaps given populist and alt-right pressures on 'freedom of expression', this might well be a defence that we should be very grateful for from our public servants.

For it is a mission that replicates in peculiar symmetry the foundation of the Museum of Modern Art in New York in the early twentieth century itself. There the curators of ground-breaking shows such as *Modern Architecture* were establishing a dichotomy between as Colomina puts it 'art and life, the artwork and the everyday object, by maintaining a hierarchy between architecture and building'.[80] It was MOMA who first understood the museum as a function of modern media, something that their founding director Alfred Barr had written extensively about in catalogue essays. Here was a 'new building for a new age'. Publicity was, through the 1930s, understood as central to its aims in which catalogues were only one form of print media that operated as propaganda as much as documentary with shows having left MOMA often touring for years after, much as we would expect the super shows of today's museum culture to tour. And at the heart of many of these architectural shows was precisely the image of the 'private house' and domestic architecture. For instance in *Modern Architecture* a show conceived at MOMA for 1929 Beatriz Colomina catalogues this domestic bias:

> the exhibition was made up almost entirely of domestic architecture: Frank Lloyd Wright presented the model of his project for a house on the Mesa and photographs of the Robie house, Roberts house, Millard house, and Jones house; Le Corbusier, the model of Villa Savoye and photographs of the Beistegui apartment, Villa Stein, and Double House […]. [etc. etc., and the list continues to the bottom of the page.][81]

Here MOMA understood the significance of the domestic realm to a truly contemporary collection that has been our locus for this chapter since setting off past that Degas painting via Elmgreen and Dragset's *architect's* apartment.

A century later in an uncanny inversion of their distinguished ancestors, Tate has understood the power of the domestic but in a show of originality inverted its direction, framing the *exterior* domestic space of Neo Bankside apartments as critical to their mission. It is not as though they have any longer to mount an exhibition called *Modern Architecture*, they have a prime example from Rogers Stirk Harbour and Partners outside their south-facing side and the viewing platform operates as a means by which it can be accessed by those who, like their ancestors a century before, are detained by the domestic interior and its awful fascinations. If the house has since that MOMA show been recognised as a media-centre in its own right, as it has with the growth of home entertainment technologies since Mildred's desire for that fourth living room screen in Ray Bradbury's novel *Fahrenheit 451*, then its incorporation by Tate Modern is an inverse staging of that mediatised relation. Here ironically the everyday life of those who are perceived least likely to have any such thing, the super-wealthy, is restored to the view of those who most definitely do have an everyday life just like you or me. Sometimes even in our underwear. If as Le Corbusier said, 'The true museum is the one that contains everything' then what better way to operate at such inclusionary levels than to incorporate not just the panorama of London in your sights, but curated examples of domestic life in that city too.[82] At a moment that the very media that have brought this about are threatening the existential identity of the museum with their facilities for sharing everything in greater and greater detail with all, the spectacle of attendance might be expected to incorporate increasingly hard-to-get experiences of which this viewing platform would appear to be some kind of cultural zenith.

There can be few high up there who reach for their camera who do not know of Alfred Hitchcock's film *Rear Window*, and if they don't they might already have guessed Walter Benjamin's link between the interior and crime: 'The criminals of the first detective novels are neither gentlemen nor apaches, but private members of the bourgeosie'.[83] By this Benjamin means the residents of these spaces, the ones we have been working over for clues since we last left Constantius (and Kierkegaard) in Berlin some pages ago. We have already traced the genesis of the crime scene that has likely happened there in walking our way through *Die Familie Schneider*. But what are the clues that those on the viewing platform are seeking out? It is as though the developers in resisting tenants' wishes to screen their windows are asking those who invest in Neo Bankside to come clean about something in their past that if visible to all might in some way ameliorate the ways in which capital has been accumulated (primitively or otherwise) to invest in such high-end property.

The theatre box was long thought by Adolf Loos to exist at the interface between claustrophobia and agoraphobia and the much-contested winter gardens at the heart of the crime scene at the legal hearing on Neo Bankside, would appear to have offered just such a liminal space on to the exterior from a private inside. The incorporation of that viewing device into the interior realm brings with it complex disruptions to this relation. The apartment effectively turns back in on itself, losing its peripheral vision to a reversed view of, well just more, interior. 'It is no longer the house that is the theatre box; there is a theatre box inside the house, overlooking the internal social spaces'.[84] Here the relation between acting and spectating is further troubled for those involved in this psycho-drama while the traditional relations between outside and inside are intensified by the existence of the world's largest theatre box, the Tate viewing platform, overlooking all and everything, like it or not.

Here Søren Kierkegaard's Constantius from *Repetition* comes back into view one more time. Where the Konigstadter Theatre box for Constantius had provided for the privileged, and he was certainly privileged given his regular theatre-going habits, 'a private space within the dangerous public realm' of the theatre, for the residents of Neo Bankside, who have inverted their boxes to look inwards not outwards, are left exposed and trumped by a public institution able to offer the private view of all private views. Beatriz Colomina is in fact describing Adolf Loos' Moller house in Vienna of 1928 but she might as well have been writing about Neo Bankside when she says: 'The intruder is "inside", has penetrated the house, only when his/her gaze strikes the most intimate space, turning the occupant into a silhouette against the light'.[85] It is as though Loos in this design understood something of what Ms Fearn *et al.* were going through with regards to the silhouetted shadowing that prevented them from screening themselves from the public. Colomina continues:

> The 'voyeur' in the 'theatre box' has become the object of another's gaze; she is caught in the act of seeing, entrapped in the very moment of control. In framing a view, the theatre box also frames the viewer. It is impossible to abandon the space, let alone leave the house, without being seen by those over whom control is being exerted. Object and subject exchange places.[86]

In this very respect Mrs Urquart could not have said better what Jacques Lacan understood of this predicament, and indeed said on her behalf:

> I can feel myself under the gaze of someone whose eyes I do not even see, not even discern. All that is necessary is for something to signify to me that there may be others there. The window if it gets a bit dark and if I have reason for thinking that there is someone behind it, is straight-way a gaze. From the moment the gaze exists, I am already something other, in that I feel myself becoming an object for the gaze of others. But in this position, which is a reciprocal one, others also know that I am an object who knows himself to be seen.[87]

Without being quite aware of the gender-morphing irony Mrs Urquart would now be reversing the Lacanian direction of the gaze as the one who 'knows themselves to be seen'. The architecture of Neo Bankside is not only a platform that accommodates the viewing subject (her) but it produces that subject and makes that subject susceptible to another architecture turned into a larger and more impressive platform of scopic control, the Tate viewing platform. The problem for Mrs Urquart and where her narrative differs in some degree from the history of modernist architecture as media I am proposing here, is that almost no photographs of those modernist interiors ever included human figures in them. Beatriz Colomina who has done more archival work than most on the period can find just one Adolf Loos interior that includes a human figure. That lonely soul stands in the entrance to the drawing room in the Vienna Rufer house of 1922. But even here the male figure is barely visible as though shy of the camera and disappearing into the threshold of the wall rather like Degas' ghosts in the Opera of Muyerbeer still hanging in that corridor of the V&A where we started on these domestic matters. Embarrassed perhaps that the *female* occupant of the scene, present and correct on all but the day of the photo-shoot, has gone missing in action once again.

There is no such discretion nor resistance to human publicity in the version of Neo Bankside that Tate stages for its visitors. Here there are a myriad of images available of interiors without, but also often *with* their female residents insecurely in place. It is possible of course that in a few years it will be announced to a public utterly immune to any further art-world shock, that in a *Truman Show* scale operation Neo Bankside had been built by Tate following a joint proposal from Tino Sehgal and Richard Rogers for a Turbine Hall show that needed to be bigger, better, longer and more expensive. It would not surprise anyone if this were the case and it would not surprise those in court 16 in the Rolls Building either, so unlikely the narrative that unfolded there over that Autumn week in 2018. Indeed it is the measure of our art-world expectations today that it will be disappointing when we discover that Neo Bankside was not a relational art work at all, that the 'net curtains speech' by Nicholas Serota was a speech about net curtains, with no further resonance intended nor hermeneutic work required.

That public 'immune to art-world shock' could have been nothing but shocked at the news that comes from the Tate viewing platform on the day I am completing this chapter of innocence. I have referred to the relations between the platform and the domestic residences as that of a crime scene, requiring the court of law to untangle its complex filigree of disappointment. But as we know from the outset of this work, loss is a relative concern, and the apparently arbitrary act of one young person of 17 years throwing another child of six years over the much-discussed parapet on the afternoon of Sunday 4 July at 2.40 pm, can only strike those who hear about it as a brutal coda to such minor skirmishes. That the perpetrator of this act is described within a few hours of the incident by the BBC as having 'special educational needs' implies that State responsibility for the welfare of those in their care might in the wake of savage austerity have exposed the public to undue risk once again. At the time of writing there is no name given to the 'French national' who has dropped 100 feet from the tenth to the fifth floor roof of the Blavatnik Building, where the emergency services have somehow found a way to stabilise his critically threatened life-force and brought him to the hospital that will have seen much worse, but are unlikely to have encountered many more arbitrary injuries. This wilful act has taken place to the North side of the Switch House pyramid and it is possible that it is the angled incline of the architecture, and the levitated Turbine Hall that has saved the life of this child on this occasion. But the child lies stricken in a London hospital with multiple injuries that irrespective of the psychological effects of such an act, are certain to change his yet-to-be-lived life. In the meantime, Tate Modern administration have re-opened the gallery but have kept the viewing platform closed until 'further notice'. One might reasonably think they have recalled that just downriver their sister institution, Tate Britain, hosts some of

148 The loss adjustor

the world's most sublime panoramic images of London, such as Turner's *Richmond Hill on the Prince Regent's Birthday* (painted exactly 200 years ago in 1819) so that we ourselves do not have to go there, but glory in a 'way of seeing' there. The whole idea of the viewing platform begins to appear a banal solution to a problem that had already been solved, by artists. It would perhaps anyway be too much to ask in this age of 360 degree vision that our appetite for recording unhindered vistas of our sovereign dominion be sacrificed until such a time that that young victim of transparency has had the opportunity to convalesce his injuries without his family having to imagine the selfies being taken high in that same cloud-skudding sky.

Notes

1 See 'Everyday Life' in Read, Alan. (1993). *Theatre & Everyday Life*. London: Routledge, p. 121.
2 Ibid. p. 136.
3 Ibid. p. 147.
4 As published by Unbound at the remarkable Live Art Development Agency who along with the London International Festival of Theatre, Arts Admin and Artangel through the 1980s, 1990s and 2000s have made living, working and engaging with performance in London such a golden era of serious challenge.
5 See Kierkegaard, Søren. (1983). *Fear and Trembling* and *Repetition*. Ed. and Trans. Howard V. Hong and Edna H. Hong. Princeton: Princeton University Press; Kartsaki, Eirini. (2016). *On Repetition*. Chicago: University of Chicago Press.
6 See Choonara, Joseph. (2017). *Unravelling Capitalism: A Guide to Marxist Political Economy*. London: Bookmarks Publications, p. 30.
7 See Federici, Silvia. (2012). *Revolution at Point Zero: Housework, Reproduction and Feminist Struggle*. Oakland: PM Press.
8 Bhattacharya, Tithi. (2017). 'Introduction: Mapping Social Reproduction Theory', in *Social Reproduction Theory*. London: Pluto Press, p. 1.
9 Ibid. pp. 1–20, for a crystal-clear exposition of both these questions but also their recent histories in feminist thought. See Valencia, Sayak. (2017). *Gore Capitalism*. Cambridge: MIT Press.
10 While *oikonomia* refers strictly to that economy of the household sphere the *Dictionary of Untranslatables* edited by Barbara Cassin, Princeton: Princeton University Press, 2014, traces its etymology through nine centuries of use back to Xenophon, pp. 728–732.
11 Nancy, Jean-Luc (2008). *Philosophical Chronicles*. Trans. Franson Manjali. New York: Fordham University Press, pp. 37–44.
12 See Phelan, Peggy. (1993). 'The Ontology of Performance', in *Unmarked*. London: Routledge, pp. 146–166. See Kierkegaard, Søren. (2009). *Repetition*. Trans. M. G Piety. Oxford: Oxford University Press. Further references to *Repetition* from this edition unless otherwise noted.
13 Ibid. p. 2. Constantine Constantius's 'voyage' as Kierkegaard puts it begins at p. 20. of the Oxford University Press edition.
14 Rose, Gillian (1992). *The Broken Middle: Out of Our Ancient Society*. Oxford: Blackwell, pp. 22–25.
15 See Katz, Marc. (1998). 'Rendezvous in Berlin: Benjamin and Kierkegaard on the Architecture of Repetition', *The German Quarterly*, 71.1 (Winter 1998), p. 7. This brilliant exposition of the unnoticed relations between the work of Kierkegaard and Walter Benjamin has provided the context for this discussion.
16 Katz, Marc, op. cit. p. 3.
17 Katz, Mark, op. cit. p. 3.
18 See *Repetition*, op. cit., p. 21.

19 Søren Kierkegaard, *Repetition* quoted in Marc Katz, op. cit. p. 3.
20 *Repetition* op. cit. p. 28.
21 Katz, Marc, op. cit. pp. 3–4.
22 Katz, Marc, op. cit. p. 4, see *Repetition*, op. cit. p. 33.
23 *Repetition*, op. cit. p. 33.
24 See Ridout, Nicholas. (2013). *Passionate Amateurs, Theatre Communism and Love*, Michigan: University of Michigan Press, for a wonderful exploration of this apparent oxymoron. I also look forward to Ridout's forthcoming work *Scenes from Bourgeois Life*, Michigan, 2020, having shared a number of these ideas for some years stretching back to Eirini Kartsaki's 'Repetition' conference in Cambridge where we first discussed bourgeois interiors in convivial company.
25 *Repetition*, op. cit. p. 33.
26 *Repetition*, op. cit. p. 33.
27 *Repetition*, op. cit. p. 37.
28 *Repetition*, op. cit. p. 37.
29 For a marvellous discussion of these 'warped spaces', through Lacanian as well as other figures, see Vidler, Anthony. (1994) *The Architectural Uncanny: Essays in the Modern Unhomely*. Cambridge: MIT Press.
30 Ibid. p. 173.
31 See Roger Caillois, 'Mimicry and Legendary Psychasthenia', Trans. John Shepley for *October* and latterly edited and translated by Claudine Frank for the marvellous collection: *The Edge of Surrealism: A Roger Caillois Reader*. Durham: Duke University Press, 2003, pp. 91–103.
32 Ibid, pp. 91–103.
33 *The Edge of Surrealism*, ibid. p. 100.
34 Martin Welton of Queen Mary, University of London, has also been doing some fascinating work on this recently, you can see him talking about it on *Faculti Media* by entering his name into their search engine.
35 Amongst many examples fine work includes; Racz, Imogen. (2015). *Art and the Home: Comfort, Alienation and the Everyday*. London: I. B. Tauris; Perry, Gill. (2013). *Playing at Home: The House in Contemporary Art*. London: Reaktion; Briganti, Chiara and Mezei, Kathy. Eds. (2012). *The Domestic Space Reader:* Toronto: University of Toronto Press; Lauzon, Claudette. (2016). *The Unmaking of Home in Contemporary Art*, Toronto: University of Toronto Press.
36 At a conference curated by Dr Eirini Kartsaki, Anglia Ruskin University, Cambridge, UK, 30 November 2013, with keynote addresses from Keith Potter, Joe Kelleher and Alan Read.
37 *Tomorrow*, Michael Elmgreen and Ingar Dragset, Victoria & Albert Museum, London, 1 October 2013–2 January 2014. www.vam.ac.uk/content/exhibitions/tomorrow-elmgreen-dragset/video-elmgreen-and-dragset/ (accessed on 25 August 2019).
38 Accessible from the V&A digital collection here: http://collections.vam.ac.uk/item/O17815/the-ballet-scene-from-meyerbeers-oil-painting-degas-hilaire-germain/ (accessed on 25 August 2019).
39 Given this is the V&A rather than the international art Biennial context Elmgreen and Dragset would be instantly familiar within, on entering this space it should be noted when I arrive at the installation I am in fact accompanied by a diverse audience amongst whom there are inevitably a number of the unsuspecting accidental tourists in search of Tipoo's Tiger, by general agreement the museum's most extraordinary colonial artefact and by far its biggest audience generator. Nobody leaves for some while however, and over time we realise that what we share is a space that was the V&A Textiles Gallery, long-since faded and emptied and now repurposed as the domestic realm of a fictional failed life.
40 See Read, Alan. (2000). *Architecturally Speaking: Practices of Art, Architecture and the Everyday*. London: Routledge.

41 See Sassen, Saskia. (2014). *Expulsions: Brutality and Complexity in the Global Economy*. Cambridge: Harvard University Press; Rogoff, Irit. (2000). *Terra Infirma: Geography's Visual Culture*. London: Routledge; Massey, Doreen. (1994). *Space, Place and Gender*. London: Polity Press.
42 See Lyotard, Jean-François. (1993). *Political Writings*. Trans. Bill Readings with Kevin Paul Geiman. London: UCL Press, p. 97.
43 *The Unmaking of Home in Contemporary Art*, op. cit. p. 4.
44 See Agamben, Giorgio. (2011). 'The Mystery of the Economy', in *The Kingdom and the Glory*. Trans. Lorenzo Chiesa. Stanford: Stanford University Press, p. 17.
45 Lyotard, op. cit. p. 100.
46 See Colomina, Beatriz (2000). *Privacy and Publicity: Modern Architecture as Mass Media*. Cambridge: MIT Press, p. 10; Nietzsche 'On the Uses and Disadvantages of History', www.sackett.net/NietzscheHistory.pdf (accessed on 25 August 2019).
47 See Gucbilmez, Beliz. (2007). 'An Uncanny Theatricality: The Representation of the Offstage' (May 2007). *New Theatre Quarterly*, Volume 23, No. 2, pp. 152–160.
48 See Rancière, Jacques. (2009). *The Emancipated Spectator*. Trans. Gregory Elliott. London: Verso.
49 Also see: Image: Rachel Whiteread, *Ghost*, National Gallery of Art, Washington, DC, 1990 for another inverted take on the domestic interior. Archived at National Gallery of Art, US, www.nga.gov/collection/art-object-page.131285.html (accessed on 25 August 2019).
50 Michael Landy, *Semi-Detached*, Tate Britain, 2004, see Tate Britain site for archival images: www.tate.org.uk/whats-on/tate-britain/exhibition/semi-detached-michael-landy (accessed on 25 August 2019).
51 Racz, Imogen, op. cit. p. 26.
52 Mike Kelley, *Mobile Homestead*, 2011 for access to archive images see Artangel: www.artangel.org.uk/project/mobile-homestead/ (accessed on 25 August 2019).
53 *Uncanny Encounters* ICA Programme, Rachel Whiteread, *House*, 1994, Artangel site: www.artangel.org.uk/project/house/ (accessed on 25 August 2019), which reminds me that there is little new that we work on but much that we repeat, hopefully not too obviously, the second time as farce.
54 Lauzon, op. cit. p. 22.
55 Federici, Silvia. (2012). *Revolution Point Zero: Housework, Reproduction and Feminist Struggle*. Oakland: PM Press.
56 Ibid. p. 28.
57 Bhattacharya, Tithi. 'How Not to Skip Class: Social Reproduction of Labor and the Global Working-Class' in Bhattacharya op. cit. p. 69.
58 Ibid. p. 70.
59 See Giorgio Agamben's reading of this poem in 'What is the Contemporary?' in *Nudities*, (2010), Trans. David Kishik and Stefan Pedatella, Stanford: Stanford University Press.
60 See Wills, David. (2008). *Dorsality: Thinking Back through Technology and Politics*. Minneapolis: University of Minnesota Press.
61 Ibid. p. 7.
62 Ibid. p. 59.
63 See Review of *Introduction to Cambridge Performance Studies*, Contemporary Theatre Review, Volume 19, 2009, Issue 3: www.tandfonline.com/doi/abs/10.1080/10486800903000177 (accessed on 25 August 2019).
64 Fisher, Mark. (2015). *The Weird and the Eerie*. London: Repeater Books.
65 See O'Hagan, Andrew. 'The Living Rooms': www.artangel.org.uk/die-familie-schneider/the-living-rooms/ (accessed on 19 August 2019).
66 Marx, Karl. *Economic and Philosophical Manuscripts* of 1844 quoted in Vidler, Anthony (1994). *The Architectural Uncanny: Essays in the Modern Unhomely*. Cambridge: MIT Press, p. 5.
67 Bloch, Ernst. (1954/1995). *The Principle of Hope*. Trans. Neville Plaice *et al*. Oxford: Blackwell.

68 Tate Modern had just been announced as having overtaken the long-running 'top attraction', the British Museum, with a staggering head-count of more than 5m visitors a year. Whatever my criticism they must be doing something very right if sheer numbers speak to any kind of measure of success.
69 All observations as recorded in writing by me and checked with court stenographer at each day end.
70 Fearn vs. Tate Modern, Monday 5 November 2019, Neo Bankside resident witness statement.
71 For a development of the 'full O'Hagan' see Chapter 7.
72 See Federici, Sylvia. (2019). *Re-Enchanting the World: Feminism and the Politics of the Commons*. Oakland: PM Press, p. 27.
73 Native Land web-site can be found here: www.native-land.com/development-portfolio/neo-bankside (accessed on 28 August 2019).
74 See Colomina, Beatriz. (1994). *Privacy and Publicity: Modern Architecture as Mass Media*. Cambridge: MIT Press.
75 Ibid. p. 6.
76 Ibid. p. 7.
77 Ibid. p. 8.
78 Barthes, Roland. (1981). *Camera Lucida*. New York: Hill and Wang, p. 98, quoted in Colomina op. cit. p. 8.
79 Op. cit. p. 8.
80 Colomina op. cit. p. 203.
81 Ibid. p. 207.
82 Ibid. p. 212.
83 Benjamin, Walter. (1986). 'Paris, Capital of the Nineteenth Century', in *Reflections*, Trans. Edmund Jephcott. New York: Schocken Books, pp. 155–156.
84 Colomina op cit p. 244.
85 Ibid. pp. 249–250.
86 Ibid. p. 250.
87 Lacan, Jacques. (1988). *The Seminar of Jacques Lacan: Book 1, Freud's Papers on Technique 1953–1954*. Ed. Jacques-Allain Miller. Trans. John Forrester. New York: Norton, p. 215, quoted in Colomina, op. cit. p. 250.

INTERLUDE

Dreadful trade: the vertigo of attractions

Forgive me for marking the half way stage of this book with another anxiety, but I rarely write about Shakespeare. I took Edward Bond at the Royal Court in 1974 seriously when he suggested in a play called *Bingo* there had been dubious accounting by 'the Bard moonlighting as landlord' and I knew that episode did not end well for the national poet. In the same year that *The Family* hit our television screens, this was one of the first plays I had seen in London, and, as it followed the seminal work on small-business accounting, *The Sea*, I was determined not to miss it despite the cover price. Such anxieties are slow to subside when it comes to Shakespeare, despite all that work of the Early Modernists, and some 40 years later I am still nervous about 'canonical masterpieces' that seem impervious to criticism. So I take my place in the theatre stalls well before the ones on the stage, the paid ones, turn up. I have time on my hands to take in the surroundings. I am confronted by a vast map of a kingdom, on what appears to be some kind of heath.

As I wait, looking up at that raised platform which for all its flatness appears to represent the border to a precipitous cliff, another worry sweeps over me, not wholly irrelevant to that embarrassing detail concerning the Shakespearian fiscal landscape that Edward Bond wants to draw our attention to. My vertigo precludes a first-hand experience of what it might be like to stand on such an edge.[1] That is for the simple reason that vertigo, for me is *not* a fear of falling. Vertigo is the profoundly felt sense that the ground is coming up to meet me, to embrace me, or to engulf me. Despite all signs to the contrary in the previous chapter, it is not architectural heights, such as the tenth-floor public viewing platform of Tate Modern that worry me. It is proximity. So, I have never been to Shakespeare Cliff in Dover, at the southeast edge of England's green and pleasant land. A sheer chalk edge, as high as a 50-story building, a place of tall-tales, that ends England, presenting its white face to those beyond. But then again I don't have to go there to know it, for I am sitting here waiting for it, as I understand it is on the horizon in the three hours traffic of this stage. At least to know it as Shakespeare *imagined* it, almost exactly 400 years ago. That is the land-owning Shakespeare to whom we owe a significant debt as to how the rest of the world receives and perceives this sceptered isle, this disunited kingdom.

The son, of an old man, who is not a king, but who is blind, a son who is feigning to be mad, and yet finds marvellous words to describe this place I have never been, and where *his* father will never go except in his mind, puts into words what I will never see:

> Come on, sir; here' the place. Stand still! How fearful
> And dizzy 'tis to cast one's eyes so low!
> The crows and choughs that wing the midway air
> Show scarce so gros as beetles. Halfway down
> Hangs one that gathers samphire – dreadful trade!
> Methinks he seems no bigger than his head.
> The fishermen that walk upon the beach
> Appear like mice, and yon tall anchoring bark
> Diminished to her cock; her cock, a buouy
> Almost too small for sight. The murmuring surge
> That on th'unnumbered idle pebble chafes
> Cannot be heard so high. I'll look no more,
> Lest my brain turn and the deficient sight
> Topple down headlong.[2]

If we have ever heard Edgar's speech to his father, Gloucester, in Shakespeare's play *King Lear* (1606/7), we will know that place, that cliff, quite well. Edgar is in fact imagining the cliff for his blind father, as they are nowhere near it. They are on an elevated stage just in front of me, playing out the final scenes of a tragedy, thought by some to be the height of literary and dramatic culture. Notwithstanding spoilers, Gloucester blinded as he is, his eyes have just been gouged out, seems to have none of my own vertiginous fears. I am not sure this is just because he cannot *see*, he is, palpably, given what he has endured through the congress of this play, more courageous than I am, though probably of similar age. He says to his son Edgar who he thinks is the raving mad-man Poor Tom: 'Set me where you stand.' And his son replies: 'Give me your hand. You are now within a foot of th'extreme verge.'[3]

I am now on that extreme verge, and if not that one, one of my own making, my own imagining. For, despite my vertigo, I *will* see this cliff, I do see it, but differently. It is not that representational theatre of this kind is somehow illusionistic, that's plain silly. I did not sit in the theatre, just before this cliff episode in Act 4 Scene 6, worrying that the storm blowing Lear's brains in, will threaten me in the auditorium. I know it's his storm, not mine, though I do have a number of very minor personal gusts as a father with daughters that I bring to the experience. I have paid to watch it, and he is paid (as an actor who happens to be on this occasion Jonathan Pryce) to endure it. And we both presume the health and safety people have checked the systems to ensure that, unlike in the Belarus Free Theatre's magnificent water-logged *King Lear* mash-up that came to London's Globe Theatre in 2012, the two don't get confused. Rather, in this scene on the cliff, I am being invited, by Shakespeare I suppose, to see, think and feel about one thing, in terms of another thing. Some might call this metaphor, but I would take my lead from the botany of the cliff itself and call it *meiosis* – that is, a form of understatement that diminishes something significant for the purpose of heightened effect elsewhere. We only have to wait a few minutes following the cliff scene for Lear to appear garlanded with flowers to know why the cliff scene operates as it does. The real end is nigh in this last human venue.

Having never been near the edge of a cliff, this experience of being on a cliff edge that I am having in the theatre, must have come from somewhere else. And in saying this I am suggesting it is not from Edgar's description. I want to suggest such theatrical imagining offers us a way to practice, or to rehearse, other ways of imagining that outside the theatre might have some consequences for the ways we live now. Not least of all how we live now, economically and politically that is. We after all live on an 'extreme verge' of another sort, at a time of great precariousness. It is precisely our precarity, prey to the vicissitudes of febrile global capital, that either as consumers of *more* than we need, or producers of what others don't know they need, has become the defining inequality of our age.

When Edgar conjures up a tiny figure, no bigger than a head, hanging from the cliff harvesting samphire, he describes that man's work, as 'dreadful trade'. If this person is hanging from this cliff, then one might imagine them as I do, tethered by a rope, working across the sheer surface of the chalk. Edgar imagines them no bigger than their head, distance and perspective collapsing the scale of the body to its rational part. This head, and for some reason I think of it with dark hair, set off against white, moves steadily in pursuit of their dreadful trade. They move steadily because otherwise they will fall, like others, including fine, much-missed actors of their generation, suicidees who later became subject *to* dreadful trade, and bankrupted, who cannot escape this vertigo. As this head moves across the sheer of the cliff, it marks a sequence of points, pausing here, then there, then there, then there, working their way, away from us, from our embrace, our reach, collecting samphire, from there and there and there, into the white distance. As they go the rope, tethering them to the cliff face, follows their trajectory, joining the dots between their itinerary, between there and there, between there and there, and between there and there. The rope forms a visual connection between the wild growing plants on a surface, now picked and placed in a basket on the back of the figure. Dreadful trade. A trade marked by a set of points, on a white incline, joined by a line that drops, vertiginously, across the white surface, towards the bottom right hand corner of the cliff.

Here a *graph* has been drawn, a sequence of points on a grid with two axes, of cliff and beach, joined by a line that describes, in the form of a gradient angle, the nature of trade, dreadful trade indeed. But Edgar, who draws our attention to this graph, now, when we hear these words in *King Lear*, has not always drawn attention to proceedings in quite this imaginary way. When Edgar first said these words, at the premiere of *King Lear* in 1606 or 1607 (there is as with all masterpieces some disagreement as to their exact origins), at the first Court performance, no one in the audience would have conceived of a graph, nor brought to mind any such thing, as graphs as we now know them only came into use in the 1800s.[4] Whoever said these words, in their earliest rendition, an actor called Henry Condell *might* have played Edgar, though it could as easily have been an actor called John Lowin, graphs could not have been on their minds, but they could, at the nascent stage of capitalism, the beginnings of the capitalocene as we know it, already have been *in* their bodies.

So ubiquitous have graphs become that it is hard to imagine a world without them. And I would suggest here we cannot imagine our world without them because they are now part of 'our' world, and shape our world in the manner of a series of corporeal encounters with sheer drops, vertiginous planes, precarious points of insufficient rest, toppling over into the abyss of debt. But how did we start to move this way? How did graphs begin to describe life and death? Well, not only would Shakespeare have never known a graph, the Scientific Revolution of the European seventeenth century did without graphs too. It was only with the publication of the extraordinary statistical atlases of William Playfair, in the early nineteenth century, that the shaped overview of the graph would have been widely available. And, Playfair never referred to 'graphs' but to 'Atlases'. The word graph only came into being in 1878, enthusiastically picked up by the first cinematographer, Etienne-Jules Marey, who thought them the natural language of science that would one day replace everyday language itself.

If Shakespeare's plays are sometimes simplistically thought of as a form of 'universal language', I do not share this imperialistic view, then Marey certainly thought graphs to be the 'universal language' of the future. I *have* begun to accept Marey's view irrespective of its homogenising claim. As a pioneer of photography and widely considered a key figure in the foundation of cinema, he developed animated photography in the 1880s. His revolutionary idea was to record several phases of movement on one photographic surface, rather like Edgar's picturing of the samphire collector, working across the face of the cliff. In his laboratory Marey's 'birds and choughs that wing the midway air', would emerge against the white photographic papers in a tray of hot salt-water processors. His work was always close to the saline of the sea in this respect. Marey seems to think that these processes are more than just the mechanics of engineering images. They are, as I have been trying to suggest, rather inscriptions that affect us in a bodily way. This is how Marey put it in 1885 in his work *Methode Graphique*:

> Our senses, with perceptors that are too slow and confused, can no longer guide us but the graphical method substitutes for their insufficiency; in this chaos it reveals an unknown world. Inscription apparatus measure the infinitely small pieces of time; the most rapid and the most weak movements, the slightest variation of forces cannot escape them. They penetrate the intimate function of organs, where life seems to express itself by an incessant mobility.[5]

I am sure that something of the graph's stark, sheer, cliff-like quality has done more that entered our popular imaginary since the first decade of the twenty-first century, it has become the shape of our very being. Its contours are the collapse of the World Trade Tower and its fluttering paper trail, the collapse of Lehman Brothers, the collapse of the stock market, the collapse of the life aspirations of those young people in countries referred to condescendingly as the PIGS: Portugal, Italy, then Ireland, Greece and Spain. King Lear knew a thing or two about swine having lived amongst them after his storm-tossed nights on the heath. Cordelia weeps for him. Pity now those for whom the World Bank fails to weep.

Others might have expressed these feelings too, but frame them somewhat differently, with more *austerity* you might say. Tom Carper, US Senator from Delaware calls it like this:

> Without Congressional action, automatic tax increases and spending cuts will begin to go into effect. Both the suddenness and the extent of these changes to government policy relative to previous years have led some economists, business leaders, and politicians to associate this event with 'driving off a cliff'. While there may be disagreement as to whether the economy is headed toward a cliff or a slope, there is broad agreement that failing to adequately confront these challenges will weaken the economy, perhaps even leading to another recession.[6]

And yet others, perhaps better-looking others, treat that cliff with more abandon. Thelma and Louise in their plummeting 1966 Ford Thunderbird, Butch Cassidy and the Sundance Kid in their 'great escape'. There is a well-known story that the novelist Louis de Bernieres has recounted of a driver, riding their top of the range motorbike, off the edge of Dover cliff, shouting "Geronimo" as they went. This was the 'triumphant' cry of someone who took their own life in their hands. When Gloucester falls, however, his life is in his *son's* hands. Just feet from me in the stalls he lurches forward, across the bare stage, in a way that leads the influential Polish theatre critic Jan Kott into a rare and, I think, serious error of critical judgment. He describes this move, on the stage, as necessarily comic, pantomimic, when, in my experience it is always in its miniature, disappointing awfulness, the tragic fulcrum of the play that is thought to be Shakespeare's most tragic.[7] As an example of *meiosis*, a trick of relative scale, a reduction where an apparently small thing signifies a very much larger thing, this cliff becomes the place for a *graphic* encounter.

Immediately upon Gloucester's fall, his son, Edgar puts into strangely economic words, his feelings: 'And yet I know not how conceit may rob/The treasury of life when life itself/Yields to the theft [...]'[8] Here 'conceit' could mean imagination, or it could mean delusion. The slippage is telling. But what this speech draws upon is another rich economic imaginary that numbered the pages of the first Folio edition of *King Lear*, that graphically demonstrate in their own way how Gloucester's suicidal intentions at the verge of this cliff are very much more than a matter of comic mistiming. When Edgar describes the samphire collector's dreadful trade one's thoughts are drawn towards what trade? For whom is this samphire being picked, for what table and whose Early Modern digestion? To grace which dish one might ask? Jamie Oliver has made samphire one of the ingredients of his profitable cooking career prior to his later financial reversals, a staple in his signature Scottish Salmon Salad dish, but in Elizabethan times it would have been eaten with white-wine vinegar, coriander powder, ginger, cinnamon and mustard seed. And it would have been eaten by the well-to-do, indeed by an Earl like Gloucester, or a King like Lear, before they both lost the use of their un-fitted kitchens. Here the *commodity* of samphire as distinct to its natural, complex origins on that cliff, Karl Marx would later say, have had to deny its relations to those persons whose dreadful trade was to harvest it. It would at all costs, and it was a costly process, have had to efface its origin in *social* production. It has been widely recognized that when Edgar first spoke these lines in London it was not that the theatre was like a market, it was a market, where commodification and consumerism were rife. And Shakespeare himself has been acknowledged as operating during a momentous transition between feudal and capitalist modes of production and living.

Before his leap, that is not a leap, Gloucester disburses his wealth to a mad man who is in fact his son. He gives Poor Tom, who being mad is by definition without property nor identity, a precious token. He says to his son who he believes to be in need: '[…] Let go my hand./Here, friend's another purse; in it a jewel/Well worth a poor man's taking […]'[9] When he lurches forward I imagine, perhaps because I have vertigo, the awfulness of a sheer fall. But as he does not fall, I fall *for* him, and as I do so, I cross another line, that is the graph, that cuts across the cliff, Shakespeare's cliff that is. The graph reaches down to the beach, to the sea, where Edgar describes the chaffing of the 'unnumbered pebbles'. They are 'unnumbered' because they are beyond the imagination of mathematics, and beyond the diagramming of science of the time, and still, our time. But they are also unnumbered because they are an 'infinity of sandy species' locked in the embrace of a last and fatal intimacy.

My vertigo does not preclude me from standing on that beach. But here, amongst those extinguished species, looking up, having left the theatre for the flat-world, I realize I am not alone in my *acrophobia*, my fear of edges. Infants and all other animals, when presented with a visual cliff, real or simulated, are reluctant to move towards it. This is for a good reason, well known to Shakespeare, but not apparently those responsible for our mad world, our economic masters, who have left us to live there, while they scuttle below, as Edgar says, 'gros as beetles'. Creatures it would seem, do not thrive close to the edge. It is samphire that grows so well there and might be left in peace. Dreadful trade indeed.

Notes

1 This passage was first commissioned by the BBC Radio 4 Producer Sarah Blunt for a series on *The Cliff*, and I am grateful for her editing of that work for transmission. The essay as it was performed can be found here: www.bbc.co.uk/programmes/b051rnlg (accessed on 25.08.2019)

2 William Shakespeare, *King Lear*, Act 4, Scene 6 in Shakespeare, William (1997). *King Lear*. Ed. R. A. Foakes. London: Thomson and can be accessed here: http://shakespeare.mit.edu/lear/lear.4.6.html
3 Ibid: http://shakespeare.mit.edu/lear/lear.4.6.html (accessed 19/08/2019)
4 I am grateful to Clare McManus whose writing on economy in *King Lear* influenced me, and to Lucy Munro who alerted me to this subtlety which was way beyond me. I am indebted to the Early Modernists at King's College London who have tolerated my resistance to Shakespeare for years and especially Ann Thompson who first invited me to apply for the Chair in Theatre at King's in 2006.
5 Etienne-Jules Marey, *De La Methode Graphique* accessed here: www.larevuedupraticien.fr/histoire-de-la-medecine/etienne-jules-marey-de-la-methode-graphique-au-cinematographe (accessed: 25.08.2019)
6 Tom Carper, Senator for Delaware, the economy on a cliff edge: www.carper.senate.gov/public/index.cfm/economy-and-jobs
7 Kott, Jan (1964). *Shakespeare Our Contemporary*. London: Methuen.
8 *King Lear*, op. cit.
9 *King Lear*, op. cit.

PART II
Living currency
Scenes from the last human venue

In the summer of 2008, three months before the collapse of Lehman Brothers Bank heralded what some had foreseen but few 'financiers' wanted to acknowledge, the sub-prime fiasco in the US property market was about to sweep outwards from its relatively contained real-estate berth and inundate all those 'rats and mice' that the doer-upper Candy Brothers had so endearingly referred to in the High Court during their bankruptcy battle with Mark Holyoake, tracked in the first chapter of this book. From that vantage point a decade ago the 'theatre' of the financial crash was, or perhaps should have been, self-evident to those looking on. It was hiding in plain sight in a century-spanning dramatic repertoire that, since Balzac's theatrical sketches of insolvency in *La Faillite* in the 1830s, and Ibsen's study of property loss in *An Enemy of the People* of 1882, had long forecast the dynamics if not the detail of what was about to happen on Wall Street. *The Game* by Harold Brighouse (1914) and *Serious Money* by Caryl Churchill (1987), both preceded the banking meltdown with their own form of predictive text.[1] In the case of the latter of course, the City brokers in braces took the riotous musical irony of the work to be a paean to the joys of their dynamic trade and flocked to Sloane Square and the Royal Court for more than just the high-end shopping.

The 'crisis' of that year was swiftly followed by *Money* (2009) from the novel by Émile Zola, conceived and staged by SHUNT in a disused tobacco warehouse in Bermondsey (since the eviction of our own theatre just half a mile away in 1991 the area had been rapidly repurposed as a zone of arts-led gentrification). Here was a company that understood that the facile adoption of the descriptor 'immersive' to characterise any performance that appeared to resist the immediate attraction of selling seats to sitting audiences in serried rows for reasonable prices, really was falling short of the potential to shake things up a bit for those who paid to participate. And how SHUNT shook things up in their inspired incubator to the forces of liquidation. I recall coming out of that miraculous, noir-fairground apparatus, shaken and stirred to the immediate aftermath of what had, until warily stepping into their gargantuan theatrical contraption, appeared a somewhat distant threat of somebody else's monetised meltdown. It was now mine, all mine. In a more formal and very different concrete staged-environment, *The Lehman Trilogy* by Stefano Massini (2018), 10 years later, with its starry cast flattered to deceive at the National Theatre promising to return punters to where they expected to be, in the stalls looking on at other's dilemmas, perusing NT programmes that even for work that brilliantly illuminated the savagery of austerity, such as *Faith Hope and Charity* by Alexander Zeldin, carried prominent advertisements for the wealth fund managers that such audiences would no doubt need to diversify their at-risk Brexit stocks.

Wall Street crash

In the late days of editing this book, but 'just in time' as the supply-line entrepreneurs would have it, London has been threatened through the summer of 2019 by the promise that 'money bags are on their way' for an 'immersive spectacle' at £70 a shot, after Jordan Belfort's bull-market memoir *The Wolf of Wall Street*.[2] By the time I get to enter the repurposed city building at 5–15 Sun Street, hard on the back of Liverpool Street Station, on a rainy Sunday evening for the 6.00pm show, repeated announcements of delays and cancellations have been made on social media 'apologising to audiences and ticket-holders' regarding the challenges the producers' have faced in commissioning the site, water damage and cast sickness, and most predictably the way the running of the show has been affected by 'aggressive behaviour from some heavily intoxicated patrons, all of whom were removed from the building, with the safety of our cast, staff and audience members in mind'.[3] Given *The Wolf of Wall Street*, and Jordan' Belfort's own erratic saga within that sorry narrative can only be described as the epitome of 'aggressive and intoxicated', it occurs to me on listening to the moralising warning made to the assembled audience at the outset of this show that there will be a 'zero policy towards such conduct for the duration of the evening', that the much hyped immersive quality of the event is about to suffer its first serious bifurcation. And indeed it does, from the floor of the sparsely furnished 'trading floor' of Stratton Oakmont Inc. in the basement of the retooled building, the thin crowd of about 50 or so newby 'Strattonites' who have dutifully paid the now reduced admission charge of £58 (+£1.95 fee), are at something of a loss as how to respond to the cast's cajoling to enter into the bull-market 'craziness' before them. They look more sober than the punters one might come across most nights in the nearby, upscale, Barbican Theatre bars, and that does not auger well for anything other than the most alluring of all possible spectacles. Unforgiving appears to be the dress code here. Some seem to have clicked on the web booking page offer of a bottle of Champagne for £49, so I am presuming as those fallen ones pre-load in the bar that that kind of rarefied intoxication is to be tolerated throughout, in the generous interval break when the bars reopen, and indeed at the miserable, dramatically botched end of the show when the newly fired traders (us) are invited to drown our sorrow for being so bad at what we never asked to be.

Throughout the evening we have been warned that our, that is the audience's, behaviour is being monitored by four security cameras in each room and that we have an extra 'duty of care' given there is a six-year-old girl in the cast whose safety and well-being is 'everybody's responsibility'. I cannot help thinking this is a curious form of deferred parenting, they were the ones who presumably invited her into this hell. The as-yet unseen girl is evoked again by one of the bar tenders in the interval who tells me (when recovering from the surprise that my only order is a tonic water without ice) that this very Sunday evening a couple have been ejected from the premises at 5.45 pm for having sex in one of the makeshift cubicles before the show had 'even started'. It *is* Sunday we agree. His concern is again for the girl who he says, 'could have heard everything if she had been nearby'. Apparently, the sated couple left the premises at 5.55 pm complaining that they had 'lost £140.00 on the evening' which suggests they had booked before the flood and plague and the steep drop in ticket prices, and rather cheaply had not opted for the Champagne offer. No class. I am beginning to wonder what happened to that earlier generation of city boys that Caryl Churchill nailed so decisively in her decidedly non-immersive show, *Serious Money*? Things were clearly not what they used to be at the time of their Big-Bang.

We have after all (in the room I was in at least) been treated to a late show attempt to rescue some theatrical pulse which has been missing in the foregoing 3 hours, that takes, for me, the queasy retro-fitted form of a memorable scene from Thomas Ostermeier's celebrated production of *Richard III* that had been touring Europe for some years to rather more acclaim than this not wholly disconnected narrative of betrayal, conceit and deceit. When the much touted 'young girl' finally arrives in the midst of this tawdry, orgy-like scene to confront (I think) her father, and to witness the slurry of Wall Street at work, the degraded deployment of a minor in this theatrical car-crash is as close to dramatic abuse as one could imagine. The presence of the girl is obviously solely to deliver some kind of innocent *deux ex machina* to 'adult proceedings' that otherwise, without dramatic or narrative pulse of any discernible kind, simply might be expected in the absence of her arrival to go on and on, given there apparently is 'no alternative' to immersive theatre of this kind, like capitalism itself.

The dramatic intent of the work, if ever there was any intention to have such a theatrical thing, has gone missing hours before with a series of meandering scenes up and down endless flights of stairs (apparently directed by the long-suffering but presumably well-remunerated Alexander Wright) taking place in the upper rooms of the building to absolutely no cumulative effect whatsoever. These involved a series of spin-off issues to do with financialisation, accounting and business protocols that you would have to be a wannabee government accountant to have any interest in. At one low point, despite hiding in what I thought was a dark corner, I am shoved a ledger by Jordan Belfort's accountant father (I think) and asked to read out-loud those entries that look suspicious. I read out the $2,056 spent on a trampette, and the three bills at the Ivy restaurant of ($210, $128 and $67 respectively), on the grounds that trampolines are so passé and no decent meal could be had at the Ivy for such preposterously low amounts. Mr Belfort (I think) shouts at me: 'NO, fuckin' stupid Strattonite! Look at those initials, they are obviously sex workers, that's where the money's gone!' If the initials had read SW then I might have clocked this obvious fraud, but they don't so I don't, and from then on I am not invited to participate again while others, deservedly given their noble efforts at subservience, flourish in this spotlight. I feel like that bit in Tom Wolfe's truly epic take-down of these precise 'master of the universe' delusions, *The Bonfire of the Vanities*, where a star turns abruptly from ascent to descent.

These interminable scenes take place around tables with, in one case, half an hour spent being harangued by an FBI officer (I think) grooming us to expose the wrong-doing of the Belfort brand (I think). But each of these scenes might as well have been played on a raised stage with lush red curtains where we could see and hear them as to all intents and purposes there is about as much 'immersion' going on here as at the premiere of Chekhov's *The Cherry Orchard* at the Moscow Art Theatre on 17 January 1904. Indeed it is all too obviously apparent given the strict protocols of behaviours and necessary distance established at the outset of the show that the only 'immersion' at work here is the immersive, drowning feeling of being £70, 'early bird' rate (*sic*), or £59 further in debt by the end of the evening, if you resist the copious offers of alcohol along the way and were fortunate enough to come without travel costs. It is unlikely anyone in this room is wealthy enough to live nearby given the escalation of real-estate costs since the arrival of immersive cultural events of this kind started drawing attention to the shabby chic of the urban realm, around the time our warehouse theatre was being closed down in Docklands by these very speculators and bankers in 1991. I am not sure I was their ideal audience member.

Well before the ever receding 'end' of the show my mind has turned to Jordan Belfort's famous *cri de coeur* that his one great regret about ever being 'the wolf' of Wall Street was the losses that he inflicted on those 'rats and mice' investors that trusted in his dodgy financial offer. It is to them he says that a generous proportion of future proceeds will go that are generated by the post-jail-term literary and cinematic afterlife career of his 'Wolf'. Although I am told, by the same barman recovering from my abstemiousness, that Belfort has had to 'sign off' on the script, which begs the question what kind of script he would *not* have signed off on, there does not appear to be anywhere, in any and all of the avalanche of literature and web-site pages dedicated to this 'major event', any mention, not one, of that very heartfelt *cri de coeur*, that those who have lost everything in the fine cause of financial freedom (to lose everything) will latterly be compensated. I suppose we have all been warned that investments can go down as well as up. Very down is how I suspect the Angels are feeling about this charade. Given the righteous homilies regarding our behaviours that these producers press upon us in a moralising spirit that would have turned Nietzsche's stomach, it surely cannot be the case that this event, planned to run for many months and perhaps aspire to the 'immersive' record run of the producer's other show in town, *The Great Gatsby*, which is just about to transfer to spanking 'old' premises in Mayfair after three years of excess, that there is nothing, no contribution being made to those losers who are after all the offstage victims of this dramatic debacle. Notwithstanding the horror-show of problems catalogued by the company in their frequently tweeted apologia to discontented customers, one might be forgiven for thinking that this production marks the moment when not just good old Capitalism, but new improved 'Immersive Capitalism' eats itself, destroys itself, as Marx himself forecast the first time round before this farce. Drowned out you could say. I have to admit going to see the show on that Sunday evening was prompted by the selfish fear that *The Wolf* would be pulled off to save further losses before I had had a chance to see it, to experience it and if not immerse myself in it, then to look on in abject misery for the state of the financial art in order to make critical capital from it.[4] That was their point surely, to profit at all costs from other peoples' distress in their moment of loss.

This financialised aesthetic realm is vast and well worth immersing oneself in for clues as to the conduct of the capitalocene, stretching way before and beyond this wimpish *Wolf Of Wall Street*. Indeed this form of 'cultural cruelty' inflicted on paying customers would appear to mimic in uncanny measure an amplified version of the financial embarrassments already suffered in the 'real world' it purports to represent. But however much sport it offers it is decidedly not my focus in the following second part of this book, given it has already been widely written about in post-crash lamentations of late-capitalism, jeremiahs to the injustice of debt (to which a book called *The Dark Theatre* is self-evidently a footnote).[5] What is more this litany of theatrical representations *of* economy (such as *The Wolf*) does not, with the noble bone-shaking exception of SHUNT Theatre's *Money* noted above, begin to engage with what I seek here, what Daniel Heller-Roazen might call the 'inner touch' of the bankrupted, the 'dance of the derivative' as Randy Martin talked about the financialisation of everyday life.

Rather than settle for the easy affective hit offered by the immersive trend then, I will explore here in Part II of *The Dark Theatre* the more elusive but perhaps sustainable sense of a 'living currency' that performance registers. A living currency that performances of all kinds (with the possible exception of immersive work given what I have just witnessed) recounts and resists from what has become the dead-serious show-business of our precarious lives. Now that storm of unaccountable feelings would surely be the whole *raison d'être* of making a serious attempt at a form for which one might claim the grandiose title 'immersive theatre'? But as I suggest above with sly evocation of the always already immersive nature of the canonical *theatrical* repertoire, one-trick-pony performance has long been superseded by an innate and sophisticated sense of circulating lives that is the living currency of the dramatic domain.

Should one wish to subscribe to the idea that all theatre is political (as I once did in a book called *Theatre, Intimacy & Engagement* by arguing strenuously the counter-intuitive corollary that none of it is), then, furthermore I would suggest here all performance self-evidently has *economy* at the heart of its circulatory systems. The philosopher Michael Marder recognises this task as pre-eminently important in our current, precarious moment: 'to tackle one of the root causes of today's political predicament, it is imperative to draw new lines separating economics from politics [...]'.[6] So in this part of *The Dark Theatre* it is the inner *economic* touch of the work that I am after in a sequence of reflections on disturbed states of attention in the theatre:

1   In another version of 'vertigo'
2   In the act of 'abandonment'
3   In the state of the 'amnesiac'
4   And in the condition of the 'irreparable'.

It is these contingent conditions that might account for the 'state of insecurity' I have been describing in dramatic action, precisely the kind of 'dramatic action' that is wholly missing from *The Wolf of Wall Street*, but readily appearing elsewhere as I will demonstrate without nearly so much fanfare and far cheaper entrance costs. As Isabell Lorrey puts it: 'If we fail to understand precarisation, then we understand neither the politics nor the economy of the present'.[7] In this sense I am adopting Lorrey's term and tracking the affective charge of something called *precarious performance* through Part II of this book. The 'living currency' I was seeking in that dread-full Shakespearian scene from *King Lear* in that interlude just passed, happens to take the temporary form of a human samphire-collector, harvesting their precarious livelihood from a cliff-face. But from that relatively simple Shakespearian observation the living currency I am after here will now take various forms of 'accounting for the real' that each theatrical scene from the last human venue seeks. Encouraged by Milo Rau's 'Ghent Manifesto' the work I will be exploring in the coming chapters is perhaps less about depicting 'the real of loss' as its capacity to make the 'representation of loss itself real'.[8]

Living currency

The provocative idea of a 'living currency' is one drawn from the artist and philosopher Pierre Klossowski, somehow better known for being the brother of his more famous painter-brother Balthus than the leading interpreter of Nietzsche of his era. But in his own time, prior to his turn to the visual arts and drawing after 1972, a period he later referred to his 'mutism', Klossowski was recognised by a boy's club of philosophers including Michel Foucault, Gilles Deleuze, Jean-François Lyotard and Maurice Blanchot for having found the discrete relation between Freudian libidinal economy, and Marxist political economy in his 1970 text *La monnaie vivante*.[9] This dry-dream hope for the philosophical fusion of the two grounding epistemes of European modernity was somewhat misplaced given that Klossowski was always already writing between two quite different pillars of alternative influence, Friedrich Nietzsche (as evidenced in his seminal collection of essays, *Nietzsche and the Vicious Circle*) and the acrobatic erotic exertions of the Marquise de Sade. Given the challenges *Living Currency* poses (not least of all in translation) it would be as well to articulate some of its key features here before launching into the scenes from a post-crash decade of performance that offer twinklings of its treasury for theatre thinking.

The title of *Living Currency* was in fact drawn from the final short passage of an elliptical essay of that name, barely 30 pages long written in 1970, in which Klossowski imagines a kind of 'classical utopia', in fact a counter-utopia that the author makes clear already exists in contemporary capitalism, and one that I suggest has not changed since its first identification by Klossowski just before the OPEC oil embargo of 1974. This is how Daniel W. Smith, one of the translators of the work, and largely responsible for making Klossowski accessible to an English-speaking audience, summarises what might at first sight appear something of an outlandish proposition, but in fact, on closer scrutiny, could be considered an apt descriptor of theatre business-as-usual in an immersive spectacle with a name not unlike *The Wolf of Wall Street* where one finds oneself subjugated to the role of a dealer for Stratton Oakmont:

> Klossowski imagines a phase in industrial production where producers are able to demand 'objects of sensation' from consumers as a form of payment. These objects would be living beings. Human beings, in other words, would be traded as currency: employers would pay their male workers 'in women', female workers would be paid 'in boys', and so on. This is neither prostitution nor slavery, where humans are bought and sold using monetary currency. Rather it is *humans themselves* that are used as currency, a living currency, and they can function as currency because they are sources of sensation, emotion and pleasure. [my emphasis.][10]

Pierre Klossowski's conception of a living currency was never intended as a descriptor of theatrical practice, but was really an exploration of a long-running philosophical speculation that the monetary economy providing the trading medium for modern industry, is always and everywhere merely a simulacrum, or as Klossowski nicely puts it, a *parody* of the economy of the human passions. It is in this sense neither debt nor barter that secures that financial economy but the existence of humans themselves, whose very being, not just their labour as figured in Marx, is the rationale of any economy for which the gold-standard has become merely one of numerous historic substitutes for 'ourselves', that is our own bodies.

In theatrical terms, to make this dense idea more accessible, one might resist thinking of the 'cost' of performance solely in terms of an exchange in which money is passed over for a ticket that buys time with an actor or actors, (though star-vehicle shows might invite us to think otherwise) but rather a contribution to the balance of expenses that accrue to all the *extra-human* aspects of the event, that is, venue, light, warmth, technical support, marketing. The 'cost' of the actor or actors in an economy in which living currency was recognised would be quite distinct from such infrastructure and would be payable through one's *own* presence as audience member. You could call such participation a form of 'balance of trade' or 'balance of payment'. One's corporeal and affective presence to the spectacle, one's body, one's feelings and one's memories (in Klossowski's terms) would be made available to the actors in a reciprocal exchange of spectation with its attendant affects of appreciation and dismay. This is not so much to return to Rancière's 'emancipated spectator', but rather the isolated figure in company often called an audience, finding themselves through their relation with the traffic of the stage in debt to those performing others. I am not of course here talking merely about the excrescence of 'immersive theatre' such as *The Wolf of Wall Street* in which one is cajoled into participation with one's own 'self' at stake, though this parasitic form has played fast and loose with precisely this model of living currency without really admitting it. But I am talking about *any* form of performance in which the presence of one human is validated in their expressions by the presence of another making felt-sense of them.[11] A version of such exchanges was later called 'libidinal economy' by Jean-François Lyotard, and while there has been precious little theatrical commentary on that work's potential for thinking about relations between performers and spectators through theatre practice, its obvious predecessor, *Living Currency*, has had precisely no attention whatsoever. The following pages will make a start at just such a recovery.

There is not sufficient leg room here to delve too deeply into the complex background and context of Pierre Klossowski's canonical work on these polymorphous passions of corporeal human exchange, but a small anecdote might set the scene for what is about to come by way of explanation. As Pierre Klossowski was the author of the notorious *Sade My Neighbour* (1947) we felt it sufficient when we invited him to the Institute of Contemporary Arts in London in the Spring of 1997, when he was still a spritely force in his early 90s (and fully five years before his death just before 9/11), to work on a public event under the agreed title: *Philosophy in the Bedroom*.[12] In this project, as Deleuze recognised, Klossowski was introducing the category of 'production' into that of 'desire' while simultaneously and inversely attending to the nature of desire in our infrastructural social arrangements. Indeed anyone who has encountered the first pages of Deleuze and Guattari's ground-breaking work *Anti-Oedipus* will have effectively read Klossowski on these passionate matters given the influence his writings had on these seminal (*sic*) pages of French philosophical enquiry.[13] According to Daniel Smith, Pierre Klossowski's principle themes with regard to these abstract 'passions' can be characterised in four, marginally less abstract sub-sets of critical analysis as: impulses, simulacra, phantasms and stereotypes.[14] In brief these states can therefore be identified theoretically before we return to them in practice, threading as they do through the theatrical work of Romeo Castellucci over the last decade that I am about to explore through the lens of Klossowski's unusual 'method'. They offer a vocabulary for expressing the affective charge of performance that beyond Lyotard's quite well-known 1970s work on the *Libidinal Economy* have had nothing like the influence on performance study one might have expected in such an affect-friendly environment.

The first of the four categories, *phantasms*, for Klossowski, derives from the Greek 'phantasia', as in appearances and imagination, or, as Daniel Smith puts it, 'an obsessional image' that is produced in us by impulsive life, amongst which *love* and its serial returns would be the most obvious example.[15] Unlike other philosophers for whom phantasmic states are those liminal conditions *beyond* which one seeks for coherent expression in various versions of rationality, for Klossowski there *is* no recourse beyond phantasms and the impulses that bear them. One is left, in and outside the theatre, with the eternally vicious-circle of attempting to represent these phantasms in some form of simulacra, but that is as good as it gets and it is often, for anyone who has experienced being in and out of love, not nearly good enough. In the following theatrical examples 'phantasms' in all their evanescence will be readily identifiable, for ineffable as they are in theory, in the practices of Romeo Castellucci's staged performances they are always everywhere present. The continuous condition of such inadequate expression would anyway be another way of describing what we already experienced earlier in this book where Kierkegaard's anti-hero Constantius endures in his attempt to express the repetition that he eternally seeks but cannot secure in the theatre.

An understanding of Klossowski's second category of the sensation of *impulses* derives from his extensive readings in theology and amongst the Christian mystics where 'impulsive forces' are not about the will of the subject, but the constant disintegration of the 'self' in what Klossowski figures as the 'depth of the soul'.[16] This 'soul', again as with phantasms, is teasingly incommunicable, and while productive of forms that are consequent upon simulacra and recognisable in such echoes, their soul will itself always remain unformed. Representation, understandably given how sceptical performance studies has always been of it, operates by way of *betrayal* of its object for Klossowski, a condition that will become apparent in the following theatrical analysis in which a human female body, at the limit of her life, is asked to stand in for all those who are in their own different way 'irreparable', beyond the virtuosity of medical care. This physiognomy is precisely what engaged Klossowski in his later work, following Nietzsche (and obviously the Marquis de Sade) whose corporeal emphasis over the 'mental state of philosophers', intended to cut through the superstitions attached to the psychological sphere, in preference for the immediacy of the body's works and impairments. In the case of the irreparable body whose bedside we will be invited to attend later, the passions at work are ones that fulfil the true identity of the passionate act (from the Latin *pati*, to suffer or endure) which is *done* to someone, rather than the consequence of their own doing.[17] I think it is in this sense that Joe Kelleher talks about the 'suffering of images' in his book *The Illuminated Theatre* though Klossowski, perhaps mercifully, does not make an appearance there.[18]

Klossowski's conceptions of *simulacra*, the transcription through some form of representation of phantasms, and *stereotype*, the presupposition of a set of prior forms, can be considered together as they are interdependent. Klossowski conceives of the stereotype as a form of fatigued, or redundant simulacrum, the washed-up image-version of an abandoned practice, what Hito Steyerl would call 'the wretched of the screen'.[19] In this botched relation between simulacra and stereotype Klossowski articulates the peculiar contradiction of all theatre, especially the kind of theatre that does not know any better when seeking to identify that which is strangely efficacious about the failure of such stereotypical characterisations. I have annotated Klossowski's words here with my own intentions to make clear what otherwise might seem rather far-fetched:

> Practised advisedly, [by Romeo Castellucci for instance] the institutional stereotypes of syntax [with theatrical names like *The Divine Comedy, Go Down, Moses* and *Orpheus and Eurydice* in the coming chapter] provoke the presence of what they circumscribe, their circumlocutions conceal the incongruity of the phantasm but at the same time trace the outline of its opaque physiognomy.[20]

Thus all such traces, such physiognomies, sometimes given the name 'drama', 'play' or 'performance', have their own style that will always, for Klossowski, and the theatre makers I am most attracted to, betray the phantasms and impulses that gave rise to them.

The index of my pleasure in the following three performance works by Romeo Castelluci, over a decade since just before that financial crash of 2008, is the degree to which this coefficient of disappointment is laid bare as the theatrical experience of living currency. Here we are invited to invest in that currency not just through our ticket price as I have said but with our present affections. And it is that contract that inscribes an unusual measure of accounting for taste. In each of the following productions what is notable is the degree to which theatrical endeavours involving phantasms, simulacra, impulses and stereotypes, apparently immaterial phenomena after all, are engineered through the stone, wood, concrete and resin of the stage architecture in three different venues, to account for and press upon the fleshy, actorly, precarious lives that are exposed through performance as having been subject to bio-political governmentality. There is no promise nor hint of any offer of 'immersion' in any of these proceedings, and that is very much for the better of all concerned. Immunity from the scene is as necessary an affect here as any placebo of community. In the theatre, and it is the *theatre* as we might have expected it and foreseen, such lives are rendered by Romeo Castellucci as a child-abusing sovereign of a suburban 'home', a mother grieving her lost baby to the poker-face of 'social services', and a stricken bed-bound figure of bare life beyond repair. Here the theatre itself becomes a waiting room, or a corridor of such spaces through historical time, between such State governance and personal passions, where accounting for such bodies in jeopardy, a stock taking of insecurity, is all that fills the necessary duration. There is no need for a faux-retro-fitted *Wolf of Wall Street* 'bar' here to sell us drinks while we wait. There is quite enough to be thinking about in the meantime. Isabell Lorrey articulates just why that theatrical waiting room might be making a play to become the last human venue:

> The assumption that life, because it is precarious and endangered, because it is exposed to an existential vulnerability, must be or even could be legally or

otherwise entirely protected and secured, is nothing other than a fantasy of omnipotence. Although they need protection living bodies can never be completely protected, specifically because they are permanently exposed to social and political conditions, under which life remain precarious. The conditions that enable life are, at the same time, exactly those that maintain it as precarious. All security retains the precarious; all protection and all care maintain vulnerability; nothing guarantees invulnerability.[21]

Theatre is just another economically expedient exposure machine in this respect and as such, for its normative accounts of such lives as much as its exceptional means of rendering those lives theatrically present (as we are about to see), demands scrupulous attention to its special apparatus of revelation amongst multifarious competing traders in corrupted, contemporary forms of carceral currency: pimps, theatrical impresarios, immersive producers, gang-masters and slave traffickers.

Notes

1. www.theguardian.com/stage/2010/aug/22/harold-brighouse-football-play-revived (accessed on 25 August 2019).
2. Belfort, Jordan. (2017). *The Wolf of Wall Street*. New York: Bantam and for extensive details about the immersive London production of 2019 see: https://immersivewolf.com/about (accessed on 12 October 2019).
3. See *Twitter* Thread, 3/6: 13.30, 10 October 2019 The Wolf of Wall Street, @ImmersiveWolf (accessed on 12 October 2019).
4. In this sense I am a collateral debtor to those defrauded ones too, though I think Routledge would be surprised to find that debt recognised in the contractual arrangements for this book.
5. See Watkinson, Philip. (2018). 'Staging Money: Theatre and Immateriality following the 2008 Financial Crisis'. *Theatre Journal*, 70 (2018), pp. 195–208, for an engaging essay on this legacy.
6. Marder, Michael. (2019). *Political Categories: Thinking Beyond Concepts*. New York: Columbia University Press, p. x.
7. Lorrey, Isabell. (2015). *State of Insecurity*. Trans. Aileen Derieg. London: Verso, p. 1.
8. See Rau, Milo. 'Ghent Manifesto', One: 'It's not just about portraying the world anymore. It's about changing it. The aim is not to depict the real, but to make the representation itself real'. www.ntgent.be/en/manifest (accessed on 12 October 2019).
9. See *La monnaie vivante* (1970), Paris: Losfield, and the excellent translation with notes I have relied upon here: Klossowski, Pierre. (2017). *Living Currency*. Ed. Vernon W. Cisney, Nicolae Morar and Daniel W. Smith, with a helpful introduction from Daniel Smith and translated by the editors.
10. Smith, Daniel W. 'Introduction' in Klossowski, ibid. p. 1.
11. See Alston, Adam. (2019). 'Safety, Risk and Speculation in the Immersive Industry', *Contemporary Theatre Review*, Creative Commons, 29.3 for one of the very few commentators on immersive theatre who know what they are talking about and available in its entirety here: www.contemporarytheatrereview.org/2019/safety-risk-and-speculation-in-the-immersive-industry/ (accessed on 25 August 2019).
12. I am grateful to Helena Reckitt who worked alongside me at the ICA between 1994 and 1997 curating more than 500 talks of this kind. Having succumbed to a contaminated batch of Polio vaccine following the booster taken to accompany the immunisation of my first child, this was the only event in four years at the Institute of Contemporary Arts that I had to cancel due to sickness. The *Evening Standard* ran a diary entry on the irony

that having set up the promise of a public gathering that celebrated polymorphously perverse philosophy in the bedroom, the curator of the event was too fatigued to see it through to a 'satisfactory climax'. 'Buck up, back to work'. I am grateful now as I was then to Sonu Shamdasani and Alphonso Lingis whose encouragement to collaborate with the elder and near-forgotten Pierre Klossowski, almost delivered such a remarkable occasion.
13 Deleuze, Gilles and Guattari, Félix. (2009). *Anti-Oedipus: Capitalism and Schizophrenia*. Trans. Robert Hurley. London: Penguin, the first two chapters of which clearly mark the influence of Klossowski.
14 Klossowski, Daniel Smith, op. cit. p. 4.
15 Ibid. p. 7.
16 Ibid. p. 4.
17 Ibid. p. 5.
18 Kelleher, Joe. (2015). *The Illuminated Theatre*. Abingdon: Routledge.
19 Steyerl, Hito. (2012). 'In Defense of the Poor Image' in *The Wretched of the Screen* London: Sternberg Press.
20 Pierre Klossowski quoted by Daniel Smith in op cit, p. 9.
21 Lorrey, Isabell. (2015). *State of Insecurity*. Trans. Aileen Derieg, London: Verso, p. 20. For an empathetic and incisive discussion of care and performance via Alphonso Lingis see: Groves, Rebecca. (2017). 'On Performance and the Dramaturgy of Caring', in *Inter Views in Performance Philosophy* Eds. Anna Street, Julien Alliot and Magnolia Pauker. Houndmills: Palgrave, pp. 309–318.

4

IRREPARABLE STATE

Compensations of performance

'Je m'appelle Romeo Castellucci'. *My name is Romeo Castellucci* introduces the *Inferno*, from Dante's *The Divine Comedy* in Avignon, in those innocent pre-crash days of summer 2008, and plunges this audience in the vast, stone-layered Cour d'Honneur of the Palais des Papes into a vertiginous aesthetic adventure.[1] The man who has entered centre stage rear and walked to the apex of the playing space dons a padded suit and tenses himself. Downstage, seven Alsatian dogs from Les Cavaliers Voltigeurs de France are led on howling, by their handlers, and chained close to the customers, while Balkan, Bonzai and Robin are unleashed to set about the Director of Socìetas Raffaello Sanzio (SRS). Self-scapegoating on behalf of us, the spectators, the director on this earth, as he once referred to himself and other terrestrials in the same image-render-trade, would appear to be guilty of something, but heaven knows what.

The faux theatricality of the scene, the dogs are manifestly trained to within an inch of their canine senses and are possibly the best-paid living organisms we will see in the next 24 hours, mixes humility with the grand gesture. Humility in the announcement: 'Je m'appelle Romeo Castellucci', a fact not doubted by a well-informed, festival-going, theatre-expert public in Avignon who in annual succession have witnessed his direction of *Giulio Cesare* (1998), *Journey to the End of the Night* (1999), *Genesi* (2000), *Tragedia Endogonidia Episode A2* (2002), *Tragedia B3 Berlin* and *Tragedia BR4 Brussels* (2005) and *Hey Girl!* (2007).[2] The definition of a grand gesture might as well be this centre stage introduction in Jean de Louvres' 1352 *Cour d'Honneur* with the founding text of Italian culture in the founding seat of Papal peripateticism.

Between this miniature announcement and this inconceivable architectural magnitude another man emerges to take the skin of the director (an animal pelt passed on like so many other identities in this quixotic show). As unassuming as the earth-bound director, this figure begins to scale the windowed, sheer-face wall of the Palais des Papes. Without apparent effort and little ceremony (a quality shared by Romeo Castellucci's work over more than a quarter of a century) this climber, who I guess from the programme to *Inferno* is Jeff Stein, works his way at an acute angle diagonally traversing the seams in the fourteenth-century masonry. Given what I have said about such elevations elsewhere, I watch this scene warily through splayed fingers.

Obviously secure destinations such as window sills and the ornamental rose are passed without a second thought for us who from our seats offer concern, who will project care through the night towards the diminishing figure, but who accept the inevitable. On the way he swaggers in a manner that suggests Romeo Castellucci has bartered a strict allowance of showmanship in return for the climber tempering his excessive ease with this phenomenally daring act. It is not that this director on earth would ever remind this sure-footed ascendant above the earth that to be able to fall is a prerequisite for our theatrical affections; rather, it is so that his rate and manner of ascent might more literally play with our expectation of what it means to scale the largest domestic architectural structure we are ever likely to inhabit.

On the acutely angled porcelain roof, 150 feet above us, unhooked from his safety wire (this is theatre, it is not about the suspension of disbelief in unlikely lines but the suspending of our belief on a line) the climber holds a bright orange standard-issue basketball above his head and calls to a boy in spectacles way below who has wandered onto the stage.[3] We are still recovering our stomachs from a reverse vertigo that, as the climber has climbed unfeasibly high towards the night sky, pitches us, the audience, somehow upwards to the building itself which in homeopathic symmetry comes falling down to meet us halfway. There has been some talk of theatrical affects but the direction of this particular manoeuvre, in this infernal place on earth, introduces us to the deepest, most interior sense of being fixed to our seats while being propelled from them.

The ball, meanwhile, familiar from Castellucci's earlier work *Tragedia Endogonidia R07 Rome*, in which a group of seminarians play a miraculous game of hoops, is lobbed towards the earth and, following a line of flight that can be counted in 1,000 heads, one, two, three, four, terminates with an authentic-sounding thud and bounces to the second-storey window, to the first-storey lintel and, this being a well-directed ball, on a third bounce into the hands of Jean. We know the boy in spectacles is Jean because, like other entrants to this *Inferno* who have introduced themselves, Jean has helpfully graffitied his name on the wall facing us (the one the climber has just climbed). This is the last time we hear the authentic bounce of the ball, because from this bounce on, each time Jean propels the ball to the stage, the stage and the ball unleash an amplified version of what a bouncing ball in this place (now not Earth but palpably some unearthly place) must sound like. This in turn unleashes a terrifying spectral presence in the building itself as though to remind us there will be no shelter there. Gregor Schneider would approve. That this is more *Exorcist* than naturalist introduces us to the first of many cinematic directions essential to this director's work.

By this time, perhaps 20 minutes into Romeo Castellucci's trilogy from Dante's *The Divine Comedy*, we have been introduced to the director, the Papal edifice and the *Inferno*.[4] There is little summative imperative, as this bare description attests, but rather a sequence of realised spectacles, gestures and sounds that begin to hint at a job description for a director on this earth. The director's role would apparently be to remind us in hell that before we reach the inevitable stars (étoiles) of Dante's final stanzas, stars that in this version sit high above us on television monitors that crash to earth with their flickering linguistic sign of the heavens blacked out, that before that fall *we* have some accounting to do for our human life on this earth, the living currency circulating right here amongst us.

Phantasms: *Purgatorio* and *Paradiso*

A short bus ride to the outskirts of Avignon from where *The Divine Comedy* started I am in Purgatory, for the second part of the promised trilogy, where we are decidedly 'at home'. Or at least what the director Romeo Castellucci has decided 'home' might stand for. You know you are in Purgatory because there is a sign outside that says *Purgatorio*. The inferno is now outside, 40 degrees in the shade as you wait with 600 hot souls to enter the Parc des Expositions in Chateaublanc on the outskirts of Avignon. We are now apart from the historical traces of the city, beyond the city limits of the night before and the archaeology of vertical differences that site contains. Here it is all similar, not similar to anything, just similar. There is another Salle next door, and another and another. Horizontal existence. The serial waiting room for whatever is to follow. For all you know in this heat this is an endless suburb of exposition and exposure, playing an infinite loop of human abuse night after night. It is the perfect setting for the repetitions and uncanny similarities of naturalism with its violences in the world we think we know, the quiet betrayals of the really-real.

As you enter *Purgatorio* from the inferno outside you first notice, on your skin and then in your head, that it is cool. It must be air-conditioned in here. The first and perhaps only prerequisite for Purgatory is that it should maintain conditions appropriate to its continuation. A limbo has to offer a condition of lasting – never last as in an end, just lasting. We are in the waiting room with nothing to read except something which is offered to us that we are not sure we want. We have then gone indoors, and 'her indoors' (La Première Étoile played exquisitely by Irena Radmanovic, and this being naturalism one might respect an unusual admission of acting here) is washing up dishes in an acoustically-enhanced sink. Like but not quite like, just similar to that sink in *Die Familie Schneider* we encountered in Whitechapel some years earlier and visited in Chapter 3 of this book. The clatter of porcelain is keyed up by Scott Gibbons and the SRS technical crew to a register just one notch above nature's true ordination of scale. It is instantly recognisable as such and confirms we are still sentient beings whose sense of being alive is precisely calibrated through the registration of such niceties. This is the first of a series of plays with scale and proportion that domesticate and naturalise the vertiginous shifts of perspective that characterised Hell. But this Purgatory is a lower-case hell we can all have and already do. Being Purgatory, this is much, much worse. Yesterday, in

Inferno in Palais des Papes they knew they were in Hell and played out their solaces there. The 'je t'aime' passed choreographically through the 'community' of a 100 occupants on that stage the night before would be inexplicable in the truer isolation felt here.

The first and only word in this wallpapered chamber is 'chérie' spoken by the woman at the sink to another room in which we are to assume there is a loved one. But the call hangs unanswered in this house. Our previous experience of an enlarged domestic interior in *Inferno* at the Palais des Papes was a demonically occupied interior that vomited objects through its epidermal skin. Here the ghosts are closer to domestic-scale Ibsen; by the end of this play, if not Purgatory, an abusing father of that object of love, chérie, is rendered as the reduced dissembling progenitor of a St Vitus dance that is now what a distended child would appear to have inherited. Or maybe just, like father like son, the primordial power of mimetic contagion is shown to be in good working order?

If this is premature and risks spoiling the surprise, Romeo Castellucci himself finds a way through projective surtitles of telling us what will happen at each stage without telling us what *does* happen. What does happen, what is fated to take place, is the abuse of a child (La Deuxième Étoile played exquisitely by Pier Paolo Zimmerman) in an upstairs, offstage room, where the deep-throated imperative 'Open your mouth!' punctuates screams, cries and paternal groans. The father (La Troisième Étoile played exquisitely by Sergio Scarlatella) has arrived 'home' from work and sets about toying with a reheated supper. He appears to be intimate in his exhaustion with his wife, but when he asks for 'le chapeau' the way she responds suggests she knows he means his rancher's hat and not a condom. Both would be possible at this point in the action if we were anywhere else. But we are not. For at this point the surtitles rest on *la musique* (the hands not playing the notes) which is only fulfilled as a promise (unless one is willing to accept anguish as a certain form of human melody) when the father returns downstairs and, with the back of his hands resting on the keyboard of a grand piano we last saw the evening before burning in Hell, gives rise to Arvo Pärt's elegaic *Für Alina*.[5]

At this accompanied moment the boy does something predictable, logical and, for the liberal seeking a quick prosecution of the unspeakable, terrible. He sits on his father's knee and embraces him. He can do this because while the act was unspeakable, he has spoken it, voiced it over from offstage, and while we are left dumb-struck he can fill the ensuing bars not with forgiveness – this is Purgatory – but with tenderness. The man sitting behind us in the audience, who at the reappearance of the father on the landing after the abuse bellowed out: 'Was that good, was it?' has already left Purgatory for the inferno outside. But meanwhile, and unusually this far into a Romeo Castellucci show, almost everyone is present and correct, unified in a scattered way in a willingness or necessity to stay. This distended naturalism, sort of David Lynch *circa Mulholland Drive* (2001) but much better than that film's moral paucity, would appear to have absolved the witnesses from recognising this as Romeo Castellucci's cruellest drama.

Purgatory is cruel because it is not exceptional. The extreme world of catastrophic politics borne by the *Tragedia Endogonidia* episodes directed across Europe by Castellucci over the previous four years (with the exception of the final bed-bound episode) is gone: there is no obvious political foe such as Mussolini or Charles de Gaulle from those productions left behind here to vent anger upon. This is the limbo of Inferno, that had a day before been characterised as a glass room, a viewing chamber, lead-rimmed, sealed equally from gamma rays or infernal sounds, transparent yet mirrored to the incarcerated three-year-olds who gambol in this transparent play-pen. Here in the Parc des Expositions the room with no view has become the house that, as with the Neo Bankside apartments adjacent to Tate Modern, demands *to be viewed*. As we do that viewing the boy does his own from within a tower of optical devices. His father emerges from a sugar-beet forest, to the incessant beat of one of Castellucci's preferred composers, Scott Gibbons's, most persuasive tracks, and is scrutinised through a magnifying lens, a robot amplified from the boy's hands to gigantic proportions in a cupboard is illuminated by the boy's pocket torch.

This repertoire of shifting phantasmic states is destined to continue because, despite the Vatican Council's cancellation of Limbo as a topography of soulful excursion in the prosaic 1960s, we know now that this is all we have to look forward to. Indeed, not only are we directed by this director on earth to look forward to it, the surtitles deny us the excuse of ignorance before the act, but we are also directed to see what is taking place *as* phantasm. A vast lens descends at right angles between us and the stage action through which we are compelled to watch a final, awful and beautiful choreography. A cerebral-palsy dance by a man who would appear to be a reduced version of the abusing father is inherited and amplified by a shaking fit from an enlarged version of the boy who was once, and again, abused. The lens has become an eye, a dark eye (such as the ones that will reappear ten years later amongst the blind-women chorus of Castellucci's production of *Die Zauberflöte* in Brussels), through which we now see what we have been seeing *as seeing*. These are the same people, played by different people (Juri Roverato and Davide Savorani, exquisitely) but the director plays havoc with our expectations, by directing our looking as much as that object of attention requires our embarrassed witness. Indeed, this director would appear to invest everything in *our* care while crediting those on stage with an absolute freedom born of trust. A man with cerebral palsy with a hat will be trusted to be perfect, which he is, while we as spectators are utterly incomplete, we, YOU, are as-yet unfinished.[6] There is, it would appear, more work for us to do than might have been imagined of the leisured spectator, our currency is not quite meeting the needs of those who have offered everything they have to give. They are stars, les étoiles, numbered but stars nonetheless, we are a black hole called audience whose gravity folds in upon itself. It is all we can do to leave so ghostlike have we become.

As for the narrative, and Romeo Castellucci is never without a good story, even if that story often simply brings perfect acting to stage rather than troubling us with reiterating why the action is perfect in the circumstances, the potentially distressing lack of a terminus for spectatorship in *Purgatorio* ought to be resolvable after a fashion. *The Divine Comedy* is a trilogy after all, and if Dante Alighieri is to be any kind of guide we could expect Paradise to follow. Resolution obviously awaits if narrative arc is anything to go by. Dante might offer *Paradiso*, but there is no *Paradiso* in Avignon (well at least judging by the apologetic notice outside the venue, not until Sunday). The intractability of theatrical deadlines clearly effects the genre's most celebrated exponents. *Paradiso* is cancelled because paradise is still 'under construction' by the director, the director who is busy on this earth. And while the earth was made in six days, Hell, Purgatory and Paradise will take this director a couple more to resolve adequately for audience consumption.

So what to do in the absence of redemption? Well, rather literally as invited by another utopian some years ago, I imagined Heaven, it was easy when I tried, Hell was below me and above me only sky. *Paradiso* is after all *an installation* at Église des Célestins. In the absence of paradise, which was ticketed strictly for 1pm entry (we were to be the first to enter Paradise perhaps on the presumption that Hell is other people); we gather to eat lunch nearby. A director called Romeo Castellucci walks up and greets us individually in a familiar, warm, generous way that respects our own solitude. A breath, an open vowel that sounds like a soft 'aaah', and then the name by way of embrace: Joe, Nick, Becky, Piersandra, Céline, Alan. He is with his composer Scott Gibbons who tells us, quite straight-faced, that Romeo is taking him away to be decapitated. Given that I know that Scott's score for *Inferno* was partly made up of the grinding and chiselling of an autopsy worthy of the gruesome *Berberian Sound Studio*, this seems like too much information on this good Friday lunchtime.[7] As the director who is Romeo Castellucci walks away from the Église des Célestins, in the opposite direction to Paradise, I am left wondering what Scott could have meant by this. It is not a problem of translation, Scott Gibbons is from Chicago, and he would appear to know what he means by decapitation – he smiles and as he goes gestures a florid, suicidal version of the cut-throat action that punctuated the latter half of *Inferno* with the residents of this city falling to the floor one after the other, despatched there by a civil-war of thumb strokes administered by one citizen advancing behind another cutting across their windpipe between their Adam's apple and their chin.

On reflection, when others have packed for home and I am left looking through the fourteenth-century church venue's keyhole to Paradise, to see what its construction looks like, like everything else in Romeo Castellucci's universe, which includes this earth but would also appear to transcend it, it is perhaps sensible to take this departing comment quite literally. If Scott Gibbons does expect to be decapitated by his director it would suggest that he at least believes the director to be sovereign. Or at least he expects to experience the sovereignty of the director. The sovereign makes the law and is above the law, he, in this theatrical instance, is the exception to the rule that requires those who kill to be killed. To be set upon by dogs and to walk away to join us on the audience side, yet above us in a glass box from which his word is heard by all who wish to participate in his theatrical anti-republic, would therefore appear to be a demonstration of that sovereignty.

There is no doubt now, in the shadow of this suspended Paradise, on this late afternoon in Avignon that Romeo Castellucci is absolutely exceptional. He *is* the director on this earth, at least until tomorrow.

That is not to say there are not other directors on this earth, and have not been others – in the middle of all this unforgiving Avignonaise afternoon glare I have seen a production by the Latvian director Alvis Hermanis called *Sonia* that in its transcendence of exquisite naturalism throws the harshest comparative light on everything about it, including Romeo Castellucci and what on earth he is doing with all that dramatic freight. But this one, Castellucci that is, in one subtractive sense, is the true heir to that other director who in this European hinterland set the pace for everything that followed. On the way back to the festival hotel on a scorching bus ride, Carl Weber, a member of Bertolt Brecht's Berliner Ensemble in the late 1940s and early 1950s is able, on this day, to remind those of us who have experienced fewer directors on this earth, quietly and wisely, that history has a habit of repeating itself – I would just add, as divine comedy. Weber tells us, and he was there so he knows, that on 6 October 1954, on the eve of the premiere of *Der Kaukasische Kreidekreis* (*The Caucasian Chalk Circle*) in Berlin, Brecht cut his losses and abandoned most of the scenery that had been designed and built for that first production. In this willingness to change (almost) everything Romeo Castellucci at least follows an honourable directorial precedent.

And change everything he does on that day just before the financial crash. There will never be another reduced premiere of *The Divine Comedy* in Avignon in the summer of 2008 but many more Divine Comedies in which nothing here will be recognisable and in which all will be amplified to suit the rapidly deteriorating economic circumstances. That is as it should be. The musical notes by Scott Gibbons in the programme for *Paradiso* (and in our case the programme is all we have) gives us a modest sense of what we have missed:

> The deafening roar of angels' wings, of incomprehensible speech and song. Such saturation of the senses as to be at the edge of comprehension and beyond the limits of human description or poetry. Exclusion.

Well, that is at least accurate and again quite literal. Scott concludes: 'The music for Paradiso is created from [...] cicadas (in swarm and singularly)'. I am, then, writing this in Paradise, with just the sound of cicadas, loving and lonely, for company. Above us? Only stars.

Simulacra and stereotypes: *Go Down Moses*

If there is one thing we all know about Moses, it was that he was found as a baby in a basket, floating in a river, in reeds, abandoned. We are sure we have seen this one before. Christian Bale comes to mind in Ridley Scott's *Exodus* (2014) for instance.[9] But abandoned by whom? A mother one might imagine, somewhere. Well, this is what Romeo Castellucci imagines in *Go Down Moses*, at the Theatre de Ville in Paris in 2014. And we are not so sure we have seen this one, quite like this.

We begin on the stage, in a gallery of some sort, with well-to-do suited people attending to, and discussing a work of art. Well, at least a *simulacra* of a rabbit of some sort. Although I have said Castellucci is not interested in theatre as illustration or simulacra, when it is an actual illustration of this representational quality, things are different. The work, that is somehow familiar but not quite, happens to be a picture of a hare, with very large ears, an animal that you might know if you have ever seen one in its natural habitat, flees very fast. It is a great listener, something that will be lost on most of the officials of authority figured in the coming production. But it was also a totemic animal for the artist Josef Beuys who 'explained pictures to a dead one', and is of course, in Albrecht Dürer's remarkable gouache on vellum of 1502, a must-see masterpiece of the Albertina Museum in Vienna, already top-heavy with visual glories. So it is already a much-discussed animal in art circles. And it is being discussed here, and will be.

A white industrial roller machine the size of a small car slides onto the stage from the wings and begins to rotate furiously. A woman's hair, a wig or something worse, is lowered down towards the stage from the rig above and as it meets the machine it is whipped into its mechanism and flies around in front of us. The machine leaves without apparent assistance and an aperture opens towards the rear stage revealing a cubicle that is a brightly lit public toilet open to us on one side reproduced with naturalistic precision. A woman is in the toilet, slipping and sliding on a white tiled floor in her own blood, lots of blood. She is haemorrhaging violently. She is calling for help. She is frantically trying to clean the cubicle with lavatory paper and towels from the sink. There are repeated and urgent knocks on the locked door. She activates the hand dryer and flushes the lavatory in a semblance of hygienic protocol as though the keeping-waiting is more significant than the staying alive.

The woman is lying on the floor exhausted and unable to stem the blood. As she does so the spiritual *Go Down Moses* from an early recording, possibly by Roland Hayes of 1922, is amplified through the auditorium. The sound is not coming from the cubicle but appears to reach the cubicle from elsewhere, from *us* maybe for the refrain is surely amidst us? A builders' skip, piled high with rubbish, is lit to midrear stage. A black bin-bag on the top of the skip is crying and moves gently. There is something small inside, alive: the woman's baby. Moses.

The scene switches without you noticing. Moses' mother, who was lying on the toilet floor, is now in a psychologist's office being interviewed as to the whereabouts of her lost baby by the officials who cannot get her to tell them. The woman is left alone. She pulls a felt blanket around her shoulders, like an artist not unlike Josef Beuys before her, and cradles a picture of a hare. The one the gallery visitors were looking at with aesthetic respect in the first scene, but cheaper. She, unlike the hare, cannot escape and no one is listening. The white machine reappears and rotates furiously with hair lowered again into its workings. The hair is familiar now. It is the woman's hair. The machine leaves the stage and a hospital setting is lit to middle stage in which a body-sized MRI neuro-scanning machine sits central with an aperture facing us. The woman is led into the ward and lies on the bed of the machine and then slides slowly into its workings. A vast naturalistic scene opens up at the back of the stage filling its huge depth depicting a caves complex within which Neanderthal figures are eating the limbs of a small animal. One of the Neanderthals carries a dead baby across the cave floor and buries it tenderly in a shallow grave.

A woman Neanderthal approaches the downstage gauze screen, that has veiled the whole action of the play so far and slaps the screen with a bloody or pigmented hand. The palm prints left on the screen are familiar from a 1,000 cave painting pictures. (They have become more poignant for Europeans since, in April 2019, following the murder of journalist and writer Lyra McKee in Derry and the daubing of red handprints on the Saoradh headquarters, the political wing of the 'New IRA' who admitted responsibility for the killing.) The woman writes SOS in huge figures on the screen. A male Neanderthal fucks a woman Neanderthal on a raised stone platform to the rear of the stage. The rear aperture of the cave fills with the machine from the hospital and delivers the woman who has entered the machine some minutes before to this scene, 40,000 years before. She lies down in the trace of the bodies that were on the stone. The performance ends.

I would like to ignore the denouement's dramatic pre-history (sometimes called 'the play' and understandably what critical writing tends to concentrate upon) and dwell in this last scene of subterranean pre-history itself. "Pre-history is an essential, unavoidable aspect of any lived moment".[8] When humans first blew earth-red pigment from their mouths towards their hand placed upon the cave wall, *they* were doing what *we* have been doing to the walls around us ever since. They were seeking a simulacrum of them*selves*. In this act we are destined to repeat ourselves and to fail ourselves: putting things of our own upon walls that surround us. But 40,000 years ago, in those caves of Pech Merle and Chauvet, humans stepped back, and away from that wall, removing their hand, and in that moment witnessed themselves at a distance for the first time, now an onlooker to what was their own hand print, but now part of a larger composition.[10] Now, then, this was new. This is what Castellucci's cave figure does, but with a subtle shift in perspective.

This shift has something to do with the common experience of *déjà vu*, otherwise known as the 'mnestic faculty'.[11] The performances and pathologies of this faculty are what Paolo Virno ascribes to any account of historical experience. That is historical experience not conceived in the soft-core glow of a psychological or personal atomism, but within a public realm marked by the formation and deterioration of memory. I will for reasons of clarity call this public realm the theatre. In this theatre, with that manual act in mind, it is less that we could ever be expected to 'remember' such a thing, but rather as Virno says: 'it is historical in that it is that faculty that distinguishes individual existence'.[12] On this stage we are witnessing a mode of 'being historical' that happens to have marked itself out by its absence in script as precisely 'pre-historical'.

A performance is *not* a *déjà vu*. A performance has rather everything to do with the re-playing of a past scene subject to renewed recognition. And this is not *déjà vu*. Rather for *déjà vu* to occur as Virno says: 'we have an only apparent repetition, one that is entirely illusory'.[13] It is a form therefore of *false recognition* where memory's sovereignty does not just extend to a 'past' but infelicitously to the present, which takes on for memory's sake, something of that past as though as to ameliorate its newness. What we see in this staged finale of *Go Down, Moses* is a form of false memory syndrome in which a Neanderthal figure writes out a message for help, that I am sure I recall from somewhere if not prehistoric, then at least a while back. This may be to do with the dramatic lexicon that operates between performances directed by Romeo Castellucci that I am putting into play in this chapter (and displaying on the cover of this book), or it may have more to do with the appearance of figures behind this kind of scrim, or veil, that masks what they do to precise sight as though mimicking the mnemonic mists of memory.

Perhaps because Andy Warhol makes an auto(motive)-biographical arrival on the stage of *Inferno* (2008) as discussed above in that production in Avignon, Romeo Castellucci's own work has been associated elsewhere with a certain Warholesque literalness. But this would be too literal an association. Certainly there is nothing in Castellucci's commentaries that would give succour to those who seek semiotic meaning in metaphor or allegory. But the artist who most readily comes to mind in this veiled space set by Castellucci is Josef Beuys' student and neighbour in Dusseldorf, Sigmar Polke. By appropriating and deploying the pictorial shorthand of advertising, with Gerhard Richter, in a method that assumed the name *Kapitalistischer Realismus*, Polke foregrounded the pointillist archaeology of newsprint in a series of works that effectively 'screen' the subject matter from the viewer. Castellucci's common theatrical screening of his subjects from exposure effects an equivalent volume of obscurity that comes to some sort of zenith in the veiled final prehistoric scene of *Go Down, Moses*. This veiling simultaneously softens the act of representation while removing any presumption as to what such simulacra might actually be similar to. Here Polke's defence against determinist reading of his images as 'stereotypes' of commercial advertising, is channelled by Castellucci in defence of his actors against claims of simulation.

Whatever my recollection of this veiled signalling figure comes down to, the 'memory of the present' I have just described as being foundational to *déjà vu* takes a 'past form' and, having applied that to the present, replaces that form with a *past content* which in the present act of theatre is repeated with what Virno describes as an 'obsessive loyalty'.[14] But of course despite the fact this gesture appears to have arisen as though by way of some sort of archetype, or exemplary action, this gesture has never taken place, until now. We 'falsely' recognise it because, precisely, it is false. It is a false gesture but one that alerts us as spectators to our potential to become something. That is, a figure amongst others who signals meaning. That figure, Homo Sapiens you could call them, by the very paucity of their rhetorical means of gesturing (when compared with other limber and loquacious species) is the living thing working within the limits of language that follows the signaller in the cave.

The complications that arise from this scene do not stop at *déjà vu* and false memory syndrome. They are compounded by a sign that, should Bertolt Brecht have been directing this production, would have hung prominently over the stage: Pre-History. We know this is pre-history because of the rocks, the light, the costumes and the actions that figure barely-human-animals practising doing what will one day become recognisable as 'human things': eating other animals, burying their dead, procreating their life, marking their walls. But this catalogue of events does not tell us it is pre-history in any other sense that we take these events to be some sort of *a priori* for the human species that follows these figures. These are the 'fundamental mode of existence', and 'immovable background' that Virno ascribes to the prehistoric condition.[15] Here it is all a matter of potential. Just as before, for Moses' mother at least in the traffic of the stage, it was all 'impotential'. How the one got to the other over just 40,000 years, is the social timeline of *Go Down, Moses*. All the 'inability' of Moses' mother to call for help, to express herself to psychiatrists, to reason with her doctors, was at this prehistoric outset there for the making. This linguistic faculty, or capacity to speak, is for nothing when encountered by those on this stage with no capacity to hear. They are not hare.

While *déjà vu* might commonly be ascribed to those dedicated to 'watching themselves live' as Virno puts it, in this scene it is rather a case of those of us dedicated to 'watching others live', theatrically. Yet the same anomie takes hold where this experience becomes one of recognising the best we might hope for is the playing out of a present over which, with Moses' mother in a solidarity of submission, we have absolutely no influence. We have been reminded of this necessary passivity through two millennia of un-emancipated theatre-going, and not much has changed in the living currency exchanges of *Go Down, Moses*. We are where we are. They are where they are. And they get to wear the costumes of power in that opening private view scene while we feel aggrieved by the conduct of that power as the scenes pass before us and beyond us.

Any hope for change consequent upon these actions is foreclosed in the knowledge, as Henri Bergson has put it, that 'the future is closed'. At least it would appear to be for Moses' mother. And this despite the cruel fact that *déjà vu* might trick us into thinking we are still somehow attached to these matters, this history, and her history. But Bergson also reminded us that it is not so much that *déjà vu* should strike us as interesting because it occurs occasionally for some, but rather that *déjà vu* 'is not being produced at every moment in everybody'.[16] Of course if it were it would be impossible to live, for all but Kierkegaard's Constantius in search of his repetitive fix, each happening recognised in its reiteration would become overwhelming to any action in and on the present, drowned by the echoes of the past. One would become in such a state the equivalent of one of those serial repeaters (fandom you might call it) who stalk each of Ian McKellen's performances from the same seat, or 'live' for their next fix of *The Phantom of the Opera* after a quarter-century of Phantoms.

Is it fanciful, the writer Marie-José Mondzain asks, to consider this very action that we see reprised in the caves on the Théâtre de Ville stage as being the 'invention of the spectator'?[17] Is this the moment when *Homo Faber*, the one who works, or *Homo Ludens*, the one who plays, becomes *Homo Spectator*, the one who watches?

It is all very well for everyone to work, and everyone to play, Karl Marx and Johan Huizinga would have appreciated the equality in such an arrangement, but such continuous equality of action does not account for the commensurate degree of reaction upon which a performance economy could be built. If this is the case then I want to ask: What might the *Homo Spectator* be looking at? In the case of the cave figures in *Go Down, Moses*, it would appear to be *us* beyond the scrim in the haze of the future, rather than as Mondzain suggests, themselves. Who are 'we' other than the artist formerly known as audience?

Performance in the last human venue, the venue given hopeful names like *Théâtre de Ville* that we are currently inhabiting before our inevitable ecological demise, thus becomes not that different to the spectatorial process of adjustment described by Marie-José Mondzain in the *first* human venue: that is the constant recalling and testing of the faithfulness of the representations made there in the cave, the fidelity of the theatrical event, and of course listening for the signs of animals and others there-out who siren-call our inevitable fate. In this sense we perceive echoes of a cave and a spectator as imagined by Castellucci, checking their hand against its representation on a wall. It is no longer a question of whether the story is true or not, but rather the degree of faithfulness his telling has to the fidelity of the event he describes.

For those caves would appear to have something of the character of the performance space about them, and a rather more relational space than Plato allows for in *The Republic*, with his riveted customers. Such caves would appear to subscribe to the origin of the word *venue* in its French ancestry: the recognition of something 'coming to' (from *venir*) the community of the cave in this more material, less mythic sense. The cave was, after all, presumably the primordial venue for such human 'coming to' and together, not as Plato suggested in serried ranks, in forced entertainment, but in three-dimensional disordered depth and amongst, not against or contra to, animality. The geological and palaeontology record suggests a variety of ways this would have been the case, not least of all in the form of collective cooking and ceremony, but also in the remarkable number of child handprints that indicate such places were wholly cognisant of the imaginative intensity of the 'yet to be adult' and gave due regard and prominence of position to these playful expressions.

The presupposition I would then like to contest here having watched this last scene of *Go Down, Moses* with the last human venue in mind, is that communities of this, or any kind, are necessarily *human*, and that it is through community that humans register something of that which is essential to their humanness. Reversing this egoistic, hyper-humanistic, goal-oriented ambition, Jean-Luc Nancy suggests a far more enigmatic but useful velocity for performance, and proposes the opposite of the dynamic from 'self' to 'collective', that we might have expected: 'the individual is merely the residue of the experience of the dissolution of community'.[18] Or in our own terms of *déjà vu*, Marie-José Mondzain's imagined spectator working solo against the wall is not the origin of anything, but the retreating solo individualist *remains* of a collective who once watched together. By becoming spectator this Homo Sapien cleaves the collective called community.

Like the ruins and fragments of Rome that Sigmund Freud so loved for their uncanny premonitions and pictured on his consulting room-walls at Bergasse 19 in Vienna, and 20 Maresfield Gardens in London, like the stone pediments scattered to the side of the stage at the Théâtre Antique in Arles, the parts of the whole only become singularly visible on the dissolution of the entity they were once were. This is what we see when we see the bones and the stones in the caves. It is in this historical reverse of their later arrangement that they become apparent, and they really have no identity prior to that forming. The collective or the assembly in this sense only understands itself on its dissolution into the 'singular identity' of what we have called *Homo Spectator*. It is only when we perceive the lonely spectator stepping away from the wall that we understand the group from which they undoubtedly depart to make such an act readable as singularly artistic in its motives. SOS indeed given there is no longer any community to count on here.

The caves I have been talking about have names, unlike Plato's idealised subterranean world, and they can be found, and were, are and will be (not least of all as I live through the summers just a few miles from their most glorious iteration at Chauvet and in their uncanny faked doubling in the replica-kitsch simulacra of Chauvet II). And they have histories as they, at least at a late point in their development, became humanised by those who occupied them. It is in Chauvet and Lascaux in continental Europe, that (pre-French) human-animals first made representations of their own strangeness in the melée of another collective of figures with something in common. The self-knowledge of humans here was of their inherent *strangeness* to those others depicted there on the walls, bison, horses and stags. Their hands were different when they looked back at them. The human, Jean-Luc Nancy says in this context, is the stranger, but 'monstrously similar'. The human is already associated with its prey.

The history of human-animals and their strange relations with other animals, their community of being in common in the caves that Castellucci figures at the close of *Go Down, Moses*, is a happening and an event that took its first performative place in chambers such as Lascaux and Chauvet. And according to Georges Bataille, from whom Nancy drew significant aspects of his work in this prehistoric sense, this site was a privileged site of 'pre-history'. For Bataille, the very images that Nancy refers to announce a generational moment for human being not just for spectation and performance, but for the ontological category marked as the social animal, the human assembled, including somewhat later theatrical assembly: 'The passage from animal to man announces the birth of the subject, the birth of the human community, the we'.[19]

But if one looks more closely at the evidence, at Lascaux for instance, these earliest depictions of 'man', this 'we', were significant not for their humanist centring of the subject but for the way that humanity is *remaindered*, at the edge of everything else which is actively occurring in communication. Bataille figured this edging out in the following way: 'Far from seeking to affirm humanity against nature, man, born of nature, here voluntarily appears as a kind of waste'.[20] Here, long before Moses' mother experienced her loss, humans are already seen apologising for their status, at the edge of this collective, having not yet prevailed in the order of things. They marginalise themselves in these first pictorial significations and, tellingly, they are always alone, unlike the other animals in their herds, flocks and prides. They are literally *wasted*. At least Moses in the garbage waste bin is where humans perceived themselves to be from the outset. Of course this is just another, rather illustrative, act of performance, a 'feigned apology' Georges Bataille calls it, so that the human predator can continue to do what he (*sic*) has to do, kill other animals, without remorse.

As a witness to this remorseless history you have a nagging feeling that this is not the first rendition of *Go Down, Moses* you have experienced. You feel this of course in your own way and with a degree of privacy preserved for the recognition of *déjà vu*. You know, amongst others imagining likewise, that Romeo Castellucci is not the first to sample this spiritual for its historical resonance and echoes. And then you recall William Faulkner named a seminal series of short stories *Go Down, Moses*, Bob Dylan's friends The Band wrote a song *The Weight*, which in its third verse references the spiritual, and more recently amongst hundreds of restorations of this song as rendered by The Band, Bryan Saner in a valedictory production with his group Goat Island called *The Lastmaker*, sampled the lyric of 'Go Down, Moses' while he played a carpenter's saw. I happened to know these various renditions, and of course there were a 1,000 other people there with me, in that Parisian auditorium that night, drawing upon their own reservoir of musical, if not maternal, memories in a publicly secret act that one might describe as the living currency of 'theatre'. Amongst which despite the demographic of this auditorium, it might not be impossible to recall the roots of this spiritual in a history of human slavery. It is these recollections of acuity and intensity of expression that create a form, a pattern, to whose very existence within an act of déjà entendu experienced by those gathered alone I would want to assign the name, *Go Down, Moses*, 2014, directed by Romeo Castellucci.

Impulses: *Orpheus and Eurydice*[21]

My seat in the Brussels Opera House, la Monnaie, might be the cheapest one, but Søren Kierkegaard would have liked it for its solitary nature to the rear of a discrete box. You can see some things but not everything. You can hear everything and see who is producing that sound and how. On the far side of the empty stage perches some kind of stacked communications, or data box, with flashing lights. I was there in May 2014, the same year as the performance of *Go Down, Moses* I have just discussed. You may or may not appreciate Romeo Castellucci's stage exertions, but you would have to at least note his work ethic. I have a programme in my hand that appears to list those who are about to labour, not for us, but in various degrees of reconfiguration of operatic expectation, with us. Still no talk of immersion though.

You do not have to know the opera *Orpheus and Eurydice*, nor its cast, to notice something unsettling about the cast list, offered by Romeo Castellucci, for his production. Beneath the leading part of *Orpheo* and to the side of *Eurydice* is the name, Els. You can see it here between Eurydice and Amour but do not recognise it. That

Amour is the personification, the characterisation of the love that Orpheus has for Eurydice, that makes dramatic sense, but Els? Who is Els? Her name is unsettlingly closer to our names, the ones we brought into this opera house, than those others from the classical repertory who might be expected to populate a drama with this title. The opera has barely begun when this message appears on the screen covering the back of the vast stage:

> Today, at this very moment, Els listens to this interpretation of *Orpheus and Eurydice* by Christoph Willibald Gluck in a version by Hector Berlioz. The music played at the *Théâtre de la Monnaie* is being transmitted directly into Room Number 416, in the Centre for Neurology, Inkendaal Hospital, about 40 kms from Brussels. Audio is connected via wi fi, video is broadcast through broadband via a mobile transmission. A film-crew has been dispatched to Els to transmit direct images back to us, live, during the coming performance. The name Els has been chosen to conceal the name of the family.[22]

The opera continues to the forestage in the simplest possible rendition without any of the spectacle nor virtuosic scale one has come to associate with the quarter-century theatre work of Romeo Castellucci, not least of all that monumental trilogy for Avignon of Dante's *The Divine Comedy* we alighted upon earlier. But something quite riveting is happening as we listen. The story of Els is scrolling in large font text across the vast cyclorama at the back of the stage. We learn this way that the woman lying in the neurological ward at that hospital was born on 15 July 1986. She lived in a working-class district on the outskirts of Brussels. We discover what her parents did for work and the background to her family. Apparently mundane details continue to scroll across the screen like so many film credits for an insignificant life. Els marries Daniel and has two children, Adriano and Alessio. So far now, like us but less like us than we might have imagined.

We are now about 20 minutes into the opera that continues to swell and churn beneath this textual narrative. The opera is being rendered in as theatrically spare a way as one can imagine with Orpheus at a simple, broadcast studio microphone. On 18 January 2013, the screen tells us, Els is struck by a sudden and catastrophic malaise. She is alone with her children at home. She calls Daniel for help, but Daniel cannot understand the words she is saying. He rushes home to find her lying on the kitchen floor, immobile but with her eyes wide open. He thinks she has been poisoned by carbon monoxide. But when the ambulance has come and taken her to hospital it is clear she has suffered a stroke and has cerebral damage, leading to a condition called 'locked-in syndrome'. Locked-in syndrome is a rare neurological collapse in which the patient is fully conscious of events around them, but their body is completely immobilised, a total paralysis, with the exception of the eyes that continuously flutter, and move. Like ours, but not like ours.

On being transferred to the Inkendaal Hospital it becomes clear that as with most locked-in-syndrome patients her intellectual faculties are not impaired, yet she is unable to move, nor to speak. Els's senses are intact, she can hear, see, smell and remember. We are told of Els's daily regime in the hospital, we understand that Daniel visits her daily and that she communicates with him through movements of her eyes, and the use of an alphabet board hanging on the wall. This has now been the situation for a year and a half. At some point in that year and a half Els has agreed, via this alphabet board, to her involvement in this production, as has her family. Not quite as we have done by buying a ticket, but not wholly disassociated from our act. Cheaper in one sense, exuberantly expensive in another.

The text has been rolling for fully half an hour. Text now gives way to some blurred film or video images that appear to show the passage of a vehicle moving through suburban streets to some destination. It is obvious that this is the film crew, in real-time, on their way out to the hospital in which Els is lying stricken. We could well be meeting soon if the traffic is not too heavy. The opera continues telling its own story which you may or may not know.

Based on Christoph Willibald Gluck's masterpiece *Orfeo ed Euridice*, the opera is being presented in Brussels in Hector Berlioz's 1859 version in French. Hervé Niquet is making his debut conducting the orchestra and Stéphanie d'Oustrac and Sabine Devieilhe are playing the title roles. The myth of Orpheus and Eurydice is, as Joe Kelleher has reminded us in his work, *The Illuminated Theatre*, if anything a myth that would appear to trouble some presumptions of 'theatre watching'. It is essentially an injunction 'not to look', an anti-theatrical imperative in its most notable classical retellings in Virgil's epic *The Aeneid* and later in Ovid's *Metamorphoses*. Eurydice is bitten by a snake and dies, shortly after her marriage to the musician and poet Orpheus, who is unable, or unwilling, to abide the situation. His music, which even the deaf are not immune to, enables him to enter the underworld, where Eurydice's shadow now resides. Orpheus may bring back love to the world he has left but he must not look back at Eurydice as he does so. Orpheus is incapable of fulfilling this demand and in looking back consigns her to the nether world for a second time and forever.

The myth tells of the impossible return to the land of the living by a woman who has been mortally wounded. The poet-musician Orpheus's eventful journey in the world of shadows, searching for the one he loves and cannot let go, takes him to the Elysian Fields. This is an unexpected place of peace, composed of countryside and those in its thrall. It is here that Eurydice is now installed. During his journey Orpheus is thus introduced to a surprising reality: an enclave, a protected place, both near and yet inaccessible, disturbing, between life and death. With this in mind the location of Els, now, becomes perhaps more comprehensible.

With this work in two parts, in Vienna as well as in Brussels, the programme tells us Romeo Castellucci sets out to explore poetically and scientifically one of the last unknown continents, the human brain, with the music of Gluck as a guide. But for me this event appears to be much less about the brain than it is about the insistent, whole, bed-bound figure of Els, in all her stricken materiality. Where we have so far in this chapter been exploring the vertiginous (in Dante) and the abandoned (in *Go Down, Moses*), I want to call this associated but extreme material malaise in *Orfeo ed Euridice*, the irreparable.

By the time we get to the hospital where Els is lying, with the film crew, we are in the depths of the opera, we follow the crew through the corridors of the hospital, noticing as we proceed clocks that tell the time that is our time, in the rather different auditorium that is the Brussels Opera House. Below me the conductor, Hervé Niquet resplendent in a three-quarters tail-coat is the dynamic, moving image of life-lived, cajoling his orchestra to render the lyricism of the work with precise but forceful sweeps of his arms.

As we enter the hospital's ward, number 416, the camera comes into focus for the first time, we see the bed and cannot bear to look but of course we do, the image is vast, filling the whole of the backstage area of the opera house, 30 by 20 metres. And while we are first aware of a figure in the bed, Els, we are instantly aware of her head being somehow larger than expected, or at least her ears. She is wearing headphones listening to the opera that we are listening to. She is the 'act' we have come to see. We are now aware that we are listening together to this opera, in two quite distinct venues. I have called the theatre 'the last human venue' for reasons I will explore in the next chapter on ecological threat, and barely a few paragraphs ago we were considering the way a subterranean cave that was once the first human venue might, at the time of its discovery in 1940 in the same year as the inauguration of the death camps, also be construed as our last. But here you are forcefully reminded of some other pretenders to that title, the hospital ward having a poignant claim to its finality, but not the only one as we shall see.

The singers, singing the parts of Orpheus and Eurydice are raised at this point in the production, as though in perspective behind the screen, but are tiny in comparison with this vast face, Els's face. We don't want to look, in a sense we know we *should not* look, but we have to. Orpheus and Eurydice sing their dialogue with what appears to be Els 'listening in' from another world, or at least another place, 40 kilometres but a world away from where we are now listening from, in our seats. When the singer singing Orpheus turns to look around at Eurydice, as he is forbidden to do, the screen whites out immediately. Eurydice and the woman's face disappear. Everything shuts down to darkness, including the rather worrying bank of technical monitors that have been bleeping their hybrid amplification or medicalisation, voice-sustaining lights, through the whole of the opera to the side of the stage. Sight has gone yes, but so has voice.

There follows a sensational theatrical reveal in the dark initiated by the figure of love, Amour, who enters with an electric candle and wipes it against the screen covering the rear area of the stage. Eurydice is exposed, or at least a body double of Eurydice is revealed to us. Romeo Castellucci suddenly opens up the stage space to its huge depth, making appear a fantastically naturalistic rural, Illyrian scene, in which Eurydice bares herself to us, unclothed, launching herself into a vast lake where she cavorts giving the myth the happy ending our times demand. But I am not going to dwell on that spectacle here having some more modest gestures to concentrate upon 40 kms away.

As the opera nears its searing, soulful end, Els reappears in her hospital bed on the screen. We withdraw quietly from the ward through the lens of the live-feed camera, where we have been observing Els listening to the opera. Her eyes are flickering, it is obvious she is responding to what we are responding to, in the time we are responding, but we will not be discussing the production together any time soon. It is very rare for patients with 'locked-in-syndrome' ever to emerge from the state that captivates them.

In such a suspended state what might there be to say about such a condition of impulses as much as a work, that does not further load in a hermeneutic act more labour of critique onto Els's young shoulders? The production has been castigated by some for what is perceived to be its insensitivity to her stricken body, and the way she is exposed through the live camera eye of the lens to distant scrutiny. I have been endeavouring to avoid repeating that act here of course and there are no photographs in this book (save the diptych of my grandmother's milliner's shop whose legacy I am partly responsible for recovering) for this very reason. Well, the condition I am describing might well be the most poignant *contrary* to something that I have previously written about as the *sine qua non* of all performance, 'the Lazarus Affect'.[23] In something of a perverse reversal of that potential infinitely to 'begin again' I am going to gently approach the contours of that state by suggesting what its antinomy might be.

That contrary to the Lazarus Affect has a name and it is a name which perhaps begins to account for the situation Els finds herself in, and more pertinently here how we come across her in this opera. We would after all not know Els unless Romeo Castellucci had introduced us to her life, if not to her, for there *is* a troubling voyeurism that attends to the visit we variously make to her ward. By joining Els through the media of the screen in her room we are not just invited to consider her immobility, we are invited to relate in some serious way to her state. And not just to her state but to the kind of act that she offers us as witnesses. And her active state is, here, now somehow the opposite of the potential that performance always promises, it is by definition, *irreparable*. It is a state that cannot be repaired. Els cannot be repaired, mended nor cured. There is no known cure for 'locked-in-syndrome'.

But for all that the irreparable is of course not nothing. For Els it is in a sense 'all'. This is how the philosopher and actor Giorgio Agamben describes the condition of the irreparable:

> The irreparable means that things are consigned without remedy to their being thus. They are precisely and only their *thus* [...] irreparable also means that for them there is literally no shelter possible. In their being thus they are absolutely exposed, absolutely abandoned.[24]

If the way we think about the world is commonly caught between the two poles of necessity and contingency, demand and accident, the world that this opera presents to us is that of 'the not being able *to not be*'.

The necessity that despite and perhaps because of everything, Els goes on living, the potential of being able to not be, that is the contingency, that hovers over all such situations exemplified by those high profile court cases that seek the right to end life in such situations, becomes obvious and haunting. But here, what we are shown is an extraordinary situation in which Els is capable of 'not, not being', she is precisely capable of the irreparable. And it is this capacity, this potential that is built on the vastness of her impotential that faces us in the ward and the live-feed back into the auditorium I am sitting in now. In the end in that same seat, alone amongst others in our rather different, though not wholly unrelated state of impotential audience.

I will say just a few more words on this state of the irreparable as it would be such a thing that would demand that we construe that which is somehow 'not irreparable' you could say, the voluntarism of the Lazarus Affect that haunts performance. The state of the irreparable is that 'things are just as they are', consigned without remedy to their way of being. States of things are irreparable whatever they may be: sad or happy, atrocious or blessed. As Agamben puts it: 'How you are, how the world is – this is the irreparable'.[25]

Spinoza called the irreparable two things: confidence of safety and despair. In the figure of Els, both are at play in a troubling simultaneity, you do not fear for her, she is in the safest place possible, but you might despair at such a situation. The one thing that has been removed from this situation, and it is the one thing that makes human situations so anxious, and exhilarating, is doubt. Every aspect of doubt has been removed in this scene as it is obvious from what we know, and what we see, that things will be thus. In that sense it might appear we have reached the anti-theatrical state of impotentiality *par excellence*. It does not matter whether this brings joy or sadness. Hell and Heaven might as well be the same thing here, or you might want to substitute both for the middle term that Castellucci has demonstrated in his work on *The Divine Comedy*, that he is something of an expert in, that is the state of Limbo. It is thus. Things stand, or in this case, lie, thus.

All performance is of course only or always thus, it is 'as such'. Thus means 'not otherwise'. Which might as well be a definition of performance. As Agamben says: 'Seeing something in its being thus – irreparable but not for that reason necessary; thus, but not for that reason contingent – is love'.[26] I obviously cannot speak for others but I love this performance. That much is obvious. It *is* all there is, on this day becoming night at least. If this dreadful dilemma describes the parallax of the performer, then the paradox of the actor is more accurately the 'absence or suppression of any property', the caesura, or failure, of the anthropological machine to activate a propriety, any property, for the human. It is therefore not just the disappointing man, the underachieving human that marks the actor, that would in the end be rather dull. Rather this paradox would suggest that the performing man and woman must be a 'man and woman without qualities', somebody who is literally beside themselves, their part played by those who have no part. It is nature that has given this sense of nothing to the human, simply, what philosopher Philippe Lacoue-Labarthe calls: 'a perpetual movement of presentation'[27] This gift, our birth-right, is the gift to be improper on every occasion. That is I would suggest precisely the kind of impotential that infuses the figure of Els in that bed in that hospital in the outskirts of Brussels in 2014, being relayed to us in the Opera House, prostrate.

Given this impotential, when I say Els *is the Act* we have not come to see, but have been invited to look at, I owe you an explanation. You might want to say her apparent physical immobility precisely *precludes* her from any such act, but as I stressed earlier, amongst many candidates she has asked to be present to us in this production. When various protests coalesced around her involvement, as they tend to around Castellucci's work, her family made this agency-to-act explicit to those few willing to suspend their faux outrage and listen to the woman who has chosen actually, really, to act.

'What is the human and how does it appear' is as Esa Kirkkopelto makes clear, a philosophical question to which every theatrical performance offers one possible answer, and the figure of Els in *Orpheus and Eurydice* is certainly no exception to this iron rule.[28] The answer to this question almost always goes unnoticed, but here it *is* the point, the whole point of what we are watching and listening to. Here in the simplest sense Els's presence expands our conception of personhood way beyond any trite definitions of ableism, disability or inclusivity.

As Joseph Roach puts it in his irreplaceable work *The Player's Passion* 'the history of the theatricalisation of the body' has at every phase been closely braided with the evolution of the natural sciences, physiology and psychology. And, of course, in Roach's version of events the philosopher Denis Diderot plays a foundational role in such relations. Here, with Els, that theatricalisation of the body has arrived at the impasse of science in the face of the irreparable. But to be clear, as Kirkkopelto is on these matters, one would have to admit that the relations now are less of an overtly scientific nature, rather more I would say of a political culture. Here it is less to do with explaining anything through the restorative scientific regimes of the stage and the underworld of the hospital unable to offer any cure, so much as perhaps changing our perception of their possible relations. Here Els becomes politically charged as a new site or articulations (not least of all ventriloquised by those arguing over the ethics of displaying her prostrate body to an audience). And that of course, as Jacques Rancière reminds us, is down to us as 'spectator citizens' as much as it is to do with her. We after all have some currency to expend too.

What nature, that is animals other than humans for instance, cannot do as I have made clear at length in my book *Theatre Intimacy & Engagement* is make a work of its own way of appearing. It cannot 'merely appear', which is the birth-right of only humans, who have the gift of nothing. The kind of appearing that Els is doing renders such a 'merely appearing' to its zenith, or its depth, depending what you consider this form of appearing to be doing 'for you'. What we do recall from Diderot is a concern for the withdrawal of the comedian in relation to 'his' (*sic*) roles, his distance from the behaviours of other characters, his insensibility that is so upsetting, and his coolness with regard to the passions, all writ large on the figure of Els one could say. In this sense she becomes the actor *par excellence*. She absorbs the effects of the citizen-spectators and become possessed by us. We fulfil our classical roles here. On the one hand we *pity* her, indicating our excessive identification with her, on the other hand we are terrified by her, we are driven apart both after the event but also now, in the longer term as we argue about the merits of Els's inclusion in the act.

Joseph Roach in *The Player's Passion* emphasises the physiological significance of the diaphragm for Diderot, an actor being somebody with talent for controlling the diaphragm in ways others cannot, but only ever in relation to the brain as Diderot himself makes clear. It is this necessary relation that has been complicated by Els's catastrophic stroke. Where an actor might be expected to control these relations with a dexterity unavailable to mere offstage mortals, no such control can be presumed in the case of Els. We are human I would suggest because we are enabled as human-animals to control an extended, unbroken, outward breath. It is this uniquely human capacity that has allowed us to develop language. It is this privilege, should language be conceived as a privilege, that is no longer extended to the stricken figure of Els. In witnessing Els we are brought face to face, with our fate as subjects, unable to ever appropriate, master or control our exposure totally. Our fate as human-animals is then to set about trying to *conceal* ourselves from any such exposure, however partially, which is why we are peculiarly well-suited to the veiled screens of all performance, but especially Castellucci's recognition of such obscurities. Theatre is always thus the art of the hidden.

This vertigo ceases, for Diderot at least, with a decision, a decision concerned with affects, that is, when one becomes subject to affects, pre-eminently through performance, one becomes subject. In the case of Els lying in that bed, the constant fluttering of her eyelids, her eyes are decidedly and observably *not* closed, operates as an immense affect machine, inscribing on us from its amplified form at the back of the Brussels Opera House, the intensity of engagement between this suspended life and that music. When possessed with oneself through affects the subject-less mimetic actor, who is by definition active becomes the uncontrolled and unmanageable subject of a passive mimesis.

The final act for Els is indeed an act of extreme passivity. We watch as the headphones that she has been listening to *Orpheus and Eurydice* through, are gently removed by a nurse from her ears. They are put away for another night. They will be back on tomorrow, for the next night's performance, and there is a frisson of jealousy of this stricken figure, that she will get to hear this wonderful work again, and you will not. I have never seen anyone do this before. To remove or place headphones upon another person. It seems at once the most intimate and yet out-of-place act, given you might associate these very headphones with the ultimate agency of running and listening simultaneously. But it reminds me of something else that has stayed with me from catechism classes as a young, now lapsed, Catholic. That is: in the Kingdom of Heaven, everything will be exactly as it is now, just a little different. This subtlest of displacements would be so hard to achieve by mortals, that the Messiah would be required to effect its minimal movement from what we know to what needs to be. The idea that the Absolute would be identical with the world, just different, describes again the parallax of the minimal difference that characterises performance. This tiny displacement cannot of course really be down to the state of things, that I would have a bit more hair in heaven, though I would have liked it. It does not refer to such states of things, but rather to their sense, and their limits. It does not take place *in* things but at their periphery, in the space between everything and itself.

This periphery in Christian iconography was represented as the halo. Nothing can be added to the perfect of the redeemed world, but there is something that can be added as a surplus, what Saint Thomas described as an 'accidental reward that is added to the essential', that is not necessary for beatitude, but that simply makes it more brilliant. As Agamben describes the halo: 'The halo is the supplement added to perfection – something like the vibration of that which is perfect, the glow at its edges'.[29] Els's headphones form this dark halo around her head, this 'inessential supplement' to her irreparable state. They are the acoustic zone in which possibility and reality, potentiality and actuality are made manifest and become indistinguishable. The beatitude of Els is not therefore some sort of abstract performance of belief, some blind hope, it is that of a performance of potentiality that only comes after the act of the opera, a matter that does not remain *beneath* the form that we have witnessed and heard, but surrounds it with a halo of its own making. That SONY rather than BEATS by Dr Dré is the branded logo clearly visible on the side of the headphones as they are momentarily held towards the camera by the assisting nurse, is to remind us of our debt to those god-like technologists of acoustic perfection who work beyond the medical expertise of the good doctor, and the musical profession.

The theatre, the opera, whatever we call it, that traffic of 'the illuminated stage', comes to an end with this act of acoustic retreat from the subject of or attention.[30] This should not go without saying before we leave this Brussels night. Indeed, this is saying something quite different to the various, complex, 'ontologies' of performance where that traffic is figured as ephemeral, as disappearing, as unrepeatable, all those loss-making ghostings that have come to define the melancholic fixation of theatre's sister act, performance study. Here we are not dealing with the metaphoric deaths of performance with its faux losses, having just faced up to what some of us might imagine is a kind of living death. Indeed after the resounding applause for the soloists and the orchestra a single name appears on the screen:

ELS

And of course we applaud while knowing that Els cannot hear us, having had her headphones put away for another night. But we applaud anyway, and loudly, perhaps for ourselves, for being alive and able to leave the theatre, this last human venue. We all know her name is not really Els after all.

We also know the theatre always comes to an end, not least of all when we watch the people we thought we knew for a while, take a bow and leave, before we leave. And we do go, despite the inclination to stay just where we are. We leave quite rapidly, irrespective of how decent we think the show was, and we leave as closely as we can to the others who are leaving despite our best intentions to tarry, to delay a while. Gaps in aisles are surreptitiously filled. There is little love lost in departure from a spent auditorium, La Monnaie, Théâtre de Ville, Palais des Papes, where we have just spent the last accelerated theatrical decade taking account of this living currency we call the theatre-going human.

Or is there? By way of concluding thoughts as I leave this theatre, is there a way to consider this sense of an ending to the circulation of such living currency and the love lost right there? Quite how it feels, and how much of it there is that has been lost? The balance of payments you could say. Richard Yates offers us an anatomy of such departures in *Revolutionary Road* (1961) and figures everything that follows in his celebrated novel upon the way a shattered, bewildered, gaggle of individuals who before this night had imagined themselves some sort of community, find their way to leave each other, in the auditorium, in the parking lot, under stars that Dante might, if he had lived in a Connecticut suburb, have offered as the canopy for Romeo Castellucci's *Divine Comedy*. But what happens when those, albeit lesser things end, when 'the open', the 'coming community', the 'expanded collective', all hopeful names for performance politics becomes closed? Theatres 'go dark' as we encountered at some length in the first pages of this book, but what if they were to 'stay dark'. If theatre has a vocabulary it is surely an insanely hopeful one: 'opening night', 'corpsing' (turning a death into a synonym for uncontrollable laughter) and 'resting' (as in out of work and depressingly under-employed) are indicative of the eternal optimism of the theatre mind. Philosophically the language adopted by theatre theory is no less affirmative. Natalist terms, pregnant with expectation are delivered by philosophical midwives: 'birth to presence', 'emergent appearance', 'becoming' are all dramatic commonplaces. I suppose it was all this untrammelled joy that in the end got the nascent discipline of Performance Studies down so seriously and prompted its morbid excesses cultivated by its 'loss leaders'.

But what, without submitting ourselves to the ever-present performance studies couch, about the potential finality of this exchange, extinction itself as the ultimate un-dialectical event for the author and the actor? Surely the face of Els requires us to think of such a thing? In *Theatre & Everyday Life* as I discussed in Part I of this work, I undertook a survey of what I called the 'first human venue', the quotidian, the everyday, and demonstrated how theatre had become removed from the everyday in return for its privileges as a cultural artefact. It had traded its origins for a specious respectability among other excised arts practices it had little affinity with. The status of theatre often rested on the maintenance of these distances rather than their recognition and dissolution. In the second part of that book *Theatre & Everyday Life* as I am doing again a quarter of a century later in the next chapter of *The Dark Theatre*, I wrote about the relations between the given and the created, pointing out that beneath the depths of the everyday lay an even more threatening remainder to cultural production, the natural, which if admitted might overwhelm all the coordinates of what performance might be considered to be. When I said inundation, I did mean drowning, but not quite in the spirit that the philosopher Adi Ophir means when he says: 'The planet of the drowning is our planet'.[31]

I was fearful of that inundation myself and I did not take this further at the time. Later, in *Theatre, Intimacy & Engagement* (2008) I resumed that task and did so in the company of the theatre examples of amongst others, such as again here, Romeo Castellucci and Socìetas Raffaello Sanzio. The significance of what I call 'the last human venue' in that book, that is theatre in the age of urban modernity, is that this theatre, our theatre, has been the first theatre to understand itself as an 'epochal theatre', with a sense of the present, yes, but also for the first time a sense of its newness is braided with a vivid sense of its ending. Such an end, as Martin Heidegger cautioned in his own writing on ending, would not be signified as an 'event', rather a certain acceptance of finitude, an anticipation of it, and not a completion of it.[32] It is this finitude that Adi Ophir describes as 'laying a common ground' for the recognition consequent upon ultimate loss.

In theatre terms, we *can* act ethically, we can lay a common ground in the name of Els, and others, who *cannot*. We can do that by simply keeping their company until such a time as they have departed us. When we truly start to feel *their* loss. In the very face of the ethical impotential that Els offers us by her presence, as the human face is washed from the sand by the tides of day and night, the insistence of the potential that has to be inherent to any ending, is realised: the opportunity to return to the shore and draw out another human face is staged upon the sacrifice of a million sandy 'faceless' species that, for the Surrealist author Roger Caillois, have long-ago died, and drifted to that beach below Shakespeare Cliff and its dreadful trade, where those unnumbered pebbles lie amongst the shells in their 'first and fatal intimacy'.

Back on earth, with the director on this earth, in a curious room called theatre, the small gel-covered box on the wall above the door at La Monnaie glows green with the word I was looking for:

EXIT

It reminds us where we are if not who we are. It can never be turned off when we are there and we have no idea who turns it off when we are not. If ever they do.

Sigmund Freud, whose early hypnotic excursions took him nightly to the theatre, describes the composition of his last work *Moses and Monotheism* in recalcitrantly conventional theatrical terms. Close to death, on the publication of this concluding volume that 'completes' his complete works in 1939, Freud noted in his diary: 'Quite a worthy exit …'[33] I wonder what makes an exit 'worth' something and another less, or even nothing? I suspect it was what went before. But, unlike the summative remorselessly cumulative narrative of the talking cure, there is always an opportunity to recover oneself in the theatre, to begin again. Who after all in an aisle on the way towards that glowing sign has not done an involuntary dance, a feint to block an interloper, a last look back to check the satisfying distance climbed, away from the stage towards the light of the 'front of house' before the dark outside. Not the same 'outside' but certainly the same stars that preside over the hospital in which Els lies, *still*, tonight.[34] Like animals, leaving the ark, the audience flees the Laurel Players' *The Petrified Forest*, on their way out towards Richard Yates' *Revolutionary Road*, the one that until the end of their world, Els's world, and then *the* world, will go on going, around and around:

There was nothing to watch now but the massed faces of the audience as they pressed up the aisles and out the main doors. Anxious, round-eyes, two by two, they looked and moved as if a calm and orderly escape from this place had become the one great necessity of their lives; as if, in fact, they wouldn't be able to begin to live at all until they were out beyond the rumbling pink billows of exhaust and the crunching gravel of this parking lot, out where the black sky went up and up forever and there were hundreds of thousands of stars.[35]

Notes

1 Between 8 and 11 July 2008 during the run of *The Divine Comedy* at the Avignon Festival I interviewed Romeo Castellucci in preparation for a commission by Dan Rebellato and Maria Delgado to contribute to an edited collection: *Contemporary European Theatre Directors* (2010). London: Routledge and in 2020 due for republication in a new edition. I am grateful to the editors for their work on that manuscript from which I have lifted the opening reflection on *The Divine Comedy* for this rather different chapter.
2 This decade of festival appearances, less than half of the two-decade repertoire of the company Socìetas Raffaello Sanzio, marks a sequence of preoccupations that could be described as indicative of the work of SRS and Romeo Castellucci as director: radical adaptation of Shakespeare involving professional and non-professional performers at the extremes of physical range and versatility; literary transformation from the canon of European literature from chamber scale to great magnitude; biblical and Catholic liturgical interest; long-term research exploration involving peripatetic, Europe-wide coproduction and the centrality of Castellucci family members in performance; installation and site-sensitive sculptural manifestations indexing concerns evident in the theatrical repertoire.
3 Directors for stages on this earth have more commonly concerned themselves with finessing our disbelief in a character's lines that try as they might do not quite add up to the person named in the *dramatis personae*.
4 Castellucci acutely conscious of the always already self-reflexive intertextuality of the theatre machine, announces himself within the drama as director prefiguring Dante's own self-reflexive identification at the outset of *The Divine Comedy*.
5 There is also a longish period where the 'stage directions' in the surtitles diverge from what we see on stage. Castellucci would appear in this commentary to be less concerned with glossing an action that has the inevitability of tragic fate about it than interrupting each stage of a reading (our witness) that might presume to collapse sounds, spoken words and writing to a consistency that conceals multiple abuses elsewhere.
6 The actor who 'has' cerebral palsy might be described by some as having disabilities away from this stage. The 'dis' here I would take to refer to strategies of locomotion, presumptions as to the momentum and direction we as able humans might consider standard. But on this stage on this earth (Avignon, then latterly Barbican where the production was seen in the UK in April 2009) these actions are exposed as perfect: they are beautiful, strange, revealing, obsessive, clear, funny, flowing, in other words all the things that dance has tried to work on over a few years but finished up rather missing the point, which is what this performer shows us.
7 This mortal sound track also found live expression recently at the Donmar Warehouse in London: www.donmarwarehouse.com/production/6885/berberian-sound-studio/ (accessed on 26 August 2019).
8 Virno, Paolo. (2015). *Déjà vu and the End of History*. Trans. David Broder. London: Verso, p. 186.

9 www.theguardian.com/film/2014/oct/27/christian-bale-moses-was-barbaric-and-schizophrenic (accessed on 26 August 2019).
10 If you are elsewhere, beyond this Eurocentrist view of origins one might add names beyond France and Spain such as Sulawesi in Indonesia, or Arnhem Land in Australia. But care is needed as the distinguishing feature of the 'pre-French' cave is the presence of precisely the human spectator, whereas in most other cave systems there are representations of multiple animals but no human representations. This might imply that the objectification of the animal by the human, and hence the origin of our ecological dilemma, was a profoundly Eurocentric shift and one that simultaneously announces the recognition of the viewing spectator upon this very tragedy of exclusion. See Bataille, Georges (2009). *The Cradle of Humanity: Prehistoric Art and Culture.* Ed. Stuart Kendall. Trans. Michelle Kendall. Cambridge: MIT Press.
11 Virno, op. cit. p. 3.
12 Ibid. p. 4.
13 Ibid. p. 7.
14 Ibid. p. 18.
15 Ibid. p. 184.
16 Bergson, Henri. (2002). 'Memory of the Present and False Recognition', in *Key Writings.* Ed. Keith Ansell Pearson and John Mullarkey. London: Continuum, p. 143.
17 Mondzain, Marie-José. (2007). *Homo Spectator.* Trans. Patrick ffrench. Paris: Bayard, pp. 11–58. I am grateful to Patrick ffrench for his beautiful translation of the Introduction to Mondzain's otherwise untranslated text for the occasion of her visit to King's College London for our seminar series, *Caves,* 14–17 February 2011: www.academia.edu/21460562/CAVES_Anatomy_Theatre_and_Museum_King_s_College_London_14–17_February_2011_co-curated_with_Prof._Alan_Read_King_s_College_London_ (accessed on 19 August 2019).
18 Nancy, Jean-Luc. (1991). *The Inoperative Community.* Trans. Peter Connor. Minneapolis: University of Minnesota Press, p. xxxvii, and p. 3.
19 Bataille, Georges. (2005). *The Cradle of Humanity.* Ed. Stuart Kendall. Trans. Michelle Kendall and Stuart Kendall. New York: Zone, p. 16.
20 Ibid. pp. 31–46.
21 In September 2013 I was invited to contribute to the *Homo Novus Festival* whose curator Gundega Laivina had selected the subtitle of my book, *Theatre, Intimacy & Engagement* as the thematic umbrella for artists to work under. The sub-title read: 'The Last Human Venue'. I have returned to some 'loose ends' here that were first developed in two works: Read, Alan (1993). *Theatre & Everyday Life: An Ethics of Performance.* London: Routledge; Read, Alan (2008). *Theatre Intimacy & Engagement: The Last Human Venue.* Houndmills: Palgrave. I am grateful to both publishers for their permission to return to this work and explore it in this new context, if of course, not to resolve it, and am grateful to the editors of *A Life of Ethics and Performance* (2013, Cambridge: Cambridge Scholars Press) John Matthews and David Torevell, for their invitation and insight with regards to an earlier version of this part of the chapter.
22 Backdrop text projected across La Monnai De Munt, Brussels, cyclorama for *Orpheus and Eurydice* (2014). Dir. Romeo Castellucci.
23 See 'The Lazarus Affect', an epilogue to Read, Alan. (2008). *Theatre, Intimacy & Engagement: The Last Human Venue.* Houndmills: Basingstoke.
24 See 'The Irreparable' in Agamben, Giorgio. (1993). *The Coming Community.* Trans. Michael Hardt. Minneapolis: University of Minnesota Press.
25 Agamben, ibid. p. 89.
26 Ibid. p. 105.
27 Ibid. p. 259. Nature has given man nothing but the 'aptitude' for presenting.
28 Kirkkopelto, Esa. (2014). 'The Most Mimetic Animal: An Attempt to Deconstruct the Actor's Body' in *Encounters in Performance Philosophy.* Eds. Laura Cull Ö Maoilearca and Alice Lagaay. Houndmills: Palgrave, pp. 121–143.
29 See 'Halos' in Agamben, Giorgio. *The Coming Community* op. cit. pp. 53–58.

30 The 'illuminated stage' is a misheard appropriation of an idea developed by Joe Kelleher via Edmund Husserl and Søren Kierkegaard, figured as 'the illuminated theatre' and developed at the 'Traces of …' seminar series, King's College London, March 2010.
31 Ophir, Adi. (2005): *The Order of Evils*, Cambridge: Zone Books, p. 625.
32 Ibid. p. 620.
33 Freud, Sigmund. (1997). *The Diary of Sigmund Freud. 1929–1939*, Trans. M. Molar. London: Hogarth Press, p. 255.
34 I wrote this line on 4 August 2019 and it occurs to me it will not be true at some point in the future, perhaps before the acid-free paper this book has been printed on begins to perish in about 300 years' time.
35 Yates, Richard. (2006). *Revolutionary Road*. London: Faber, p. 10.

5
ARRESTED LIFE
Ecology of the new enclosures

Before one of the planets amongst those 'hundreds and thousands of stars' seemed as threatened as the earth would appear to be now, when I was writing *Theatre & Everyday Life* at the outset of the 1990s, environment and ecology were barely mentioned within performance study. The prescient work of Bonnie Marranca *Ecologies of Theatre* (1996) was some way off, the ground-breaking *Between Nature* international cross-disciplinary symposium was yet to be staged at Lancaster University in 1999 (followed by my editing of *On Animals* published in 2000 that grew from my keynote talk at Lancaster), and Baz Kershaw with the comprehensive overview *Theatre Ecology* (2009) was fully two decades away. No one thought of publishing Jacques Derrida's musings on his cat first discussed at Cerisy in 1997, nor Donna Harraway's thoughts about her dogs and other 'companion species' that later appeared in 2003. So it surprises me now that having addressed Everyday Life in Chapter 3 in that work (as I have done again rather differently here in Part I of *The Dark Theatre*) I chose not to dig deeper into the domestic realm but rather decided to launch outwards towards a wider 'world' that I scarcely knew anything about, save the evocation of its colonial spoils in the naming of the docklands wharf buildings we worked in through the 1980s. As I wrote at that time:

> While the landscape of the preceding pages [of *Theatre & Everyday Life*] has been the urban I can […] no longer artificially deny the contingency of this realm, dependent as it is on the country […]. It remains to locate theatre again within an understanding of its relations between nature and culture.[1]

And again, as then in *Theatre & Everyday Life*, so now, but differently, in Part II of *The Dark Theatre*. Where previously I placed theatre as the mediating term between nature and culture, ferrying back and forth converting apparently 'natural' elements into culturally realisable phenomena, here I take the same three terms but with the hindsight of a quarter-century of ecological, feminist and economic theory concern myself with three common scenarios of the capitalocene: the loss of land by those bankrupted by development (as already traced in Docklands in Part I, and in the coming chapter forms of assembly that resist such forces of expulsion); the natural historical relations of 'cheap natures' and capitalism and the *mise en scene* of their staging; and the co-option of 'creativity' by conservative readings of history and the collateral cruelty of that culture-class.

The significance of what I call 'the last human venue', that is theatre in the age of urban modernity, is as I began to outline in the previous chapter, that this theatre, 'our' theatre, has been the first theatre to understand itself as an 'epochal theatre', with a sense of the present, yes, but also for the first time a sense of its newness is braided with a vivid sense of its ending. Here I am opening a much wider field of operation than the disappointments of the bankrupted neighbourhood theatre I directed through the 1980s, but I am keeping those disappointments in mind as the loss of one venue remains a signifying, material force in what follows to tether what I say securely in historical evidence that will resist the always present threat of metaphoric abstraction. The significance of this venue that I would like to give the name the last human venue has been the way in which its *time* did not correspond solely with 'its *times*'.[2] Its contemporaneity in keeping with Nietzsche's propositions in his 'Untimely Meditations', might be said to have been precisely its disjuncture *with* its times, its state of being out of joint allowing it to become aware of its own contingency.[3] As the philosopher of evil Adi Ophir puts it: 'In the present time, the end of the world appears as a common horizon of the whole world that determines a common future for this era'.[4] Such an end is predicated on the wholly secular, commonly available proliferating data of pollution and global-warming, that is represented through the present discourses of scientific truths. There is no messianic quality to the evening news now, but a rather prosaic adaptation to circumstance for the neo-human wedded to a catalytic converter here a low carbon-emission freezer there. Inconvenience, as Al Gore might have once said, has now become the key register of a certain future discomfort.[5]

Human extinction is available in at least three relatively accessible and well-documented contemporary modes: by nuclear accident or endeavour, by the ratcheting up of mass exterminations common to genocides of the last century and, what I am going to concentrate on in this chapter, ecological disrepair. Each has their own time and, apparently, site of conduct. But however they operate, they would appear to converge at 'an end'. Whatever landscape you might imagine for such an end my hunch is that this end for all but the most pluralistic and inclusive cultures will be one staged within a graveyard of abandoned practices that once might, should they have been preserved against the forces of disciplinary exclusion, have saved the human from their own worst instincts for self-immolation. The ultimate fire sale you could say, these long-lost knowledges, intuitions and sagacities would have been just what the doctor ordered should the physician themselves not long-ago have disappeared alongside their once-trusted homeopathies, pharmacognosies and complementary cures (and I will come to the fraught responsibility the twenty-first century Western university has for such losses by the end of this chapter). It is perhaps a petty solace to speculate whether it is performance or thinking that is extinguished first, just before this end, but such thoughts on theatrical closure certainly sharpen the tired debate regarding the relationship between practice and theory. If as Adi Ophir says: 'The end is a being without witness', then it is that witless, witness-less, condition, that marks the end as one from which performance will be a relatively early casualty.[6] In this sense it is quite the opposite of the saturated and well-judged theatre curtain call with which we familiarise ourselves with the haunted human look of the soon to be out-of-contract actor. The ends that I am talking about here are the kinds of end where there is nobody left to conduct the fire sale that follows more prosaic finales and attends to other interruptions in business-as-usual, marking out those interruptions as something *less* than final, something therefore, however traumatic that might be cause for some hope, however slim.

My concerns here are hardly marginal as I write them out today. Within minutes of images of the Notre Dame Cathedral fire in Paris appearing on Twitter on the early evening of Monday 15 April 2019 the theatre researcher Katie Beswick had posted the following:

> Like in 10 years or less there will likely be such massive ecological disaster that you will be watching your own house burn down and your children starve to death. So I wouldn't waste what time you have left mourning architecture.[7]

Within a matter of minutes 'Flaming June' replies: 'Later please'. To which, in a dystopian riff worthy of Caryl Churchill in *Far Away*, Katie Beswick returns:

> I Mean … all I think about every day right now is how the planet is suffocating in plastic and no real action is being taken, insects dying, mammals falling dead out of trees, very few real fucks given by powers that be, so forgive me if I don't care that an old church is burning.

Given Beswick has started the day with a drop-mouth emoji announcing 'I'm sad' it is not as though she has not alerted us already to the sincerity of her feelings regarding the world 'we' share. By the end of that day she had suffered the cruellest fate of Twitter having lost followers while not picking up the kinds of numbers that generate new audiences for future arguments that her always persuasive posting deserves.

The lack of responses (including me) on Beswick's commonly busy mentions indicates not just the fragility of people's feelings about this complex response to a fire, but the rapidity with which it has been posted. But Beswick is only saying what David Attenborough has been feted for years for saying over rather longer hours of natural history broadcasting, and in a language whose timing and lack of euphemism is in its own way admirably candid, precisely because it has measured itself against an apparently inviolable and obviously Western Judaeo-Christian cultural 'loss' of 'civilisation'. On that very morning Beswick was hardly alone in thinking about extinction so clearly, and certainly not without the force of hope that always accompanies such commitments to the labour of precise expression (which this tweet clearly has in its favour irrespective of its apparent lack of responsive feedback). Waterloo Bridge in London on that Monday morning has, after all, just been occupied by the environmental activists of Extinction Rebellion (prompted by the courageous school-strike interventions of Greta Thunberg) constructing a verdant 'garden bridge' with plants of their own choosing, not only to close down the bridge and disrupt the continuous commerce in the toxic city for a day, but to troll the British Prime Minister wannabee Boris Johnson and his failed Garden Bridge across the Thames at Temple that 'spaffed' £53.5 million of public funds 'up the wall' (as Johnson himself referred to police-funding for child abuse enquiries).[8]

These urgent demands on our attention need not necessarily be the 'last word' however. By definition, before any such end, not *all* is lost. That after all is the precarious historical accident in which I and we find ourselves in 'our' times however dark these times are supposed to be. If this is our assigned place we should surely commit ourselves to practising and thinking our way through this, with as material a response as we can manage, and that might, surprisingly, not exclude theatre thinking. When we were asked on Twitter what could possibly account for the survival of the Notre Dame altar crucifix amongst the fallen roof 'forest' of transept beams on the morning following the devastating fire of April 2019, other than 'belief and faith in God', more than one rational soul posted the relative combustible temperatures of metal and wood: 300 degrees Celsius for wood, 1,500 degrees Celsius for metals. So, religion is not required in that calculation, if indeed it is required at all in this seriously terrestrial context. The late loss of witnesses after all reminds us that each of these modes of extinction are measurable, and are being actively measured, in the present era. There are attempts to measure nuclear proliferation, historical repetition of genocides and ecological disaster as so many varieties of act and accident. And it is, perhaps inevitable that the arts are co-opted and corralled to this end, playing the siren warning to these apocalyptic scenarios.

Performance has played this trigger role under the guise of 'political theatre' for so long it has forgotten quite what that responsible position within the culture under threat might necessarily demand by way of critical intelligence, nuance to circumstance, or *any* considered stance beyond the Arts Council of England's well-meaning but naïve 2019 call for increased 'relevance' from its portfolio funded tranche of nationwide theatre makers.[9] Again, the chasm between political reality and aspiration are obvious not only from years of academic writing on such lost nuances, but also from today's Twitter feed where a playwright well known for 'relevance' with more than 27,000 followers, Simon Stephens, tweets: 'Imagine if Extinction Rebellion persuade the police to support them. That is the tipping point of most revolutions'. To which within 11 minutes Shane Boyle, a theatre academic at Queen Mary University London with (presumably) a less 'relevant' 972 followers has responded: 'You're joking right? The tipping point is always the army joining up. The cops historically are on the side of the ruling class'.[10] There is no doubting here where the historical wisdom regarding efficacious revolution appears to rest, and it is not with the author of *Wastwater* (excellent as that play is). In the quite proscriptive words of Adi Ophir 'If there are still poetry, science and thinking, they should sound to us as the music played on board the Titanic would have sounded had the passengers only known how to see the iceberg'.[11]

The last human venue I would propose then, is the place where the position of the human-animal in relation to such an end became measurable for the first time. We can always estimate this distance through thinking and lengthen this distance, from or to an end, not only through acting, but through action, and here the distinction between the gerund and the verb is moot. The time that remains, in this scenario (and in this book), for theatre at least, would then appear to be one of *hope*. Having begun to measure these distances, having begun to act in the interests of their lengthening, the last human venue to which here I have given the gloomy title the Dark Theatre would appear to be a venue with a purpose, even if that purpose, in my imagination, always falls short of claims for the political that were once routinely placed at the feet of the 'most social of the arts', that is theatre.[12]

Informal assembly

With these hopeful thoughts in mind it is not so much then a question of 'how to act', the great conundrum of classical Athenian theatre, that is the ethical touchstone of this chapter, rather here more modest questions of what forms of action, what shapes our conduct might take in acting on behalf of others for whom 'the burden of images', as Marlene Dumas titled it in her paintings of 2015, is no longer an aesthetic nicety.[13]

Indeed by way of articulating one such form and shape of action one of the first events which I hosted at the Institute of Contemporary Arts during a period of directing the talks programme there during the 1990s, involved the group therapist Féliz Guattari, who had come to London just before he prematurely died of a heart attack, to discuss his newly translated and published essay *The Three Ecologies*. On finally shoe-horning a considerable audience into the modest ICA theatre space (*A Thousand Plateaus* in the translation by Brian Massumi had been doing brisk business at the ICA bookshop for years) I recall him insisting, before he could possibly speak to the assembled expectant group, that this kind of seating arrangement just would not suffice for the democratic purposes of his work. It was the wrong kind of assembly, the kind that Judith Butler does not encounter in her own work on the performativity of assemblies that we will come to shortly, that would appear to have to fulfil some kind of metric of assembled attainment. When the co-author of *Mille Plateaux* says he does not like the seating set-up you take note.

I am sympathetic to the idea that one's political ends and means should be linked formally and so readily agreed that we should spend an hour removing the rising bleachers that were designed to ensure everyone could see, and seat everyone on the floor in a circle around Félix, who promptly positioned himself sitting at their centre, therefore by definition with his back to a significant proportion of the audience who had come to listen to him. Félix had a quite soft voice and started with this passage from the work he was with us to discuss, *The Three Ecologies*:

> Now more than ever, nature cannot be separated from culture; in order to comprehend the interactions between eco systems, the mechanosphere and the social and individual universes of reference, we must learn to think 'transversally'. Just as monstrous and mutant algae invade the lagoon of Venice, so our television screens are populated, saturated by 'degenerate' images and statements. In the field of social ecology, men like Donald Trump are permitted to proliferate freely, like another species of algae, taking over entire districts of New York and Atlantic City; he 'redevelops' by raising rents, thereby driving out tens of thousands of poor families, most of whom are condemned to homelessness, becoming the equivalent of the dead fish of environmental ecology.[14]

Well, that was Félix Guattari at the ICA in the early 1990s. Prescient, at least. No one either knew what he was talking about, never really having heard of Donald Trump, nor could they get the analogy to algae, as they could not hear what he was saying, and his pronunciation of algae was quite baroque anyway. It took a brave heart to suggest at this stage that given we were all there to listen to Guattari we might want to return to a seating arrangement in which he *could* be heard. A less democratic proposal maybe, but a functional one at least. So we, or I should say the stage managers and I, spent another hour putting the theatre back into the shape it had been specially put into just an hour before, pulling the retractable seating out again, much to the exasperation of the ICA technicians who muttered something about their labour clearly being the one absolutely infinite resource available to intellectuals who require optimum circumstances for their own labour, with little respect for the pressure these demands place on others tasked with putting out chairs, taking them away, then putting them out again, in pursuit of the ideal democratic arrangement. The point Marx might have said, was not to change the world, but to administer its seating.

I thought that Guattari's idea of transversality, the pre-eminent place afforded institutions, institutionalisation and the critical 'act of instituting' in his work, was already underway within that room, there and then, as much in the *form* of the discussion and disagreement about the precise arrangement of assembly we should be staging, the seating, and ways of resolving that local dispute. His startling theoretical diagnosis, his forensic analysis of the newly empowered rentiers of the Reagan and Thatcher years, those beyond any constraint of something once called society, Donald Trump's instinct for gated communities, camps of the uber-elite that like algae would proliferate across the fetid lagoon of the cosmopolitan class, was so interesting, but principally for me because of what had just taken place in that very room as a model of like action.[15] I was aware as early as the mid-1990s that another elite, an educated elite that circulated through the theoretical groves that I was responsible for organising here at the ICA, had little sense of the question posed to them by those who were responsible, in *this* institution, for moving those chairs around at their will. A question of the disaffection of labour and also a question that Donald Trump himself would notice provided him with an opportunity and an electoral mandate of 52% some years hence. I also noticed that at that time a certain 'will to power' was manifest within a liberal elite who were beginning to deploy intersectional theory to constitute themselves as polymorphously free of wearisome identity formations (for which feminists had strived for years to empower) at the same time as forgetting to re-inscribe their own, evangelically relativist analysis with any due regard for those long left behind by successive government attacks on education and the welfare state, a working-class who were still apparently expected to rearrange the seating on the Titanic without comment from those going down.

Judith Butler has recently attempted to give shape to such 'performative assemblies' in a small catalogue of political gathering that this chapter seeks to amplify (and contest) in all kinds of ways. The 'nature' of assembly is what I seek to examine and expand in the coming pages with a close-eye trained on the expansion of the collective to meet the kinds of radical inclusion that would be the test of any viable socialist endeavour. Judith Butler's work on 'assembly' is far more focused than this, in short measure it represents an extension of Hannah Arendt's meditation on 'material supports for action' with the significance of the *infrastructural* capacity of the peoples' assembly as its focus. As Butler says:

> Assemblies assert and enact themselves by speech or silence, by action or steady inaction, by gesture, by gathering together as a group of bodies in public space organised by the infrastructure – visible, audible, tangible, exposed in ways both deliberate and unwilled, interdependent in forms both organized and spontaneous.[16]

As with the work of Shoshona Zuboff and her concept of 'surveillance capitalism' discussed earlier, the question as to quite *what* practices might contribute to such assemblies is nowhere made apparent in Judith Butler's otherwise useful analytic of gathering. In my view such action will always require us to take careful accounting not just of those evidences of existing practices that performance study has for five decades made its rightful measure, but critically those abandoned practices we might once have presumed to have access to in the event of such an emergency, the kinds of practices that will equip those seeking performative forms of assembly to act in desired ways.

In a series of linked essays Butler returns to themes close to the question of grievable lives in her earlier work, but with attention in this instance focused on how the field of appearances that regulates grievability, its infrastructure, is organised in such a way that certain kinds of bodies appear to be able to appear while others in complex ways cannot.[17] There is 'no alternative' as Margaret Thatcher the ferocious exponent of relative grievability might have said, to acting politically where one's ungrievable body is only ever able to secure its means of existence *by* such political endeavour. In this thinking Butler is echoing Hannah Arendt in *The Human Condition* whose principle of political action required those acting to occupy 'the space of appearance' for the sake of their survival.[18] Bodies on streets for Butler stand together to contest what she calls 'existing forms of political legitimacy' yet in an echo of the thinking on corporeal exposure of Adriana Cavarero these bodies are always constituted as vulnerable, yet passionate.[19] Indeed there is in this model of assembly no sociality without a precarity that exposes it as such, assemblies are in their ontology, their very being, an arrangement of interdependency. As in all masculine infrastructural theory (from Brecht on the street scene, Benjamin on the sidewalk and Debord on the beach that lies below the stones), for Butler the pavement is the privileged site of occupation in this imaginary of action, the support to any rights to mobility that we as protestors may wish to redeem. Indeed as the expressly non-violent Extinction Rebellion are finding out to their committed but perhaps naïve cost in Spring 2019 in London, as I write this chapter, every claim such assemblies make to the public sphere are, as Butler says, 'haunted by the prison'.[20] They are discovering Antonio Gramsci was right in his prescient linking of spectacle and arrest: "The theatre is merely the continuation of your life and your life is all written in the police's black book".[21]

In Butler's work on assembly, protest and activist groups coming together in the early 2010s such as in Gezi Park, Tahir Square and Occupy at Zucotti Park in New York (and I might add on the West Front apron of St Paul's in London) are figured as a 'source of hope', discovering what Butler calls their 'political potential' in 'unpredictable assemblies'.[22] Yes such appearances mark a caesura between those who are able to make their appearance felt in such masses, and those that are in no position to do so (as Peggy Phelan identified some years ago in *Unmarked*). Certainly yes, there are mobilisations of 'vulnerability in concert' as Butler puts it nicely that complicate any presumption of strength in resistance.[23] But there is also an insistent disavowal of *theatre* (if not the always already useful performance) in what Butler is referring to. As Hana Worthen points out, in her thoughtful review of Butler's work in *Critical Inquiry*, she troubles 'this readerly performative, this interdependent 'we', [that] aims to establish its force':

> In Butler's vision, the assembly is constituted by a 'new "between" of bodies', a sociality 'never reducible to one's own perspective', always already exceeding the unconnected and unencumbered individual. In its relational materiality and spatial appearance, the assembly seizes upon 'an already established space permeated by existing power', a 'theater … unproblematically housed in public space' (p. 85). 'Theater' appears in the *Notes* [*Towards a Performative Theory of Assembly*] as shorthand for the organising power of the state apparatus, somehow obliquely performing, too, as an antithesis to the assembly 'not circumscribed in advance' by design or identity. By implication, Butler's 'theatrical' seems to separate theater from the power of the 'unchosen dimension' of assembled plurality, I assume because theater's 'brokered' character

might appear to be consistent with the 'deliberate agreements we enter knowingly', in accord with the contractual dimension of liberal state power relations. Through Butler's *Notes*, then, theater comes into sight implicitly reduced to a single scene, an inherently disavowed space incapable of the queering work of other assemblies, even the assembly of Butler's readers, 'we'.[24]

Judith Butler is certainly not alone (think of Chantal Mouffe in previous chapters) in losing sight of the detail of the defining diversity of performance acts at the very moment they should be most pertinent and precise within any general cultural argument of this kind. Given the work the word performative is being asked to do on behalf of establishing how assemblies come into their complex being, the loss of theatre as 'we' might have taken pleasure in it, is peculiarly untimely if not understandable given amongst theorists it still carries the anti-theatrical prejudice that Jonas A. Barish (via Plato) made so clear to us years ago.[25] There are very few twentieth-century arrondissement philosophers after all, including Alain Badiou and Jean Baudrillard, Jacques Rancière and Jacques Derrida, whose *theatre* examples are as critically nuanced as Hélenè Cixous, who tellingly of course had the advantage of working so closely from the mid-1980s *within* Ariana Mnouchkine's Théâtre du Soleil at the Cartoucherie in Paris.[26] That said, Judith Butler has hardly been *without* theatre, working closely for some years with Shannon Jackson in Berkeley whose own book *Social Works* demonstrates the detailed way theatrical and performance practices can be embedded within, and inform theoretical speculation of, precisely this order.[27]

It is as though performance study might have learnt from the lesson of the performative (in large measure thanks to the early work of precisely Judith Butler to whom performance will always be indebted) but somehow performative theory such as *Notes Towards a Performative Theory of Assembly*, has not learnt in turn from material nuances of performance histories themselves. No wonder we find ourselves in our theatre and performance field the 'least-cited' academic discipline in the UK in 2018. It is as though we are 24/7 available for others without the simple respect of return citation. Try as you might you will very rarely find specific theatre practices discussed anywhere in books that lionise the performative nature of all else (with the noble exception of Miranda Joseph). That cannot only be to do with J. L. Austin's own anti-theatrical prejudice, whereby he peculiarly and inaccurately excluded theatre from precisely his first lectures on performative utterances. These kinds of queerings of performance *itself* (as theatre, as 'not theatre' and those common states in-between that 'we' commonly enjoy *as* theatre) are wholly absent from Butler's *Notes Towards a Performative Assembly*, as Hana Worthen astutely draws our attention to.

McKenzie Wark also usefully contextualises Butler's thinking within a broader tradition than is commonly offered (other than the obvious influence of J. L. Austin and performatives themselves): 'One could think of Butler's performativity as starting from Althusser's famous theory of ideology as interpellation. Ideology works by calling to us, addressing us. We misrecognise ourselves in the address, adopting the point of view provided for us'.[28] Tracing a rethinking of precarity in this context Wark notes how, for Butler at least, precarity is about a 'differential exposure to suffering'. Those 'unspeakable people' whose appearances disrupt the smooth working of the state are forced to act politically to 'secure the means of existing':

> Butler makes this a problem for critical theory. Who are these needy bodies that don't appear as subjects? What do the excluded call themselves? Can the illegible form a group? Can they be recognized? Full recognition may well be a fantasy for anybody. As Althusser and Laura Mulvey would insist, when ideology hails us, we misrecognize ourselves in its calling. But what would it feel like to not be called at all? To be a subject, to become a political being, means being about to perform some version of the norms that call us.[29]

Here the forms and assemblies that Butler prioritises are bodies that already exist in spaces together. They are made manifest in forms of appearance and Butler is especially interested, as noted above, in the precarious versions of such gatherings, where bodies are in some way restricted, limited or fragile, a politics of bodies assembling is in its own way always a politics of precarious and vulnerable bodies at further risk. But these human bodies, despite their apparent precarity, are nevertheless only figured in the form of a species-being that we recognise as resolutely of 'our' own kind. It is not as though Donna Harraway's spirit is amongst this number, nor her dog, never mind myriad representations that ecologically trouble the recent work on animality that has been central to performance studies for at least two decades. I will be testing Judith Butler's resolutely humanist limits to precarity with the arguments on 'phyto-performance' that follow. It is not that expanding the collective negates nor delegitimises such human centric arguments, the demand of priorities to action might after all be made in this instance of asking how assembling becomes a form of acting, but when such assembly is precisely gathering to alert us to the coming storm of climate change, it might be as well to have recognised that it is the capitalocene not the anthropocene that has driven demand for cheaper and cheaper natures and brokered in the surplus life that was once called human agency to act.

McKenzie Wark with an eye to the capitalocene, without referring to it given I don't think they like the word, notes in Butler's work the assembly of minds and bodies in various forms of action and meeting but recognises a manifest lack amongst all those bodies, a lack which has to do with *labour*:

> infrastructure appears as that which supports a political body; it is not that which a laboring body also builds and maintains. Like media, infrastructure is not really performative. In Butler, political bodies perform with public spaces, making them part of their assembly, but the reciprocal kind of performance is lacking, in which infrastructure makes labor part of itself [...] the (laboring) body is not a requirement of the pavement.[30]

Indeed the labour of species, of the dead, of the living, has gone missing in this account. With this lack in mind while Butler's work is always 'exemplary', as Wark puts it, at extending the account of 'political theory' it cannot account at all for the complexities of the category of what constitutes the '*polis* itself'. It remains in that sense within the horizon of the humanist universals of the Greek site that the location of this chapter seeks to contest.

Indeed, and most critical to this account, it would appear that for all the theory of assembling it is far from clear quite what *theatre* has to do with any such act of resistance. A doubt that might trouble Judith Butler herself, though given the lack of caveats in her writing regarding this yawning gap it would not appear to have done, but a doubt that would of course be fatal to a book of this nature given that Part I of this book committed itself to such an extended work out of precisely what *kinds* of theatre might operate in such circumstances of assembly that operated in contexts of intense political turmoil in which houses and homes were being co-opted by the State. Presumably all of which would be of interest to Judith Butler. It should therefore not be impossible here to continue with that project of precise discrimination of ways of working that *do* meet Hanna Worthen's quite reasonable expectations. The first of these is, in human terms, is a queering of expectation for performance that even the recent rush of animal theorists might find beyond the pale, given the way it will shake out any presumption we might have as to the very conditions of the verticality of assembly, the free locomotion of its subjects, and the expectation that when those subjects die they are not dead, and if they are dead, they are completely dead and not dead *and* alive.[31] These are some of the characteristics of performance I am about to address, question and call out in an expanded, and hopefully more radically inclusive, theory of, more precisely *perform*ative assembly.

Phyto-performance

One infinitely variable shape we might wish to consider as worthy of some attention to launch some new or undervalued perspectives for theatrical inclusivity might then be, plant-shape. Caring for plants, or less patronisingly, concerning oneself *with* plants, in the practice of gardening say, might be to stray as far as one could imagine from the intense urban and domestic assemblies that have formed the grounds for the arguments of this book so far, and appear to constitute the limits to Butler's 'field' of operation. But abandoned practices of this nature have long formed imaginary association for those gathered for performances in those very places. Matthew Goulish some years ago in a seminal (*sic*) performance with the Chicago-based performance ensemble Goat Island, called *The Sea & Poison* (1996), was already tending to a runner bean, seeded on top of his head, watering it with a child's watering can, well before I began thinking about the significance of abandoned practices in the cityscape, from the botanist of the asphalt Walter Benjamin, to the everyday theorist of the commons, Silvia Federici.

We all know the English love their gardens, but more empirically, last year in 2018 there were 86,000 British people on waiting lists for an allotment, a modest plot of land to grow vegetables and flowers, in the UK.[32] It is not that such practices therefore have in any way been abandoned, the statistics suggest that indeed they accelerate and proliferate in the era of climate change, despite the best efforts of Christopher Alexander whose *The City is Not a Tree* illuminated the ecologically sparse 1970s, it is rather that they have never been considered worthy of attention in the hierarchical realm of performance study in which everything from the minutiae of the urban gutter to the grandeur of the world's highest mountains are given due regard, while the prosaic and the popular are neglected to the point of abandonment. Here it is more a question of disciplinary abandon that loses sight of precisely those practices that could foster modes of assembly beyond those urgent human arrangements visualised by Judith Butler. Indeed, in keeping with the original wellspring of the abandoned practices project, long forming the curatorial frame for the Performance Foundation in London, now flourishing with summer schools at the School of the Art Institute of Chicago and in Prague,[33] in the work of the philosopher and historian of science, Isabelle Stengers, one could perhaps make an argument for the reconsideration of plants along such 'abandoned' lines while insisting on the new dimensions such phyto-performance offers a theory of political assembly. Stengers encourages us to take seriously that which has been abandoned for precisely such political purpose, in order to resist a globally rampant phenomenon that she calls: 'eliminativism'.[34] I have chosen to give another name to this wasting process, 'Abandoned Practices', but notwithstanding the subtle distinctions between the descriptors, what might such words mean in this vegetal context?

The *a priori* question Stengers always asks is: how can an event, such as a performance in this context for instance, be correlated to the need and concern for 'unity in struggle', or the 'production of the common' as she calls it? Hers is a fundamentally political question at all times – her thinking has underpinned a wide ranging reappraisal of the claims of laboratory science and its presumed 'objectivities', while contributing to a broad three-decade European movement that I would wish to align my own theatre work with, that of 'radical inclusion'.[35] For Stengers this problem of struggle, and you can add here struggles that one is oneself absorbed by on the ground, should be addressed in materialist terms, as practical ones, not simply as theoretical problems, the solution of which must be conceptually coherent. Language will help us here but the language theory at the root of deconstruction, less so. Such practice might just allow us not to 'see' the systematic destruction of practices, or of commons, as part and parcel of the power of capitalist expansion that both conditions that expansion and feeds it. Stengers' sources do not include Silvia Federici in this respect (though do rightly give a keystone place to the eco-feminist Vandana Shiva), but to ensure the obvious links to the earlier chapter on everyday life and social reproduction are kept fully in mind it is Federici who most persuasively argues for what she calls a 're-enchanting of the world' through the feminist politics of the Commons: 'Not only have commons existed for thousands of years, but elements of a communally based society are still round us, though subject to constant attack that recently has intensified. Capitalist development requires the destruction of communal properties and relations'.[36]

This challenge, which Stengers (and Federici) deems to be a materialist challenge, is that whatever the mess and perplexity that may result, we should resist the temptation to pick and choose among practices – keeping those which appear rational and damningly judging away the others, tarot-card reading, voodoo, hypnotherapy for instance, or here 'vegetal practices', that might at first sight appear bucolic or romantic, or most dangerously for pragmatic political purposes, utopian. The need for such a resistance is something naturalists have already learnt, when being careful to avoid judging animal species as either 'useful' or 'pests', or how botanists have sometimes, but not always, been able to avoid the presumption that something green, doing some mass-excluding of other species across a vegetable patch, is a 'weed' to be exiled and exterminated . This does not mean that some animals or plants cannot be considered as destructive or dangerous, it rather depends 'to whom' and with what kinds of pre-emptive powers. In the same way, some practices may well be considered intolerable or disgusting, often 'by others'. In both cases, the point for Isabelle Stengers is to refrain from using general judgemental criteria to legitimate their elimination, and to refrain from dreaming about a clean world, an un-fuzzy paradise with no cause to wonder nor alertness to alarm.

Stengers' clarion call is not for 'another science', but for a *relevant* science (perhaps attracting the same opprobrium that the word relevant attracts from artists in the art-world). A science that would actively take into account the knowledge associated with those agricultural and vegetal practices that are in the process of being destroyed in the name of progress. I will call this a Plant Science for reasons that will become apparent by the end of this chapter. The thesis that Stengers is defending – that materialism should divorce from eliminativism in order to connect with struggle – does not deny that elimination may have been utterly relevant when it entailed struggling against the allied powers of State and Church in the past, or racism and homophobia now, for instance. Today however, as Stengers is swift to stress, the situation has changed. Elimination has become the very tool of power. It is not only a tool for capitalism, but also for what Stengers would call: 'bad science'.

Phyto-centrism would in light of this marginalisation describe a project, and an opportunity, for something to happen by way of a small and gentle correction, in a deep very dark theatre of its own, an adjustment that one might imagine for the purposes of this book as performance-led. It has long been said that cities and theatres came into being at the same time and cannot do without each other. This might have something of a Western, Graeco-Roman bias about it, but across the limited landscapes of Europe and North America it is largely true. At the same time it should not escape our notice that there is barely a major European urban conurbation without its necessary alter-ego: the botanical garden. These glass-houses cling to the edges of almost all great cultural centres: Paris, Madrid, London, Rome, Prague, Edinburgh, Lisbon. At the very least one could therefore say that phyto concerns are by their nature defined by a measure of marginalisation to the city itself. But the degree to which a city inevitably asphalts over its phyto past is rather obvious (indeed Heinrich Goebbels at the height of the Third Reich designed a political programme upon just such asphalting), and we should attempt to deepen our discussion here between 'city vs. country' binaries if only to resist the threat of future totalitarians.[37] The word 'country', in English at least as Raymond Williams reminds us in *Keywords*, comes from the Latin word *Contra*, meaning 'against something'. In this sense it was only with the invention of the city that anyone cared to notice what the city was set against, it was set against something else that became the largely green thing called country, *after* the event of the urban you could say.

More interesting than these binaries, phyto interests, from the Greek word for 'things that grow', have most recently been championed in all their unpredictability by the Russian philosopher Michael Marder, in his ground-breaking book *Plant Thinking*.[38] Phyto-thought you could call it, has been common to the literary and philosophical imagination and vigorously spreading its tendrils, since Plato. It is now relevant to the philosophy of a number of thinkers whose broad interest is in vegetal life, a decentring of the human from plant perspectives, among whom the French philosophers Gilles Deleuze and Félix Guattari's work on the Rhizome would be the most obvious example.[39] But that casually metaphoric use, and some might say philosophical and interpretive abuse of plants, turning them back to their humanist use-value, is not where I intend to take us in this chapter. Encouraged by the generative phenomenological writing of Michael Marder I am going to look and feel elsewhere.

The coincidental relation staged at the ICA on that day in the company of Féliz Guattari, between transversality and assembly was one that was brought about by a discussion of ecology and the presence of plant life, in this case algae, within that phyto-sphere. Extending this relation for the purposes of this chapter and thinking about some of the performance concerns that might engage us with a book of this title *The Dark Theatre*, namely movement, awareness of the surrounding world, and life itself, Michael Marder reminds us we do not tend to associate with plants in quite the way that Guattari has reminded us is possible. We perhaps, if we think of them at all, think of plants 'shrouded in obscurity' to quote Thomas Aquinas. They predominantly live in continual darkness after all. We perhaps fail to recognise ourselves *in* plants, and I would add to that we fail to recognise politicians in plants (as Guattari so presciently was able to identify in Donald Trump's second algae-life). Thus, plants provide us, Michael Marder would suggest perhaps unwittingly, with a welcome short-circuit in the anthropocentric machinery. That is the machinery that ceaselessly compares us with other animals and having found comparisons wanting, co-opts other animals in *our* interests for our instrumental ends. It is perhaps, therefore, Michael Marder proposes, a good thing that we do not recognise ourselves in plants. It is their foreignness that might trouble us, but it is this otherness that protects us from too easy assimilation of what they intrinsically are. They are palpably and unmistakeably, 'not us'. I would stress here that this chapter will have failed if you think what I have been promoting is an appetite to cast, to draft in plants to performance (such as Audrey II the carnivorous cross between a Venus Fly-Trap and a Butterwort in *The Little Shop of Horrors*), to squeeze them for their pips, to mimic their movement or to transplant their roots.[40]

But, I would suggest at this stage of such a humancentric book, that a fresh approach to movement, to surroundings and to life itself, in the spirit of Michael

Marder's vegetal thinking, might be recognised in plants if we look and listen carefully enough. And that might not be such a bad thing when we seek ways of performance that can draw upon abandonment for their nourishment towards more sensate forms and fashions of assembly than Judith Butler has been able to offer us. But in this context, just so we can check some of our zoological bias at the door, movement itself immediately throws up some problems for thinking phyto-centrically. Our ideal movement we might though have to admit at the outset *is* an animal movement, by which I mean, we have the capacity for locomotion (as detailed at length in the discussion of dorsality in Chapter 3). The whole rhetoric of human 'disability' with regard to movement is based upon just such a spurious norm. Just think of words like crawling and striding for their comparative vertical place within an unwritten hierarchy of power to measure something of this loco-normativity. In saying this, and celebrating human locomotion over other movements, we forget as Michael Marder is at pains to point out, that plants move at their edges, their leaves, at their centre, their stem, and indeed, most voraciously, underground, in the dark. Growth itself, though in its own time and always patient compared with our pre-emptive leaps and impatient spasms, *is* a kind of movement. The life of plants is after all largely the life of a very dark theatre.

That said, it should be remembered, Michael Marder stresses, that the life of plants are virtually inaccessible to our senses. Plants were commonly placed between dead things and living things in the classical orders for this reason, they resisted easy assimilation to one or other realm. Logic does not allow philosophers (or lawyers) to think life and death at the same time for instance, one of the extraordinary capacities of plants that we take for granted at our peril. As I write these words scientists at Yale University have just announced that they have discovered a way to re-stimulate electrical capacity in the brain of a pig that has been 'dead' for four hours, but given the ethical implications are quick to reassure us that this is far from consciousness being restored in any sensible way.[41] The intense debate since 1968 as to when human death occurs is conducted in a language that cannot tolerate the nuance of the simultaneously alive and dead. An animal dies instantaneously, dead, or not dead, alive, as it is an integrated identity, whereas a plant can live *and* die at the same time. A lizard can shed a dead skin but this is an unusual zoological capacity for simultaneity, and in a sense we are all in the process of shedding ourselves, sloughing our human epidermal, given the tonnes of shed skin found by the 'fluffers' in the London Tube network each night. But more seriously and poignantly, the troubled history of what is described somewhat inaccurately as a 'persistent vegetative state', for those such as Terry Schivo suspended for years between life and death, or the 'Bella Addormentata' in Italy, Luana Englaro, whose 15 year incapacity after a car-crash engendered film and theatrical responses, requires medical practice and the law to legislate in the end on an 'appropriate *moment* of death' with the switching off of a life support apparatus (as we touched upon in the last chapter). Contractual neatness requires certifiable closure, not least of all when human life is at stake in the ambiguity of indecision.

So, while we might not be able to recognise ourselves in plants we perhaps, should be able to recognise, Michael Marder ingeniously suggests, the *vegetal inside us*. The otherness of vegetal life in us is a good antidote to anthropomorphism, we should begin here to recognise something of the plant in us, not us in them. And this perhaps is where the affective response to performance might begin to make sense vegetally. It is no small conceptual fry after all. The sustainable development of the earth relies on this inversion, of course. The assumption that it is up to human beings to sustain all that is 'natural' is deeply presumptuous. There is a grain of truth in this as humans have the most widespread impact on earth. But it is a delusional arrogance that it is humans that should be sustaining the earth alone. To be sure, as any history of weeds and their durability will tell you, some plant life is, really, quite negligibly dependent on us. The possibilities of life thus lie elsewhere. What difference does it make to our thinking if we begin to consider that, compared to the significance of plants for the biosphere, human stewardship of the earth often called the anthropocene, is almost superfluous when in our human-centred realities we think we are the most essential? Early cave dwellers, as we traced in the last chapter, understood this marginality of humans in the realm of other flora and fauna, they pictured the first human in Lascaux as shamed by their separation from other species who were 'like water within water', to borrow Georges Bataille's immersive phrase.[42]

There is an inequality in the sustaining and the sustained. Vegetable life, plants, provide material sustainability for human life, but there is in this process a form of 'ideal sustainability' occurring when the most superfluous being, the human declares, themselves central, the most essential thing imaginable. Material sustainabilities are thus preserved behind a veil of metaphysical abstractions, which bedevils the environmental and the ecological cause. Michael Marder has done more than anyone to break down such idealism with his meticulous material-horticultural hermeneutics. Plants provide for so many pressing perspectives: Are relations of instrumentality between humans and plants as straightforward as this? Do we just *use* plants? Do they use us? Is there feedback in this looping influence? Well, as Michael Pollan made clear in his book and film, *The Botany of Desire*, we work on the plants' behalf without realising it.[43] Where would the humble potato be if it had not been exported, to the corners of the earth, by people not unlike us just with bigger hats and ruffs? Honey bees no less exploit the human love of sweetness. They make sense as part of an evolutionary framework. We perhaps largely overlook the subtle ways plants determine *our* human behaviour.

Phytocentrism thus halts the anthropocentric urge of humans, that is for us to situate ourselves as central to a biosphere which got on quite well before us. The decentred nature of plants themselves then poses some interesting questions for us in performance. By putting plants in the centre, Michael Marder insists, probably in the light of a familiar and repeated questioning of his project, do we not just repeat anthropocentrism and its humanist ills. Well not exactly, as they, plants that is, are not unified organisms. It is difficult to tell where a part of the plant begins and ends, it is difficult to pinpoint coherent identity in vegetal life. The truth of the matter for Michael Marder at least is that to place the plant at the centre of our life is to 'decentre the centre', the centre implodes along with the penumbra.[44] That disruption to humanist service as 'normal' or business-as-usual, is especially interesting when we return to the question of the politics of assembly that we opened with.

The English Garden Effect

Given the apparent invitation this decentring might offer our theories of assembly, I want now to move onto the frictions that occur when plant-thought is practiced within material limits. And I will do this with recourse to a performance, *Lost Gardens* (2013) with which I was directly involved as a participant. Henry David Thoreau spanning the nineteenth century created an image of 'virgin nature' in which such limits were to be resisted at all costs. As he wrote in *The Maine Woods*:

> This was that Earth of which we have heard, made out of Chaos and Old Night. Here was no man's garden, but the unhandseled globe. It was not lawn, nor pasture, nor mead, nor woodland, nor lea, nor arable, nor wasteland. It was the fresh and natural surface of the planet Earth, as it was made for ever and ever.[45]

Well, Thoreau detested gardens, the geometric lawn was anathema to him, he celebrated those who burnt fences on behalf of the forest. Thoreau's deep intelligence understood that paradise was always 'paradise lost', his was a reaching for nature in its wholeness not in its picturesque, aestheticised scenery, what you could call the English Garden Effect.

This phrase comes from a short story by the American writer Walter Abish, who in turn borrows it from a suite of verses, *Three Poems* (1970), by the language poet John Ashbery. In that story Abish writes: 'Remnants of the old atrocity persist, but they are converted into ingenious shifts of scenery, a sort of "English Garden" effect to give the required air of naturalness, pathos and hope'.[46] I am interested in what such an English Garden Effect might mean for us as artists, outsiders, visitors, to this phyto-place, perhaps looking for a way to work that eschews the opportunistic occupational mode of the site-specific, and thinks itself into site in a more responsive and responsible fashion? In Abish's short story, an American writer visits Brumholdstein, a new German town built on the site of a former Nazi concentration camp. The writer carries with him on his visit a child's colouring book and some pencils to transcribe an interview he is conducting to find out how the local citizens have familiarised, neutralised and reified both the past and their present worlds as well. The narrator says:

> When one is in Germany and one happens not to be German one is confronted with the problem of determining the relevancy and to a certain extent the lifelikeness of everything one encounters. The question one keeps asking oneself is: How German is it? And, is this the true colour of Germany?[47]

This short story and its horticultural/aesthetic title came to mind amidst the potting sheds and allotments of the documentary theatre project *Lost Gardens* staged as part of the *Homo Novus* Festival in Riga in September 2013. The curatorial umbrella Gundega Laivina the artistic director of the festival had chosen was 'The Last Human Venue', from my work in *Theatre, Intimacy & Engagement* (2008) that opened this chapter. Christine Umpfenbach from Munich, the director of *Lost Gardens*, explores social realities in her performance pieces, focusing on migration, labour and the realm of the city. The performers one meets in *Lost Gardens*, as in other Umpfenbach projects, are mostly non-actors, people engaged in other professions, older people, children. They could be your neighbours. Umpfenbach works on this occasion with Latvian video artist Katrīna Neiburga and Austrian artist and scenographer Rudolf Bekic who had been living in Latvia for a number of years, working with hand-made objects and mechanisms. Zane Zajančkausk, a Latvian editor, curator, producer and a researcher of communities worked as director's assistant on the *Lost Gardens* project, researching what the promotional material for the piece called 'small garden culture', and helping in communication with the local groups and individuals who wished to be involved in the event. The festival programme puts the context like this:

> In May 2013, a lane was cut through the allotment gardens in Bolderāja to free up the space for railway tracks as a part of the Riga Free Port development plan. Gardeners lost their gardens, fences were knocked down, trees were cut, garden houses were burned down or were demolished by bulldozers. The traumatic event had a considerable impact on the lives of these gardeners, who after spending every summer there, now have no place to go. Many of them started 40 years ago as young families to cultivate this area from being a swamp into the place in which trees, fruits and vegetables could grow and flowers would bloom.[48]

The group were therefore seeing the first fruits of their labours in the early 1980s when I was starting work in another contested docklands port at Rotherhithe Theatre Workshop. The 'English Garden Effect' comes to mind as we group here amidst a landscape of 'rearranged' structures, gardens and fences. It is clear that there has been some rebuilding for the purpose of this event but not so much as to conceal the shattering experience these carers for the soil have experienced. We gather hesitantly, in loose assemblages of between ten and 14 folk, a community of those who have nothing in common while looking on at a community who most definitely do. Loss.

We are split into separate witnessing alliances rather than anything approaching an 'audience', and gently are asked to follow one of six leaders. We are given a piece of cut fruit or vegetable, something with a distinctive colour to mark us out from the other groups as though we might not remember to whom we belong. And indeed as we walk together slowly through the gathering twilight gloom of a late summer Rigan evening, there is something to be said for this small token of identity. For as one engages with each 'station' in the landscape in turn, a small shed here, a makeshift stand there, a soup being cooked here, a television playing an episode of some injustice there, the sense of one's own self begins to dissipate and mix with the horticulture that this land was once given over to, before the bulldozers came and made way for the Free Port Authority development that will asphalt 40 years of shared nurturing from this land.

The protagonists in this performance are the displaced gardeners and, peculiarly democratically on the invitation of the artists a representative from Riga Free Port (who presents his talk to us on the bus *en route* to the location). This is how these participants are described:

> Asja bought her garden 30 years ago for her father in order to help keep him busy and give him a purpose in life. After his death, she continued to maintain the garden to help her relax. One day, she returned to the garden to find it had been burned to the ground. She wrote to the Free Port authority asking for explanations as to why she was not given notice of the demolition. Anatolijs and his wife grew fruits and vegetables in their garden so they never had the need to go to the market to buy fresh products. He and his wife stood there watching his fruit trees being cut down. Together with his granddaughter Liza he explains how his garden house was relocated by a crane to an area 30 meters away from the original location. Kostja, a sailor, loved his garden house. This house was used as a place for friends and family to celebrate with music, food and drinks. He talks about the oak tree he planted in 1976 when his son was 2 years old and the shock when the tree was uprooted 40 years later. Gaida would visit her garden every day after work to relax by working in the garden, swimming and fishing in the nearby river. Now she does not know what to do with her free time after her garden was destroyed.[49]

Each of the stations one visits as part of the two-hour event is a small bricolage edifice within the landscape, hewn from the materials at hand. Each station is attended to by one of the residents, who in several cases prepare food from the ground nearby and serve a hot bowl of broth or salad and fruits as we perambulate. The time of this event is one that would appear to be closer to that of those growing things I have so far been calling plants, but here appear more like co-actors in a network of distributed performance capacities. The evening ends in as much as it can end, in a tent in the landscape, with a fire glowing outside, and inside a supper served by those who have been telling their stories of displacement. They stand in a simple tableau in the opening of the tent as we watch on from inside, looking beyond them to the long sunset across the landscape that is now not theirs. The coaches wait for us in the discrete distance as though to remind us that this country, this 'contra', is only what it is because of the other it is not – the city, to which we are about to be returned via the advertising lights of the petro-chemical companies and banks that edge Riga's urban fringe.

Saying what we mean with regard to politics is not quite as obvious in this horticultural context as it might appear in the first quiet words that get spoken to us on our walk through the allotments. Speech act theory has long taught us 'how to do things with words',[50] but as becomes evident in the landscape of the Lost Gardens of Riga 'arresting language' as I want to figure it here, turns its attention in another direction – toward the surprising things that language can undo and leave *undone*. Arresting language is seen amongst these plants as language at rest, words no longer in service to the project of establishing conventions or instituting legal regimes, where language itself – without any identifiable speaker – arrests otherwise continuous processes and procedures, including the processes of performative representation. The representative of the violating Riga Free Port, who had already lectured us at length on the bus, and who explains the Port Authority's perspective on what has happened, is an obvious example of such misapprehension. This loquaciousness of the 'entrepreneurial in action' is set off a little later by something else entirely, the resistant speech of the 'subjected under arrest'. Each of those who work this land at some stage whisper the word 'sapinats', a word that I do not recognise until asking later. It apparently means 'sorry'. Critically, the gardeners are recovering the recipes of the earth while at that very moment expressing some kind of bare apology for such appropriation of plants in the interests of human nutrition, expressing something of the fraught relationship that they well understand might be of some significance to the future of the land. Vegetal matter is setting the pace in this environment, as Asja is unable, or unwilling, to turn the flame up under those root vegetables and expect them to hurry along for the sake of theatre. She is sorry, 'sapinats', we will have to wait. They will take their own time to simmer, and that, for me at least, feels for the better.

Lost Gardens as convened by Christine Umpfebach digs a vegetal environment and in so doing constructs a site of *uncertainty* if it is anything, and therein lies its eloquence. The people doing the small and foreshortened speaking here, who happen to go by the names of Asja, Zeta and Kosta, are, in their doing, in their stilted saying, the word sorry for instance, *sapinats* which they repeat quietly at each station over the modest meals they offer us, marking their own *infidelity* to what lies in those propagation beds. Here that labour of oratory on behalf of plants and humans is self-evidently being marked as an improper performative process, it is a phyto performance that in so doing recognises and measures the degree to which it falls short of its subjects. Hence the murmured apology that arrests over easy affiliation, that arrests pseudo-association and action that used to go by the weirdly premature name of political theatre.

The only participant under 60 years of age, Nina, the granddaughter of two of the gardeners, who is about 14, demonstrates with great articulacy what she will do before the heavy machinery returns, she will rebuild against the storm. While we are there she is not doing theatre labour, she is doing a quite different thing called labour-labour, she is craning in a new replacement structure for her grandparents to sit in. She knows it won't last long against the developers, but she's all about the meantime for them as they are in the twilight of their lives at an age that can only count *on* that meantime. We ask her where she will go while her grandparents watch the land disappear? Unlike her older neighbours on this land she does not say sorry, 'sapinats', she is not sorry. She says 'Barbados', to open a beach bar.

The site that interested me in this work of assembling is not so large, more or less visible to its boundary half a mile away as we perambulate through the twilight together, and not nearly as auspicious as those historic protests selected by Judith Butler for scrutiny, but through this performance this 'lost garden' becomes an incalculable, or infinitesimal ground. This performance analysis occurs within the 'continuum of appearances' of this threatened landscape and the cyclical seasons of its growth. The question of *arrest* hovering over those who wish to participate here (given their continued presence is now deemed illegal trespass and reasonable 'grounds' for eviction) makes a special demand on any such apparent continuity. Arrest and the dark of incarceration would after all imply an irreversible and irrevocable interruption of everything that has hitherto appeared here, in the phytocentric form of blossom and fruits, seeds and stems.

In the poetic realm such arresting interruption would be called the *caesura*, the pure word or counter-rhythmic interruption. Here in this brackish landscape it is no longer the changing nature of representation that is at stake but representation itself that appears as a thwarting of expectation. The caesura of that breathed sound, 'sapinats', does not simply mark an interruption, it carries the interruption out. Although it cannot be experienced within a continuum of representations it structures this continuum by interrupting it and dividing it into unequal parts, or stations that we encounter on our way. Language not only arrests the succession of representations in these stations, 'sorry' is no longer here the hardest word, rather it is language that has been arrested in turn.

This double-sided arrest would be altogether paradoxical if the language that arrests the succession of representations were the same language that was arrested, but it is not – or not quite. The arresting language is what the Germanist Peter Fenves would call the 'pure word', but I would prefer to call the 'barely there' word, the sound of sorry, 'sapinats', is there but bare, so bare it is 'just so', no more no less, it is *thus*. The 'arrested language' on the contrary is the empirical word, which is to say, the word through which appearances are represented, as for instance in the expansionist language of the Port Authority representative with their reassuring maps of 'regeneration', or indeed in Nina's brave and irrational resistance and escape, voiced as 'Barbados here I come!'.

The 'barely there' word by contrast *says* nothing, beyond 'it is thus', it cannot begin to articulate an apology to plants from the humans that have used them and subsequently betrayed them. For this reason it is by no means certain that the 'barely there' is even a word – one word among others. Rather the 'barely there' word here interrupts the process of judgement through which words are separated from, and connected to, one another, and prompts us to think again about the impotential of performance. If it is thus, what is left for performance to do one might ask? In this case I would suggest, bide its time, and thereby expose the lie of this land in ways that would otherwise be quite unfathomable.

In these chapters *The Dark Theatre* gravitates towards such resistant figures, those who are 'just so', those who interrupt the continuum of representations without being in a position to justify this interruption. They are weak after all; they have no power. Which of course does not mean they don't have strength. The strong-willed gardeners of Riga have found a way to act in accordance with a 'lawful calculus of justice', not as an arbitrary whim or expression of egocentric will, but as their own number, an association of loss, a curious company, those who are amongst their plants yet recognise the pathos and hope that separates them now they are so 'barely there', in the asphalt twilight.

Critical commons

I take it that a concluding set of questions for this chapter that arise from work of this nature might refer to where we are, or where we find ourselves and our relations to others, and the forms, modes and comportments of practice we deploy once we have found ourselves through our work *with* others, which of course necessarily includes realising we are always lost, dazed and confused, but necessarily adjusting to the demands of the horizon. That symmetry between means and ends (that we explored on Féliz Guattari's fateful visit to the ICA discussed earlier) inasmuch as it shapes our practice today, is by no means one that can be taken-for-granted when it comes to imagining and realising forms of assembly that will make any kind of difference. And perhaps it is the precise challenge of ecology and environment that most presses upon our responsibility to such self-reflexiveness.

Again it takes Silvia Federici to have preceded us in this work given that her writing has always braided questions of everyday life, the commons and the future of the university as coeval, critical and crucial and as a great pedagogue as Federici is, always to be thought together whatever the sense of entitled embarrassments that might accrue to reflecting on the relative privileges of the university in such circumstances. As though to emphasise these links Federici places an essay on the 'Commons against and Beyond Capitalism' next to her exploration of 'The University: A Knowledge Common?' in the recent essay collection *Re-Enchanting The World*.[51] In the first her concern is with the diminishment of the commons at the behest of capital, a diagnosis wholly in keeping with the experience in Docklands that forms the first part of this work. By way of summary as though foreshadowing everything said of the dictatorship of the performatariat in Chapter 2, Federici concludes: 'It is almost a law of contemporary society that the more commons are attacked, the more they are celebrated'.[52] If as Federici asserts history itself is a 'common', a shared experience that connects us to a 'vast expanse of struggles' then in the terms of the university that this last part of the chapter occupies, those struggles are inevitably ones of disciplinary inclusivity and curriculum plurality, but rather characteristically given Federici's concern for the pragmatics of social reproduction that undergird all such knowledge production, these connections are certainly not all that is at stake.

Where elite US university libraries describe themselves as 'information commons' the very sites of London's historic universities, including my own current academic berth King's College, can with very little archaeological work be found to be sites of struggle. As Walter Benjamin said all historical documents in the end are documents of barbarism, and that would especially well apply to those documents that record the Royal establishment of 'our' historic university campuses. When invited to talk about 'the university' Federici is acutely aware of such violent legacies, returning to the 'grass and the land under the cement on which the classrooms and the libraries have been built'.[53] Wholly consistently Federici perceives the university as a 'sort of enclosure'. I share with Silvia Federici the obvious qualification that:

> if we want to change the university [which given its recent decline into financialisation, securitisation and militarisation we obviously do] and construct a 'knowledge commons' we need to be concerned not only with the content of the curricula and most importantly the cost of studying, as crucial as these undoubtedly are. We need to question the material conditions of the production of a university, its history, and its relation to the surrounding communities.[54]

In this specific context of adjustments to circumstance I was touched by the experience of sharing an evening with the gardeners on their Rigan allotments, but I was also fascinated by their continued capacity to avoid arrest, to retain their potential for political change precisely by avoiding incarceration. In this sense they were, despite their relatively senior years, the more nimble version of the Extinction Rebellion activists who today, as I write this, are still offering themselves up for mis-treatment by the police three days into their occupation of Waterloo Bridge in the centre of London. With regards to *resisting arrest* I was especially interested here in what James Martel has recently called 'misinterpellation', the way that however one is 'called upon by power', there will always be those who find ways to subvert the force of that call.

The Rigan gardeners were some way from the passive aggressive 'I would prefer not to' refusniks that orientate Herman Melville's 'Bartelby', they were far more subtle than that in their de-voiced apologies to power who could not quite work out a way to deal with their continued presence on land that they had presumed they had long-since put under the enforced sign of enclosure. Louis Althusser (as we briefly touched on at the outset of this chapter in our discussion of Judith Butler's performative assemblies) outlined the force of this calling by power, otherwise known by the word *interpellation*, in his celebrated work on Ideological State Apparatuses of the 1970s.[55] To put it simply as imagined by Althusser: when a police officer, or figure of state authority, hails a figure *on the street* with the words 'Hey You There!', the subject turns to face the appellant, knowing it is them that is being addressed. But significantly for Althusser, wary of pure origins, it is only in nine out of ten cases that the force of law subjectivises its subject of attention in this demanding way, which of course means that in at least 'one in ten' cases that violence of attention between state and subject *misfires*. This misfire I would propose, provides opportunities for resistance, re-empowerment, play and in the case of the Rigan gardeners, cultivation and cooking. This flaw in the mapping of State and subjecthood gives rise to the promising possibility that not only the site of the street at least (the privileged location of Althusser and Butler's theory of interpellation), but also in the commons at large (as represented by those allotments) there may well be all kinds of latent, or excessive space for performances of identity and politics that complicate at the very least those supposedly all-embracing State definitions.

But what kinds of subjects emerge from such misinterpellation? It is Nietzsche, who helps us with this in his work by continuously offering a form of counter theology in which our own deep desire to be delivered to some authority that is at the core of interpellated subjectivity is repeatedly thwarted by a form of anarchic messianism, the misfiring messiah, whether that force is given a name like Zarathustra or the Overman. In such failed callings and returns, our expectations and unacknowledged hopes for great political endings, heroic teleologies that we might ordinarily wish to operate by, are constantly thwarted. The whole point of reading Nietzsche against the grain, in the spirit of a book about loss, is perhaps to observe the detailed mechanics of how it is that a 'hope for salvation' might be, and will be, dashed at every turn. But such disappointments inherent to such failed returns, are much more than disappointments about thwarted aspirations, they constitute a continuous and sometimes complete collapse of subjecthood, as Nietzsche himself experienced in that Turin street as he turned beyond his own species to a horse, not just for solace but to save him.

Indeed the contention I am making here amongst the gardeners of Riga is that the interpellation of the State that Althusser rightly identified as the workings of ideology, does not have anything like a hit-rate of nine out of ten as Althusser suggested, it more often than not gets it wrong, it renders subjects in all of their multiplicity and anarchic complexity, manifestly unknowable by projecting onto them a single unitary self that, being false, offers nothing 'to know' at all. Reading theatrical figures and *mise en scene* in this way I would suggest can then without voluntarism operate by way of a form of a modest *training*, as Nietzsche certainly espouses in his own modus operandi, for larger and distinctly political applications of that way of reading across from events to the questions in hand, in this case we might say the camps where mis-interpellation is rife.

I suppose any mention of exhaustion insists anyway that we, however grudgingly, return to Nietzsche again, whatever reservations we might rightly have about so doing. Nietzsche dwelt very precisely upon the entanglements of the vegetal, variegated species and what he called 'the jungle', or as it has been more recently translated by Kevin Hill in Nietzsche's newly translated notebooks, 'primeval forest', in his notes on *The Will to Power*, which were without his permission, and indeed against his expressed view, collected together and published after his death by his sister, Elisabeth Forster-Nietzsche in 1901. But Nietzsche turned to the vegetal only after a detour through the 'arrant misrepresentations' and 'counterfeits' of psychology. In fragment 704 in 'The Will to Power in Nature' (written between November 1887–March 1888) Nietzsche questioned 'Man's' striving after happiness. But to understand anything about life, Nietzsche, unusually perhaps for the philosophical tradition, insisted on an expanded sense of *botanic* life, a 'formula that must apply to trees, and plants and animals'. Nietzsche even takes the trouble to notice the structural problem when asking what a plant might strive after, a false unity which does not exist given the 'fact of millionfold growth'.

When Michael Marder, the author of *Plant Thinking*, and *Through Vegetal Being* (with Luce Irigaray) visited us at King's College in 2013 he discussed this tangled Nietzschean excerpt fleshing it out with some fascinating material insights borne of his own commitment to thinking-through 'plant practices'. Without being presumptuous I hope, unbeknownst to themselves who know little of Nietzsche's view perhaps, scientists confirm Nietzsche's hypothesis in examining the pronounced kin-recognition of plants. Specimens of the plant *Cakile Edentula* for instance produce more roots when they share a pot with *strangers* (that is plants of the same species, grown from seeds that derived from a different mother plant) than when they germinated in the same pot as their kin (defined as plants grown from seeds collected from the same mother plant). Perhaps then Nietzsche's interpretation of the 'fight' amongst trees in a jungle is also a theoretical fiction which in turn naturalises the struggle for survival in human societies, rather as the work of Konrad Lorenz had done with supposedly 'red of tooth and claw' animalities of his markedly post-war mid-twentieth century thinking, against the conclusive research of Ashley Montagu that reframed atavistic nature as altruistic nature. But having said that we ought to look for a philosophical rather than bio-anthropological sense of Nietzsche's 'will to power' in order to assess its significance here.

Such striving, such 'will', will always occur in the face of something that Nietzsche says 'resists': 'For what do the trees in a jungle fight each other? For happiness? – *For power!*'[56] But amongst these competitive columbines there are other millionfold symbiotic forms of species *co-existence* which with some plant thinking, some properly environmental thinking of the kind I have been reminding us of in each of these practices from Rotherhithe to Riga, could be taken into account when considering what kind of assemblies phyto-performance invite us to think and act through. It is not that 'the jungle' offers another metaphor with which to squeeze the pips of the vegetal, rather it offers a material/historical site where kinship relations between plants have been observed, where to strive to 'be in the sun' could be conceived as more than an ontological imperative against entropy, where to *persevere* in being is itself the genesis of the performative comportment.

That performative comportment in practice, and its study, informs what I can do now with the energy that I have for assembling amongst others for commitments that demand something more than this kind of theoretical attention (that is most commitments that want to do more than speculate on what the 'Left' might now be getting on with). For instance work I do now (and have been doing for some years) as an advisory board member, participant and maker for the activist artist group Platform whose work as part of Liberate Tate is very well known given it, spectacularly and with due regard for the big theatrical occasion, brought an end to BP Sponsorship of that well platformed institution. Our occupation of Tate on the weekend of the Paris Climate Talks Summit of December 2015 cannot have been the sole cause of the sudden withdrawal of Tate's BP funding, but neither was it irrelevant given that when Liberate Tate began their work on exposing the hypocrisy of this institution and its funding streams there was barely any public consciousness of the propositions that such institutions always work only when they have a 'licence to operate'.[57] When that licence is revoked by a public through their rejection of that company's terms of business, or brought into question by their continued flaunting of evidential reason, there are serious corporate implications for those who commonly consider such matters marginal to their conduct. Volkswagen, Coca Cola and Dasani and the corporate excavators BHP Billiton have all been made aware of such implications recently in the standing of their share price and the precarity of their executive boards.

In the case of BHP Billiton there has been some local house-keeping to do (stone throwing in a glasshouse you could say) and I have been committed on the picket line, in meetings and student support, in raising awareness of the peculiar, yet wholly predictable fact, that King's College London thought it appropriate in full sight of students also graduating with hard won degrees, to award the one honour they had to bestow, an Honorary Degree, on Andrew Mackenzie (FRS) the long-standing chief executive officer of the international mining conglomerate BHP Billiton prior to his succession in 2020. Dr Mackenzie has done much for charity causes in his long and distinguished career as a chemist and industrialist, but the principle that King's was promoting that they were working towards a 'sustainable campus', did not for me at least sit well with the evidence of Billiton's international extraction projects amongst which the Samarco Dam collapse in Mariana, Brazil, in 2015 (a joint venture of Vale and BHP Billiton) has been described by authoritative sources as 'Brazil's worst environmental disaster'. It is a disaster that wiped out an entire eco-system, killed 19 humans, directly affected 240,000 individuals, 24 municipal governments, 11,000 (smaller) businesses and 200 members of the Krenak indigenous community, and has led to a £5 billion legal claim those combined parties launched from Liverpool in the UK on the reasonable understanding that under UK law the plaintiffs might stand a chance of swifter, or indeed, any justice to begin to compensate for the toxification of their lives, their livelihood and their land.[58] If there was ever a landmark (in the form of a tomb or grave) that spoke more powerfully to the claims made in Part I of this book about the exploitation of 'cheap natures' by colonial forms of capitalist expansionism, I very much hope I will not be witnessing it in my own lifetime.

Drawing attention to a university senior management and council that such ironies have been noted is only to note those ironies, it is to do nothing more than to pay witness to injustice. Silvia Federici would be the first to remind us of that hard fact. But perhaps such witnessing and retelling, in the spirit of Federici, contributes to the weather-front of actions being conducted courageously each day anyway, in the much derided, apolitical university for instance, amongst courageous and committed students, by precarious and generous early academic career staff fighting for labour rights for others, and minimum-wage cleaners seeking the justice of being brought 'in-house' from the outsourced companies that fail to provide them with the most basic health and safety protection, a triumvirate who have my attention and support now, given they have nothing like the securities as a tenured professor that I enjoy. The only comment a member of my senior management had about this particular incident as they negotiated our picket line was: 'What are you looking so jolly about?' It's as though they don't mind us being on picket lines as long as we look like unhappy picketers should. One even suspects they might prefer oppressed picketers. Our assembly, as largely irrelevant academics even, is not just agonistic therefore, it is destined to be anxious and agonised. Modes of political representation would appear to have to be melancholic if at all today. Forgive me for smiling at the obvious irony that politics has always been, or at least since human record began, our second most-pleasurable pursuit.

Notes

1 Read, Alan (1993). *Theatre & Everyday Life: An Ethics of Performance*. London: Routledge, p. 149.
2 See Ophir, Adi (2000). *The Order of Evils*. New York: Zone Books, p. 615.
3 See Agamben, Giorgio. (2008). 'What is the Contemporary?', in *What is an Apparatus?* Trans. David Kishik and Stefan Pedatella. Stanford: Stanford University Press.
4 See Ophir, Adi, op. cit. p. 619.
5 Al Gore, *An Inconvenient Truth* (2006). Dir. Davis Guggenheim.
6 Ophir, Adi, op. cit. p. 624.
7 Katie Beswick, tweeting as @ElfinKate, 15 April 2019 (see thread for response). I am grateful to Katie Beswick for agreeing to my inclusion of her sober and prescient short-form writing here. Her equally challenging work in longer form can be found in a number of books including the excellent: *Social Housing in Performance: The English Council Estate On and Off Stage* (2019). London: Bloomsbury.
8 www.theguardian.com/science/2018/sep/01/swedish-15-year-old-cutting-class-to-fight-the-climate-crisis (accessed on 28 August 2019).
9 Arts Council of England 'Shaping the Next ten Years' strategy document, at www.arts-council.org.uk/nexttenyears included metric of 'relevance'.
10 Twitter, Wednesday 17 April, 8.41am and 8.52am.
11 Ophir, Adi, op. cit. p. 625.
12 To see why I think this turn to: Read, Alan. (2008). *Theatre, Intimacy & Engagement: The Last Human Venue*. Houndmills: Palgrave, p. 208.
13 See 2015 record of Tate Modern exhibition: www.tate.org.uk/whats-on/tate-modern/exhibition/marlene-dumas-image-burden (accessed on 28 August 2019).
14 Now included in: Guattari, Féliz. (2000). *The Three Ecologies*. Trans. Ian Pindar and Paul Sutton. London: Athlone, p. 43. I am grateful to Tuija Kokkonen who reminded me of this occasion when she wrote and presented about this work herself: www.uniarts.fi/en/newsroom/seminar-philosophy-and-politics-ecology-8–9112016 (accessed on 28 August 2019).
15 On Transversality and the institution see Andrew Goffey in *Radical Philosophy* 216, Jan/Feb 2016: www.radicalphilosophy.com/article/guattari-and-transversality (accessed on 28 August 2019).
16 See Butler, Judith. (2015a). 'We the People' in *Notes Toward a Performative Theory of Assembly*. Cambridge: Harvard University Press, p. 156.
17 See 'Grievable Lives' discussed at: www.versobooks.com/blogs/2339-judith-butler-precariousness-and-grievability-when-is-life-grievable (accessed on 28 August 2019).
18 Butler, Judith, op. cit. p. 72

19 Ibid. p. 85 and p. 97.
20 Ibid. p. 185.
21 Antonio Gramsci (1985). 'Avanti!', Piedmont edition, 11 September 1917, in *Selections from Cultural Writings*. Eds. David Forgacs and Geoffrey Nowell-Smith, Trans. William Boelhower. London: Lawrence and Wishart, p. 67.
22 Butler, Judith op. cit. p. 1.
23 Ibid. p. 140.
24 See Hannah Worthen Review: https://criticalinquiry.uchicago.edu/hana_worthen_reviews_notes_toward_a_performative_theory_of_assembly/ (accessed on 28 August 2019).
25 See Barish, Jonas A. (1985). *The Anti Theatrical Prejudice*. San Francisco: University of California Press.
26 www.theguardian.com/culture/2012/aug/10/ariane-mnouchkine-life-in-theatre (accessed on 28 August 2019).
27 Jackson, Shannon. (2011). *Social Works: Performing Arts, Supporting Publics*. Abingdon: Routledge.
28 See Wark, McKenzie, 'What the Performance Can't Perform: On Judith Butler', *Critique and Praxis*, 13/13, March 25 2019, accessed 01.08.2019 at: http://publicseminar.org/2016/06/butler/.
29 Ibid.
30 Ibid.
31 As I write this the question of Dead/Alive that Forced Entertainment reflected upon so beautifully in their performance work over a number of years is being contested once again as scientists at Yale University inject into dead pig's brains and find them electrically charging despite all expectations that a dead brain starved of oxygen for four hours, cannot be revived. *O Lucky Man!* (1973) Directed by Lindsay Anderson also explored these questions with alacrity.
32 See National Allotment Society, UK: www.nsalg.org.uk (accessed on 28 August 2019).
33 See Abandoned Practices Institute at http://abandonedpractices.org (accessed on 28 August 2019).
34 Stengers, Isabelle. (2007). 'Diderot's Egg' in *Radical Philosophy*, 144, (July/August 2007).
35 See Read, Alan. (2008). *Theatre, Intimacy & Engagement: The Last Human Venue*. Houndmills: Palgrave.
36 See Federici, Silvia. (2019). 'Commons Against and Beyond Capitalism', Silvia Federici, *Re-enchanting the World: Feminism and the Politics of the Commons*. Oakland: PM Press, p. 87.
37 For a detailed philosophical discussion of this asphalting see Blumenberg, Hans. (1996). *Shipwreck with Spectator: Paradigm of a Metaphor for Existence*. Trans. Steven Rendall. Cambridge: MIT Press.
38 Marder, Michael. (2013). *Plant-Thinking: A Philosophy of Vegetal Life*. New York: Columbia University Press.
39 See Deleuze, Gilles and Guattari, Félix. (2004). *A Thousand Plateaus: Capitalism and Schizophrenia*. London: Continuum.
40 https://en.wikipedia.org/wiki/Little_Shop_of_Horrors_(film) (accessed on 28 August 2019).
41 www.theguardian.com/science/2019/apr/17/scientists-reboot-pig-brain-hours-after-animals-died-yale-university-researchers (accessed on 28 August 2019).
42 See Bataille, Georges. (2005). *The Cradle of Humanity: Prehistoric Art and Culture*. Ed. Stuart Kendall. Trans Michelle Kendall and Stuart Kendall. New York: Zone Books.
43 Pollan, Michael. (2002). *The Botany of Desire*. London: Bloomsbury.
44 See Marder, Michael. (2013). *Plant Thinking*, op. cit. especially the Introduction in which this manifesto is laid out with incisive flair.
45 Thoreau, Henry David. (1916). *The Maine Woods*. Boston: Houghton Mifflin, p. 78.

46 See Abish, Walter. (1980). 'The English Garden Effect', in *In The Future Perfect*. London: Faber.
47 Ibid. p. 37.
48 See *Homo Novus* web-site archive: www.homonovus.lv/eng/performances.php?s=lost-gardens (accessed on 10 March 2019).
49 Ibid.
50 See Austin, J. L. (1962). *How to do Things with Words*. Oxford: Oxford University Press.
51 See Federici (2019), op. cit. pp. 85–98 and pp. 99–101.
52 Ibid. p. 86.
53 Ibid. p. 99.
54 Ibid. p. 101.
55 Louis Althusser discusses interpellation in *Lenin and Philosophy and Other Essays*. Trans. Ben Brewster. New York: Monthly Review Press, 2001.
56 See Michael Marder, 'Nietzsche's Jungle', in *The Philosopher's Plant, Los Angeles Review of Books*, https://philosoplant.lareviewofbooks.org/?p=59 (accessed on 19 August 2019).
57 As part of the *Deadline Festival* at Tate Modern, 5–7 December 2015, I gave a talk with a title not a great distance from the nature of this chapter. The full programme can be accessed here: https://deadlinefestival.wordpress.com/programme/ (accessed on 28 August 2019). I am grateful to Platform for involving me in this work and their ongoing commitment to critical causes: https://platformlondon.org (accessed on 28 August 2019).
58 For a reliable summary see: www.theguardian.com/environment/2018/nov/06/bhp-billiton-facing-5bn-lawsuit-from-brazilian-victims-of-dam-disaster (accessed on 28 August 2019).

6
CULTURAL CRUELTY
Extraordinary rendition and acoustic shock

The sounds in my head began with a vengeance on the evening of Thursday 6 October 2016. I was in the audience of the first night of Christopher Brett Bailey's *Kissing the Shotgun Goodnight* at the Oval House in London, accompanying a group of students who were anticipating work by the celebrated auteur of *This is How We Die* (2014), at an event that made quite explicit the intended extreme amplification levels of the imminent show with a helpful graph indicating the contours of noise we would experience – with or without the orange ear plugs provided by the venue, I wasn't sure. At the foot of that sheet Chris had enthusiastically added: 'We will send you home with ringing in your ears'.[1] That seemed a confident claim from a practitioner whose commitment to do what he said by way of performance I never doubted. I readily wore the garish, fluorescent-cheap ear-protection from well before it began, having previously experienced Scott Gibbons' compositional work with Romeo Castellucci and Socìetas Raffaello Sanzio over a number of years, (and discussed at length in Chapter 4), with on one occasion an admirably noisy, stage-filling volcano that occupied the second half of a work called *The Four Seasons Restaurant* at the Odéon Atelier in Paris.[2] The coefficient between the complex meanings of the staging and the corporeal and psychic demands it made on those attending, was, as with all Castellucci's work, well within the margins of pleasure one might expect for an exhilarating hard-night out at the theatre. I have lived a life of such (comparatively leisured) 'hard' nights out and never subscribed to John McGrath's titular appeal for 'A Good Night Out' for the working classes. I presume we all deserve our fair share of the harshest representations of hard lives that might make some sort of difference when it comes to not just interpreting that world but changing it.

On this very different occasion at the Oval House, the much-loved original venue in Kennington that had been formative in the spirit of London's Fringe theatre scene from the 1970s, and where I had been countless times before without hint of calamity, it was volume and volume alone, that appeared to be covering up for something that seemed to have gone missing from Chris Brett Bailey's consummate theatrical practice. Searing guitars filled the hour, with a brief, mysteriously opaque barely audible spoken interlude in the middle, by way of concession to those for whom guitar bands were passé, without apparent sense nor reason, at the end of which there *was* no reason, nor sense of hearing as I had previously experienced it left in me.

It was not that thrash-metal was new to me, as a guitarist with a 50 W Marshall amp who had spent an adolescence in Essex at the time of the great strafing diagonalist, Wilko Johnson, and his heavy-duty rhythm and blues band Dr Feelgood, that was unlikely. Indeed, since well before that adolescence my life had been marked by the *recovered* gift of hearing so I had long protected it assiduously in the manner of those who have lost something. My earliest memory after all, at four years old, was being carried into Rochford Hospital in Essex by my widowed mother, with a vertigo-inducing pain that I thought was in the middle of my head but was in fact diagnosed as mastoiditis and surgically treated with the insertion of grommets in my ears. After a week away from home, the first time I had ever left home, sitting forlorn, head bandaged, on a faded eau-de-nil ward, I was discharged with artificial bones in my flaps and a year-long schedule of consultation appointments. On that first night back at home I marvelled at the gas-poker that roared into life and lit the coal-fire with a warmth that I could hear for the first time in my memory without pain. I suppose that what follows in this chapter, 58 years later, is then some kind of reckoning with risk, an apology to the Consultant who with his NHS standard caring-expertise preserved my hearing then, and gave me the freedom to choose what I did with it for the rest of my life, until late in the day I made a serious error of judgement on that Thursday evening in South London.

I should be grateful, I know, that's how I was brought up by my working-class grandparents, the Oval House theatre box office *did* provide ear plugs which I wore throughout the 'Shotgun' show, presuming as I had done since that childhood experience, that my ears were susceptible to noise. Though as I later discovered, listening to an expert witness on the critical matter of hearing-protection in the High Court, those plugs were not fit for purpose, and made little measurable difference to the tumult on offer on that evening. My ears have been ringing away day and night ever since (two and a half years at the time of writing) which is how certain forms of hearing impairment make themselves manifest, as some of you reading this with noise in your head will know. I cannot find the words to describe the sound, and we are all sonically different anyway, so my acoustic evocation should I find a way to put language to it here would be *sui generis* to the point of partiality. Indeed by its nature sound is a phenomenological experience of rare ephemerality (which is presumably why such hard loyalties are felt for bands we enjoy), but the celebrated music journalist Nick Coleman has a valiant and wholly recognisable go in the first pages of his shattering memoir, *The Train in the Night: A Story of Music and Loss*:

the *pffff* evolved into a wild humming and the inside of my head began to resound like the inside of an old fridge hooked up to a half-blown amplifier [...] *Pfffff-zzzzzz-mmmmnnnn*. Such are the excitements of tinnitus. Soon, every outside-world sound that went in one good ear produced a balancing, then overwhelming noise response in the other one, on top of the basic fridge noises. It was deafening in there. A fight. A riot. I began to be frightened of any sort of ambient sound and of people who threatened to make it by scraping chair legs or laughing or handling paper bags. I began to treasure the thought as well as the actuality of silence.[3]

Some three months after the shotgun had been kissed goodnight by Chris Brett Bailey there had been no improvement in my hearing, certainly no silence to speak of, and I knew why. I had been examined by Dr Harriri, an audio-consultant in a specialist clinic on the Cromwell Road in West London, who drew an image of my aural faculty and its recent impairment. As his wrist angled across the page, as though joining a giddy samphire-collector's route across the cliff, it had the unmistakeable dip of loss, or at least diminishment about it. The plunging roller-coaster graph tracked under the doctor's index finger was mute and failed to capture the sounds in my head which, triggered by the theatrical occasion at the Oval House, had brought about the condition that audio-specialists most fear because there is absolutely nothing they can do about it. The condition is irreparable. They pronounce the prognosis softly so as to recognise its lasting impact without unduly surprising you: tinnitus. I knew about this elusive condition because one of my favourite performers, Richard Lowdon of Forced Entertainment, had on the occasion of the group's 30th birthday party at the London Toynbee Hall base of Arts Admin, shared with me that he had sustained something that sounded quite similar as a consequence of a theatrical act that had gone wrong. And Richard knew he was not alone, we unfortunately never are. On the day I wrote these words the inquest into the death of the *Inspiral Carpets*' drummer Craig Gill is reported in the *Guardian* newspaper. He apparently took his own life after suffering the debilitating side effects of 20 years of 'living' with tinnitus. When Bella Bathurst recently researched her unusual aural work, *Sound: Stories of Hearing Lost and Found*, she tried to interview rock musicians about tinnitus, but none would speak to her despite its prevalence in the profession. 'Deafness is too aging' she concludes.[4] Well at my age those considerations seem less compelling, so I might as well continue now I have started in this somewhat exposing way.

The worker at play

To be crystal-clear from the outset, there is no revenge tragedy at work here, no rancour nor righteousness towards Chris Brett Bailey for whom I hold the kind of uncertain admiration reserved for those 'originals' I have had the great good fortune to work with over three decades. An artist cannot be to 'blame' for anything (within reason) given I presume they do what they have to do and I meanwhile choose to attend to what I choose to attend to as a writer. I have spent many years defending that human 'right of expression' with the obvious caveat that it should never have been historically restricted to self-identifying artists who grant themselves a pass to behave as they wish, while all-too-often policing the line which might prevent others from joining them. Everyone has something to say and all, equally, deserve to discover and enhance the form they might need to say it in, not least of all when that requires amplification to reach above the numbing, lo-fi static of the everyday.

But a producing venue, an institution, whose arrangements will determine the experience one has of any such freedom, *does*, it seems to me, have a duty of care to those artist workers, such as Chris Brett Bailey himself, as it does to those others who have paid to be present. And in this instance we are sitting together at a place called Oval House, you could call us an audience, who have put their trust in a venue, amongst which I am the one with the ringing ears, the ones promised in the programme. I am secure and relieved in the knowledge that none of the 15 students I sat with experienced any ill-effects on that evening, (indeed given this is CBB at work they have as I expected, thoroughly enjoyed themselves), and nor did my occasional colleague, the writer Tim Crouch, who happened to be sitting close enough to me in the row in front, to act as a kind of unwitting control test for those who were not students in the audience. In the foyer after I approached Tim to ask if his ears were ringing, but other than responding with the quite funny joke 'pardon?', he appeared to be immune to the special consequences I had suffered. I had it coming you could say.

This diversity of response to sound is very well known, the diagnosis for the onset of this continuous aural state of tinnitus is of course a contested one as by definition, it is like, but really nothing like other syndromes such as Iraq War Syndrome. Acoustic Shock Syndrome, one possible trigger of tinnitus, has long been misunderstood. Just because one person does not experience it in a shared space with others who do, Tim Crouch and me in this instance, has commonly disqualified it from serious attention. Its consequences are therefore actively resisted by the medico-legal profession seeking tidy arrangements and clear causality. And its symptoms are so unnerving I did not even have the courage or clarity of thought to return to the venue and alert them to my predicament. It felt too much like 'blame', something I have never associated with the mutual agency of art, an impulse that I swiftly converted into 'shame'. My own, for being injured. I knew the venue, much loved over five decades, was about to be demolished anyway so was relieved of the fear that I would ever be reacquainted with it in the future where it had previously stood.

During the writing of this chapter over the last year, between 2018 and 2019, that state of universal denial regarding acoustic shock has changed dramatically, led by the legal case I am about to recount in the following pages, for its myriad meanings through the High Court, and it is that fundamental transition that forms the motor for this chapter on an 'artist' in proximity to their work.[5] And as a consequence, for the first time, we now have a definition of what acoustic shock is, namely: 'An index exposure to any sound or cluster of sounds of short duration but at a high intensity'.[6] The legal 'Authorities' that might conceivably provide precedent for a claim to acoustic shock, on the rare occasions it has been allowed to reach the courts (and following my own experience I'm not about to expose myself to the barbarity of the legal-real any time soon unless a lawyer reading this would like to defend me on a no-win no-fee basis), are therefore rare and relatively recent.

The only industrial precedent for an action concerning acoustic shock in the UK is Baker vs. Quantum Clothing Group Ltd of 2011, in which a group of female textile workers in Nottingham in the UK Midlands claimed for noise-induced hearing loss, sustained from the machinery in the knitting factory in which they had worked for, in some cases, 30 years. It is Quantum that provides the 'Authorities' that legal-defence for the orchestral musician Chris Goldscheider, in Court Number 12 of the Royal Courts of Justice draws upon during March 2018. And it is Quantum that provides the landmark case for the leading disabilities-equalities' solicitors, Fry Law who act for the claimant. I heard the Quantum precedent evoked several times over the weeks of the trial, from where I was sitting observing proceedings, interested as I was in my writing on law and theatre and those incapacities, those sink holes of law, when law tries to understand or even engage sensibly with aesthetic questions and finds itself flailing at the very first mention of imponderables such as artist, beauty, genius and virtuosity.

So, this chapter responds to that experience of witnessing another kind of 'musician', the name we give to a virtuosic form of work, who has been stopped from performing and is now being 'put to work' somewhat differently in a court room. His *non-performance* as it is being inscribed in law in front of me in the real-time of the court proceedings requires me to address, as François Laruelle has done with his thinking on what he calls non-philosophy, what it is in this encounter that is concerned with practice, affect, existence, as all performance thinking is, but here exposed to a field of legal precedent where performance appears to lack a rigorous knowledge of itself, where it exposes itself as a field of objective phenomena not yet subject to theoretical overview. Such instances of non-performance then become central to my understanding of 'cultural cruelty' as developed in this chapter, where non-performance of various kinds comes as a consequence of those who would maintain, sanction or enhance violations of the human right to expression.

Chris Goldscheider whose non-performance I will explore, is (or perhaps more accurately now, *was*) a viola player, one of a remarkably 'talented' North London musical family, who had in 2012, when the incident took place that forms the substance of this court hearing, been playing with the Royal Opera House orchestra for close to a decade. In that time he has, as he said in the witness box, played in at least two, if not three full productions of Richard Wagner's *Ring Cycle*. He does not seem to know for sure quite how many, but more than two would appear likely. He was first involved in the celebrated Keith Warner Production of 2007, and then again was in rehearsal on the 1 September for its revival in 2012 when, on a Saturday afternoon, just prior to the opening night, he succumbed to the acoustic event that is at the centre of this unique legal case.

This is how David Platt QC, council for the Royal Opera House, puts it in his opening skeleton argument for the hearing:

> The operas of Richard Wagner often provoke strong emotions. Whilst probably the greatest musical theatre ever written, they have been appropriated by German nationalism and engender controversy to this day. Nevertheless it is unprecedented for it to be alleged that they cause actual injury to its participants.[7]

Despite my occasional attendance at Romeo Castellucci's operatic productions as tracked through Chapter 4 in this book, I am certainly no regular opera-goer, not at £1,400 for a stalls ticket as was being charged for this 2012 London Olympics feel-good fuelled *Ring Cycle* at the Royal Opera House. I am only here interested in this *Ring Cycle* and specifically the second of its four parts, *Die Walküre (The Valkyrie)*, in as much as it has industrially injured the viola player Chris Goldscheider. Peculiar as this ghoulish interest might sound to those from the Royal Opera House ranks, who sat to my side during the weeks of the High Court case, I later discovered from one of their number, that the ROH management presumed I was a professor of theatre who was researching the contemporary influence of Wagner in performance. I hesitated to break it to them that I am no more familiar with Wagner than I am with the sound of an industrial sewing machine in a Nottingham garment factory, where women have worked for years, been deafened for years, and have gained recourse for that damage in law some years before this rearguard action by the ROH against equality with general standards of UK employee protection. This aesthetic ignorance makes me something of a rogue respondent to these proceedings, largely immune as I am to the special pleading of arias.

The Royal Opera House defence, a defence that its sponsors clearly perceive as constituted by what François Laruelle might call 'higher and more intelligible principles', is indeed built on drawing a strict line between the association between music and machine that I am insisting on here:

> unlike heavy industry where noise is an unwanted by-product of an industrial process, 'noise' *is the product*. The quality of that product is of the highest importance, with all its highs and lows, cadences, harmony, light and shade. Hence any system of regulation must recognise this fundamental divergence from the normative target (i.e. it should not damage or unreasonably inhibit the purpose of what the Royal Opera House does by the blunt application of regulations largely designed for others).[8]

I am intrigued here quite whom might constitute such 'others' and how their labours might differ from the 'not others' who form the work force for institutions such as the Royal Opera House, who in the opening to their defence have created this peculiar divide between one worker and another. It will not have escaped you that in evoking *my* Quantum machinic model, by drawing on these authorities in law that constitute minorities, I am toying with a slippage between industrial worker and virtuosi which will offer the conceptual leverage for this chapter. Indeed the origin of the word *Opera*, lies at the very root of the word Operaism. 'Operaismo', as in the name of the Italian political Autonomista movement in the 1960s, comes from 'operaio' – the worker. Hence the epithet: the Workerists. This in turn is derived from the term 'opera' itself – the concrete result of a process of material labour, which in turn derives from the Latin 'opera'. The neutral, plural form of 'opus' therefore holds a reified meaning, in that it describes the objects resulting from physical, concrete labour. Opera in Italian, now, is curiously both used to indicate highbrow, intellectual production, but also very material labour, as in 'manodopera', manpower/labour, composed of 'mano', hand, and 'opera'.[9]

Continuing with the genealogical association between operatic production and work 'Workerism' (Operaismo) was the Italian movement that rethought Marxism in the 1960s and 1970s, long foreshadowing ideas of immaterial labour that were later to be developed by Maurizio Lazzarato in his work 'Lavoro Immateriale' of 1997,[10] and became co-extensive with critique of the neoliberal sphere within which work-time became synonymous with the lifetime of those persuaded as to their own responsibilities for the maintenance of the labour markets. Of course, Workerism inverts the logic of labour as the unquestioned rationale for life. Thus Workerists are counter intuitively precisely at odds with work 'at all costs', seeking ways in which to reduce workload through automatic, technical means that increase forms of social intelligence. Distinguishing themselves from the orthodox, popular Marxism of Antonio Gramsci's early influence in Italy, Operaists made a point of learning from 'the workers themselves what the reality of production was'.[11] In order to draw attention to systems of production and to counter those practices, strikes and sabotage in the workplace were the preferred political means of action, a preference that we will return to in a moment when we discuss forms of 'exit' and civil-disobedience with regard to the orchestral environment and its soft-power tyrannies.

In keeping with our discussion of the 'dictatorship of the performatariat' in the second chapter, the presumed centrality of the proletariat to political action is brought into question by the Operaists, who agitated for a new conjunction between the university and the factory as sites for struggle. Helpfully, given the place we have given the question of the performative assembly in this part of the book, Virno's thesis regarding the Operaists, is indeed a *performative* one drawing analogies between virtuosity in art, work, speech and politics. As Virno puts it:

> They are all political because they all need an audience, a publicly organised space, which Marx calls 'social cooperation', and a common language in which to communicate. And they all are a performance because they find in themselves, and not in any end product, their own fulfillment.[12]

For the Operaists and those who followed such as the anarcho-libertarian Autonomia, whose strapline was 'We are the front of luxury', performance would appear to constitute a 'luxury that we should be able to afford: the luxury of imagining a future that would actively bring together what we are capable of'.[13]

The virtuosi

I am interested in thinking through this unusual legal case at precisely the curious conjunction of an aesthetic necessity, you could say 'luxury' for risk (if the opera house team is to be believed) or criminal neglect (if the claimant is to have his way) where X, that is the position of the musician's work-station in the pit, marks the spot. The rehearsal where the injury has allegedly occurred takes place on the afternoon of Saturday 1 September 2012. Goldscheider notes in his witness statement that the rehearsal was loud and uncomfortable, though this is apparently not 'uncommon' for orchestral musicians in *Die Walküre*. Goldscheider is sitting, as indicated by the orchestral plan passed around court, immediately in front of the principal trumpeter, and in view of the conductor. The viola player is intermittently in response to the progress of the work inserting and removing his ear plugs as advised by the management. But in the loudest passages of the *Ride of the Valkyries* he begins to feel 'uncomfortable and strange', finishes the session and returns home. He is not alone in discomfort. In a critical witness statement, evoked at paragraph 217 of Justice Davies' final judgement an anonymised viola-playing colleague, on the same desk, has made the following damning observations to the intermediating legal team:

> The claimant's desk partner wore personalised 25 db earplugs throughout the entire rehearsal and performance period of the *Ring Cycle*. She described the noise on 1 September as 'unbearably loud' even with her 'very heavy duty plugs in'. Following the two rehearsals on 1 September she felt physically sick, her hearing was affected. She stated that she was much more sensitive to noise for a number of weeks after these rehearsals.[14]

The decibel level of the orchestra as recorded on that afternoon has been hovering in the low 100s reaching 120–130 db at peak moments (as with the rather more prosaic *Kissing The Shotgun Goodnight* at the Oval House), well above the 90 db limit that pertains to UK building sites for those working without hearing-protection. Despite the corroborating statement from the second viola player, legal-defence for the Royal Opera House, David Platt QC, insists in cross-examination it is Chris Goldscheider's ears that are the problem, 'not the sound'. But on the train returning to his home later that afternoon, it is reported Goldscheider becomes physically disorientated and begins to feel a 'pressure like a brick' behind his right ear. I recognise that feeling too though might have given it a less workerist metaphoric object by way of description. I do though, painfully, understand the idea of weight and stress being expressed here.

By describing Chris Goldscheider as a virtuosi I am making a quite specific claim that should not go untroubled, as much in the treatment of acoustic phenomena by the court in the coming days will rest on a misunderstanding as to quite what artists *do*, and the language we use to explain that conduct that hinders rather than helps sensible critical reflection on their practices. What is a virtuosi? By 'virtuosity', Paolo Virno is primarily referring to 'the special capabilities of a performing artist', but such special capabilities (unlike vague ideas of mystical artistry) are never entirely separated from their association with other conceptions of work.[15] It must be admitted that the virtuoso is one who carries very specific characteristics that on first sight would appear to separate out their conduct from other 'workers': 'theirs is an activity which finds its own fulfilment (that is its own purpose) in itself, without objectifying itself into an end product, without settling into a "finished product", or into an object which would survive the performance'.[16] On first sight this might appear to exclude Chris Goldscheider given his output would necessarily include the production of ROH recordings for sale and distribution. It might also appear to exclude him on the grounds that he is an orchestral player rather than a soloist, one who is quite capable of taking a principal role in recitals elsewhere, or at home, but whose current position on the second-strings desk at the ROH makes him susceptible to the principal trumpeter who most certainly is a virtuosi, and don't we know it when he starts up in *Die Walkürie* without so much as a mute.

Second for Virno, and this is most certainly a characteristic borne out by Goldscheider, the activity of the virtuosi is 'an activity which requires the presence of others, which exists only in the presence of its audience'.[17] Here performance theory from Peter Brook's opening line of *The Empty Space*, to Peggy Phelan's 'Ontology of Performance' appears to have been rehearsed some years before its later reiteration for theatre. In the absence of any kind of outcome, Virno wants all political action to have a virtuosic character that associates itself with such expressive acts without end, but also wishes those aesthetic acts themselves to intrinsically bare the germ of all political action. The productive material evidence, any after-effect you might say, from the practice of the virtuosi necessarily relies upon contemporary witnesses to their acts to confirm the nature and value of those acts. This rationalisation of praxis through spectatorship is hardly a new idea having already been tried out some two millennia before by Aristotle in the *Nicomachean Ethics* (VI, 1140 b), then some centuries later by Marx himself in the Appendix to *Capital* Volume I in which he distinguishes between 'immaterial or mental activity' which results in commodities separate to the producer, and those whose acts are inseparable from the act of producing', and subsequently by Hannah Arendt who has always linked the nature of political action in the public sphere to its witness by specific audiences.[18]

The celebrated pianist Glenn Gould emphasised the *labour* values in what he did, countering the charisma of public appearance with the work and output of the recording studio, short-circuiting the fetish audiences make of those it wishes to elevate to stages they would necessarily choose for themselves. Chris Goldscheider sitting in front of me at the Royal Courts of Justice is Glenn Gould's soul-brother in some respects, underplaying at every turn what the Royal Opera House defence team want to pronounce as the 'artistry' or the 'beauty' or the 'uniqueness' of what he does. Goldscheider knows that to accept this mystification of his labour is to accept defeat in his claim for damages, as the ineffable of art will never, however high its volume, be considered anything but an ornament on our souls as happy listeners irrespective of the damage it wreaks on our bodies. Of course the work of Chris Goldscheider is presumed to be that embarrassing kind of immaterial labour for Marx that would appear to produce a super kind of surplus value, not just as in any capitalist society by way of producing profit for the ROH (though it clearly does given the value they later put on losing three rows of prime stalls in the interest of extending the pit) but it would seem to be quite different to that value produced by servile labourers, which cannot in and of themselves produce surplus value.

For Marx then the virtuoso who is unable to produce a product slides towards the functionary mode of the servile labourer, theirs is a form of wage labour that does not conform to productive labour. This is precisely what would then appear to have opened up the opportunity for the Royal Opera House to resist Chris Goldscheider's claims against them. The claim of the Royal Opera House defence would seem to be that artistic work is somehow special while at the same time those who produce the fruits of such acts, the musicians in this case, are treated as servile figures no better than anyone else who labours. I like this defence of equal rights at work here but rather think the ROH has measured their standard to the lowest possible common-denominator. Given the health and safety protection for all those other 'servile workers' in the same institution, it would be unthinkable for a waiter for instance to tolerate a regular sound (noise though the distinction might be moot) in the bar that threatens their hearing without that racket being checked out, rectified and stopped within the shift they are working. But in the High Court the relation between that kind of industrial sound (noise) and musical sound is being resisted at all costs. The Royal Opera House know exactly what they are doing, and they have the backing of the Association of British Orchestras to do it.

It is clear from the claimant's evidence that it is the lead trumpeter from amongst the four-person trumpet section behind his right ear that has, as he puts it, wreaked 120 db havoc on his hearing, his profession, his life, his health and his mental wellbeing. When Chris Goldscheider takes the witness stand to recount this sorry story he necessarily becomes 'speaker' rather than the 'musician' (he once was). This verbal role would not appear to be his chosen professional idiom and he follows a litany of professional speakers into a box which appears to have been designed precisely for those who wish to represent themselves in words rather than subtle tones, cadences or refrains. The sound quality in the 76 courts of the Royal Courts of Justice on Strand is uniformly dreadful, and though Court 12 has been chosen with care as it has an orthopaedic chair that suits Justice Nicola Davies, it is notably sub-standard as an acoustic chamber in which to discuss acoustics with an alarming number of people present who appear to rely on hearing aids to establish what is going on, acoustically, not to mention those of us sitting there with ringing in our ears. But Goldscheider shares with all of us who can speak in any way whatsoever, what Virno calls 'the activity of the speaker' and all speakers by definition do what musicians do which is to fulfil oneself through the act of doing rather than involve themselves in the physical manufacture of any 'object' that might be construed beyond such speaking. There *is* no object beyond speaking (short of recording the voice and selling it on, bought or distributed, which is the same as the musician's work in that respect). For Paolo Virno, language is 'without end product', every utterance is a 'virtuosic performance'.[19]

On the witness stand Chris Goldscheider might not quite speak to as many listeners he once played for at the ROH, but there is surely an audience of listeners here and we are, in our various states of hearing impairment, listening as carefully as we can to his quiet voice as he bears witness to the manner of his own injury. Paolo Virno asks, as though sitting in the High Court amongst us: 'what is the *score* which the virtuoso-workers perform? What is the script of their linguistic-communicative *performance*?'[20] According to Marx the score of the virtuoso is the 'general intellect', that is the abstract thoughts that support social production, and the faculty of thinking itself. Thought forms itself only as it enters the public realm and becomes part of a productive process, evidenced as here in the testimony Chris Goldscheider makes to the court about his own predicament. Since 2012 that predicament has been largely private, though supported toward this challenging form of public expression by family, friends and the ever-present, and, in respect to this case at least, much to be admired, Musicians' Union. It has certainly not been encouraged by the Royal Opera House which is quite different to saying they have not been supportive in other ways. It is just they have not been supportive in quite this way. This 'going public' kind of way that institutions often find so threatening and so diminishes the likelihood of so-called whistle blowers blowing-time on unjust practices.

The true relation between Chris Goldscheider's two scores therefore, his score for *Die Walkürie*, and his score for his testimony, is that they are both regulated by the norms of a cultural-capitalist enterprise. But in the latter case of spoken testimony while the first has given rise to faculties of profit for the Royal Opera House, the second vocal score appears to be at the very least destabilising any such presumed labour relation. This is what appears to be so troubling to some of the ROH executive and management staff who, while courteous to Goldscheider from the witness box, cannot prevent themselves, so shaped as they are by loyalty to the institution, from betraying their deep disrespect for what he has endured on their behalf. Not in speech of course, they would not be that obvious, but in their dogged continuation with defending this indefensible litigation. In law and in the very act of resisting his claim to damages they are, by legal definition, unwilling to recognise the suffering, hurt and loss that he has experienced on behalf of their 2012 Wagner *Ring Cycle*. The more virtuosic his appearance might be the more he is equated to the servile work of others, his true legacy as a *second-row* player. This should not be surprising given the fundamental link between the performance art of the waiter and waitress at the ROH and the work of the so-called virtuosi. They are in all respect the works of performing artists with somewhat different histories but inseparable roles in their subjection.

The obvious question, given the relations being articulated between musician and orchestral management in this court is as Paolo Virno asks: 'How is non-servile virtuosity possible?'[21] Chris Goldscheider offers us two ways forward that chime uncannily with Virno's own prognoses. His choices under extreme duress are civil-disobedience and exit. Rather than the common state of a 'gloomy dialectic between acquiescence and transgression', a surly conformity to circumstance, Goldscheider opts for a courageous version of Hermann Melville's 'Bartleby' resistance, that greets all invitations to return to work with the push back response of all push-backs: 'I'd prefer not to'. I suppose he 'prefers not to' sit in front of a principal trumpeter in order to have his hearing blown out in Die Walkürie, and on making that preference known, he literally exits the orchestra, and goes home. Taking up Albert O. Hirschman's well-known proposition that the voice of protest should give way to the *act* of exit, Goldscheider would appear to conform to that unusual departing spirit as characterised by Hirschman: 'Nothing is less passive than the act of fleeing, of exiting'.[22] It is clear at the moment that Goldscheider leaves the rehearsal on that Saturday afternoon and does not come back, that this defection has altered the rules of the orchestral game which presumes at all times that there will be manoeuvres in the dark to put things right before the show must go on for patrons who are not amused by disruption to the schedule of operatic loss and the cancellation of their human right to feel emotions.

Here exit or defection is the opposite of 'losing one's chains'. If there is nothing else to lose than one's chains, as the Autonomista group reminded us, then it would appear there is nothing much left. Rather in the act of exit Goldscheider wages a 'latent kind of wealth [...] an exuberance of possibilities [...]' that disrupt the smooth running of the operatic apparatus.[23] Goldscheider's exit from one place (the orchestra) after all is the precondition of his entry to this place (the High Court). It is unthinkable that anyone would be here now if he had stayed in his seat in the second tier violas having his hearing further damaged by that trumpeter. Thus Goldscheider finds another way to express his 'dramatic, autonomous and affirmative surplus' that was once directed towards the virtuosity of playing his chosen instrument, the viola, but here is expended on, or invested in, a reparatory political action, for himself, yes, but also clearly for numerous others. In this act Goldscheider impedes the seamless transfer of his own surplus value onto the bullish, much trumpeted stock of the Royal Opera House, and thus excludes it from the serene progress of a capitalist enterprise, otherwise known as Covent Garden PLC.

But who are those 'other's', and in what sense does Goldscheider's political action respond to the demand of their own predicament? Looking around the High Court I catch sight of a woman I do not recognise. In the well of the court sits the representative of Zurich Insurance Company, the global corporation who should this test case be lost will have to pay the million pounds end-of-career lost earnings that this claimant is claiming, but more significantly cover all those other consequent claims that past and future will cascade upon them from other orchestral players who have been similarly brutalised 'by' Wagner. A colleague in the well of the court whispers to me that there are apparently something like 47 such contingent claims in the pipeline in London alone, waiting on the outcome of this landmark hearing. A historic avalanche of claims that the Royal Opera House, should they fail in this defence, seriously see as jeopardising the future of live orchestral music in the country at large and a threat that eventually draws the Association of British Orchestras into the Appeal fray.

Summing up

What kind of prosaic Real am I evoking here in that most intimate of dark theatres, the one that is playing out in Chris Goldscheider's, and my inner-ears, right now, amongst those fridge sounds channelled through a half-blown amplifier? First of all it should be acknowledged that this viola player while ostensibly a virtuosi by nature of his instrumental prowess, he could not find a berth in the Royal Opera House orchestra without such peer recognised expertise, is in fact a *Second* Desk Viola player and therefore treated by the authorities responsible for his management as lower status than the his *First Desk* colleagues, who presumably practised more when they were young, and of course yet more so, a lower class than the soloists, one of whom, the trumpet player is so virtuosic with the sustained upper registers of *Ride of the Valkyries*, that he has deafened him. Indeed I have heard it said by a well-known orchestral player I will not name that such second-string musicians are routinely referred to as 'pond life' in orchestral circles. They are after all commonly subjected to the immediate attentions of the brass section that others can distance themselves from. This question of status or caste is not just a given in the order of orchestral manoeuvres, the higher one rises in the ranks of the sensitive strings the further *away* from the brutal brass section one moves. Goldscheider is in this sense a human shield to those who play better than him, who are more virtuosic than him, a baffle to the sound of the brass section, and he is *baffled* having played that baffle and not been rewarded for his protective altruism.

Second when confronted with the argument by the Royal Opera House defence that he could not claim to have suffered 'acoustic shock' because by definition he would know the score of *The Valkyrie* so well as to prohibit any such surprise at the contours and likely volume spikes of the music, an affinity with the score that would allow him to place the regulation health and safety ear plugs in his ears in good time for any such spikes or crescendos that might otherwise damage him, the claimant quite surprisingly makes the serious claim that he does not know *The Valkyrie* that well at all, that he last played it five years before, has not seen it once in the intervening five years, and indeed has no orchestral score of *The Valkyrie* because he only has his *own part* on his music stand. In this legal process disavowal of expertise by the virtuosi becoming non-performer, has become standard.

Third *his part* is not *the* score. Here contrary to Jacques Rancière whose political claims 'on the part of those who have no part' are so well known, this, rather, is a legal claim on the part of one who *has* a part.[24] That is the whole point he *is* a part and a part only. But he is also, palpably, and sadly, 'One' and one who is 'Alone'. It is noticeable that with the exception of the Musicians' Union representative sitting next to him no other orchestral players from the *current* ROH orchestra are present and showing support of this ex-viola player in the court. Chris Goldscheider is the exception that proves the rule, who has found a line of flight from the industrial apparatus given the name 'orchestra' to cover its industrial scale volumes, and contested the claim of the Royal Opera House that it has 'done all it can reasonably be expected to do to safeguard those who occupy the pit'.

Fourth the *pit* is the name given in all seriousness to the place of work of the orchestral players. They are literally 'down the pit'. They do not appear when naming it thus in the eighteenth century to have foreseen that Kafka's parable of *The Penal Colony* would take its place at the lip of another pit in the desert, in which the law is inscribed on a body stretched across an apparatus that scores that body with inked needles. Indeed, as though bearing out these Kafkaesque continuities, on a site-visit organised by the Crown Prosecution Service with the two defence teams and the judge to the Royal Opera House on Friday 2 February 2018 to examine this pit, the court party are asked to don bright yellow hard-hats on entering the auditorium on the grounds that for 'health and safety' purposes it is the responsibility of the management to protect them from any harm. Chris Goldscheider, the claimant, who is of course present, and returning to this pit for the first time since his sudden deafened departure five years ago, can only smile at such 'duty of care', towards those who are not required to present themselves to this workplace each day of the week, and Saturdays, the legal teams on this one-off visit (but precisely when it most mattered, not to him the lonely protagonist in this obscene, meaning literally *offstage*, drama).

As the court party enter the pit in their hard-hats they are shown the instrumental stations, the desks, the seats, the areas where the strings would have sat for the *Ring Cycle* (though I think the actual seating arrangement is set for *Giselle* that is currently playing in the repertoire), the viola stations and the proximity of the brass music stands to those seats. An unlikely staging of a trumpeter and viola player, supposedly in their *Valkyrie* rehearsal positions, is played out for them, and the once viola player I am now sitting next to, hearing about this outing on the Monday morning following their return to the High Court. It is obvious that someone on behalf of the opera house has been in early doing their very best to expand the 75 seats into as much of the pit as is physically accessible, including the alarmingly low under-croft in which players sit in just six feet of headroom from floor to the stage underside. But it is pointed out by the defence council for the claimant who knows his Wagner well, that despite these best bureaucratic efforts the seating of 75 is nothing like the seating of 120 that would be expected for the *Ring Cycle*, the opera in the whole repertoire that by definition requires the greatest possible amplification without electronic means. It is not the machinic that has wreaked havoc on hearing say the Royal Opera House, it is individual humans with instruments. 'Accidents will happen' as Elvis Costello once crooned at a modest volume. And human musicians in the end cannot be accounted for irrespective of how they got hold of their instruments. I have heard this before somewhere. Oh yes, it's a familiar argument from the National Rifle Association in America following mass shootings of innocents.

The visiting party are also shown two (or three) rows of stalls seats that would have to be removed should the advice of the hearing-specialist in defence of the claimant be adhered to, that is to expand the pit in such a way as to ensure that instrumentalists are given more room to distance themselves from their deafening colleagues. The combined building cost and loss of revenue from opera house closure, over five years of such a removal of seating, has been estimated at £50 million and is therefore presumed in court by the representative of the ROH speaking in the witness box now, to be prohibitive. But this is said as though it is a self-evident inference, and solicits a waspish response from the claimant's defence, Theo Huckle QC, who asks *what* price the Royal Opera House management *would* put on the hearing and well-being of their employees? Once council has found his contrary funny-bone he doesn't let it drop, he ramps up the logic: Indeed, why would the Royal Opera House insist on staying in an old building in Covent Garden that has been demonstrated not to be fit for purpose, if fit for purpose describes the continued well-being of its instrumentalists, or its workers as the defence council puts it?

In his summing up, on the final Friday in court, defence for the Royal Opera House David Platt QC suggests that what he has been defending is the continued existence of the ROH as a world-leading venue capable of attracting the best musicians and audiences, and that this will come under threat should this claim for damages be lost. He insists that what he is talking about 'is not a steel works in Ebba Vale, it is a music venue'. He wonders whether the pit is the workplace after all or the station at which the musicians stand? In what would appear to be a philosophical turn on the 'ontology of the event' that could well owe its opacity to Alain Badiou he suggests that the defence for what happened to Chris Goldscheider at that work-station can only stand up if there is an 'event' that would change the burden of proof, and that acoustic shock would only be arguable in the event of any such 'event'. Mr Platt (challenging what he calls the 'snake-oil charmer', actually the 'expert witness', Mr Parker, who has articulated at length the scientific proofs that have accrued to diagnoses of acoustic shock over a number of years) wants to insist for the purposes of his argument that acoustic shock is a *psycho-social* phenomena, and unverifiable in law unless consequent upon a single catastrophic injury (as one might experience say as an airport worker in close proximity to a jet-engine at maximum force). He claims that what is actually in operation in the 'event' of *Die Walküre* and that that is something quite different to any such unpredictable event, is rather in his view the delivery of a 'score' very well known to the orchestra.

Defence for the ROH David Platt continues his summing up by suggesting the score is *always* manifestly predictable, not just to the musicians but to audiences too: 'This is music that people pay large amounts of money to hear and they all know where it is going'. I am not sure quite what this says about the supposed 'widening participation' accessibility successes of the ROH. For the viola player to claim the experience of playing this canonical work is random is therefore in defence council's view, 'absurd' and *causation* of injury, the turning point in law, cannot therefore be proven. Warming to his apparently common-sense theme David Platt QC insists:

> If there was something like a hole in the middle of the pit and the Royal Opera House had not assessed that risk and someone fell in, well that would be clear, but acoustic shock is not a hole in the middle of the pit.

Here Mr Platt raises the key question for us in this chapter: 'No one is disputing the claimant is suffering what he's suffering' but given the outcome of this case and the Appeal that follows that vain protestation of empathy with the victim might be questioned, and we will question it in some depth below given no one has in the press, cultural commentary or academic sphere, begun to address the dreadful ramifications of this case for any reasonable measure of the cultural cruelty that pervades artistic institutionalisation today.

Theo Huckle QC then sums up for the claimant, Chris Goldscheider. He opens by pointing out there has been no serving musician called to testify by the Royal Opera House, which is curious in a case of this significance. He does not quite say it but it is as though the opera house could not risk exposing a single one of their other musicians to scrutiny in this setting, given the widely held qualms that many would feel as to the management of the risk of sound. He asks how any noise policy could be sensibly separated from the fundamental health and safety issue and responsibility of the ROH. The obligation of course is not to eliminate noise in the opera house per se, that would be impossible and unwelcome, rather like a continuous version of John Cage's 'silent' *4'33"* composition of 1952. The obligation is to eliminate risk. Do you start from the proposition that you have to place this number of musicians in the pit, or do you start from standpoint of the 'safety of the musician'? While Theo Huckle recognises that what we are dealing with here is professional people and artists it is the *employer*, the producing venue, who is responsible for their health and safety. It is palpably a question of *managing* sound in the orchestra pit, that is what managers might be expected to do in the interests of their workers and, in his view the ROH adopted no serious measures, or not enough adequate measures, to mitigate the risk. Either the orchestra could have been configured, or the rehearsal postponed, but this would obviously undermine the 'keep on keeping on' contract of the business model of show-business. Since the Factory's Act of the 1930s, factory managers in the UK have not been able to simply argue 'well this is what we do'. The excuse of 'reasonable practicability' cannot apply to everything in such contexts.

The judgement in Goldscheider vs. ROH from Mrs Justice Nicola Davies arrives on 28 March 2018. It is easy enough to jump to the 235th paragraph to short-circuit the outcome, but it is nevertheless a surprise: 'By reason of the above findings there be judgement for the claimant on the preliminary issue. Damages to be assessed'. And I have to admit a relief, for Chris at least. In short Chris Goldscheider has done the impossible and set a precedent in court that will have ramifications within not just the music industry but across any public venue for the rendition, showing and reception of performance, for the foreseeable future. Or at least until the Royal Opera House consider their options and decide to go to Appeal, which despite the stated sympathy for Chris Goldscheider they now, perhaps inevitably given the culture-class have recently become unfamiliar with being bested, do. In the meantime, we are left with Justice Davies' coruscating take-down, in its own quiet way, of a defence launched against these claims by an institution that appeared 'tone-deaf' to the prevailing health and safety climate.

The opening paragraphs of the judgement reiterate key findings of the hearing and summarise the ROH position in stark terms.[25] Justice Davies makes quite explicit her recognition of the impossibility of severing those orchestra workers from others:

> The reliance upon 'artistic value' implies that statutory health and safety requirements must cede to the needs and wishes of the artistic output of the opera company, its managers and conductors. Such a stance is unacceptable, musicians are entitled to the protection of the law as is any other worker. The employees are subject to instruction, set rehearsal times and performance hours.[26]

In paragraph 219 Justice Davies summarises her position on responsibility:

> In my view there is a clear factual and causal link between the identified breaches of the Regulations and the high level of noise which ensued at the rehearsal. It commenced with an inadequate risk assessment, continued with a failure to undertake any monitoring of noise levels in the cramped orchestra pit with a new orchestral configuration which had been chosen for artistic reasons. Even when complaints were raised the three-hour afternoon rehearsal was commenced and completed in the absence of any live time noise monitoring. All of this was done against a background of a failure by the management at the ROH to properly appreciate or act upon the mandatory requirements of Regulation 7(3) of the 2005 Regulations when it knew the noise would exceed the upper EAV.[27]

As if this demolition of the Royal Opera House's defence is not sufficient, in Paragraph 229 Justice Davies concludes:

> I am satisfied that the noise levels at the afternoon rehearsal on 1 September 2012 were within the range identified as causing acoustic shock. The index exposure was the playing of the Principal trumpet in the right ear of the claimant whether it was one sound or a cluster of sounds of short duration. It was that exposure which resulted in the claimant sustaining acoustic shock which led to the injury which he sustained and the symptoms which have developed, from which he continues to suffer.[28]

Unexceptional victim

Identifying a singular figure amongst an orchestra for a study of this kind reverses the collaborative presumptions at the heart of the previous theatre-going chapter in the Lost Gardens of Riga. But this case really is a fraught example of 'solitude in relation' as Nicholas Ridout would describe all performance assemblies.[29] The degree to which a viola player at the second desk in an orchestra pit is visible at any sensible level to an audience is anyway worthy of conjecture. The sound is collaborative in outcome, yes, but questions as to quite 'who' is responsible for making those sounds is, as this sorry saga suggests, not quite as straightforward as one might have imagined. It is clear in a Foucauldian sense that this viola player's body has been highly 'disciplined', the subduing of the body takes its place amongst others in its meshing with a machine of social reproduction that you could give the name 'elite orchestra'. Chris Goldscheider's own erupting body, its intellect, language and creativity, are not only the primary tools for the production of its value to the ROH, but also a form of immaterial labour that these proceedings operate to remind us of.

But is there a critical or even philosophical vocabulary that could be developed to offer a language to proceedings of this kind in the future? A language that could serve others, in other culturally driven scenarios of suffering and loss? It is starkly obvious that this opera business has pushed the law to its limits of expression, though it has to be said, it only takes a cursory reading of the various proceedings and judgements in Goldscheider vs. ROH to recognise how ill-equipped the law has been to encounter aesthetic nuance of any kind whatsoever. This would not be an issue should *this* mode of justice not depend upon precisely these faculties and elisions, and the following coda to this case offers a first attempt at sketching out what any such vocabulary of the artistic victim might sound like.

So what of the victim? To adopt some words from François Laruelle, the question for Goldscheider might now, during this interregnum, be one of a *vain hope*:

> Ordinary man does not have to search for the real in the possible of the Law, for it is he who gives his reality to the Law and can therefore transform it; he brings with him the primacy of the real over the possible, and the primacy of life over ethics.[30]

The real in the case of Chris Goldscheider, that is the ordinary man brought to court to claim damages from his employer, is a peculiar kind of 'real' that could in this instance be characterised in four specific ways: as a matter of loss, as an event of disappearance, as an instance of damage, and as an experience of suffering. I am sorry to say, with respect to institutions and their sometimes barbaric histories, each is predicated upon a manifestation of what the philosopher Adi Ophir would call, 'an order of evils' within an ontology of morals.[31] Where *Theatre & Everyday Life* assiduously avoided any hint of moralising cant by distancing *an* ethics of performance from the proscriptive ordering of the moral realm, here I will join Adi Ophir in looking as unflinchingly as I can at two not-unrelated events that have *differently* (in degree and damage) effected Chris Goldscheider and myself. In doing so I seek some order to that chaotic acoustic disturbance by inverting the common presumption of the 'goodwill' inherent to all those communities responsible for creative acts to consider the degree to which culture always bears with it a certain cruelty for which the descriptor, 'evil', obviously cannot necessarily be discounted. Don't worry, if there is evil, despite everything Nietzsche counselled, good, its necessary other, will follow to conclude the chapter.

Adi Ophir in his magisterial work *The Order of Evils*, draws our attention towards what he calls 'paradigmatic situations and institutions in which the logic and production of evils becomes manifest – for example, a concentration camp, an army base, a regime of occupation, a state of war, a disintegrating family'.[32] For 'evils' simply read here: 'any injury irreparably worsening someone's condition'.[33] The idea that one might add *cultural* institutions, whether the opulent Opera House or the precarious Oval House, to any such demonic mix in which a human condition could be 'worsened by injury' would appear to be fraught and contestable, but as we have seen in some painful detail above, there is no necessary reason why cruelty in any place should be legitimated by the aesthetic quality of what any such institution believes it is in the business of producing. The commandants of the camps prided themselves on the quality of their orchestras after all. Adi Ophir's project, with specific reference to the extermination of the Jews in Europe, is to make possible the 'knowledgeable representation of superfluous evils in different cultural sectors and to pay attention to social struggles over the calculation of the accumulation and dissemination of evils'.[34] That 'paying attention' is what is underway in this book, and specifically this chapter, where an individual has been isolated by injury (the 'disappearance' and 'loss' of his hearing as he once knew it) from an orchestra, and is now seeking 'damages' for his 'suffering'.

You will notice that the four categories I have identified for discussion with regards to the implications of the Chris Goldscheider case above, are ones that readily, and without apparent abuse to their integrity, sit quite logically with any right description of the wrongs visited upon the claimant in the Royal Opera House pit. Perhaps the only disjuncture one might reasonably feel is when one arrives at the end of that sentence and I choose to situate such cruelties within an orchestral pit rather than an industrial warehouse, a place of wonder one might commonly remove from the realm of possible damages caused by occupational, health and safety law, preferring to protect its sensibilities amongst quasi-aesthetic interests such as personal commitment, talent, resilience and so forth. But these are precisely terms and categories that simultaneously dehistoricise humans while idealising the musician as something more than 'man', 'woman' or however one might identify what 'they' in their labour clearly are, workers. I give orchestral music its legitimate identity back in this chapter by insisting it is something very much more beautiful than a vague abstraction of divinely inspired genius. It is first, foremost and fundamentally, in the forms discussed here incontrovertibly part of 'the world of work', and its various managements need to start acting as though it were. In this sense for all his virtuosity Chris Goldscheider is the epitome of the unexceptional victim.

The logics of evil that Adi Ophir identifies have, as all logics such as the logics of expulsion and loss discussed in Chapter 1 of this book, have a definable dynamic from their outset to their cessation. If there is no cessation, in Ophir's discussion of hurt, then the word for what one is witnessing or engaged in is torture. When a by-passer comments to me outside Court 12 that this viola player has been 'going through torture' by being present to this case that represents his injured life, I think this is exactly what they might mean. Adi Ophir summarises his logics of loss turning to evil, that we will follow with regard to the treatment of Chris Goldscheider in the following way:

> The transition from one category to another results from an addition, accumulation, acceleration, and intensification of the simpler, more abstract experience, and its more general conditions: an intensified presence becomes an excitation, an intensified excitation becomes suffering; a disappearance to which an interested person is added is a loss; a loss whose value is estimated in terms of a certain exchange system is a damage. Suffering that is not prevented or compensated for is an evil; when evil can be prevented but is not, can be relieved but isn't, it is a superfluous evil.[35]

The specific lower-case 'evil' that Adi Ophir refers to at the end of this dreadfully familiar litany, then becomes for Ophir a category which he capitalises as Evil, that is Evil itself. A category that all but the most reductive thinkers might recognise through the staggering breadth and depth of Ophir's work on the ontology of morals, as having been earnt. This is not some base-line knee-jerk swerve around complexity by way of avoiding subtle characterisations of wrong-doers through history, but the awful truth that stares one in the face when each of the previous manifestly preventable stages of a logics of Evil have been played out. Some court cases in their chronology have traces of such evils at work, cultural cruelty in their arrangements, but few are quite as stark as those that mark Chris Goldscheider's 'fight' for justice in the High Court.

An evil is not just any wrong, but a specific act which worsens someone's condition so that no compensation is possible. You might say that the whole point of 'going to law' allows for precisely the merits of any such compensation to be judged, in the case of Chris Goldscheider following the first hearing those damages were set at around £750,000, but of course those damages are only payable should the defence not choose to Appeal, which they summarily did. Here the Royal Opera House, paid for largely through tax payers' revenues and income collected from tickets sales and other on-site sales to the public, of which you, me and Chris Goldscheider might also be considered constituent parts, appears to be a peculiar use of the limited funds that institutions in the arts commonly call up as the spectre of our austerity days.

Compensation is only possible in states where there is any recognised system of exchange whose terms as Adi Ophir puts it 'make it possible to assess the value of the injury'.[36] But again here it should be noted that the Royal Opera House defence is predicated on precisely the denial that the injury exists, and if it does exist they claim, without irony, that the claimant cannot have it (in the meantime amateurishly alternating substitute conditions that the claimant clearly does not have that will not make them liable for the payment of damages). The attempt to discredit the claimant's expert witness on hearing impairment, Mr Parker, as a 'snake-oil merchant', as defence for the ROH Mr David Platt does, rings loud around the court room in its awfulness and does not appear to have dented the credibility of Mr Parker's robust defence of the existence of 'acoustic shock' as a phenomena categorisable in the medico-legal literature, and one that might reasonably be adjudicated as worthy of the payment of damages should it be experienced by a worker in one's duty of care.

If Chris Goldscheider's hearing is 'damaged' in these terms, then the 'loss' of that hearing is by default assessable in some kind of compensatory or even monetary terms. But the loss of his hearing, as Goldscheider makes clear with a testimony from the witness box, that is as moving as it is appalling (he cannot listen to his children who now themselves play instruments), is like all true loss an irreversible disappearance of some irreplaceable thing. It is not as though anyone in the court can offer back Chris Goldscheider his hearing as it was before the accident, and I am as familiar with that as anyone else in the room. Loss means loss. The disappearance in question here is like all other disappearances whether it is the *desaparecidos* (disappeared) of Chile or the wedding ring that falls irretrievably through the floor boards, a transition from something that 'is there' to 'is not there'. In the case of Goldscheider's hearing it is not that the hearing has simply gone, he does not experience silence that would be a mercy, in as much as the ring that has dropped from the finger leaves no trace but for an indent or skin tone difference, but rather that the musician's hearing that was there is now no longer there, replaced by a cacophony of others sounds, noises and roaring fridges that we identified at the outset of this chapter with the help of Nick Coleman's own dreadful debilitation.

Chris Goldscheider is the one who has experienced loss. This should not be forgotten in the welter of claims and counter claims that fly around Court 12. It is recognised in the words of the Royal Opera House press-release on the matter, but the conduct of the case and the following Appeal do not quite meet that base-camp standard of empathy with the one who has suffered. This is critical to the question of evil itself, for the one who has an interest in that loss (Chris Goldscheider) experiences the disappearance of the hearing they once had as not just a plateau of interest, equal to all intents and purposes as when he first set foot in Court Room 12 of the Royal Courts of Justice, but rather, as we experience when we are left to fight for justice, the presence of the disappearance grows *more* intense. It becomes in this sense a form of continued torture and one that most humans would not seek to endure by conducting a court case that by necessity returns them again and again to the scene of the crime, the act of cultural cruelty that has brought their predicament about. It is only with the recognition that damages have occurred, that compensation might be due, and damages paid, that some form of reparation might, just might, begin to make the presence of that original loss less, not more, intense. Any delay to such recognition, simply by definition, given the logics of temporal suffering we have outlined here, will escalate the sense if not the actuality of the disappearance and its felt loss.

Adi Ophir explores the consequences of such reparations and their delay in the following further summative set of affects that pursue such disappearances and losses, of which hearing is the one we are exploring in detail: 'Injustice will appear when the damage or loss is perceived as superfluous, unnecessary, preventable; wrong will appear when there is no possibility of demanding the restoration of what has been lost, or when the damage remains without expression or compensation'.[37] While no one in their right mind, or with an eye on the case outcome, would have ever claimed that Goldscheider's hearing loss was 'superfluous', there is something in the conduct of the ROH defence as outlined above that suggests there might be room for some misunderstanding here. And I will insist one had to be there to see this and know this. Performance study is useful in this respect at least, liveness is all on this occasion. Their defence team certainly chooses to leave this doubt hanging in the air. The judge looks genuinely surprised to hear representatives for the Royal Opera House express their own surprise, even shocked hurt you could say, that given the chaotic conditions obvious within the restraints of their current orchestra pit, they might be minded to move their base of operations from the Grade I listed Royal Opera House in Covent Garden, to a building that might be fit for orchestral purpose. One more like the capacious Sydney Opera House for instance. Indeed on one of the days, half way through the proceedings when matters might have appeared to be swinging their way, one of their team jokes with me that they have seen a 'To Let' sign on an edge-city industrial warehouse that might well 'fit the bill' for the judge's preferred removal option. The argument seems to run that losing £50 million for the closure of the building to allow the pit to be expanded to an accommodating size is £50 million too much, or some sort of 'too much' that is left hanging in the air. The obvious question alongside any such valuing of turnover and profits would be to ask precisely *what* value would one then place on the safety of the musicians one is hiring to deliver these spoils (which do have names like the *Ring Cycle*, but those names should not become a veil for any number of cruelties along the way to production and profits)? All activities have costs attached, but some activities such as opera it would appear, have costs attached that are just not equal.

Disappearance, loss, damage, compensation

Let us briefly by way of conclusion expand on each of the four categories arising in the Goldscheider vs. Royal Opera House case that could be extrapolated for thinking about forms of cultural cruelty and loss.

Disappearance is perhaps best known to theatre amongst the four as it has long stood for the ontology of performance as articulated by a counter-intuitive argument in 1993 by Peggy Phelan in her work *Unmarked*: 'Performance's only life is in the present [...] it cannot be saved, recorded, documented, or otherwise participate in the circulation of representations of representations: once it does so it becomes something other than performance'.[38] If it cannot be saved, then it must have disappeared. Here Phelan offered theatre studies a line that has ricocheted back and forth ever since giving rise to its own side branch of studies concerning the problematics of liveness through the work of Philip Auslander, Rebecca Schneider and more recently Jonah Westerman.[39] But disappearance as I am evoking it here has little to do with this sport of sparring of effects in the aesthetic realm.

It is obvious that there is a certain kind of uneasy symmetry between the ephemerality of Chris Goldscheider's beautiful playing of the viola, which disappears onto the air while it is not being recorded, and recognising the abrupt distinction between any such niceties and the disappearance of his hearing as he knows it. The problem as Goldscheider discovers to his personal cost is that while it might be relatively simple to identify the moment when something is present and the later moment when it is not, or that it exists manifestly differently, convincing *others* of this experience is a rather different challenge. There is no certain expression of the identity of that disappearance that has become the presence of an absence, the absence you feel when you no longer hear as you once did. I struggled to find words to express precisely this distinction to the consultant who cared for me.

What disappears can only disappear once it has been given a name, and in testimony it is left to Chris Goldscheider to struggle to give his hearing the name it deserves. This is the same with the disappearance of all precious ephemeral things, not just humans with names who are mourned more readily than those ungrieveable ones that Judith Butler has done much to recognise. Those, such as the unnamed 'stowaway', who fell from the undercarriage of an inbound plane, a fall that opened this book and closed an unknown life-story. Hearing amongst the senses is rather like a species that is threatened with extinction because it has not been clearly enough named to be recognisably at risk. There is little understanding of the threat to hearing that sound in venues risks daily, as a matter of course. The difference between extinction and the disappearance of hearing in this instance is that extinction as suggested in the previous chapter on the last human venue is identified at *all* times 'within time' whereas disappearance is recognised as potential for all time, but *particular* to the person in question. 'Disappearance is always for someone' as Adi Ophir puts it succinctly.[40] It is precisely disappearance for you, or of you, or of your faculty of hearing.

Disappearance (for the claimant at least) is a fact, but one that ironically rests on the testimonial of its occurrence to be made to appear in the court. The work of the ROH defence is to rubbish that claim and in so doing deny the facticity of the disappearance. For all the niceties of legal procedure that abound that is the cruel reality of these proceedings. There is just no way to get around this brutal truth. No amount of genteel courtesy, and sometimes even that disappears from the proceedings, can cover for the fact that an institution is challenging a musician's testimony that something has disappeared. Goldscheider is plainly told he does not have what he claims to have, that is acoustic shock, which is the name that describes the disappearance of his hearing as he had previously enjoyed it and lived off it. His hearing, unusually perhaps, is his means of livelihood after all. This is his own special loss.

Loss, in the form of 'loss of hearing' that I am describing here, is like other losses: 'a singular type of disappearance'.[41] It can only be loss if is the 'irreversible disappearance of some irreplaceable thing' and as such should not be confused with other temporary and restorable losses, keys and suchlike. Keys are not only replaceable in the form of copies, irritating as this might be, they are also not irreversible in that a lock in a door is itself infinitely changeable for a surprisingly large amount of money. Hearing is not this kind of loss when it is in the form of an impairment that is irreversible and irreplaceable. While I might get by, might survive following a disappearance of something with the promise of a replacement, loss announces the end of any such hope and the inauguration of a wholly different economy of effects. It is unlikely then that the Royal Opera House, however long they delay these proceedings with their various tactics, appeals and suchlike, will persuade Chris Goldscheider to give up his 'interest' in his lost hearing. They could persuade another musician that they should give up on their hopes for an unwarranted bonus for working on a public holiday, but it is unlikely that Goldscheider is about to give up this kind of interest in the fate of his hearing any time soon. This is what some people give the name 'perseverance' to, a much admired but somewhat Kafkaesque quality that often loses support as it proceeds. This is what Adi Ophir calls 'an economy of forgetting. The one who forgets loses the loss'.[42]

In the history of orchestral music there will be countless occasions on which those injured as Goldscheider has been injured will 'choose' to forget all about it, it is all that they have left in the absence of an economy of reparation that I am proposing here. Forgetting becomes the only protection against protracted grief. Goldscheider's precedent allows for future injured ones *not to* have to forget but to choose to remember if they wish to (and many wisely do not). Given that the kinds of institutions I am talking about with regards to cultural cruelty, libraries, museums, archives are in the business of preservation, it is not surprising that those who work within them, such as musicians at the Royal Opera House, might have a heightened stake in recalling those faculties they entered the institution with, and keep some sort of rough tally as to how those faculties are doing by way of survival as they proceed to go about their labours. The very act of participating in that revival of the 2012 production of the *Ring Cycle*, is not only a preservation of Keith Warner's earlier 2006 version, but also obviously an echo of all those other *Ring Cycles* through time at the Royal Opera House, and elsewhere, that describe the ghostings, the natural history of the theatre machine.[43] Indeed having the capacity to account for such losses is a critical component of subjectivity, and an immediate mark amongst subjectivities where life has become so routinely dispossessed or precarious as to mark the irrelevance of any such taking-stock of one's future. Losses presume the existence of humans interested enough in what is worth keeping, to signal the resistance to further loss, or, in courts such as the Royal Courts of Justice, who have the means to take account of such losses and seek damages.

Bankruptcy was the form of loss that I chose to examine in the first part of this book, here in Part II other kinds of subjectivised precarity have come into play, including orchestral play.

In the case of Chris Goldscheider, the one after all who has lost something precious, what has been lost does not reside solely within the domain of his hearing, but more prosaically, in the predicted income from any future work he may be able to do. Goldscheider goes to law to seek the 'representative mechanisms' that any such claimant has to turn to (short of personal reprisals which are not unknown but tend to end badly for the wronged). Such conditions cannot in Goldscheider's case be put down to the common claim of 'bad luck' but are themselves, as we have seen with the meticulous reconstruction of the court proceedings, a structural logics of a pit that is too cramped, prey to insufficient health and safety care, a prevailing ambivalence to right management in other words.

The proceedings I am witnessing are interesting precisely because they irritate a capitalist system, with a cruel logics of its own, that cannot tolerate the kind of 'social association' being built up around Chris Goldscheider's loss as it is being represented in Court 12 of the Royal Courts of Justice in London. We are certainly not having a good time in our buzzing social worlds in there, but we are finding ways to express our association in a curious community of those with something, acoustic shock-induced tinnitus, in common. Adi Ophir recognises this problem of association for capitalism in the following way: 'The capitalist market is characterised by sophisticated mechanisms that introduce every loss into a cycle of exchange relations and do not allow it to be preserved as a problem for too long'.[44] Buck up. Seek closure. Move on (and pay for some Cognitive Behavioural Therapy if you can't). It just would not do for a system built on profits to have to make appear too readily all those instances where no such thing accrues to those who have bought into the system. This system is made up of a myriad fluid-losses that are never allowed to stabilise for long enough to cohere into a rallying cry. Before their brutal undermining unions once mediated such atomisms into purposeful, collaborative action. Now that really does sound like the essence of well-being.

While Chris Goldscheider quietly but courageously attempts to give appearance to his own loss, the market is working overtime to offer substitutes for all such losses everywhere, often in the game of privatising such losses in the form of non-disclosure agreements and other diversions from the open truth. The losses being privatised here might also extend to those memories that are turned into nostalgia by the State (or more reprehensibly cultural curators) for the purposes of memorialisation and *political* as distinct to traumatic forgetting. Grenfell Tower and its aftermath will offer a final, extreme version of such politics to end this book. But before we go to that infernal place, the more local, individual case of Chris Goldscheider has now reached the rather more prosaic question of damages. Here we begin to see the far side of an argument that when he took up his complaint must have seemed a very distant and nebulous thing. The human capacity to imagine such things as relevant to oneself is a mark of the political potential of all of us to call time on injustices that injure us, and others.

In the court system 'damage' is conceived as a 'harmful loss that is assessed as depreciation in terms of an exchange system'.[45] That system in the UK is represented in the Tort branch of Common Law, but whether the discourse that identifies someone as having a losable thing can include the loss of hearing, is in the case of acoustic shock, very uncertain. That is precisely what makes Goldscheider vs. ROH so significant a case. Is it possible for a judge in law to estimate the depreciation consequent upon the damage to Goldscheider's hearing? Though the question is complex, law is quite commonly asked to adjudicate in the context of complex damage cases, not least of all where nations are held accountable for wrongs in the conduct of war. It is obvious over years that the exchange system that allows for the measure of the depreciation of, say, a film star (should they suffer disfiguring accident) or a footballer (should they sustain a serious knee injury) is in the case of the orchestral claim somewhat more conjectural. While damage might itself evidently be attributed to a loss of some occurrence, the problem for Goldscheider was that defence for the ROH insisted on bringing into question the very occurrence that brought about his claim for damages, that did damage to him. The defence for ROH was indeed built on an exchange system that recognised *no* place for 'acoustic shock' in its vocabulary, nor in its pathology of verifiable symptoms. That seems careless given its other, acoustic pleasure, would appear to be its core business.

Those vested with the responsibility for representing these losses in court are often expert witnesses, such as Mr Parker who seeks to secure the diagnoses of acoustic shock to the claimant Chris Goldscheider. If damages are the assessment of the depreciation resulting from a loss then any such loss is surely relative to the value placed on that capacity in the instance of the claimant. As Adi Ophir puts it:

> The damage suffered by a person who has lost about 20 per cent of his hearing varies in accordance with his occupation and his hobbies: a musician will incur far more damage in such a case than the operator of a tractor, and an opera lover will incur more damage than a football fan. All this is self-evident and trivial.[46]

Trivial, and contestable, as it might appear at first sight, this equation runs through the Goldscheider case like a luminous thread throwing shade across a musician whose capacity has been brought into question. It ties together the judge's comments on the degree to which the loss might have been preventable (in her opinion it was) and the measure of what it would take to mend it (the loss that is, not necessarily the cause which is the responsibility of the venue in law). The Royal Opera House would appear to have made arguments that imply the loss is inevitable, a part of the 'privilege' of playing Wagner, the judge in her statement appears to perceive the loss, the injury, as preventable. Goldscheider is not claiming for some vague deterioration in his hearing due to age, he is claiming only what he can and should claim is the measure of loss attributable to an occurrence that was preventable by the orchestral managers at the ROH.

There is then a stark incommensurability between a defence team for the ROH who do not accept that any occurrence occurred, and those for the claimant who most certainly do. It is their responsibility in law to establish precisely where that injury occurred and through meticulous reconstruction of that fateful rehearsal they appear to do so in such a way as to convince Justice Davies of the reality of the event. And still the ROH can and do fall back on the tried and tested entertainment principle of 'exorbitant cost' as a reason to avoid responsibility for what has, now patently and in full view of the public gallery, taken place. This seems harder to fix than it might otherwise have been, given the already significant budgets and economy, the exchange system that the Royal Opera House currently works within. It might not have wholly helped the ROH's case that exactly symmetrical with the timing of this hearing they were grandly opening a major overhaul of the liminal café and other Champagne-grade spaces adjacent to the Opera House itself, on a budget of about £60 million that was wholly raised from their uniquely well-endowed private donors. That this has done nothing to improve the conditions of those actually *working* in the engine room of the opera house, the orchestra pit, could not have gone unnoticed within this particular system of economic exchanges. It brings back to mind the provocative 1988 Saatchi and Saatchi claim made for the Victoria & Albert Museum just down the road in South Kensington: 'An ace caff with quite a nice museum attached'.

Goldscheider in seeking compensation knows he is entering a pact with the devil that will inevitably lead to the silencing of a number of other adjacent issues that the case will throw up. This is the 'loss' that is inbuilt to any compensatory claim and takes the following form:

> The compensation sought, which defines the value of what was lost, ends the semiotic chain, and usually represses whatever is left without compensation. If the damaged person [Chris Goldscheider] agrees to compensation, this cancels the mediating role and the semiotic value of the damage. What is left is what was lost, the compensation, and what was lost and has no compensation – the aura left by the loss.[47]

Those who seek compensation are by definition announcing themselves as those who have a problem. While this might appear an inconsequential and colloquial reality in life it has a significant impact upon the conduct of the court case in which the claimant has to enter into an exchange system, a discourse, that often simply cannot account for the acute impact of this 'problem' on their lives. It is such 'problems' that cases are designed to close down, to bring under bureaucratic control on behalf of a State that is allergic to frayed ends. And it is precisely in the inability to close down Chris Goldscheider that an uncertain aura begins to hover around the proceedings of that which will not go away. The symptom of the problem, or at least of articulating this problem, is that those who enter court as an observer, cannot enter the exchange system of the legal process and finish up movingly but ineffectively 'loudly lamenting a loss'.[48] I have experienced this often in courts where a claimant, frustrated with the exchange system of the chosen barristers, breaks free from the constraints of the strictly ordered ceremonial of the law and shouts out to those present (as in Holyoake vs. Candy & Candy discussed earlier) or indeed in one case leaves the court room entirely, wailing as they run down the corridor on an injured leg that is the limb under legal scrutiny. In a fashion not unakin to Walter Benjamin's evocation of the 'aura' in his essay 'The Work of Art in the Age of Mechanical Reproduction', it is then my role to open up that aura, to consider what it is at the margins of this case that might endure for further speculation. I will do that by considering how Chris Goldscheider's case advances our thinking of performance and its relationship to suffering.

Cultural cruelty

Suffering is 'the duration of the encounter with the unbearable; the unbearable is precisely what one bears when suffering, what one suffers from'.[49] For Chris Goldscheider what is unbearable is sound that happens to take the form of 'music' as composed by Richard Wagner. Wagner has become progressively 'louder' over the last century and on Saturday 1 September 2012 in the afternoon rehearsal of *Die Walküre*, quite evidently very loud indeed. Up to 120 db loud, and then some with peaks at 130 db, close to that of a jet-engine taking off. When what is 'unbearable' takes the peculiar name of 'music', excuses appear to be made on its behalf that would not be made in any other environment of unbearable noise. Indeed, the sewing machine factory Quantum case of 2008 has set a precedent for how other workers might be able to protect themselves from such industrial brutality. But in the instance of an orchestra it would appear from the very opening passages of their skeleton argument quoted above, that the Royal Opera House defence is predicated on an economy of exchange, which is quite different to industrial precedent and apparently not legislated for anywhere. That when sound is not a bi-product but the *end* product of an activity (in this case an operatic event) this necessarily limits liability for the consequences of what might then ensue.

If the opposite of suffering is pleasure, which it is, then the logic of this defence is that the pleasure of the Royal Opera House audience would seem to have trumped (even trumpeted) the expectation of safety amongst those responsible for that pleasure. This is by no means an unusual arrangement between those who labour and their clients: sweat-shop production of fashion, sex work, pornography, boxing are just a few of the instances in which cultures of cruelty operate in and around transactions within which performance plays a mediating part in suffering. What defines suffering is the impossibility of removing 'tormenting excitation', and when that impossibility of removing such excitation continues the word for what is happening is torture. I am not for a moment forgetting the appeal and free-will of the delights of masochism here. When we discussed Pierre Klossowski in the opening to Part II of this book it would be self-evident as the chronicler of the Marquis de Sade that human freedom includes the right and capacity to choose to perpetuate such masochistic excitations and that suffering itself brings pleasure to *some* in the absence of coercion. But workers tend not in their labour relations to choose to perpetuate suffering (though neoliberal constructions of the subject might insist that our own motivations, will, drives and appetite for work are ones that now identify us as productive humans).

While 'exit' from such suffering, as we defined it earlier, is rarely an option for any others than the relatively privileged, the impossibility of retreat from harm is the ubiquitous present of those dependent on their work for a living. The unusual capacity of Chris Goldscheider is precisely his capacity for removal. While at first he has found it impossible to leave, the judge recognises that the forces of attraction to the orchestral timetable make it impossible for him to escape to sanctuary and it is only later that he refuses to return. It is important to note here that while Chris Goldscheider and his viola colleague on the neighbouring desk have both registered the pain that they have been in in rehearsal, it is not so much pain that then subsequently assails him, as the accumulated experience of damage to his hearing experienced as sound, noise, static, interference and a 'sense' of deep unease and anxiety. I suspect this is precisely the subtlety of tinnitus that escapes legislation to this point, it seems too ephemeral for serious attention, just a bit too subjective, your word of pain against my need to keep the repertoire swinging.

All performance operates through its own economy of exchange with regards to such pain and 'suffering'. One might expect a fakir to experience a different kind of pain in training for their professional life from a ballet dancer who on-point might expect a different kind of physical challenge to someone training in courtly dance at the Royal Academy of Dramatic Art. Much has been made of the ubiquity of the abject and extreme states of physical endurance in performance art and the facile assumption that such 'suffering' brings those performers in some way closer to the 'real' that other forms of dramatic representation might miss in their illusory ways. The work of Chris Brett Bailey that opened this chapter would be considered by some to somehow be more 'real' than other reals for the manner in which it confronts us with the very thing that has been familiar from the Romantic poets on (with added volume). Sir Laurence Olivier's (perhaps apocryphal) conversation with Dustin Hoffman on the set of *Marathon Man* neatly sums this presumed relationship up. Hoffman arrives on set after his 'warm-up' extended run, sweating and gasping his way into his Method-inspired role to which Olivier, from an armchair smoking a pipe, replies: 'But that is what acting is for dear boy'. Whatever one thinks about such anecdotes, they reveal a continuous economy of relative pain within performance that this court case exposes to serious scrutiny.[50]

Adi Ophir is not talking about orchestral music when he turns in his writing to sounds and suffering but his example is a useful one in the context of the Goldscheider case:

> A deafening noise can cause suffering at the moment of the encounter itself; the barely audible sound of a dripping tap becomes excessive gradually, very slowly, until the nuisance becomes torture and the one who hears it cannot take it anymore. One drop, one too many, has made it excessive. Suffering

begins when a sharp sense of 'too much' comes upon the one who is overcome by the feeling – 'I have had enough' – when something inside someone cries out, 'No more, stop it!'. The presence of what is exciting turns into the presence of a surplus that cannot be disposed of.[51]

The proceedings in Court 12 of the High Court in London suggest that the subtle yet necessary relations between these two quite different things on a spectrum between excitation and excess have either been ignored or wilfully misunderstood. Or less generously, the Royal Opera House has spent so long immured from the common ways of others, in labour law, health and safety, or just plain empathetic relations with workers, that the insistence on excitation at all costs, and it is 'at all costs' given the price of the seats, overwhelms their individual sense of palpable responsibility to others (as evidenced in the court proceedings). When we talk about 'institutional racism' and 'institutional sexism', we measure a woeful structural indifference to urgencies of equality. Perhaps now is the time to add other forms of less-urgent, but imperative change within cultural contexts bloated by their long-running isolation from the threats that others have faced. It is hard to estimate how cloth-eared, how tone-deaf to take two cruel metaphors the Royal Opera House was in a defence that was (as good as) ridiculed in Justice Davies' judgement. I have quoted the judgement at some length above in order that the *tone* of the judgement is quite explicitly available to those who are interested in such things, beyond the spin that post-Appeal failure damage-limitation kicks in from cultural institutions who can afford reputation managers. As the sufferer Chris Goldscheider has done what all sufferers do, he has become an addresser to the source of his suffering and cried out for help. That this 'help' comes back in the form of having to go to court to defend oneself in such circumstances (and, unforgivably again in Appeal) is, by any measure, a mark of disrespect of the reality of that suffering and its rightful resolution. By the time the case has been taken back to Appeal and lost again by the ROH, disrespect has turned to a sign of cruelty by any sensible human measure. If you doubt my definition of cultural cruelty as represented in this and other scenes in this book, then you doubt the veracity of all those who genuinely 'appeal' for your help when they suffer.[52] Ruben Östlund's Palme D'Or winning film *The Square* nails this cultural indifference as Claes Bang's curator spirals into the hell of those he lacks the empathy to help.

The sorry but inescapable logic of the Royal Opera House defence is that Chris Goldscheider is *simulating* his suffering. At the time of the railway crashes of the late nineteenth century that informed Freud's writing on 'railway spine and anxiety', adjudicators of insurance claims, early-starter loss adjustors, called this 'malingering'. Of course they would never say such a thing in today's hedged caution-culture, but that is the obvious inference of the defence they pay a great deal of money to mount against this claim for damages. That is the harsh but only plausible implication I can draw from their argument that acoustic shock *does not exist* and, to add insult to injury, even if it did exist Goldscheider is 'not suffering from it'. By displacing the sufferer's source of suffering from one diagnosis to another is a very peculiar act for an arts organisation to take to law by way of defence.

Going to law is itself an acceptance that a third party will decide upon the veracity, the credibility of what is being said. This deferral of responsibility for the Royal Opera House to accept as credible what Goldscheider has said, is the instigation of a costly process for all involved, in terms of resources and emotions, not least of all for the person who has (even according to the ROH) already suffered 'enough'. That the Appeal Court finds for the claimant in both cases, that it is the claimant who is credible and to be respected in this instance, is by obvious inference given the proceedings we have listened to so carefully, to judge that the Royal Opera House is *not* credible. At this juncture in public life an apology from the management to the claimant might commonly be expected. But I am not sure since the Appeal Court judgement in Goldscheider vs. the ROH that I have seen anywhere, either prominent or discrete, any apology from the Royal Opera House to Chris Goldscheider of this kind. I am presuming those came, perhaps appropriately, in a personal stamped letter to his new home that has rightly been kept private. For this is by any measure a very private matter, except in some significant public respects that will close this chapter.

It is left to Chris Goldscheider to introduce his suffering into a public exchange system that we call the courts of law. He does this through a claim for compensation: 'Suffering involves claiming compensation. By its very nature, but also and because to the extent to which it has caused loss – of time, health, quality of life, material resources, and so on'.[53] Compensation claims are made with respect to a damage that could have been prevented. But the science of such calculations is notoriously difficult, not least of all as experts who appraise suffering are often in sharp disagreement (often depending on whose side one might be on) as to the degree of suffering being endured or indeed how it might have been reasonably foreseen or prevented. The languages of the High Court are particularly etiolated in this respect, with two expert witnesses on the implications of acoustic shock and its consequences miles apart in their prognoses. Indeed most suffering of the kind that Chris Goldscheider has found ways of addressing, vocabularies to represent and exchange systems of discourse to enter, simply do not figure within legal discourse at large. That is why this particular case is being heard in the UK High Court, it is setting a long-overdue international precedent for the measure of such vocabularies, and by going to Appeal and being judged again in favour of the claimant is insisting as strongly as one can within UK law that this will not go on. Desist. Now. Whether the Royal Opera House is temperamentally suited to acting now or anytime soon, appears to be in question. Theo Huckle QC encourages them on the social networking site LinkedIn on the day after the Appeal judgement that they should draw a line under this now to allow Goldscheider to get on with his broken-backed life. This is the only liberation that the claimant might have hoped for but that the appeals process so cruelly forestalls and delays. 'Let it go, let it go' is a popular song sung by a tiaraed snow-bound Elsa from *Frozen*, but given it has not been part of the ROH repertoire in the recent past, it is unlikely their management will heed its timely advice.

One might, in any other circumstances, have expected Chris Goldscheider's suffering to remain unexpressed, unaddressed. This is an appalling indictment of the maturity of the institutions that surrounded his injury with so much smoke and mirrors. None of us are under any delusions that there have not been countless others, surely, we all know that the world is littered with those who have been injured in not dissimilar circumstances but never found a way to express that suffering. That seems rational when one considers the accelerated appetite for cheaper and cheaper labour, then cheaper and cheaper natures, that drives the capitalist enterprise. Where it becomes somewhat peculiar is its featuring within the work of institutions whose very mission might be presumed to be that of justice, welfare, tolerance, beauty, social responsibility: arts institutions you could say amongst whom opera houses appear to consider themselves a refined if apparently law-lite version.

Our social unconscious of all these unspoken acts of injury and suffering are sharpened by the sense that in the end it is to the privacies of family, a loved one or friend that one turns to when the responsibility for our suffering is resisted by those who might be best held accountable. Many would presume that the arts themselves, and theatre especially, might be best suited to take up one of the emerging mediating positions for those who suffer alongside those private partners in grief. But I am sceptical as to quite how this works in practice (notwithstanding the remarkable evidence amongst others of James Thompson on war, Paul Heritage on penal incarceration) providing just one more conversion channel through which the suffering might be reached in some helpful way. One might also expect social institutions such as opera houses, galleries, theatres to play their part in such channelling too, and the evidence of confusion here as to any such role is stark. Solidarity is the word in English we use to identify such channels of shared responsibility for those who suffer, and it is solidarity that Chris Goldscheider was seeking amongst an 'order of evils' that not personally, but cumulatively, were close to denying him his basic human rights. And he is after all a viola player on the second desk in the pit of the Royal Opera House in London's Covent Garden. Pity those who sit on the desk behind, or don't sit at all, the triangle player for instance, or those with no desk, that is all of us who never made it as far as this beautiful orchestra with its precious human parts. Those in pits elsewhere.

Demonic territory

On leaving this world of Wagner and work on the final judgement day of the hearing, it is striking that the Royal Courts of Justice on Strand in London sit opposite the sites of two talismanic buildings that shape everything we see and hear within this legal process: Britain's first bank Child & Co founded on this spot in 1599, still there doing its infernal business, and, the Devil Tavern eventually demolished in 1787 and now memorialised by a handsome aquamarine ceramic plate. Directly next door to that devil-may-care neighbour, Child & Co is one kind of future-builder that has been busy building away for half a millennia. This is the oldest bank in the UK, Child & Co, still at Number 1 Fleet Street, London, where it has been since 1559, so, well before Shakespeare got around to ensuring all children had to take theatre seriously before they needed to. This is the model business for Charles Dickens' 'Tellson's Bank', in his revolutionary novel *A Tale of Two Cities*, where the 'inconvenience' of the bank, its congenital resistance to 'rebuilding' (not unlike the Royal Opera House round the corner) is likened to the 'Country', shadowed as it is by the vast Temple Bar and its spiked, executed heads that looked back blankly at the lives 'taken' by the bank in its necrophiliac workings. Tellson's (Child & Co) is, in Dickens' words, a bank of 'death':

> very small, very dark, very ugly [...] A place of death, where the utterer of a bad note was put to death, the unlawful opener of a letter was put to death, the purloiner of forty shillings and sixpence was put to death.[54]

The bank was figured by Dickens, before Anonymous, Occupy and others drew our attention to their derivative excesses, as a 'killing-machine', and long before sub-prime, eviction, crash and expulsion, ensured those who were already precarious felt more so. Bodies and perceptions is what is at stake in this precarity of course, as it has been throughout the Goldscheider vs. ROH case, and between this bank and the Royal Courts of Justice one feels this most acutely on a street called Strand.[55] Here the odd-job-man Cruncher, never allowed through the portal of the door but always on guard outside it, the 'live sign' of the house, an early embodiment of financialisation, would, when errands necessitated his absence, be replaced by his 12-year-old son, who was his 'express image'. Like father like child-son, interchangeable as with many of Dickens' adulterised labouring children. It was via this guarded portal that a child would enter Child & Co as an aspirant apprentice, and as Dickens described it:

> They hid him until he was old. They kept him in a dark place, like a cheese, until he had the full Tellson flavour and blue-mould upon him. Then only was he permitted to be seen, spectacularly, poring over large books, and casting his breeches and gaiters into the general weight of the establishment.[56]

So, against the pressing and omnipresent 'general weight of the establishment', between a bank and the legal system as represented by the Bar I am, with others critically concerned with who is 'permitted to be seen', spectacularly if need be, and under what conditions? What are the conditions that determine whether Chris Goldscheider can be seen *and* heard? He is after all not a child, in Child & Co. who might expect (in the UK at least) to be seen but not heard. He is after all an adult who dedicated his considerable talent to being heard beautifully. That 'permitted to be seen' and 'permitted to be heard' might otherwise be described as, 'the field of appearance', one small part of which we might want to identify more acutely with the specialist name 'live art', or 'theatre', or 'performance' that I am discussing in this book, given those are modes that might be expected to offer channels of signification for such acts to be sharpened and softened as fit the purpose. I am not so concerned with what we call it, just *how* we and others for whom appearance might not be quite such a human right might be able to *do* it with more 'radical inclusivity', if indeed 'appearing' is of any interest, and it is certainly not for everyone as Peggy Phelan has made clear in her work *Unmarked*.[57]

With Judith Butler, I would ask about the make-up, the *structuring* of this field of appearance:

> Why *is* that field *regulated* in such a way that only certain 'kinds of beings' can appear as recognisable subjects, and others cannot? And why the compulsory demand to appear in *one way* rather than another that functions as a precondition for appearing at all.[58]

It is not only now that with Goldscheider's courage in mind we need to live in order to act, but that we have to act, and act politically, to secure the conditions of appearance, and therefore of existence, for those otherwise inhibited, excluded and precluded *from* such appearance. That appears to me to be the lesson that the case of Chris Goldscheider teaches us. So, a politics of possibility is at work in the narrative in this chapter of one such representation, one such appearance. And that is of course by definition also a matter of performance, always an ethics of performance as I suggested a quarter-century ago in *Theatre & Everyday Life*.[59] By acknowledging my own degree of deafness on Strand opposite the Royal Courts of Justice on that judgement day, again, quite different to others' deafness, I was not disaffiliating from the company of Child & Co, in an apparent process of ageing and retreat from appearance (as many hearing impaired people do), but rather finding a place for myself back in that company again, in the world of sonic-sensation familiar from my own childhood, indeed synonymous now I listen to it, whistling, continuous, unremitting and remarkable in its own register, if one has the courage, or is foolhardy enough to admit its comings and goings, day and night.

The financial implications of the Chris Goldscheider claim against the Royal Opera House would be of special interest to Child & Co, as £750,000 is just about the minimum credit one might require to bank with them. But those damages have come at an almighty cost to the claimant. That ceramic marker to the right of the bank Child & Co, that marks the demolished Devil's Tavern of 1787, is perhaps closer to the fiendish truth here. Thomas Mann in his novel *Dr Faustus* offers us an insight to this hell, when inspired by Søren Kierkegaard, he reached the famous conclusion that: 'Music is Demonic Territory'.[60]

As I wrote those words in March 2018 a new season was being announced at Battersea Arts Centre, an institution I have committed myself to over many years, as a punter, as a member of their Capital Board rebuilding after the devastating 2015 fire (discussed in the next and last chapter of this book), as a visitor with groups of students that number into the hundreds and as such have underwritten with their paying presence so much of the work that has yet, courageously to meet its audience. The season is promoted by *Time Out* on their web-site with the following upbeat blurb:

> Theatrical noisenik Christopher Brett Bailey presents a glorious reprise of his three most recent shows: his earsplittingly loud performance poems 'This Is How We Die' and 'Kissing The Shotgun Goodnight', plus a full-on outing for his guitar ensemble with 'This Machine Won't Kill Fascists But It Might Get You Laid'.[61]

And to back that up, on Facebook too in no less mouth-watering prose and with fonts to match:

> A marathon evening of noise-theatre and theatrical noise. For two nights only Christopher Brett Bailey brings his multi-award-winning 'cult hit' THIS IS HOW WE DIE and the 'insanely and dangerously loud' follow-up KISSING THE SHOTGUN GOODNIGHT back to London. Because his OCD manifests in a fetish for odd numbers, a double bill was never going to be enough.... The evening will climax with a performance by Christopher Brett Bailey's electric guitar ensemble, THIS MACHINE WON'T KILL FASCISTS BUT IT MIGHT GET YOU LAID. For this special occasion, they will be premiering new material and performing a surround sound concert in ear-splitting 3D audio![62]

Given the promised levels of volume (not unusual in work of this kind) I ask my colleagues in the production office at BAC whether they are aware of the recent Goldscheider vs. Royal Opera House judgement and the responsibility in law they now have, not just to offer adequate hearing-protection, but to encourage its use amongst all audience members? They don't and, typically being the always alert Battersea Arts Centre, are grateful to talk about it and open to the implications of such fundamental changes in the legal scene. I meet them two days before the scheduled opening of the 'glorious reprise' performances (in my own time and *gratis* at their premises) and discover that they are not aware of the difference between ear plugs that protect, and those that most definitely do not. So I suggest they might look into this before distributing bright-coloured but inadequate foam mushrooms to audiences that would not protect them from a madrigal concert featuring treble-recorder virtuosi. They say they will, but late on the coming Thursday evening, two full days later, I receive an email from the long-standing, indeed outstanding BAC artistic director and colleague David Jubb, that he has had to cancel the first night of the season due to 'safety concerns'. The hearing-protection has been deemed by 'health and safety' to be inadequate.

There are a crowd of unhappy ticket-holders in the bar. A banal kind of non-performance has just been staged, not the kind I have been talking about in this chapter, but the pathetic side-effect of a failure of securing not just adequate but 'right protection', that would have ensured all would proceed with the right *to* protection in place for those who chose to be protected. And after all that 'choice', an aesthetic selection amongst myriad such decisions, is itself a free choice. I offer to come and hear the public's complaints of 'censorship', the 'nanny state', health and safety 'gone mad', as best I can through my own continuous static. I convince myself I would listen as carefully as I could to these arguments before replying, 'No, it's none of these, I am as sure of that fact as I am of my own life-long support of artists to do as they wish when and where they want'. I am confident that they will be able to hear me without hindrance and confident they will choose to agree or disagree with me, reassured that they will live to listen another night given someone at BAC has had the courage to do what they inadvertently failed to do at Oval House those two years before. As they indeed *do* listen with the delight common to Chris Brett Bailey's delirious work, in the same venue, the following night, with the arrival of new acoustic protection that *is* now adequate and the show goes up and everyone, of course, given that is the point of the freedom to protect yourself, goes fine and dandy. The title of that Chris Brett Bailey Season at Battersea Arts Centre in Spring 2018? *Are You Deaf Yet?*

Notes

1. Christopher Brett Bailey, Programme Note, *Kissing The Shotgun Goodnight*, Oval House, 6 October 2016.
2. Barthelme, Donald. (2005). *Forty Stories*. New York: Penguin Books.
3. Coleman, Nick. (2012). *The Train in the Night: A Story of Music and Loss*. London: Jonathan Cape. I am grateful to Steve Tompkins who with characteristic generosity heard me out and shared this volume with me.
4. See Bathurst, Bella (2017). *Sound: Stories of Hearing Lost and Found*. London: Profile Books.
5. See the excellent work by Bojana Kunst (2015) from which I have derived this association: *Artist at Work: Proximity of Art and Capitalism*. London: Zero Books. I am grateful to Bojana for collegiality during this writing.
6. Mrs Justice Nicola Davies, Judgment, Paragraph 224. 28 March 2018, High Court Queens Bench Division, Christopher Goldscheider: Claimant; Royal Opera House Foundation: Defendant; Theo Huckle QC and Jonathan Clarke (instructed by Fry Law) for the Claimant David Platt QC and Alexander Macpherson (instructed by BLM Law) for the Defendant. Hearing dates: 30 January to 7 February and 9 February 2018. The observations here are a combination of direct reference to this judgement, and quotations from my own written daily record of the proceedings which were checked with the court stenographers at session end.
7. David Platt, QC: Skeleton Argument of Defendant – Trial, Christopher Goldscheider and Royal Opera House Covent Garden Foundation, Claim no: HQ16 PO1778.
8. David Platt, QC: Skeleton Argument of Defendant – Trial, Christopher Goldscheider and Royal Opera House Covent Garden Foundation, Claim no: HQ16 PO1778.
9. Thanks to Professor Sonia Massai for alerting me to this significant heritage.
10. See Lazzarato, Maurizio. (1996). 'Immaterial Labor', in Eds. Paolo Virno, and Michael Hardt. *Radical Thought in Italy: A Potential Politics*. University of Minnesota Press. pp. 142–157. For an interesting discussion of Lazzarato in relation to theatre see: Ridout, Nicholas. (2013). *Passionate Amateurs: Theatre, Communism and Love*. Michigan: University of Michigan Press.
11. Virno, Paolo. (2004). *A Grammar of the Multitude*. New York: Semiotexte, p. 9. These essays were first given by Virno as three lectures when he was Dean of the Ethics of Communication at the University of Calabria in 2001.
12. Sylvère Lotringer, Forward 'We The Multitude', to Virno, Paolo, op. cit. p. 13.
13. Ibid. p. 17.
14. Justice Nicola Davies, Judgment, op. cit. p. 217.

15 See Virno, op. cit. p. 52.
16 Ibid. p. 52.
17 Ibid. p. 52.
18 Hannah Arendt in *Between Past and Future*, p. 154, quoted by Virno, ibid. p. 53.
19 Ibid. p. 55.
20 Ibid. p. 63.
21 Ibid. p. 69.
22 Ibid. p. 70.
23 Ibid. p. 70.
24 See Jacques Rancière, on 'the part of those who have no part', in Jacques Rancière and Davide Panagia. (2000). 'Dissenting Words: A Conversation with Jacques Rancière'. *Diacritics*. Vol. 30, no. 2, (Summer 2000) pp. 113–126.
25 Opening paragraphs of Mrs Justice Nicola Davies, Judgment, 28 March 2018, High Court Queens Bench Division, Christopher Goldscheider: Claimant; Royal Opera House Foundation: Defendant; Theo Huckle QC and Jonathan Clarke (instructed by Fry Law) for the Claimant David Platt QC and Alexander Macpherson (instructed by BLM Law) for the Defendant. Hearing dates: 30 January to 7 February and 9 February 2018.
26 Ibid.
27 Ibid. Para. 219.
28 Ibid. Para. 229.
29 See Ridout, Nicholas, op. cit. pp. 138–162.
30 Laruelle, François. (1993). *The Concept of an Ordinary Ethics or Ethics Founded in Man*. Trans. Taylor Adkins. Available online here: www.scribd.com/document/233744571/Laruelle-The-Concept-of-an-Ordinary-Ethics-or-Ethics-Founded-in-Man (accessed on 28 August 2019).
31 Ophir, Adi. (2005) *The Order of Evils: Toward an Ontology of Morals*. Trans. Rela Mazah and Havi Carel. New York: Zone Books.
32 Ibid. p. 18.
33 Ibid. p. 35.
34 Ibid. pp. 18–19.
35 Ibid. pp. 24–25.
36 Ibid. p. 35.
37 Ibid. p. 38.
38 See Phelan, Peggy. (1993). 'The Ontology of Performance', in *Unmarked: The Politics of Performance*. London: Routledge, p. 146.
39 See Jonah Westerman on Intermedia: www.tate.org.uk/research/features/between-action-and-image (accessed on 28 August 2019).
40 Ophir, Adi, op. cit. p. 60.
41 Ibid. p. 89.
42 Ibid. p. 91.
43 See Carlson, Marvin. (2003). *The Haunted Stage: The Theatre as Memory Machine*. Michigan: University of Michigan Press.
44 Ophir, Adi, op. cit. p. 121.
45 Ibid. p. 127.
46 Ibid. p. 129.
47 Ibid. p. 134.
48 Ibid. p. 146.
49 Ibid. p. 257.
50 Also see ground-breaking work by Schneider, Rebecca. (1997). *The Explicit Body in Performance*. Abingdon: Routledge.
51 Ophir, Adi, op. cit. p. 259.
52 The word and the sound of the word 'Help!' echoes through one of the very few mainstream cinematic works to attend to the concerns of this book: *The Square*, Dir. Ruben Östlund, 2017.

53 Ophir, Adi op. cit. p. 285.
54 Dickens, Charles. *A Tale of Two Cities*, accessible at: www.gutenberg.org/files/98/old/2city12p.pdf pp. 46–47. (accessed on 1 July 2017).
55 'Bodies and Perceptions' was the title of a panel which I chaired with Harold Offeh and Evan Ifekoya at Tate Modern as part of Sibylle Peters and the Live Art Development Agency event, *Playing Up*, Starr Auditorium, Tate Modern, 4 April 2016.
56 *A Tale of Two Cities*, op. cit. p. 47.
57 Phelan, Peggy. (1993). *Unmarked*. London: Routledge.
58 Butler, Judith. (2015a). *Notes Toward a Performative Theory of Assembly*. Cambridge: Harvard University Press, p. 35.
59 Read, Alan. (1993). *Theatre & Everyday Life: An Ethics of Performance*. London: Routledge.
60 Mann, Thomas. (1999). *Dr Faustus*. Trans. John E. Woods. New York: Vintage International.
61 www.timeout.com/london/theatre/are-you-deaf-yet-a-christopher-brett-bailey-triple-bill#tab_panel_2 (accessed on 28 August 2019).
62 www.facebook.com/events/battersea-arts-centre-bac/are-you-deaf-yet-a-christopher-brett-bailey-triple-bill/122184491883326/ (accessed on 28 August 2019).

7
POOR HISTORY
Field notes from a fire sale

It is wholly symptomatic of my naïve voluntarism that when I wrote *Theatre & Everyday Life* in 1993 the book's most obvious corollary, everyday death, barely raised a mention. I did write about Sebastiano Timpanaro's ideas of the 'natural limits to life' and the challenges any such mortal realism might offer a Marxist theory of longitudinal revolutionary struggle, some way beyond the irritating closures experienced by most humans in Western Europe around three score years and ten (if we get lucky). At the time Dan Bulley had not yet written a sobering reminder as to the everyday presence of death, for some and not others:

> whilst the global nature of everyday life in many cities is accepted, far less attention is given to the global production of death. How we die and when appears a strangely local, private and apolitical affair – determined only by home-grown health politics, economics and inequalities.[1]

Indeed, some three decades before the devastating fire at Grenfell Tower in West London on the night of 14 June 2017, but after the horrifying Bradford City Football Stadium fire at Valley Parade on the afternoon of 11 May 1985, while I questioned the rhetoric of risk associated with historic theatre-attendance in the final chapter of *Theatre & Everyday Life*, I was apparently immune to the harsh reality of what any such conflagration might represent to those who perished, and those left behind in loss. There I wrote, when innocent critical-theory-confidence was king:

> The freedom from danger [when attending to theatre] has only in the last century superseded a freedom *for* danger. The contracts of Carnival have always been different, often inverted, and to be in Barcelona at the Festival of Mercé is to recognise and accept the possibility of burning, of being burnt.[2]

But that is the point, and for some there would be no point in being there without that risk. It is between the vitality of such theatrical manifestations and the conventions of Western auditoria that theatre has in its myriad alternative forms been conducting a repressed dialogue.[3]

Here I was proposing, it must be said with considerable care given the stakes, that it is in the space *between* safety and danger that theatre historically took its place and continues to articulate its demand on our attention. Indeed the previous chapter of this book explored how acoustic shock is one of the new frontiers where such delimitations are still being questioned and legislated for. In the case of fire, I had noticed, it is a contract that in the West at least is no longer debatable, it has become taboo. It has of course not always been so as the archival records show, theatres if not theatre itself, were once, thanks to the ubiquity of fire, simply dangerous.

But the way of reading this past as with all pasts, is dependent on a writing of history, which in the case of fire is to be treated seriously, but equally sceptically, if we are not to miss the real it hopes to capture in its script. Not least of all when death is in the air. I was not arguing for a dangerous or a safe theatre when I first wrote this – as I made quite clear I have no right to jeopardise life, nor to take away the other's right to death – but to recognise that, in the absence of critical thought, dangers arise from unforeseen corners and jeopardise both life and theatre. I wanted to acknowledge that historiography is one defence against forgetting, and when practiced with rigour is to be valued by the practitioner whose work is undertaken in its folds.[4]

If the meaning of fire had been forgotten I asked, what kind of history writing will adequately recall its features? A writing of the unwritten as fostered by Michel de Certeau I tentatively suggested.[5] As de Certeau says, historiography articulates the event and the fact.[6] The event according to de Certeau, is that which delimits, the fact, that which fills. The event provides the historian with the conditions for intelligibility, the fact creates the possibility of a meaningful statement being made. Thus the event defines, the fact spells out. The event provides the means through which disorder is turned into order; it permits an understanding.

To test this hypothesis and to mark a boundary between performance and the quotidian to conclude *Theatre & Everyday Life* I chose to examine three events. They all occurred in London. The litany could be extended to Chicago, or San Francisco, though the consequent analysis might be quite different.[7] The events: The Globe Theatre burns down. The Royal Opera Covent Garden burns down. The Savoy Theatre burns down. The facts: the Globe was destroyed on 29 June 1613 during a performance of *Henry VIII*, by the firing of a cannon and the igniting of the thatch. Fact gives way to conjecture. Covent Garden was burnt down on 5 March 1856, during a *bal masque* organised by 'The Wizard of the North' as the band struck up God Save the Queen, by the 'spontaneous combustion' of wood shavings in the carpenter's store. Fact gives way to conjecture later under cross-examination of witnesses. The Savoy Theatre burns down on the night of 12

February 1990. The theatre was dark at the time, the origins of the fire are not thought to be suspicious, though decorators had been completing a programme of re-gilding over the previous weekend. Conjecture, arriving late but triumphant, is that an electrical fault was responsible, a neat journalistic irony given that the theatre was the first to be lit solely by its own electric light, thus for the first time, in 1881, diminishing the historic chance of fire from gas lighting.

In the margins of this short history of the theatre on fire, where guilt and recrimination flare in equal measure, the work of the poor historian is muted. For already this site is a place where the 'other' is responsible. The gesture which attaches ideas to places is, de Certeau explains, precisely the historian's gesture. If history is the relations between a place, analytical procedures and the construction of a text, which it palpably is, the historiographical process becomes one of delimiting place, the practices therein and their conversion into writing. But fire so fundamentally affects us as to drive all reason from that place, for often the writing of the history of fire is the writing of the dead, literally. And witnesses become in this legal world, accomplices, their speaking is prejudice. It is just such prejudices that instantiate poor history.

I did not look back at this last chapter of *Theatre & Everyday Life* until exactly a quarter of a century after writing it when my colleague David Jubb, the then Artistic Director of Battersea Arts Centre (who had alerted me to the cancellation of that noisy performance by Chris Brett Bailey), wrote to the advisory board of BAC, of which for some years I had been a part, asking for reflections on the first week anniversary of the fire that on Friday 13 March 2015 had devastated their Grand Hall. I wrote back:

> When asked what quality he most admired in a theatre, the director Peter Brook replied: 'Combustibility'. The fire that took out the Grand Hall heart of the Battersea Arts Centre at this time last Friday joins a lineage that stretches back to Shakespeare's Globe that succumbed to a misdirected cannon shot in 1613. For three more centuries theatres were built, and theatres burnt. Since the invention of London's first 'Safety Theatre', the Palace Theatre in the late nineteenth century, performance spaces have been licensed along the same lines as hotels. They have to prove they are a safe place to sleep.[8]

Repeating an already tired joke about theatre and hotels being safe places to sleep neither makes the original nor the revival funny. And as, at the time of writing, Haworth Tompkins Architects' work with Battersea Arts Centre to restore to the heart of the community the Grand Hall that was the hearth of its ceremonial history, a short walk away closer to my own neighbourhood in West London stands a charred, 24-storey mausoleum to hope that Michel de Certeau would have recognised as the twenty-first century's exemplar of history as the 'writing of prejudice'. It is not quite that de Certeau would have figured that prejudice as the continuing violation of what Nadine El-Enany calls 'racialised people', though as a Jesuit scholar he was acutely aware of the forces of such racist violence, but he would have been well equipped to track the historical trajectory of European colonialism and transatlantic slavery, ideas of race and racial inferiority and as El-Enany says, 'the dispossessing effects of European colonialism' that are the true long durée history of what the Grenfell Tower fire really stands for.[9] And I am explicitly here *not* referring to Doreen Lawrence's misjudged statements in October 2019 regarding the response of the London fire services that she later rowed back on confirming that as far as the fire services went: 'I am reassured race played no part in their response to the Grenfell Tower fire'.[10] No one is really there between Latimer Road underground station and the Westway who can take responsibility for the 'statement' as to the cause of this fire, discourses about this racist past become necessarily the discourse of the disproportionately dead, the constant reference amongst those living beings presiding over this history:

> Discourse is incessantly articulated over the death that it presupposes, but that the very practice of history constantly contradicts. For to speak of the dead means to deny death and also to defy it. Therefore speech is said to 'resuscitate' them. Here the word is literally a lure: history does not resuscitate anything.[11]

Such might be the obvious inadequacy of poor history, but histories of fires, as Grenfell Tower has demonstrated to us in the most appalling circumstances, are still demanding our attention. Grenfell Tower might offer a particularly egregious example to close this book amongst the ashes, but it should I would suggest certainly not strike us as exceptional in any respect if we wish to understand its historical significance. Where theatre and everyday death might require us to think somewhat differently as to what we imagine performance can do in such razed worlds, it is Grenfell Tower that demands attention as a sobering reminder as to any kind of meaningful relation we might wish to forge between practices and politics. It is not now it would seem, if it has ever been so, that some catastrophic fires are exceptions to some complacent rule of protection, but a wholly *unexceptional* matter that demands the special attentions of a colonial history tuned to what Nadine El-Enany calls the 'slow violence' of this sudden and violent spectacle.[12]

Field notes from a fire sale

In the absence of poor history acting on our behalf then, what is left for us to do in our futures that will soon be the long-forgotten pasts? If the soft-focus sentimental poetics of this last return to *Theatre & Everyday Life* appears as a late anomaly in this tougher-minded book, not least of all when it finds itself adjacent to the monstrosity of corporate manslaughter that the fire at Grenfell Tower represents, then how might one harden up this pyro-prose to conclude? Where might politics if not performance be activated after what we have witnessed together and now cannot and don't wish to forget? The auguries are not auspicious. The UK broadcaster Emily Maitlis, in her endearingly low-bar book *Airhead: The Imperfect Art of Making*

News (2019) follows a perfectly well-meaning chapter on her exertions in the neighbourhood on behalf of the Lancaster West Estate community, on the day after the Grenfell fire, with a curiously ill-judged narrative of her preparations to interview Teresa May, the then prime minister at the BBC, the first broadcaster post-fire to secure an interview:

> Our office is on the third floor; the interview will be on the ground floor. I am crouching in the lift, trying to do my make-up on my knees as we go down. The mascara is not going well and I am wearing a white jacket. The possibilities for disaster are endless.[13]

The symmetry between the BBC lift (and other lifts elsewhere that could not be used 'in the event of fire') and the 'potential for disaster' is one that is unsettling when rendered in the explicit and unmistakeable context of a discussion of Grenfell Tower. *Airhead* is a book that is being sold in large numbers on these nuances after all, written as it is by the news presenter and journalist heading up the BBC's flagship programme *Newsnight* more recently better known for having brought about the *Pizza Express* auto-destruct of a bit player in Britain's monarchical spectacle. It is of course not the chaotic analogy of the moment that is the problem (we all have bad hair days) but the ill-judged inclusion of the passage fully two years after the event, during which time one might have imagined the author themselves, or in their absence an editor with anything but cloth ears, would have suggested caution using the word 'disaster' to refer to the application of make-up, as distinct to the matter of the life and death of Grenfell residents about to be discussed with a prime minister who throughout her draconian tenure appeared preoccupied with her own fashion choices.

At another end of an imagined spectrum between Airheaded and Wrongheaded (I was going to write boneheaded but the author is inaccurate not stupid) Andrew O'Hagan's 60,000 word account commissioned by the *London Review of Books,* filling the entirety of its issue of 7 June 2018 (exactly a year after the fire and coinciding with the launch of the Grenfell Inquiry) attracted opprobrium from a number of those who were interviewed by his 'assistants' for the piece, for being either creatively (mis)transcribed, injudiciously ornamented, or, in its lazy reiteration of a long-aired calumny concerning Mr Kebede, the occupant of the flat in which the fire first took hold, engaged in perpetuating plain and libellous falsity under the cloak of citational vagaries. An object lesson in poor history you could say 'smirkingly' referenced in the lush 40th Anniversary coffee-table sized puff to the LRB's history as having 'courted controversy'. While I think the question of the 'courts' in this narrative will soon have a rather more sombre air than the petty controversies of a publication it nevertheless seems responsible in the interests of justice to at least push back on the cultural cruelties played out in print, for those who cannot if nothing else. We will return to this account later, before spending some time at the Grenfell Inquiry itself which offers the only authoritative account of 'what happened', but the cover extract sums up the broad direction of O'Hagan's curious emphasis in this extended work-out of counter-intuitive special pleading:

> At daybreak on 14 June 2017, a large, malodorous cloud hung over West London. You could see it for miles, acrid and acrimonious, the whole country waking up with a sense of disorder. And people required an answer. So we wiped our eyes and blamed the council.[14]

If this were not the *London Review of Books*, whose mimicry of the *New Yorker*'s fearless fact-checking and editorial standard from Joseph Pulitzer's dictum 'Accuracy! Accuracy! Accuracy!', is well-known (if not always evident in practice given its continuously correcting letters page), then one might have presumed that this audacious 'we' had lost its scare quotes in the rush to publication. I for one knew so little about that 'council' I could hardly judge it. So if I was 'out' what about others? But as with the airheaded Emily Maitlis, an eternity since the fire in question had already passed before this scurrilous and wholly inaccurate generalisation as to what 'we' judged to be the matter, was inflated to front cover fonts. Before even leaving the bounteous London Review Bookshop on Bury Street, close on the British Museum, with my LRB special-issue in hand, retailing suddenly at a higher price to non-subscribers for some reason, I was already curious as to why on earth that would be the carefully selected headline feature to grace the cover of this long-awaited article.

Given O'Hagan had for a couple of years previously been my good neighbour on the sixth floor of the Virginia Woolf Building at King's College London, it was not that I did not already have an insight to the luminosity of his prose (*The Illuminations*), the imaginative articulacy of his 'history telling' (*Our Fathers*) or the courage of his convictions (his ghost-writing on his break up with Julien Assange). It was just that a side-swipe at those who held the local council partly accountable for what transpired in one of their own buildings seemed more than a touch against the grain of reasonable sense and sensitivity given all other conceivable options that were also floating in that malodorous air before the Inquiry had even begun. And given we shared a building with the name of Woolf it might have been apposite in this ashen context to recall how Virginia offered a caustic warning as to the patriarchal diversions of the apparently collegiate in *Three Guineas*:

> No guinea of earned money should go to rebuilding the college on the old plan; just as certainly none could be spent upon building a college upon a new plan; therefore the guinea should be earmarked 'Rags. Petrol. Matches'. And this note should be attached to it. 'Take this guinea and with it burn the college to the ground. Set fire to the old hypocrisies'.[15]

Well, my neighbour got out of 'education' long before I did, but the reckoning of education's expectations of veracity might surely have lasted longer in his 'journalism', if that is what 'The Tower' represents.

Pyro-politics

So, what, post the fire at Grenfell, might we offer by way of fields notes from a fire sale, how to address those 'old hypocrisies'? A pyro-politics could, tentatively, partially perhaps, but nonetheless critically and cautiously, begin to account for the three-decade gap that separates two damning symptoms that sit as stark book-ends to an interregnum of the new enclosures, the loss of public housing as evidenced in the book's opening chapters set within the 'Long Good Friday' of expulsions in Docklands, and the austerity driven cruelty towards the dispossessed as represented by the pyre of Grenfell Tower and all it revealed. At the very least the relative poverty of Notting Dale in the post-Windrush era bears out Nadine El-Enany's diagnosis of institutionalised practices of racial control and exclusion: 'This was manifested spatially with the confinement of racialised populations to sites of extreme deprivation, predominantly in the inner cities'.[16]

Michael Marder with whom we spent some time in Chapter 5 considering 'phyto performance' helpfully addresses what the broad semantic-discursive field that 'pyro-politics' might begin to account for: 'fires, flames, sparks, immolations, incinerations, and burning in political theory and practices'.[17] Where much of this book has, due to its early docklands coordinates, situated itself at the common geo-political boundary of earth and water, where for instance works such as Paul Gilroy's *The Black Atlantic* find their orientation, for Marder: 'The time has come to update the political lexicon so as to account for the elements that do not fit into the simple opposition of land and sea'.[18] Where Marx (and Marshall Berman who followed him) had previously linked the expansion of the capitalist mode of production that caused 'all that was solid to melt into air', Marder would have us think in more conflagratory measure that 'instead of evaporating into thin air, things are consumed by fire'.[19] I would add to this prognosis that those unable to escape their condition of coloniality will inevitably succumb to the consequences of extreme insecurity that marks the state-sanctioned presumption that precarity is the standard living condition for racialised people.

Such fires this time, not least of all after Grenfell, do not then simply invite us to think differently of a new-world ashen-order, but rather, following Michel de Certeau's link between fire and the problems of historical truth-telling, allow pyro-politics to register for us the means by which the political becomes conceivable and perceivable in the first place, in new conflagrated arrangements. The fire at Grenfell Tower represented such a savage sorting, such an extreme form of expulsion as articulated in the first chapter of this book, that in the UK at least, in the twenty-first century, it is hardly an exaggeration to talk about BG and AG, Before Grenfell and After Grenfell. But I am not alone in judging peoples' qualities for serious consideration (such as Emily Maitlis in *Airhead*) by gauging their responses to the Grenfell Tower fire, it appears to bring out the best in some and the worst in others. Recognising its colonial antecedents is for me and others a deal-breaker with respect to how one might begin to recover respect for those sacrificed. And it is the racialised dimension of the event that, unfortunately normalises the fire, away from the one-off exceptional 'tragedy' that suits politicians and corporates alike and returns us to examine the structural conditions that, in the UK at least, have delivered the everyday scandals of the maltreatment of Windrush British citizens, the creation of the Home Office 'hostile environment' for immigrants and the encouragement of far-right racist rhetoric under the guises of 'taking back control' in Brexit discourses of lowest-common-denominator isolationism.

Certainly my experience of the Grenfell Inquiry that followed this momentous historical moment for race awareness in the UK, the first phase of which I attended through days in late 2018 and early 2019, impressed on me not just the grave, palpable and pitiful injustices suffered by the residents, their families and their surviving relations and community members, but also the sheer racialised magnitude of an act of cultural cruelty that twice betrayed my West London neighbours, first before, and then, unforgivably *after* the fire that engulfed them. And exactly two years since the anniversary of the fire as I complete this chapter on the eve of the 24th monthly neighbourhood Silent Walk on Thursday 13 June 2019, there is no evidence to suggest that any 'lessons have been learnt', nor redress for injustice yet done. It may well be understandable given due legal process that as-yet there have been no arrests from the corporate sector responsible for the botched development programme, but it cannot go unnoticed either that, still, two-thirds of all high-rise tower blocks with similar external cladding as Grenfell that criss-cross the UK remain untouched despite being described in the Inquiry as cladding worthy of a 'fire trap'. On the eve of the second anniversary Grenfell Silent Walk a vast projection illuminates Frinstead House, a public-housing block on Latimer Road, hard upon the Grenfell site, simply and damningly stating in a font visible from my own neighbourhood: '2 YEARS AFTER GRENFELL THIS BUILDING STILL HAS NO SPRINKLERS. #DEMANDCHANGE. GRENFELL UNITED', and the Houses of Parliament are similarly lit the following night from afar with a giant script that in its limpid accusation holds those 'Members' inside to account: '2 YEARS AFTER GRENFELL THIS BUILDING STILL HASN'T KEPT ITS PROMISES'.[20]

It's not as though we (or precisely they the residents of Grenfell) did not 'have it coming'. It is not as though the expulsions that form the first dynamic of the demographics of this book, in docklands in the early 1980s, did not already infernally set the scene for what was later to happen to others on this other, apparently more affluent, side of town. From the fires that tore through the theatres that formed the first part of this chapter, it is now the 'world as stage' as it has been rearranged since the neoliberal bonfire of 'red-tape' (the Tory euphemism for health and safety laws drafted and protected with European force) that is being ignited. Of course, when Battersea Arts Centre burns down, as a theatre-lover I can write about combustion in the way I do, that is more or less flippantly, in the sure knowledge that despite all those whose work was threatened, whose creations were disrupted, whose efforts were rolled back years, not a single human was injured and confident that its listed status, and its beloved and unique position in London cultural history, will ensure its restoration, and thus its guaranteed prolongation.

Battersea Arts Centre appears to be a life-force incarnate, as exemplified by the publicity profiles that jubilantly announced its return from the ashes. It is not coincidence that BAC chose to name its Great Hall opening season the 'Phoenix Season', and indeed I took great pleasure in attending many of the events that marked that season of revival, often with large groups of students who thus, in their own not insignificant way given their straitened budgets, underwrote the expense of the rebuilding exercise. Amongst these phoenix-like events were Daniel Kitson's obsessive card-indexed memorial to the objects of a home-now-disappeared in his solo work *KEEP*, and Bryony Kimmings' rendering of her mental health challenges following the birth of her son Frank, in '*I'm a Phoenix, Bitch*'.

This reiteration of the phoenix theme, played out lovingly and overtly by Kimmings in a later gym-bound scene of defiant physical exertion, lifting weights against the demons, plays into a recuperable myth that also bedevils us for its 'self-help' symmetry with the prognostications of the neoliberal mantra of individual bravery and self-improvement at all costs. And this despite the potency of the use of the image of the phoenix in the mission-statements of a number of the deeply committed, serious and generous Grenfell 'action groups' for whom the myth of recovery from fire was always too strong a lure to resist channelling in the absence of allies they might have once expected to at least give them a fair hearing, such as the go-to author of loss Andrew O'Hagan. As Michael Marder in his characteristically sceptical mode puts it: 'In the twenty-first century, the myth of the phoenix continues to bewitch us. We still think of ashes as facilitators of new life, nourishing renewed growth'.[21] The myth of the phoenix parallels the solar recovery of the vegetal realm, after the flames have done their work, the plants by all common and popular accounts thrive in the residue of a past-burning. We have all scattered ashes in this hope of renewal. But the acceleration of slash and burn in the world's forests mean this romantic model of recovery is long-since over. Planetary burnout is the logic of where post-Amazon, in the warming age of that other Amazon and its massed-ranked servers, the world is now heading, phoenix or no phoenix. As Marder puts it:

> The phoenix forces us to forget death and finitude, even as we stare them in the face. On its wings, it carries the surplus of ideality and the empty promise of redemption, after the fire has already gone out. A political 'rebellion against the Phoenix' is long overdue.[22]

The rebellion Marder evokes is one sought by Jacques Derrida in his incendiary work *Cinders (Feu le Cendre)*.[23] One question for history (amongst others I will address here) that the fire at Grenfell Tower does not represent, so much as touch, are the parallels to the mark of the 'absence of presence' that Jacques Derrida called 'the trace'. For of all the equivalent terms that Derrida gave to this enigmatic remainder to the event, historical and otherwise, within which we might, given what I have said in the first part of this chapter wish to include the palpable event of fire, from his earliest published writings in the 1960s, it is to *ashes* that he returns most persuasively: 'I would prefer ashes as the better paradigm for what I call the trace – something that erases itself totally, radically, while presenting itself'.[24] Cinders are not perceived as offering proper, or as Ned Lukacher puts it, 'metaphorical names' for any being or entity that has been lost or found, but simply call towards or evoke another relation of 'becoming articulate' to agonism, to the conflicted *possibility* of a difficult truth.[25] And in the instance of Grenfell Tower the name for the manner by which the finding of such truth might be made public, is without prevarication nor hint of pitiful postmodern pieties to relativism, the name Public Inquiry.

Investigative journalism will surely play its noble and necessary part in such processes, but the public nature of the event of Grenfell requires a forum worthy of that name. An Inquiry after all has legal status as such, which is some way beyond the vanity of writing on the subject (whether by me or by Maitlis, or by O'Hagan) without material cause or legal effect. Indeed to think such vanity publishing in the wake of such an event should have a cause, is to wildly overreach the phantasy of writing that precludes it from touching the truth in the necessary ways that the Inquiry will take as merely sufficient. This seems to me to be the cruel confusion of the literary phantasy that O'Hagan and the *London Review of Books* sells us at a cover price that I naively presume will include a donation to the Grenfell Action Group charities. I ask this question of the LRB twice in the weeks following publication, but they choose to ignore my invitation to assuage any fear that the special issues might be profiting their well-subsidised coffers, or those who have written for them on the matter. On these matters, the common courtesy of reply to a social media enquiry is not beneath wholly commercial operations such as Wetherspoons, McDonalds and Virgin Trains, despite their apparent distance from the niceties of the cultural sphere. For the LRB comms appear to flow one way.

In *Cinders* Derrida had by contrast wanted to construct a conversation, a calling of voices, or as he put it a 'writing apparatus' that might offer just such a calling. A 'polylogue' perhaps, along the lines of the voices I tried to construct in the first part of this chapter, between my historical self in midst of a past discussion of historical theatre fires, in dialogue with a contemporary self, singed by the realities of risk seen and unforeseen in the intervening three decades. But Derrida is, as was often the case with his practical mind, drawn more in *Cinders* towards the potential of the *tape recorder*, a polylogue between printed page and tape and whose voice is heard, whose is lent to whom in support and whose speech is stolen: 'Who will decide whether the voice was lent, returned, or given? And to whom?'[26]

Poor history

Andrew O'Hagan has been involved in another not-unrelated 'polylogue' commissioned as he was, soon after the Grenfell fire, to write that much-discussed piece that would, by the first anniversary be published as 'The Tower' in the *London Review of Books*. The meticulous tapestry of the opening pages of his extended essay amounts to, or appears to amount to, a sequence of taped and transcribed conversations with those who have survived the fire, relatives of the deceased, neighbours from within the Grenfell community, and representatives of the local council and political class who within hours of the event had become the focus of attention from those most deeply affected by the consequences of that night. In these opening pages Rania from Aswan and her older sister Rasha, Naseem from Yemen, Melanie Coles from the nearby Golborne and Maxilla Children's Centre (amongst many others) feature in the opening, cascading, scene-setting. The supple fluency of this narrative is spell-binding in its apparent verisimilitude (you are acutely aware as you read that some of these profiled individuals may have survived, and some may not) until before the opening scene-setting page is out when O'Hagan makes what appears to be either a bold narrative move, or the projection of plain-fantasy as he appears to imagine a response to a poignant moment at school in which Rania's daughter Fethia has lost a flower from her white leather dance shoes. He imagines what the teacher, Ms Coles, *thinks* in this circumstance and puts the following words to those thoughts: '"Fethia gets herself all churned up about such things, but it will all be fine", her teacher said to herself as she closed her classroom for the day and made her way home'.[27]

The shift in tone while empathetic and moving is at once disturbing. As the reader one's initial presumption is that the narrative has been built from a recognisable form of documentary realism that, given the horrendous circumstances for the narratees, could be fact-checked and nuanced to suit the desperate circumstances each paragraph represents for those thus represented. But by column four of the very first page of O'Hagan's essay there is an immediate slippage between what could be known, what appears to have been recorded, and what has now been imagined on behalf of those directly involved. As the anthropologist Mick Taussig puts it, with regards to children, 'our thinking of the child could only ever be the adult's imagination of the child's imagination', but here the author's imagination would appear to be that of the teacher's imagination of the child's imagination.[28] And in so imagining, the thread of the narrative has already been way overstretched, to the point of breaking the necessary link between words and truths. Inconsequential as this might appear so early in a narrative, in which there has as-yet been no hint of what is to come (except for some portentous long views from Grenfell to the 'financial district' and the Shard which imply the common contrast between the haves and the have-nots will be borne out here) one's reason for reading is that this is not *any* tower but Grenfell Tower, and there are few people who don't know how this ends, even if many cannot agree as to how it started. It is this teleology that makes very different ethical demands on the construction of the narrative and its mobilisation of others' voices.

It might be worth repeating Derrida here who in the instance of *Cinders* is alert to the ethical claims of calling out, of recording and repeating: 'Who will decide whether the voice was lent, returned, or given? And to whom?'[29] I am imagining the answer to Derrida in this case from those who committed to interviews with O'Hagan and his assistants: these voices were 'lent' and expected to be treated with a care that Melanie Coles feels she did not benefit from. And unfortunately she is not alone amongst this community with something truly awful in common. Here is a summary of what Melanie Coles wrote in response to her characterisation in 'The Tower' as compared with, say, the local council members, and the precise, factual detail of what she actually said about what Fethia did, or didn't do:

> In the article itself, O'Hagan describes Fethia's teacher (that was me) recounting a memory from the day leading up to the fire. He writes that Fethia was upset about losing a white flower from her shoe. 'It would be there the next day', O'Hagan writes. ' "Fethia gets herself all churned up about such things, but it will all be fine", her teacher said to herself as she closed her classroom for the day and made her way home'. I do not know how much poetic licence is 'allowed' in an account like this, but to me, if you put something in quote marks, the implication is that this is what the person actually said, or at least said that they were thinking. But I did not say 'Fethia gets herself all churned up about such things', nor did I say that I thought it. I do not think I have ever used the term 'churned up' about anything. It seems like a minor thing, but if a small detail like this is fictionalised, how can we, as readers, feel sure that other, more significant quotes are not also fictionalised? Many of these quotes may include details that are far from trivial (there is a criminal investigation and a public inquiry going on). O'Hagan is being irresponsible. Also, the use of quotes (I think) has the powerful effect of giving an insight into the character of the person quoted. So it needs to be accurate. [...]
>
> Is this piece of writing to be perceived as fictional or factual? Of course it must be factual, these are real events, and highly sensitive ones; emotions are still raw, people are still traumatised, this has had a massive impact on our lives. I think that the fictionalisation of words and events is morally highly questionable, especially given the timing of the article's publication. If a small detail is questionable, what else in here cannot be relied on?[30]

Andrew O'Hagan responds to Melanie Coles the following week in the same *London Review of Books* letters page. In the interests of fairness, having reproduced Ms Coles' letter at some length, I should perhaps include the response from O'Hagan to it here. But I won't, because not everything is fair. It is a privilege for an author to have an immediate right of response to a letter critically addressing their work, and one that in O'Hagan's case, as an 'editor at large' of the LRB that positions his words with great strength against those that challenge his. He has already had 60,000 words to discuss the matter, the letter from Melanie Coles though substantial and searing, is short. Voices with cultural power are circulated far more widely than those without. Thousands have read the original writing by Andrew O'Hagan on the Grenfell Tower fire, proportionally fewer will have read the letter's page response. That is an asymmetric equation well known to those who attempt to right perceived wrongs.

O'Hagan does mount a curious defence that is worth repeating in brief (given the response is available online), that Melanie Coles, in addressing his rendition of her words in the way she does, 'wants to take them back', that she 'now wants to censor it [the material]' and 'to censure me for having taken delivery of them with a friendly face'.[31] Benign words towards his subject are apparently a hall-pass to creatively imagine what has been felt by that subject. The real issue is rather acknowledged in the sentences that follow this justification, and are as prosaic as one might imagine when working towards a deadline, even if that deadline was a generous year away when it started: 'I wish that I'd shown Melanie more clearly how I wanted to render what she told me. I know I said I would, but I ran out of time. So, that's my fault'. Perhaps understandably O'Hagan is keen to return to the taped record, but Derrida has already alerted us to the dilemma when one does this with regards to another's voice, and no amount of special pleading for the gloss put on the words, can quite obscure the pain felt by the plaintiff. Amidst the depths of the post-hoc rationalisation and excusing of what has happened in the recording process, O'Hagan comes clean as to the shift he has made, from observing an action that Melanie makes, and ascribing words to that action: 'She told us that was what she was thinking and I felt "churned up" was the exactly right rendering of Melanie's movement of her hands'. And in acknowledging both the scriptural betrayal, and the inclusion of a video online that was never meant to be there, O'Hagan offers an apology touched by a further exclusion notice that cannot but have a hint of unnecessary force about it: 'I'm sorry Melanie now wishes all this away and feels angry, but I never gave her to understand that she would be able to control the story's conclusions. I will of course leave her out of any future version'. From this point on it is O'Hagan who calls on the pity-card by speaking of the 'terrible slanders' he has received on social media since writing the piece and that those he spoke to, who he thinks did not realise he would write positively about those they 'hate', have begun to 'smear' him.

From this juncture and the oh-so-brief imagined cameo of Melanie Coles, O'Hagan's essay pivots on its axis and abruptly shifts from the tapestry-tone of its familial opening, to the rendering of the bare facts of the place and the occasion:

> Standing at 221 feet, Grenfell Tower was opened in 1974. It is owned by the Royal Borough of Kensington and Chelsea, and was managed on behalf of the council by the Kensington and Chelsea Tenant Management Organisation, which ran more than nine thousand flats and houses in the borough.[32]

Nothing untoward here, though the unusual, counter-intuitive spin that O'Hagan will put upon the actions of the council subsequently will become an irritant for some, and an outrage for those most closely associated with the various Grenfell action groups that arise from the fire. It is in the conjunction of the following lines that O'Hagan acknowledges, in his prioritisation of information, what really counts in this story, the place where a group of residents meet the consequences of a refurbishment:

> By June 2017, the tower housed some 350 people in 127 one or two-bedroom flats, a slight rise since a refurbishment completed in 2016, when new windows were fitted in all the flats and the building was covered in rainproof aluminium cladding and insulation.[33]

The details sound innocuous enough but to anyone who has seen images of the terrifying speed of the spread of the fire, vertically, up two of Grenfell's sheer windowed faces, from the fourth floor to the twenty-fourth in a matter of minutes, something that approaching fire-personnel commented on as 'unique' in their experience of fighting fires, what quite these windows and cladding contributed to the occasion is left hanging in the air. That is the nature of the artifice of literature and given Andrew O'Hagan has never claimed to be anything but a writer (or maybe 'editor at large' at the LRB whatever that means) it is hardly surprising that he should deploy the full range of rhetorical forms available to him. And they are many, and manifest and shape everything that follows in 60,000 words that, given their publication date, intervene in the very first days of a Public Inquiry that residents have waited for a year to get started. This is clearly one and only one account amongst many, very many accounts, indeed thousands and counting, not to mention the harrowing testimonies of those who were actually there which of course O'Hagan was not. But it is this narrative that is editorially endorsed by the LRB which despite being a literary mag has always given off the whiff of a kind of dependable authority from its journalism. I don't imagine that its editor Mary-Kay Wilmers imagines it does poor history. 'The Tower' would therefore simultaneously appear to stake a claim to being something more than the fantasy of a single, if unusually well-resourced, writer. Some asked plaintively at the Inquiry and elsewhere in the days after its publication why the generous word-count of O'Hagan's piece could not have been divided up between a number of different writers, whose perceptions might provide a more adequate sense of the complexity of the atrocious narrative. But that is not how a literary magazine works, it is not news, nor journalism, it is imaginative responses to the world, it is called the *London Review of Books* for a reason and hardly fair to blame it for its imaginative prose. If that is all it claims it is. As O'Hagan rightly says, it is *his* story, and equally *his* fantasy, he has control of its ending. Others did not have that privilege. It is for those others to pick up the pieces, which inevitably, now includes those after-effects for good and ill of this 60,000 word cultural intervention, with its own cruelties, which are unceremoniously scattered on site amidst the ashes 'like so much confetti'.

The fire this time

The beginnings of the fire are rendered by O'Hagan as simply as they probably began. Breughel's passing peasants (as observed by W. H. Auden in his poem *Beaux Artes*) would not have noticed them any more than Icarus falling into the sea. They were miniature in scale. The so-called 'stay-put' policy (that will come to dominate days of the Inquiry much later) rightly sets the scene:

> Inside the tower, by the lifts, there was a sign. 'If you are safely within your flat', it said, 'and there is a fire elsewhere in the block: you should initially be safe inside your flat keeping the doors and windows closed'.[34]

O'Hagan sutures this scene of safety-signs to the beginnings of the event that will eventually expose the advice to cruel scrutiny: 'Near to 12.15 am., a fire began in the kitchen of Flat 16 on the fourth floor. The flat was rented by an Ethiopian cab driver called Behaulu Kebede, a father of one'.[35] Again nothing untoward here, pass along nothing to see. Mr Kebede is reported as having appeared in the hall 'in his stockinged feet' letting others know a fire has started in his flat, he believes behind the fridge. He calls the police before alerting neighbours to the fire at 12.50 am. According to O'Hagan's account other neighbours were 'woken up by knocks at their doors' and they come out into the corridor to see what is happening.

At this juncture O'Hagan makes another injurious, if not fatal call in the narrative stream. He repeats an assertion that has already been openly made on hostile and overtly racist accounts across social media, and elsewhere since the fire (a full year before the 'LRB special' has been published but has subsequently widely been pushed back on by those with insight to the actual facts of the occasion). O'Hagan puts it like this: 'One of them [the neighbours] noticed that Mr Kebede had packed a suitcase; it was standing in the hall, as if he was prepared to leave after raising the alarm'.[36] The problem with this critical, unproven detail (the 'as if' will ring through the annals of poor history), pivotal for the whole narrative of cause and effect, given it implies some sort of intention to leave the scene by Mr Kebede, is that it is not cited as specifically the words of a single neighbour, it is not therefore traceable as a contention, it reiterates a well-known narrative that was circulating that positioned Mr Kebede within a spectrum of responsibility for the fire (rather than for instance an electrical fault due to a malfunctioning appliance way beyond his agency). Perhaps rather ominously, for the veracity of this piece as a whole, this calumny flies in the face of the actual evidence, available to Andrew O'Hagan himself if he had come to the Inquiry on the days I was present, barely a few weeks after the publication of this piece (which might have been delayed with due respect to the imminent Inquiry), in which the CCTV of the Grenfell stairwell while showing Mr Kebede calling the police, showed no sign of any suitcase, nor apparent intention to 'flee the scene'. Hindsight is a great thing, but in the case of Mr Kebede's phantom suitcase there are myriad trusted individuals from within the action groups such as Grenfell United pushing back on this kind of amateurish 'X marks the spot' bias from the outset. It seems extraordinary that O'Hagan went anywhere near its cruel implications.

The demands of narrative (for that is surely the urge that we see at work here from a writer) that situate contentious claims about packed bags and departure from the scene (albeit offset to an anonymous neighbour), fit uneasily with the clarity and care with what follows in the technical description of the fire. For as I witnessed on the days of expert evidence to the Inquiry, and on seeing the extraordinary footage from the heat-seeking helmet cameras worn by the courageous fire fighters themselves, who first entered Mr Kebede's flat to deal with the fridge fire, the consequent account written by O'Hagan is forensically accurate, with occasional flourishes as to what, or what not, might have been at fault: 'Flames from the fridge had engulfed the kitchen and were quickly licking out of Kebede's open window, setting fire to the insulation in the cavity between the building and its new cladding'.[37] Indeed as O'Hagan rightly observes, and as evidenced by the chronological, contemporary film-evidence offered to the Inquiry by the London Fire Brigade, well after O'Hagan compiled his story, it was not immediately obvious to the first responders that the flames that had worked their way out of the window of Mr Kebede's flat, were super-heating the cavity infill that, as was obvious from the camera footage which was temperature gauged, had started to heat to much higher levels than would have been expected of a normal window frame. It was this polyethylene core that, in later images screened at the Inquiry, was seen to break away from the window frame and start to flare, and then melt, dripping down the tower face.

It was hard to watch this evidence for obvious reasons, though not nearly as hard to witness as other harrowing narratives given it was essentially images of firefighters who would surely be beyond rebuke for fulfilling one of the most desperately courageous things a human can do for another human at a moment of great danger, going about their work in a way that they had been trained for and they probably considered quite routine. The problem with Grenfell of course is that while its diverse demography was anything but exceptional for public housing, there was something almost routine as well about its very fabric. The stark, apparently anomalous nature of the whole event flaring out of all human control within seconds of the first responders retreating from the kitchen, believing, in good faith that they had put out the initial fire, had already long been foretold by those residents who had watched the 'refurbishment' with horror. But unlike the residents in the know, the fire fighters were *not* to know that Grenfell Tower had been refurbished in such a way as to make it inevitable that should exposed-flame reach the cavity insulation, it would if heated to an adequate level, act as it then acted, wholly in keeping with its murderously unstable constitution. Even O'Hagan, way before the Inquiry has published anything, makes a summary conclusion to this effect half way through his own flawed piece: 'There is strong evidence that a concatenation of failures at the level of industry regulation and building controls, more than anything else, caused the inferno that killed 72 people'.[38] But that was the truth that the Grenfell Inquiry was established to pursue, led by Sir Martin Moore-Bick, and it is to the Inquiry, and away from O'Hagan's account, that we now need to turn.

Public Inquiry

Those brought under oath to testify to the Grenfell Inquiry, or indeed as announced by the London Metropolitan Police, those interviewed under caution during the first phase of the Inquiry are all as a matter of course, recorded. For the tape recorder that runs throughout makes the 'reservoir of writing' that Jacques Derrida is always aware of in the instance of *Cinders*, readable. The voices of those present do not so much 'pass away' as Derrida suggests voices do, but rather evoke those who have already and to our knowledge passed away in advance, on 14 June 2017 to be precise. Throughout the Inquiry I have noticed that as the tape machine whirls (in its now unassuming but ever-present digitally timed way), interpretation is always already also underway: 'At each syllable, even at each silence, a decision is imposed [...]'.[39] Especially with each silence given the withdrawal of agency from the Inquiry by those in the corporate sector (on behalf of the cavity and cladding specialists for instance) who claim their right to silence are painfully, powerfully and pitifully offset by the volubility of those witnesses who don't hide behind any such legalese, those such as the members of the London Fire Brigade, or the residents and relations of residents caught in the conflagration, who perhaps have very good reason to stay silent given the trauma they have experienced, but somehow, always find words, cries or sounds, that testify to what has happened there and then, in front of us. And for their trouble and their hurt they are received, responded to and called back to by the packed house from the Grenfell community that is present, those who watch and listen from the floor to every twist and turn in this minute-by-minute sorry tale. But the presiding judicial lead of the Inquiry Sir Martin Moore-Bick, is only too aware that what each signs is neither, necessarily the law nor the truth, but as Derrida offers 'Other interpretations remain possible – and doubtless necessary'.[40]

I suppose this is the Derridean nicety that Andrew O'Hagan proves in his insistence to offer his defence of a local council who to most residents would appear to have failed in their one clear responsibility – to keep them safe from burning. This part of the narrative should be no more troubling than the unforgiveable smearing of the reputation of Mr Kebede, but its blows appear to be felt as particularly low ones for a community struggling with the aftermath of the occasion. For the record I suspect O'Hagan's reading of council efforts might, as with the complex challenges faced by the fire service management, when the Inquiry makes its *full* findings known (a further two years beyond the publication of this book) prove to be somewhere as close to the conflicted reality as those who would wish the guilt of the council with its divisive name, the *Royal* Borough of Kensington and Chelsea, to be recognised without further ado. But my interest is in fact not only in the veracity of what took place on that night, but in the choices made by those who later profited from its occurrence. And that includes cultural commentators such as Andrew O'Hagan, and that includes me. It brings us together on the same corridor again in the interests of a disagreement over poor history.

There is a citational hierarchy that those who put their words to paper like to signify with nomenclature such as 'writer' (I do that myself) or 'author' (not for me at the moment) that make claims about circulation, readership and remuneration that those closest to the events simply cannot command for themselves. Given what I have said about theatre and everyday life in a book of that name a quarter-century ago, and this book now, I am not about to make concessions to those who self-identify as scribes without acknowledging a ferocious economy that a journal such as the *London Review of Books* polices as a matter of curatorial choice. Otherwise, why would the LRB not simply have approached all those writers-in-waiting in Grenfell itself, to seek their testimonies as to what happened on this occasion, without having to outsource it to an outsider who happened in this instance to be called Andrew O'Hagan for whom the detail would inevitably get the better of them. As Melanie Coles knows, misnaming the children's centre (as I was careful not to do earlier) is just something a local would not do for acute historical reasons, a bit like David Cameron announcing his loyalty to one football team that plays in claret and blue when he means the other. It just doesn't happen to those who know. And in the case of Grenfell, on the first day of the Inquiry, those who know have had surprisingly few offers of 60,000 word pieces to argue their evidence. That might account for why their appeals sound sometimes hasty, partial, gap-filling, for that is the common fate and limited column inches of those who have suffered injustice.

Andrew O'Hagan, like any writer free to sell their words, and the LRB rates are unusually appealing at, I believe, about £2 a word (60,000 × £2 = £120,000 which cannot be considered poor pay for a year's work if it was the only thing you did during July 2017 and June 2018) will be acutely aware of the responsibility to his sources (and has since as we have seen apologised for editorial decisions made in the transcription that occurred in the process of publication). But when it comes to the more nebulous matter of assigning 'blame' or not to the fire service, or the council responsible for people's care, O'Hagan seems curiously to withdraw all the benefit of the doubt from the action groups in support of the community, and those summonsed to fight the fire on our behalf, and award generous degrees of benefit of the doubt to those who were paid to be responsible for those sacrificed on the public-housing pyre. Again I think, given what I heard during the Inquiry regarding the fire service response, that the picture that emerges will be far more complex and nuanced than our shared belief that first responders can 'do no wrong' can offer. That will certainly be the case for those who 'managed' the response to the fire from a distant call centre on the far side of the city. But in the immediate aftermath of Andrew O'Hagan's *London Review of Books* essay there were dissenting voices, such as Tony Sullivan from Croydon, voices from *within* the fire services, reminding us in subsequent letters pages of, for instance the complexity of any 'stay-put' policy when it came to a fire trap as unstable as Grenfell Tower:

> Andrew O'Hagan discusses the use of the 'Stay-Put' policy on the night of the fire, with a strong implication that it wasn't abandoned quickly enough. [...] A catastrophic failure, especially in compartmentalisation, when multiple things go wrong at the same time, to the extent and at the speed they did at Grenfell, is a different situation entirely. Once the lobbies, corridors and the lone stairway were compromised, the task became almost impossible. [...] The notion that Grenfell could have been evacuated quickly, easily and without the potential for large-scale loss of life is wishful thinking.[41]

It is obvious in the cold light of the Inquiry-day how challenged representatives of the fire services were, how traumatised by their accounts of the occasion, and how sorry they were to have in their repeated words 'let down' those they could not reach (whether that was due to the calamity of the 'stay-put' policy or because of communications difficulties between the control centre on the other side of London in Stratford who had no visual live-feed of the fire in its earliest stages). We will see, even two years on from the fire, and a full year since O'Hagan's essay was published, with regards to the 'performance' of the fire services it would seem that the Inquiry, *if* the Government can resolve critical issues of local representation on the panel, is uniquely well placed to offer an overall judgement for good or ill. In the meantime, as I sit in the serried ranks in Holborn Bar during the last days of Phase One of the Inquiry, I am acutely aware that given I get vertigo and would not be able to go near a high ladder, never mind fight a fire from one, I am not about to pontificate about the courage of those who protect me, nor indeed those working under unique pressures to 'lead' in such impossible circumstances. Not least of all given the building they approached on 14 June 2017 was less a residence and more an infernal liability waiting to go up in flames at the first opportunity. It was after all described as a 'fire trap' by many at the Inquiry who were choosing their words with great caution for the record. That cannot possibly be considered a fair playing field from which to mount a counter-claim about the quality, or not, of a fire service doing its best in 'impossible' circumstances.

Authorities and activists

But with regards to the conduct of the local Council, the issue is somewhat different, and handled very differently by O'Hagan. Indeed so differently from the treatment of the Grenfell action groups in prose that one might have suspected there was a historic reason for O'Hagan to skew his take, first to ensure he *had* a take for a piece that his publisher had committed such generous resources to, but perhaps for other reasons that one might speculate about so contradictory the approach. And given O'Hagan does not for a moment flinch from speculation, why should I? Indeed we are only introduced to the Council by way of reference from those who according to O'Hagan do not like them: 'The Grenfell Action Group hate the Tory council'.[42] Well, that may as well be, I am not sure how I would feel about them, marooned high in the sky sitting in a residence that was once a robust, concrete edifice, a modest example of the utility of modernity, not without fault but broadly fit for safe purpose, transformed into an inflammable torch by a misguided and inept refurbishment process. But it is a deeply peculiar way to introduce the Council. Hatred is a strong emotion, and for most readers a residual sympathy might rest with those traduced in such terms before anything else is known about them. The reverse assault continues with O'Hagan using inflammatory terms on behalf of the action groups' perceptions of the Council such as 'stink of corruption', 'rich toffs', 'disgust' swirling around the scene of the crime. Some of these emotions, values and views are assigned to named 'local agitators' such as Edward Daffarn, a well-known and articulate surviving resident from the sixteenth floor of Grenfell Tower. The explicit warning offered by Mr Daffarn as to the potential 'catastrophic event' that might ensue from the 'ineptitude and incompetence' of the landlord, is rendered by O'Hagan as 'merely the latest in a barrage of complaints going back to 2013'[43] as though adding insult to injury, the more the residents brought their fears of the consequences of the conditions they lived in to the Council table, the less they might be expected to be taken seriously. That is the most peculiar argument I have ever heard for email economy. It smacks of an infantile 'cry wolf and you're out' approach to health and safety that just does not meet the needs of the residents nor their well-being. If you want quotas on 'complaint exchanges', you had better ensure you are not living in austerity-hit council housing in the UK in 2017 (or 2019 for that matter given nothing has changed in the two years since an event that prompted the Tory government to insist they would do 'everything in their power' to ensure nothing like this ever happened again). The evidence is that almost nothing has actually been done in the intervening years. Good intentions maybe. Little actual evidence of action as student residents of a block in Bolton discovered to their cost just a few short months later.

Grace Benton and Flora Neve are left to bat for the action groups and their reputation in the light of this assault on their motivations in the same letter's page of the *London Review of Books* that is now looking like a model for the kind of agonism that Chantal Mouffe would assign as the first priority of politics. There are O'Hagan supporters, who are readily found on the online pages that I have linked in the endnotes, and there are defenders of those who have been twice traduced by O'Hagan's perverse tale:

> Activists are said to have 'loud voices', while local officials have 'gentle manners' and are 'well-spoken'. Could this be in the ear of the beholder? Were the activists 'loud' because they had power? Or because they did not? [...] We're told that 'they seemed to be throwing accusations into the air like confetti at a whore's wedding'. Why make that comparison? [...] Is it so hard to understand why people might feel hatred towards councils ('people whose disaffection with the council went back years', 'so many people who hated councils'), who are the implementers of hated policies? [...] To say that 'the only people who could have known that the cladding was a potential fire risk were the people whose financial advantage lay in selling it' is to present a straw man. Why couldn't the councillors have known that the whole approach they were overseeing would ultimately cause harm? The Grenfell Action Group knew. Even if O'Hagan 'could find nothing to support the view that these councillors were corrupt or were trying to harm residents', why must the conclusion be that they were simply neutral actors with no more responsibility than you or I?[44]

The tide of grass-roots activism that swept into the neighbourhood on the morning after the fire was obviously going to attract attention in a way that the council representatives would struggle, in sheer numbers, or newsworthiness, to meet. O'Hagan opines that the Council should have considered the 'public relations' potential far more soberly given that a myth began to circulate that there was simply *no* Council assistance when there was as much help as could be offered within such limited numbers. If Emily Maitlis and I, though perhaps not Andrew O'Hagan, were both present on that day amongst others (as we were in different help centres) from our own not distant West London communities, then the sheer visibility of the hundreds who presented themselves and their labour to assist the recovery effort was always going to lead the post-fire story. And any other reading would be as perverse as it was arbitrary given volunteers are by definition not paid to do what they do, while council workers, and especially their leaders, are paid to do what they do and are not perceived to do. This is all well and good and fairly dealt with by O'Hagan in his essay, but at the point at which he offers an extended, largely honorific treatment to Nicolas Paget-Brown and Rock Feilding-Mellen, the then leader and deputy leader of the council, over no less than eight columns of the available space in the first half of the piece (followed by another eight later) the prism of the writing begins to shift unerringly towards an empathetic, fawning caricature of personalised authority that few others are granted individually at this length.

The leader of the council, Paget-Brown, is introduced first in sympathetic tones, he is apparently gentle, decent, fogeyish. When he arrives at the Tower, O'Hagan imagines that he imagines that the building has been emptied of its residents (though there is no means by which to credit this claim). 'Surely this was the burning hulk of an empty building' imagines O'Hagan on Paget-Brown's behalf, which nicely diverts our attention from the more likely possibility (given we can all equally speculate in fabular prose of this kind) that in his mind was a long-standing and acute sense of guilt at the continued conditions of threat that those drawn to live in the Grenfell Tower post-refurbishment lottery were now subjected to. When responding to Feilding-Mellen's broadcast interviews in the immediate aftermath of the fire, O'Hagan describes his obviously poor grasp of the implications of what he says about safety and building regulations with the inversion of the conclusion most might have drawn from such lack of coherence: 'he ventured on some of the answers without a terrific understanding of the various mistakes that were made beyond his sightline'.[45] But no one was necessarily expecting him to have a 'terrific' understanding of such detail, that would be a most unlikely bar to set a Council Deputy Leader. People, and victims' families no less, might expect simply an adequate one, and the record shows that these responses are simply not adequate to the gravity of the circumstances.

It is also glaringly obvious without needing the close-reading that O'Hagan's own students at King's College London would have been used to, that if you invert the responsibilities of a Council representative to establish their fall from required standards as 'less than terrific' you might (though I don't think they need O'Hagan's 'help') wish to offer the same largesse to those in the Grenfell action groups whose responses might also have been 'less than terrific' rather than hateful, as O'Hagan imagines and then explicitly states as fact. But in the end, as Peter Greenland, writing to the LRB from as far away as Katoomba, in Australia points out it is not so much a question of 'guilt' in such circumstances, but 'responsibility':

It is clear that the residents of Grenfell Tower were the victims of a firestorm that could have affected any one of hundreds of lethally clad residential buildings in Britain. The fire was the result of a perfect neoliberal storm of self-regulation, privatisation and cuts. So, Andrew O'Hagan asks, who's to blame? Who's guilty? Not the decent chaps heading up the local council, he seems to answer. Rather, everyone who ever voted for Thatcher and Blair. [...] Maybe that's right. But his question is wrong. It isn't a matter of guilt, but of responsibility.[45]

I certainly hold no light for Theresa May (and nor did Feilding-Mellen according to his words to O'Hagan on her parlous 1985 Housing Act) through this woeful episode, but to describe her as O'Hagan does, distancing herself from council representatives as joining 'the national hiss against a handful of pantomime villains, the unluckily posh-seeming leaders of a rich-seeming council, who just happened to have the wrong names at the right time', is plain infantile. Even for Theresa May it must have been blindingly obvious that what Grenfell represented was not just an acute breakdown of responsibility to the residents of a neighbourhood, but a grave symptom of years of neglect, racial profiling and outright hostility to the post-war ideal of public housing. Because you have a double-barrelled name has no more to do with such matters than if you choose to call yourself Stormzy, the difference is simply that the ones with the double-barrelled names happen to be in long-standing (sitting) positions of council power, preferment and pay, while Stormzy arrived to offer his words and help, alongside Rita Ora, and, yes love her or loathe her, Lily Allen, who assumes her own 'pantomime' position in O'Hagan's prose as she becomes the subject of yet another wholly gratuitous pile-on. It is as though O'Hagan had not been paying any attention to the meticulous two-decade work of Dan Gretton in a somewhat different context on the bureaucracy of power, 'desk killers', that would eventually be published as *I You We Them* just weeks after the Phase One Inquiry findings were being revealed in Fall 2019.

In announcing that he spoke to 'both sides' in this relationship, O'Hagan would appear to imply a balance to his enquiries, but he swiftly proceeds to render more fully one side of that story, first addressing the nature of the TMO (Tenants' Management Organisation) and then the council itself on the way he takes another swipe at the action group: 'But this Grenfell group was political. They hated everything the Council and the TMO did, no matter what'.[47] Well action groups do tend to be politicised along certain lines, not least of all when the stakes of public housing in a borough with the name Royal Borough of Kensington and Chelsea comes out to play. To recognise the way groups of this kind, might, as O'Hagan says, 'pursue their views obsessively' is to become aware of the height of feelings those who have less feel about protecting what they have amongst those, including me and O'Hagan, who have considerably more. Obsessiveness tends to be the by-product of not being listened to by those with more power, something that O'Hagan does not seem particularly sympathetic to, nor cognisant of, despite (or perhaps because of) his own well-represented childhood on a housing estate (*not* 'social housing' as he acutely and rightly comments) where 'tower blocks' were part of his life. Interviewed in his Primrose Hill home that the *Daily Mail* would enjoy putting a value on should one of their journalists have been visiting, on the publication of the *London Review of Books* account, it is surprising that O'Hagan is not more conscious of the potential for hurt in what he says and the fault-lined way in which he has chosen to say it. Or he is aware of the hurt he causes and the easy cultural cruelty that marks the interregnum years bounded by this book has simply bled into his demeanour and trumped more nuanced readings once again.

Anti-social housing

Legitimated by his own background in council housing that O'Hagan, in the case of the West Lancaster estate, describes as looking 'pretty noble to me', there is a welcome sense in this problematic writing of the wider context of council housing of the post 1979 Thatcherite era. The ghettoisation of council housing and the scandal associated with Shirley Porter's 'cleansing' administration in Westminster wishing to ensure, as she scandalously said, that 'the right people live in the right areas',[48] was of nothing compared with the 'estrangements' that followed the super-prime boom in London real-estate accelerating following the banking crisis of 2008: 'Too much overseas "hot money" poured into Kensington and Chelsea, as investors sought safe places to put their money. There are 44,000 properties bought solely as investments in London. People don't live there'.[49] But this absentee landlordism, signified by the darkness of entire buildings at night across London, applied as much to the warehouse building of Docklands, where the Rotherhithe Theatre Worksop had been speculated against, that was after all why I called it the 'Dark Theatre', not just Kensington and Chelsea. And O'Hagan is right to recognise that what is happening here is not so much the demographic destination of the buildings that sit on the land, as the ownership of the *land* itself that is the motor of the inequalities played out in such eviscerated neighbourhoods of gentrification. But in making these arguments O'Hagan leans on the scholarship of Anna Minton in her ground-breaking work *Big Capital* to explore what he calls a 'new politics of space', on the one hand setting up her argument as a 'persuasive thesis', on the other knocking it back down with what Minton recognises is a set of 'false oppositions;' that only serve to 'trivialise' her argument.

Given this is just one address of the legitimacy, methods and balance of O'Hagan's LRB account, and there are a number of other far longer ones, and given this letter rebutting O'Hagan was itself the object of editing by the *London Review of Books* (which is deeply idiosyncratic given the 60,000 words over 40 odd pages they have afforded the original piece) it might be worth including a part of it here again for the record:

> Andrew O'Hagan quotes the following from my book *Big Capital*: 'The zeal with which so many councils are embracing the demolition and rebuild agenda means a rapid reshaping of London is underway.... The combination

of global capital, government policies designed to kill off social housing and failures in housing benefit are configuring the city'. There is a mistake here – in the book I say 'reconfiguring' – but no matter. 'All of this is true', O'Hagan says, 'and all of it is crucial, and I wonder whether it has a defining part to play in our understanding of the Grenfell Tower fire and its aftermath'. Yet he immediately goes on to trivialise my argument by asking: 'But does this amount to a case for mass murder?' (He is referring here to the view he attributes to Grenfell activists that the 'privileged white men' of the Kensington and Chelsea Council 'were murdering ordinary people'.) [...] O'Hagan is creating a false opposition. At issue here is not simply who has direct responsibility for the Grenfell Tower fire but the way in which councils are operating to undermine the democratic process in many parts of London and the UK, not just in Kensington and Chelsea. And while O'Hagan appears to concede that the democratic deficit played a role in fuelling the anger, his overriding argument is that the longstanding hatred of local Tories and this particular council was behind the local response, rather than the exclusion from the political process that many people feel.[50]

The letter has been edited by the LRB, perhaps in the interests of economy, but in so doing reduces the necessary and well-judged force of Minton's argument. For instance, the notorious line that O'Hagan used to describe Feilding-Mellon's attitude to activists has been excised for some reason:

He is contemptuous of activists critical of him and other local politicians, claiming that at times 'they seemed to be throwing accusations into the air like confetti at a whore's wedding' and finds 'nothing to support the view that these councillors were corrupt or were trying to harm residents'.[51]

It is as though the description of activists and members of the Grenfell community being summarily associated with 'a whore's wedding' is even too much for the LRB sub-editors by now. One wonders why that standard did not apply earlier to a passage that invited ridicule and resentment in equal measure on its first inglorious appearance in the very first week of the Grenfell Inquiry. Presumably the Editor at Large has the final edit. By the end of the original, unedited letter that I have read, Anna Minton is gracious but clear in her lost conclusion: 'O'Hagan makes a number of important points but unfortunately these are undermined by the defining premise of his piece which is that it is only he who is able to see the facts as they are'.[52]

So, the evidence suggests reservations abound as to the veracity of multiple sections of O'Hagan's work, and are forcefully raised by a diversity of quite different correspondents from the most everyday to the expert directly involved in the narrative. But it has to be recognised that O'Hagan does a decent enough job at listening to the Council workers, he understandably, for what I take to be his innate sense of fairness, wants to rectify the impression that began to merge into 'dogma' in the days after the fire, that the council was 'on a mission to neglect',[53] what

O'Hagan calls a 'totemic unfairness myth' and more 'a toxic brand of cheap compassion'. O'Hagan sees this toxicity as one that will obscure the true causes of the other toxicity, the one that hovers over the landscape from the poisoned site where at the time of writing, Grenfell still stands gap-toothed and shrouded. As O'Hagan puts it: 'the clues to the tragedy were hiding in several tons of ash' by which he refers to the fittings, the 'shoddy windows', the 'failed cavity barriers' and the 'flammable cladding'. But what of the ash itself, is there anything to say by way of conclusion about the common ground for all this writing, argument and counter argument? It is the Inquiry in Holborn Bar to which one would need to go to find out, not to the LRB and its poor history.

As with Derrida's recollection of the origin of *Cinders*, where on the one hand there is a text, and on the other, a tape recording, a singular interpretation, made on a single day, there hovers over the Grenfell Inquiry an equivalent relation between statements made (as in de Certeau's prognosis always problematic given fire's banishing of reason) and the chance encounter with a tape machine, preserving that voice in its sonic sense for history. Derrida seeks a conversation about fire without 'the shadow of sacrifice', 'without the Phoenix', indeed remember what he has previously cautioned: 'There's rebellion against the Phoenix'.[54] In other words without the freight that attends to common or garden fire-talk. He seeks 'the place solely of incineration' and we understand, if we have no real comprehension of any such horror, it is to the Holocaust that he refers. But we do know the detailed identities of all those who die in the fire on this occasion, and we know now, since the conduct of Phase One of the Inquiry almost all there is to know about where that first 'took place'. 'Cinders there are, this is what takes place in letting a place occur, so that it will be understood: Nothing will have taken place but the place. Cinders there are: Place there is […]'.[55] Indeed 'cinders there are' gives the name to the place inasmuch as it was barely spoken before its immolation. Grenfell is the name.

The loss adjustor returns

By placing the evidence of Grenfell Tower next to the evidence of theatre histories, of Battersea Arts Centre, of the Savoy Theatre, of the Globe (and indeed adjacent to Derrida's *Cinders*), there is no presumption of a symmetrical relation, any such reduction between theatre, theory and the world would be another history of ill-equivalence, of barbarism, as Walter Benjamin commented on the fate of all documents destined to record injustice. But the precise history of the building 107 Rotherhithe Street that opened this book, that for 17 years carried the name Rotherhithe Theatre Workshop, is it must be said, not wholly immune to the history that I am recounting here, at two ends as they are of the neoliberal forces in the UK that dispelled the first while endangering the residents of the second. There are two forces that draw these two narratives four decades apart together, and they are public land and public housing. To close this book it is necessary to consider the demands of both for *The Dark Theatre*.

As Brett Christophers outlines in his work *The New Enclosure*, one might be forgiven for thinking that the most significant privatisation of the Thatcherite induced neoliberal era would either be that of the bailout of the banks following the financial crash in 2008, or the fire sale of council housing initiated by the Conservative administrations of the 1980s and 1990s.[56] We will return to this sell-off in a moment, but as Christophers points out it is in fact the selling off of public land which since 1979 and Thatcher's ascension to the prime ministership has amounted to two million hectares, 10% of the surface of the UK and valued somewhere in the region of £400 billion, outstripping those other contenders by a factor of ten. The privatisation of public land, that is the sale of public land to bodies that are not public, for instance the sale of land in Docklands, previously considered by the residents of Bermondsey to be publicly accessible land for recreation and play, to the third party quango of the Docklands Development Corporation who in turn sold on to the vested interests of the financial institutions, housing developers and shopping-mall entrepreneurs, is not as Brett Christophers insists *necessarily* a matter of wrong-doing. But in practice, many of the processes followed during these massive transactions of the 1980s were at the very least suspect with three substantial consequences that should concern all of us (not just those of us who lost theatres to these very transactions): 'a rise in private-sector land-hoarding; Britain's growing transformation into a 'rentier' type economy – one increasingly dominated by rents paid by the many to the affluent, landowning few; and widespread social dislocation'.[57]

We understood from the first chapter of this book why land mattered, to us and our neighbours at Rotherhithe Theatre Workshop, we always understood its apparent mobility, transferred from one to another agency with no democratic control over its eventual destination, was a matter of power. The neighbourhood was not stupid, they did not think because it was public land that they had undeniable rights to access to it, there were countless obstacles to such stately progress across brownfield docklands' byways through the 1970s and 1980s, but rather that in the last eventuality, when push came to shove which it would, then they could prove they 'owned' it, inasmuch as it was land that when they lived on it had not been transferred into the private sector shielded by off-shore tax haven accounts and dodgy paper trails as to where, who and how it was operated from. The whole animosity to the quango created by Thatcher's government in the 1980s, the London Docklands Development Corporation, was oxygenated by the local community's understanding of the basic principle and right that their democratic control over the land on which they lived would in these shady processes of sale and transfer be delegated to private companies beyond their democratic appeal.

Brett Christophers calls this broad attack on public land ownership 'the new enclosure' both to mimic the language Marx used for the first form of primitive accumulation of capitalism, and to suture the neoliberal experience of 1970s Britain onwards to these first acts of historical clearance. The links between what was perceived in the eighteenth and nineteenth centuries as 'waste land' and the demand to put it to productive use, resonates with the arguments about docklands 'surplus' land and the imperative to bring it under government control for the purposes of entrepreneurial profit. Here the apparent 'inefficiency' of the local docklands' community with its chronic unemployment (wholly beyond its control since the movement of the docks down river to Tilbury) was offset in this rhetoric by the expansive, can-do, progressive investment and entrepreneurialism of the developers. But, again, we were only too aware of the way in which this wild west, adventurist narrative, was in fact a reordering of the political economy that greased the wheels of the TINA juggernaut, that 'there was no alternative' to such *laissez faire* privileging of big money over local pace and politics. Spatial violence, as Alvaro Sevilla-Buitrago called it, was well underway in docklands becoming hyper-accelerated, capitalised 'Docklands' during the very years that Brett Christophers focuses upon in the wider UK context.[58] The eminent historian David Edgerton in the definitive survey work of the period, *The Rise and Fall of the British Nation*, indeed places this short history as pivotal within the landscape of the twentieth century UK:

> The Big Bang, and other developments, transformed London. The City rebuilt the city. [...] The financial sector spread from the City eastwards, into those parts of London which had been the home to the docks. The London that had traded things became the London that traded money.[59]

What Edgerton cannot account for given the space constraints on his authoritative but compact narrative, is to offer any insight as to what that process meant to those who experienced it. *We* were at the other end of that story and we felt it acutely. Poor the historians who do not get to feel such forces about which they write through their own feet. If this Big-Bang represented the economic devil-may-care conditions of neoliberal Britain, its endemic financialisation, its essential marketisation and the insurgence of the microeconomic mode into all areas of what had previously been non-economic life, then it was land privatisation that marked the identity of neoliberalism most obviously and uniquely. Indeed, neoliberalism, for all its inadequacy as a term, despite all its other economic valences, simply would not have got going in docklands at least, without the spatial violence of this sweeping land privatisation programme. No privatisation, no neoliberalism, at least as we would recognise it today. And beyond Brett Christophers, but perhaps in keeping with David Edgerton's contention at least, it was precisely in London's Docklands that this process was engineered, prototyped and performed as a model that would become operable elsewhere.

In the first chapter of *The Dark Theatre* I made explicit how private ownership and market-based land allocation driven by the London Docklands Development Corporation in the 1980s was wholly detrimental to the economic stability of a zone marked out for brutal development targets, and here by way of conclusion, with a charred Grenfell Tower still sitting on the horizon, it remains for me to establish how 'social well-being' has been sacrificed in the interests of profit during these interregnum years. When the highest paid Vice Chancellors of UK Universities remind us that inflated senior salaries come with the order of risk a twenty-first century university leader is responsible for in managing a super-institution with significant turnover, my answer is that given King George III gifted a sizeable portion of central London (hard on Covent Garden) to my own college on its endowment in 1829, there was little serious 'risk' in managing what had become a multi-billion pound gift of estates. Karl Polanyi might call such late nineteenth century land a 'fictitious commodity', after all, land as Brett Christophers points out was never created 'with commodification in mind'.[60] What VCs are effectively doing in this argument is replacing the gifted nature of land to the university (largely true in most cases) with a false argument about its commodity status, an argument that is essentially fictitious. It is not that there was *no* market for central London land when the college was established 200 years ago, it was simply that given the royal prerogative it was not necessary for King's College London to enter any such market to establish itself when it wished to offset the 'heathen' opposition up the road of University College London, with its own sizeable estates and god-fearing ways. As Brett Christophers says, prior to the nineteenth-century marketisation for land had 'conventionally been embedded in society'.[61]

Re-spooling now three decades to my previous place of work at Rotherhithe Theatre Workshop in fast developing Docklands, the subjection of the local land to the tyranny of the market (though logic might be a word that capitalists would use though there seemed nothing logical about what we witnessed in peoples' lives) was to observe the 'putting at risk' of anything and everything that the neighbourhood held dear about where they, and in many cases, their forebears, had lived. But as Polanyi knew, and he leavened his dystopian critique in this way, the historical response to such threats to shared land, had always been one of *resistance*. To take the land away was in itself an unnatural act, always seen as a violation of the essence of nature, and perhaps not surprisingly humans through history had been able to notice such violations to their habitats. So, here we might recognise the smaller skirmishes of the first chapter of this book as umbilically linked to the miners' fight for their own land across the Midlands and North of England (albeit as one to be excavated) and a centuries long history of such resistances to expulsion. This push-me pull-you contestation of land through history is summed up by Brett Christophers (after Polanyi) in the following way: 'The first component was the generalized capitalist "move" to marketize, to dis-embed; the second movement was resistance to this, specifically where the fictitious commodities were concerned'.[62] Such counter moves are ones of self-preservation, nothing much more, but nevertheless profound in their relationship to the ground from which such resistances spring.

The ashen ground that marks the Grenfell Tower site is one such wasted land from which such counter moves have been vigorous, thoughtful, passionate and right. These are not histories that have come lightly. They are not histories of 'the poor' (whatever such a phrase could possibly mean beyond a metric of impoverishment) for those people as is evident at the Inquiry can be seen to have their own immense strength despite lacking all power, and at every turn show up poor history for what it is and when it is. A neighbourhood steeped in its own micro-histories of expulsion, disempowerment or marginalisation, is one that is expert in such politics. The fortitude of these acts are a magnified version of the rather smaller, more modest but no less committed resistances that we experienced amongst those threatened with expulsion from their docklands homes through the 1980s. That these were public homes should not go unnoticed in this diagnosis of reasons to be cheerful, that is, reasons to act.

A spine of the neoliberal mantra during the Thatcher years in the UK had always been that surplus public land was abundant, that it represented a misuse of local authority powers in a form of lazy hording of assets that could be put to better work, and that should such resources be identified they would swiftly be put under the pressure of marketisation and sale. In a nutshell you have here the fate of the docklands community that I set out discussing in this book. There has never been a time when one could not identify 'surplus land', that would be unlikely in an island such as Britain formed by significant extremities of geological shifts, but the difference for the docklands community was the ferocity and aggression of how such surplus became entangled in rights to council housing given how much of the landscape was marked by mid-war housing of a predominantly low-rise nature. It was obvious on arrival in Rotherhithe in 1983 that much of this housing stock, including those blocks where the students who worked through the project had the good fortune to be housed for key-worker rents that would astonish residents in the area today, were at best dilapidated (Swan Buildings) and a downright health risk (Redriff Estate). But this was hardly the fault of the local Southwark Council who prior to the 1980s had been 'empowered to build and manage council housing', a simple fact that changed when Margaret Thatcher assumed office with other imperatives in mind. In shifting control of the funding for this housing away from the local council, as Brett Christophers points out: 'housing was no longer considered part of the local state's remit, council housing and the land it occupied became, in principle "surplus", and thus eligible for disposal under the famous Right to Buy program'.[63] But the broader economic environment of the Thatcher era (and it has to be noted unequivocally the Blairite Labour administrations that followed) ensured that the viability of public housing in such areas of relative poverty were also put under intense scrutiny and indeed threat:

> From the early 1980s [exactly the time of my arrival in Rotherhithe] until 2012, council house finance was strictly controlled by central government, and this period represented one long, painful squeeze as a combined result of restraints on borrowing by local authorities, limits on their ability to retain the proceeds of asset sales, restrictions on rent increases, and 'negative subsidy' payment obligations.[64]

It might represent a city-spanning ride on the underground, but it does not take a leap of imagination to get from Rotherhithe in 1983 to North Kensington and Grenfell Tower in 2017. As John Broughton puts it in his comprehensive account of social housing in the UK, *Municipal Dreams*:

> The fire at Grenfell was, above all, a personal tragedy to its residents and friends and families. But to many more it symbolised, in devastating fashion,

a crisis in social housing. It stood as an awful culmination to deeply damaging policies pursued towards council housing, and the public sector more widely, since 1979.[65]

Commercial procurement, the public–private partnership, the cost-cutting austerity agenda of post financial crash UK governments (Coalition and Tory), but also across the three decades that this book spans, can all be identified as significant markers in the fate of Grenfell Tower.

The peculiarity of this dreadful history of decline is, as Andrew O'Hagan himself points out, that since the 1890s and through the widespread inter-war years of public-housing provision, such developments had always been perceived by the vast majority of residents themselves as aspirational, upwardly mobile and often, as in the Alton East and West estates at the verge of Richmond Park in West London, beautifully positioned to capitalise on the significant opportunities of one of the world's most expensive and concentrated cities. Broughton summarises this, after much research on site of his own, as their 'essential decency', a commentary that can only be borne out by daily attendance at phase one of the Grenfell Inquiry. The anger expressed at that Inquiry as to the motives of the local Council, the Royal Borough of Kensington and Chelsea, is of course partly generated by the broadly held suspicion across the UK, that such once publicly-owned blocks of apartments will, in areas of high land value, inevitably come under the hammer of privatised interest. Those with resources, as the Barbican in the City of London shows day in day out, have nothing to fear from living in 'tower' blocks and their refurbishment is often seen as either an ornamentation for the benefit of those monied souls looking on from their stucco-fronted Kensington homes, or a prelude to privatisation.

But why such vitriol directed at the essay by Andrew O'Hagan considered at length in this chapter? It is only an essay (from the Latin for 'attempt') after all. Perhaps as Broughton points out because of a simple statistic: 'The Borough of Kensington and Chelsea, in which Grenfell is situated, has built just ten new Council-funded social homes since 1990'.[66] That is not a mis-print. Ten. Broughton's source for this statistic is an article by Ben Kentish for the *Independent* newspaper with a takeaway title: 'Number of Government-Funded Social Homes Falls by 97% Since Conservatives Took Office'. Given this was published on 20 June 2017, just days after the Grenfell Tower fire, I have no idea whether there has been a boom in public house building since, but I hardly think so. At least not from what I can see in my visits to the neighbourhood from my home nearby. The second anniversary memorials to the fire have been marked rather by a vehement sense that little has been done in the substantial work of addressing the root causes of the Grenfell Tower calamity. Given that statistic, ten, and the relative wealth of a borough with the highest per capita income in the UK, and a life expectancy years beyond other regions in the country, there can be no doubt as to why what appears to read as a memorial to the put-upon leaders of the council with their fascinating, bohemian, alternative pasts, has fallen on deaf ears.

They are not alone. To return to the landscape of Rotherhithe Theatre Workshop, here decades after its closure, and walk along the length of Rotherhithe Street, is to witness in Southwark a continuation of politics not far removed from those of its North Kensington neighbour. Yes it's house-building programme is far more ambitious than ten new council homes in two decades, aiming at 11,000 new homes in the coming years, with the demolition of the Heygate Estate and the much debated and contested 'development' of the Elephant and Castle community both on the planning boards. But throughout this work Southwark has collaborated, as in the Docklands' years, with a range of private partnerships that have skewed the transparency of who is getting what, for what. Broughton remarks that at Heygate, working with the Australian developer Lendlease, the fire sale of the estate for £50 million was later exposed as having gifted vast profits to the private sector and left the council with little or no surplus to work with. Indeed the widely read architecture critic of the *Observer* newspaper, Rowan Moore, did not pull his punches on the matter:

> Southwark Council has been played by developers. It has had its tummy tickled, arm twisted and arse kicked. It has got a poor deal in return for its considerable assets, multiple promises have been broken and violence done to the lives of many who lived there.[67]

This was written in 2016, not 1986.

And what might any or all of this have to do with theatre, the burnt down theatre that I began this chapter with, and the Dark Theatre that gives this book its name? I might be tempted to say nothing. And why should it? What possible claim could performance make on our divided attention at a time when lines of residents form at the foot of a still-smouldering, 24-storey tower to ferry provisions towards those who need them most. Surely just another form of cultural cruelty to place alongside the myriad examples offered here. It is irrelevant that Emily Maitlis and I were there that day, and our presence does not legitimate lazy words from others when it comes to representing in insufficient ways, such as writing, the loss that has been so deeply felt. And performance has, largely but not entirely, remained a distance from the matter in hand. 'Too soon' might in this instance not be an inaccurate guide for years to come. *Dictating to the Estate* by local resident Nathaniel McBride staged at the Playground Theatre at the foot of Grenfell Tower is a notable exception to this absence. And that is not to say there has not been a plethora of works that contest the broad diagnosis of what might have given rise to such a thing, the work of Sh!t Theatre, Louise Mothersole and Becca Biscuit, has been outstanding in this respect, with *Letters from Windsor House* an evisceration of the London housing crisis playing the 2016 Edinburgh Festival to acclaim.

But the art that matters in this context, like the words, remains in the gift of those for whom this represents their disappointed hopes and their lost lives. On the 22 May 2018, on the second day of the Grenfell Inquiry at the Millennium Hotel, hard upon the Millennium Casino that appropriately given the role of the casino-economy in the foregoing flashes its presence next door, I watch on as Damal

Carayol, cousin of the artist Khadija Saye who perished with her mother and her work at the top of Grenfell Tower, presented a painting he had made on the Friday morning after the fire to Martin Moore-Bick, the Inquiry lead. The painting of the charcoaled building is annotated with a vertical dedication the height of the tower: 'To Sir Martin Moore-Bick. Work until truth is laid bare. Do it for Humanity. Do it Led by Love. Damal. Family and Grenfell Community'. At the foot of the painting, beneath the tower are two small framed phrases: 'Eyesore!! Final Straw'. The painting has been hanging in the Inquiry room from the first day to the last day of Phase One, the final time I see it (now removed with the Inquiry to Holborn Bar) before the interminable break that separates Phase One of the Inquiry from Phase Two. I am struck by its insistence for right action: Do it. The second 18-month phase of the Inquiry is just beginning in January 2020 as this book is being set in the galleys for publication, and will, in the words of the commission, focus on: 'establishing how Grenfell Tower came to be in a condition that allowed a tragedy of this scale to occur'.[68] As I return to the Inquiry (now in Paddington and much closer to 'home') wondering how the corporate interests will defend the indefensible these words from Sam Stein QC, representing the bereaved and survivors of Grenfell Tower, speak for a community whose warnings went unheeded:

> Those companies involved killed when they criminally failed to consider the safety of others. They killed when they promoted their unsuitable dangerous products in the pursuit of money and they killed when they entirely ignored their ultimate clients, the people of Grenfell Tower. They knew they were literally playing with fire.

If the second day of the Grenfell Inquiry feels to me like a lifetime ago, then for those who have lost those they love it must have been an eternity. The painting is back in place: Do it.

At the end of that day when we first see the painting by Damal Carayol, that long ago day of presentations and testimonies at the Grenfell Inquiry, something happens that theatre in the UK, if not the US, finds faintly embarrassing, a standing ovation from those present, towards those who have taught, cared, created, loved and managed, for a vocation that has been brutally foreshortened. Here Debbie Lamprell, Maria del Pilar Burton, Rania Ibrahim, Mary Mendy, Khadija Saye, the Choucair family, Hesham Rahman, Hania Hassan and Fethia Hassan are remembered in words shared by those who loved them, who most acutely felt their loss. The name of Fethia Hassan will reappear in somewhat different commemoration in the *London Review of Books* just two weeks later. The words there can only pale when they follow those heard from those who do not need to imagine Fethia because they *knew* her. It is not that there are too few commemorating these lives, it is that those writings that circulate most widely and with most cultural force, are by some way in this context, it would seem for all their apparent fluency, the least reliable and by some way the less moving. Even before the publication date of the O'Hagan essay has been reached, on its eve, 6 June 2018, within the Inquiry itself

Rajiv Menon, representing Mr Kebede is attacking its shoddiness: '[Mr Kebede] did not pack a suitcase and leave with it after raising the alarm, a nasty lie that was first reported in the days after the fire and sadly continues to be peddled nearly a year later'. He means peddled by Andrew O'Hagan, via an unsourced 'neighbour'. Menon continues in front of us:

> Can I please use this opportunity to ask everyone – but in particular the press [which I suppose in this instance must include literary journals] – to leave Mr Kebede alone? He is a good man, he did nothing wrong. On the contrary he did the right thing from start to finish. Now he wants privacy for him and his family.

Something that the *London Review of Books* don't appear to offer him given the way he features in what purports to be, by its length alone, an authoritative account. On that evening's 'BBC 10 o'clock News' the claims concerning Mr Kebede are described as 'garbage'. Even that much maligned thing called 'mainstream media' appears to have called that one right at least.

Since beginning work on this book two years ago I have found myself asking about trigger warnings in theatres wondering why they are so routinely rubbished and abused? I am not sure I always felt quite this protective of those whose rights are endangered by something they would not wish to see. My writing about the risk from fire in *Theatre & Everyday Life* would suggest otherwise. I appear in 1993 to be wholly at ease with risk in the essential interests of the freedom of art to do as it must. On that same day in the Inquiry, Bernard Richmond, Secretary to the Inquiry and responsible for its conduct, apologises profusely when he misses one trigger warning amongst many, and an unannounced projected image of the burning Grenfell Tower propels a traumatised resident weeping to the corridor where outside they receive instant care from the Inquiry staff. There is no 'chaos' as is widely reported in the press and on social media. There was, from where I was sitting, a traumatised person, those who tended to her professionally outside the Inquiry room, and those of us left inside, in the profound quiet that follows serious things. Mr Richmond has opened the proceedings with a flourish worthy of Plato and his anti-theatrical prejudice: 'At times the Inquiry is not as slick as a staged production. And I'm pleased'.[69] And we are too, there is nothing more irrelevant in this current context than slick theatre and its habitual demands on our attention. It is easy for me to say and write these things. I can look up, from this script, from my study window, across Shepherd's Bush, out towards the high-vis stevedores as they pull a vast shroud across Grenfell Tower's damning, blackened, signature in the sky. And I can choose to look away.[70] Richard Yates was after all not thinking only about theatrical failure when in the first chapter of his novel *Revolutionary Road* he wrote: 'When the curtain fell at last it was an act of mercy'.

Notes

1 Bulley, Dan. (2019). 'Everyday Life and Death in the Global City', in *After Grenfell: Violence, Resistance and Response*. Eds. Dan Bulley, Jenny Edkins and Nadine El-Enany. London Pluto Press, p. 4.
2 I cannot be saying this because I had any specific knowledge of the Festival of Mercé, though I had visited Barcelona twice in the 1980s. I was not to know that in another year I would move to Barcelona for several years where what I said became known and felt retrospectively. I am grateful to the artist Beryl Robinson whose opportunity to work in an El Poblenou studio changed our lives.
3 I think I am basing this observation on the experience of my colleagues Lucy Neal and Rose Fenton who as irrepressible directors of the London International Festival of Theatre through the 1980s and 1990s had repeatedly staged, accommodated and revealed such tensions by curating the work of these companies in London. The inundation and eventual cancellation of La Cubana's (or was it Els Comediants') waterlogged version of Shakespeare's *Tempest* at Sadlers Wells Theatre was just one example of a venue whose historic prosperity had been engineered through its management of water yet was to be swept under by those same 'natural elements' reshaped in cultural form.
4 Positioning myself as a practitioner here after a decade of working at Rotherhithe Theatre Workshop I gesture to what historiography will 'do' for me and others, an expectation of resistance that I have since ascribed to all theoretical disciplines that might otherwise satisfy themselves with the sly solipsism of interpretation of others' goods. In the end I knew the pathos of history writing would always be characterised by historiographers reflecting on the power they will not have.
5 I had some years before come across a copy of Michel de Certeau's *The Practice of Everyday Life* sitting on a high shelf alongside a volume in the *Yale French Studies* series dedicated to 'Everyday Life' in a second hand bookshop in West London, one of those chance encounters with discarded review copies that guide one's own thinking for years to come. Roland Barthes recognises these ruses of scholarship when in his lecture series on *The Neutral* he openly alerts his students to the bibliography having wholly and only been drawn from the books available during the vacation before in his summer house.
6 de Certeau, Michel. (1988). *The Writing of History*. Trans. Tom Conley. New York: Columbia University Press, p. 96.
7 Indeed the Palmer House Hotel where I first gave a paper from which this chapter was written for *Theatre & Everyday Life* only stood where it did thanks to the 'Great Fire' of Chicago in 1871.
8 See Battersea Arts Centre web-site: https://batterseaartscentreblog.com/2015/03/26/in-good-company-by-prof-alan-read/ (accessed on 26 August 2019).
9 'Racialised' is the term used in *After Grenfell: Violence, Resistance and Response* (2019), by Nadine El-Enany in the context of the long durée historical disempowerments of residents and definitions of white supremacism.
10 See Twitter @DLLarenceOBE, 14.30 (accessed on 29 October 2019).
11 de Certeau, Michel. *The Writing of History*, op. cit. p. 47.
12 El-Enany, Nadine. 'British Immigration Law and the Production of Colonial Spaces' in *After Grenfell*, op. cit. p. 51.
13 Maitlis, Emily. (2019). *Airhead: The Imperfect Art of Making News*. London: Penguin, pp. 137–138.
14 O'Hagan, Andrew. (2018). 'The Tower' in *London Review of Books*, Volume 40, Number 11, 7 June 2018, pp. 3–43.
15 Virginia Woolf, *Three Guineas*: www.blackwellpublishing.com/content/BPL_Images/Content_store/Sample_chapter/9780631177241/woolf.pdf (accessed on 26 August 2019).
16 El-Enany, op. cit. p. 54.
17 See Marder, Michael. (2015). *Pyropolitics: When the World is Ablaze*. London: Rowman and Littlefiled, p. xiv.
18 Ibid. p. xii.

19 Ibid. p. xii.
20 Robert Booth, the *Guardian*, 06.00 BST Thursday, 13 June 2019, accessible at: www.theguardian.com/uk-news/2019/jun/13/this-building-has-no-sprinklers-grenfell-uniteds-12-storey-high-guerrilla-messages, (accessed on 13 June 2019).
21 Marder, Michael. op. cit. p. 155.
22 Ibid. p. 155.
23 Derrida, Jacques. (1991). *Cinders*. Trans. Ned Lukacher. Lincoln: University of Nebraska Press.
24 Ibid. p. 1.
25 Ibid. p. 1.
26 Ibid. p. 25.
27 O'Hagan, Andrew. (2018). 'The Tower', *London Review of Books*, Vol. 40, No. 11, 7 June 2018, p. 3, 4th column.
28 See Taussig, Michael. (1999). *Defacement: Public Secrecy and the Labor of the Negative*. Stanford: Stanford University Press.
29 Jacques Derrida, *Cinders*, op. cit. p. 25.
30 Reference: Melanie Coles' response to Andrew O'Hagan in LRB letters: *London Review of Books*, letters page, Vol. 40, No. 12, 21 June 2018, www.lrb.co.uk/v40/n12/letters (accessed here and below on 15 June 2019).
31 *London Review of Books*, letters page, Vol. 40, No. 12, 21 June 2018, www.lrb.co.uk/v40/n12/letters
32 O'Hagan, op. cit. p. 3.
33 Ibid. p. 3.
34 Ibid. p. 6.
35 Ibid. p. 6.
36 Ibid. p. 6.
37 Ibid. p. 6.
38 Ibid. p. 15.
39 Ibid. p. 25.
40 Ibid. p. 25.
41 Tony Sullivan in *London Review of Books*, Letters Page, Vol. 40, No. 13, 5 July 2018, (accessed here on 15 June 2019): www.lrb.co.uk/v40/n13/letters
42 O'Hagan, Andrew. op. cit. p. 15.
43 Ibid. p. 16.
44 See *London Review of Books*: www.lrb.co.uk/v40/n12/letters
45 O'Hagan, Andrew. op. cit. p. 22.
46 www.lrb.co.uk/v40/n12/letters
47 O'Hagan, Andrew. op. cit. p. 16.
48 Ibid. p. 37.
49 Ibid. p. 37.
50 See Anna Minton in *London Review of Books*, Letters Page, Vol. 40, No. 13, 5 July 2018, (accessed here on 15 June 2019): www.lrb.co.uk/v40/n13/letters
51 Original unedited letter from Anna Minton to *London Review of Books*, kindly provided by the author.
52 Ibid.
53 O'Hagan, Andrew. op. cit. p. 18.
54 Derrida, Jacques. op. cit. p. 59.
55 Ibid. p. 37.
56 Christophers, Brett. (2018). *The New Enclosure: The Appropriation of Public Land in Neoliberal Britain*. London: Verso, p. 2, and passim (this excellent work provides the basis for the analyses that follow).
57 Ibid. p. 4.
58 Ibid. p. 13.
59 Edgerton, David. (2018). *The Rise and Fall of the British Nation: A Twentieth-Century History*. London: Penguin, pp. 471–472.

60 See Brett Christophers, op cit, p. 66, for this discussion of Karl Polanyi's work on the 'social well-being' of land and its administration.
61 Ibid. p. 67.
62 Ibid. p. 68.
63 Ibid. p. 144.
64 Ibid. p. 145.
65 Boughton, John. (2018). *Municipal Dreams: The Rise and Fall of Council Housing*. London: Verso, p. 1.
66 Ibid. p. 6.
67 Ibid. p. 286.
68 See Grenfell Inquiry Official site: www.grenfelltowerinquiry.org.uk/news/update-inquiry-14 (accessed on 28 August 2019).
69 Grenfell Inquiry, Millennium Hotel, Gloucester Road, London, SW7, 22 May 2018.
70 Or not. Consigning political agency to the last endnote of a book reminds us what it would take to keep looking and acting on what we see, not as an afterthought, but as *the* thought. Antonio Gramsci helps to concentrate the minds of those of us who can act on behalf of those who cannot when he writes: 'Entering and exiting. These two words should be abolished. One does not enter or exit: one continues'. (Antonio Gramsci, *Avanti!*, 11 September 1917).

OUTSTANDING DEBTS

The Dark Theatre was always meant to be published by Routledge and thanks to Ben Piggott, it is. Laura Soppelsa and Zoë Forbes guided the project through the galleys with finesse while Martin Pettitt copy-edited with precision. Five anonymous readers critically addressed the proposed book with invaluable commentaries. I am indebted to them. The book's remaining flaws are my responsibility alone. These acknowledgements are intended to supplement the myriad citational debts that are marked by endnotes and bibliography. All such labours are equal, but some, especially when as discrete as those that give editorial and curatorial work a good name, are more equal than others.

This book is all about loss and as such owes a lasting debt to the writing of Adi Ophir. Each of its pages is touched by the critical thought of Beryl Robinson. My grandmother, Florence Cody, whose claim for compensation was refused by the War Office, was supported by Bernard Rose Cody in writing letters of appeal that were brought to my attention by Brian Renshall and Judy Lowe of the Rainhill Civic Society. My grandmother supported my widowed mother Veronica Read by securing the lease of a haberdashery shop on the Essex Estuary in the early 1960s and inadvertently offered me a textured refuge within which to while-away some childhood years amongst the patterns. Our daughter Hermione has been influenced in turn by these generational threads.

Chapter 1 owes its life to those who worked with us in the Rotherhithe neighbourhood through the 1980s. David Slater and successive years of Dartington College of Arts students and colleagues played their inestimable part. I was returned to this scene by an invitation from Andrea Phillips and Sally Tallant at the Liverpool Biennial in 2015 to talk about Rotherhithe Theatre Workshop for a conference with an inquisitive title: 'Community Arts?'. With the hindsight of history I have benefitted from decisive conversations curated by Laura Cull Ó Maoilearca and Alice Laggay as part of the Performance Philosophy Prague event *How Does*

Performance Philosophy Act? in 2017. The shape of this work was imagined on that occasion.

Chapter 2 was conceived during a seminar at King's College London, hosted by Alex Callinicos and presented by Lea Ypi on the dictatorship of the proletariat. The idea as it problematically related to theatre and social media was then road-tested at *Quorum*, Queen Mary University of London, staged by Tatjana Kijaniza in March 2019. I was grateful to Amy Borsuk, Charlotte Young and Sofia Vranou for postponing my planned contribution to *Quorum* in March 2018 to maintain the decisive UCU strike action of that year. Ella Parry-Davies, John London, Martin O'Brien, Michael McKinnie, Dominic Johnson, Martin Young, Giulia Paladini, and Lianna Mark (who has also been a nuanced PhD supervisee during the writing of this book) each made responsive contributions there. Ieuan Perkins introduced me to the perspicacity of Mark Fisher and reminded me of the pertinence of Fred Jameson. Any sense that I make of surveillance capitalism in this chapter is due to those who have leavened my timeline with their wry resistance including Tim Etchells, Katie Beswick, Tom Piper, Megan Vaughan, Lucy Neal, Annecy Hayes, Alan Lane, Shane Boyle and Vlatka Horvat. Caridad Svich influenced this book in a number of ways, and not least in this chapter through her creative and editorial interventions in defence of 'dear theatre', while Maurya Wickstrom another transatlantic ally has sharpened its politics perceptibly.

Chapter 3 begins with Bobby Baker, the influence of whose work infused *Theatre & Everyday Life* and is returned to here in somewhat different critical frame. Eirini Kartsaki not only organised the *And So On: On Repetition* conference at Anglia Ruskin University Cambridge in 2013 but produced a follow-up publication in which she edited my essay 'Theatre's Coming Home' with élan. Artangel's work appears and reappears throughout this volume and no more so than with respect to *Die Familie Schneider* in this chapter. I am grateful to Michael Morris and James Lingwood for their commitment. Having maintained a necessarily cool distance from the Tate Modern team during the High Court 'Viewing Platform' hearing I was touched when Tate Modern's Director, Frances Morris, so warmly welcomed me back on the occasion of Gavin Bryars' all-night collaboration with St Martins in the Fields Choir and their rendering of *Jesus' Blood Never Failed Me Yet* in the Tate Tanks. Georgina Guy whose work on the displayed and the performed is invaluable has generously shared her ideas from the outset. The archives of the National Art Library, one of the world's most beautiful public collections, made a substantive contribution to this chapter, as well as seat 52 providing the berth from which much of the book was written over the last two years.

The brief Shakespearian interlude that separates Parts I and II of the book, *Dreadful Trade*, was first commissioned by the BBC Radio 4 Producer Sarah Blunt and broadcast in the week-long series, *The Cliff*, in August 2016 (where it can still be heard on BBC Sounds). This is an extended rewriting of that talk and shows a debt to the research of Clare McManus at Roehampton University and the King's College London Early Modernists. Ann Thompson brought me to the critically supportive environment of King's English Department amongst whose convivial company it would be invidious to separate individuals for further recognition. Anonymity in this instance gestures to a profoundly equitable academic community of more than 80 colleagues, early career researchers and professional support staff it has been a pleasure to work within, not least of all when we were busy 'not working' on strike amongst our fine students in the Spring snow of 2018.

Part II of *The Dark Theatre* was shaped by the work of Pierre Klossowski on 'living currency' and I am grateful to Alphonso Lingis and Sonu Shamdasani for introducing me to this work when collaborating in the 1990s at the Institute of Contemporary Arts in London. Subsequently Mischa Twitchin and his work with SHUNT on Zola's *Money* offered a bone-shaking reminder as to the inner touch of financialisation that rattles through this book.

Chapter 4 is wholly indebted to the work of Romeo Castellucci and Socìetas Raffaello Sanzio. I am grateful to Romeo for the discussions over a decade that have given rise to this writing, and for the constant encouragement of Joe Kelleher and Nicholas Ridout in asking harder questions about what we have just seen. This gratitude extends more widely to other work I would have missed but for their unerring theatrical instincts, such as *Chekhov's First Play* by Dead Centre that was staged at Battersea Arts Centre and whose influence on my writing about property and land I was initially reluctant to admit. Rebecca Groves has written about care with generosity in ways that inform my discussion of the irreparable. Dan Rebellato and Maria Delgado offered an accommodating shelter for the work on *The Divine Comedy* included here in a somewhat different form. Patrick ffrench offered insights to George Bataille and translated work on *Homo Spectator* that would have remained beyond me.

Chapter 5 is written under the influence of Michael Marder whose *Plant Thinking* (and multiple follow-up works) has sustained my concern for the expansion of the collective, and Tuija Kokkonen whose reflections on the 'three ecologies' got me thinking originally. Jürgen Bock invited me to the inspiring Maumaus in Lisbon to discuss this work over three days that helped me reflect on what I had written. David Williams, Heike Roms, Mike Pearson and Carl Lavery have long accompanied me through this untilled field in a spirit of friendship. Despina Panagiotopoulou with Athina Karatzogianni invited me to present at the critically generative symposium *The Jungle Factory* in March 2017, held at the Attenborough Arts Centre, University of Leicester, and framed pressing questions that infiltrated the writing of this book. Gigi Argyropoulou hosted pertinent Biennial occasions in Green Park in Athens in extreme temperatures that invited us to think of the consequences of our actions, while Adrian Heathfield was a roof-top ally helping me to see beyond the haze of the city. Christine Umpfenbach presented *Lost Gardens* at the Homo Novus Festival in Riga that Gundega Laivina had had the generosity to title 'The Last Human Venue'. Having adopted a subtitle from my work Gundega followed up with an access-all-areas pass to ten days of the festival which profoundly affected my thoughts and feelings on the ecology of what Brett Christophers has called the 'New Enclosure'. James Leadbitter, 'The Vacuum Cleaner', shared his time and generative ideas with me there. Sibylle Peters and Paula Hildebrandt latterly organised a substantial gathering in Hamburg in 2016 under the title *Performing Citizenship* at which, thanks to the introduction of Lois Keidan, I spoke about 'The English Garden Effect', a keynote that was latterly edited by the conference curatorial team and published as 'Phyto-Performance and the Lost Gardens of Riga'. The Deadline Festival organised by Platform and Liberate Tate to mark the Paris Summit of 2015 gave me an opportunity to air this work on behalf of a cause that appeared significant then and has become critical now. Ewan Forster and Christopher Heighes along the way conjured up *Plant Science* for the newly established Performance Foundation in the Inigo Rooms in the East Wing of Somerset House on Strand in London and remain sui generis theatre makers in a crowded field. The Commune of Truinas, as with previous books, provided the landscape, climate and neighbourliness within which these kinds of words could be written, and more than enough oxygen for a dog to dream through 15 summers.

Chapter 6 has complex antecedents that demand the most careful acknowledgement. In defending the viola player Chris Goldscheider both Theo Huckle QC and Jonathan Clarke, along with their instructing solicitors Fry Law led by Chris Fry, demonstrated the power of meticulous preparation. Subsequently the defence team joined Colm McGrath, Aoife Monks and Lucy Finchett-Maddock of Art/Law Network for *Acoustic Shock* at King's College London, sign-interpreted by Richard Law. Mark Critcher discussed Tort Law with me on that evening and Teresa Critcher, with the help of Bernard (Bill) Cody and Audrey Cody, recovered the images of 702 High Road Leyton that close this book. I am grateful for their continuing support. Bojana Kunst encouraged me to think of the artist in proximity to work. Sean Mulcahy and Gary Watt invited me to Warwick University to the *Law/In/And As Performance* conference in 2018 where I first articulated these ideas to an audience that included the always supportive Carey Young. Jen Harvie edited my early writing on theatre & law with clarity. Gary Anderson, Niamh Malone and Steven Shakespeare took a serious risk inviting me to speak in the armchaired presence of François Laruelle at Tate Liverpool, where John Ó Maoilearca made some matters regarding non-philosophy marginally clearer. In the aftermath of the Goldscheider vs. ROH High Court judgement David Jubb and his team at Battersea Arts Centre were typically responsive and responsible to its implications for audiences as well as working artists. Chris Johnston QC happens to be a neighbour with significant shared interests from which I have benefitted, while Ben Bowling has never demurred from discussing the legal ideas of an ingénue.

Chapter 7 was written in the immediate aftermath of the Grenfell Tower fire on 14 June 2017. I am obviously in serious debt to the neighbours, action groups and Inquiry participants and personnel whose writing I have read, whose voices I have listened to, and with whom I have spoken when they have felt able to share their experiences. The spine of the chapter became a critical response to Andrew O'Hagan regarding the writing of history – the conversations we had at King's College London gave me the confidence to write with honesty and, in the spirit of his own writing, without undue tact. On the same corridor, but in a rather different register, Paul Gilroy has been a close-reading companion of honour. Steve Tompkins and the architectural practice Haworth Tompkins raised the roof of the magnificent Battersea Arts Centre Grand Hall after the 2015 fire had brought it low, and I am grateful to them for a sustained engagement over two decades that has flourished through shared endeavour and warm disagreement. Jacques Derrida dedicated a copy of *Cinders* to our daughter Florence at the Institute of Contemporary Arts on its publication in 1994. We have long cherished that volume with its neat signature, loving gesture, and vital struggle for life amongst the ashes.

The Dark Theatre is dedicated to my partner, the artist Beryl Robinson, and our daughters Florence and Hermione, without whom I would have been lost for words.

London, 15 June 2017 – Truinas, 15 August 2019

Charles Powell
The Milliner's Shop, 702 High Road Leyton, London
1914

The Milliner's shop 307

Florence Powell
The Milliner's Shop, 702 High Road Leyton, London
1917

LA VITA NUOVA

The cover image of *The Dark Theatre* is a photograph taken by Stephan Glagla of *La Vita Nuova*, a work conceived and directed by Romeo Castellucci with text by Claudia Castellucci and music by Scott Gibbons. *La Vita Nuova* opened on 28 November 2018 at KANAL, Centre Pompidou (Brussels), Quai des Péniches. This was a coproduction with Bozar, Centre for Fine Arts (Brussels), Kanal Centre Pompidou (Brussels) and La Villette (Paris), where the performance latterly played from 26 November 2019 until 1 December 2019. I am grateful to Romeo Castellucci and Gilda Biasini for arranging for me to be present at the Paris production, and to Stephan Glagla for his generous agreement to the reproduction of his photograph (www.stephanglagla.de).

The following extract from *La Vita Nuova* is a brief excerpt from a longer text written by Claudia Castellucci:

> New life
> […]
> There was a time when the rooms carved out of the foundations of buildings
> were used as storages for still and silent things:
> grains, larvae, must, yeast.
> These were places for seeds,
> like this garage, for example,
> with all these idle cars.
> We have gathered here to contemplate dormant being,
> To grasp the archaic origins of motors,
> far from the automobile industry.
> We are here, to extract human technique
> From the heart of the Neanderthal.
> All of these cars look normal and up-to-date…
> Do not believe it.
> They come from very far away.
> The distance we now feel between us and them is so great,
> and in spite of this, the solidarity between our words
> and their silence is complete.
> Here, in this new catacomb,
> a new and extended life is being celebrated.
> Here, in the silence of the nocturnal garage,
> I seem to hear an urge to revolt
> And embellish our conduct and the habits of our daily life […]

BIBLIOGRAPHY

Abish, Walter. (1983). *How German Is It*. London: Faber.
Abish, Walter. (1980). 'The English Garden Effect', in *In The Future Perfect*. London: Faber.
Adajania, Nancy. (2015). 'The Thirteenth Place and the Eleventh Question: The Artist Citizen and Her Strategies for Devolution', in Hlavajova, Maria and Hoskote, Ranjit eds. *Future Publics: (The Rest Can and Should be Done by the People)*. Utrecht: BAK, pp. 28–61.
Adorno, Theodor W. (2001). *The Culture Industry*. Trans. E. B. Ashton. London: Routledge.
Agamben, Giorgio. (1993). *The Coming Community*. Trans. Michael Hardt. Minneapolis: University of Minnesota Press.
Agamben, Giorgio. (2000). *Means Without Ends*. Minnesota: University of Minneapolis Press.
Agamben, Giorgio. (2007). *Profanations*. Trans. Jeff Fort. New York: Zone Books.
Agamben Giorgio. (2010). 'What is the Contemporary?' in *Nudities*. Trans. David Kishik and Stefan Pedatella. Stanford: Stanford University Press.
Agamben, Giorgio. (2011). 'The Mystery of the Economy', in *The Kingdom and the Glory*. Trans. Lorenzo Chiesa. Stanford: Stanford University Press.
Alston, Adam. (2019). 'Safety, Risk and Speculation in the Immersive Industry', *Contemporary Theatre Review*, Creative Commons, vol. 29, no. 3.
Alston, Adam and Welton, Martin. Eds. (2017). *Theatre in the Dark: Shadow, Gloom and Blackout in Contemporary Theatre*. London: Bloomsbury.
Alston, Philip. (2018). *Statement on Visit to the United Kingdom, by Professor Philip Alston, United Nations Special Rapporteur on extreme poverty and human rights*. London, 16 November 2018, accessible at: www.ohchr.org/documents/issues/poverty/eom_gb_16nov2018.pdf (accessed on 19 August 2019).
Althusser, Louis. (2001). *Lenin and Philosophy and Other Essays*. Trans. Ben Brewster. New York: Monthly Review Press.
Amit, Vered and Rapport, Nigel. (2002). *The Trouble with Community*. London: Pluto Press.

Anderson, Benedict. (1983, Revised Edition 2001). *Imagined Communities: Reflections on the Origin and Spread of Nationalism*. London: Verso.
Angelaki, Vicky. (2017). *Social and Political Theatre in 21st Century Britain: Staging Crisis*. London: Bloomsbury.
Appadurai, Arjun. (2013). *The Future as a Cultural Fact: Essays on the Global Condition*. London: Verso.
Apter, Emily. (2018). *Unexceptional Politics: On Obstruction, Impasse and the Impolitic*. London: Verso.
Arrighi, Giovanni. (2010). *The Long Twentieth Century: Money, Power and the Origins of Our Times*. London: Verso.
Auden, W. H. (1938) 'Musée des Beaux Artes', in *Another Time*. New York: Random House
Auslander, Phillip. (1999) *Liveness: Performance in a Mediatised Culture*. London: Routledge.
Arts Council England. (2014). *The Value of Arts and Culture to People and Society*. London: Arts Council England.
Austin, J. L. (1962). *How to Do Things With Words*. London: Clarendon Press.
Azoulay, Ariella. (2012). *Civil Imagination: A Political Ontology of Photography*. Trans. Louise Bethlehem. London: Verso.
Azoulay, Ariella. (2015). 'Nationless State: A series of Case Studies' in Eds. Maria Hlavajova and Ranjit Hoskote. *Future Publics: (The Rest Can and Should be Done by the People)*. Utrecht: BAK.
Bachelard, Gaston. (1992). *The Poetics of Space*. Trans. Maria Jolas. New York: Beacon Press.
Badiou, Alain. (2012). *The Rebirth of History: Times of Riots and Uprisings*. Trans. Gregory Elliott. London and New York: Verso.
Balibar, Étienne. (2004). *We the People of Europe? Reflections on Transnational Citizenship*. Princeton: Princeton University Press.
Balibar, Étienne. (2015). *Violence and Civility: On the Limits of Political Philosophy*. New York: Columbia University Press.
Barish, Jonas A. (1985). *The Anti Theatrical Prejudice*. San Francisco: University of California Press.
Barthes, Roland. (1981). *Camera Lucida*. Trans. Richard Howard. New York: Hill and Wang.
Barthelme, Donald. (2005). *Forty Stories*. New York: Penguin Books.
Bataille, Georges. (2005). *The Cradle of Humanity: Prehistoric Art and Culture*. Ed. Stuart Kendall. Trans. Michelle Kendall. Cambridge: MIT Press.
Bathurst, Bella. (2017). *Sound: Stories of Hearing Lost and Found*. London: Profile Books.
Benjamin, Walter. (1986). 'Paris, Capital of the Nineteenth Century', in *Reflections*. Trans. Edmund Jephcott. New York: Schocken Books, pp. 155–156.
Benjamin, Walter. (1976). *One Way Street*. Trans. Edmund Jephcott. London: New Left Books.
Benjamin, Walter. (1992). *The Arcades Project*. Trans. Howard Elland and Kevin McLaughlin. Cambridge: Harvard University Press.
Bergson, Henri. (2002). 'Memory of the Present and False Recognition', in *Key Writings*. Ed. Keith Ansell Pearson and John Mullarkey. London: Continuum, pp. 141–156.
Berlant, Lauren. (2011). *Cruel Optimism*. Durham: Duke University Press.
Beswick, Katie. (2019). *Social Housing in Performance: The English Council Estate on and off Stage*. London: Bloomsbury.
Bharucha, Rustom. (2000). *The Politics of Cultural Practice: Thinking Through Theatre in an Age of Globalisation*. London: Athlone Press.

Bhattacharya, Tithi. (2017). 'Introduction: Mapping Social Reproduction Theory', in *Social Reproduction Theory*. London: Pluto Press.
Bird, John. Ed. (1993). *Mapping the Futures: Local Cultures, Global Change*. London: Routledge.
Bishop, Claire. (2004). 'Antagonism and Relational Aesthetics' in *October*, vol. 110 (Fall, 2004), pp. 51–79.
Bishop, Claire. (2006). 'Social Collaboration and its Discontents', *Artforum*, February 2006, pp. 178–183.
Bishop, Claire. Ed. (2006). *Participation*. London: Whitechapel Art gallery/MIT Press.
Bishop, Claire. (2013). *Artificial Hells: Participatory Art and the Politics of Spectatorship*. London: Verso.
Bloch, Ernst. (1954/2013). *The Principle of Hope*. Trans. Neville Plaice, Stephen Plaice and Paul Knight. Boston: MIT Press.
Blumenberg, Hans. (1996). *Shipwreck With Spectator: Paradigm of a Metaphor for Existence*. Trans. Steven Rendall. Cambridge: MIT Press.
Boal, Augusto. (1979). *Theatre of the Oppressed*. London: Pluto Press.
Boon, R and Platsow, J. (2004). *Theatre and Empowerment: Community Drama on the World Stage*. Cambridge: Cambridge University Press.
Booth, Robert (2019). *Guardian*, Thursday 13 June 2019, accessible at: www.theguardian.com/uk-news/2019/jun/13/this-building-has-no-sprinklers-grenfell-uniteds-12-storey-high-guerrilla-messages, (accessed on 13 June 2019).
Bourriaud, Nicholas. (2002). *Relational Aesthetics*. Dijon: Les Presses du Réel.
Boyle, Shane. (2016). 'Container Aesthetics: The Infrastructural Politics of Shunt's Boy Who Climbed Out of his Face', *Theatre Journal*, Vol. 68. No. 1 (March 2016), pp. 57–77.
Boughton, John. (2018). *Municipal Dreams: The Rise and Fall of Council Housing*. London: Verso.
Bradbury, Ray. (1953/1993). *Fahrenheit 451*. London: Harper Collins
Briganti, Chiara and Mezei, Kathy. Eds. (2012). *The Domestic Space Reader*. Toronto: University of Toronto Press.
Brook, Peter. (1968). *The Empty Space*. London: Penguin.
Bulley, Dan, Edkins, Jenny and El-Enany, Nadine. Eds. (2019). *After Grenfell: Violence, Resistance and Response*. London: Pluto Press.
Bullough, Oliver. (2018). *Money Land: Why Thieves & Crooks Now Rule the World and How to Take it Back*. London: Profile Books.
Butler, Judith. (1990). *Gender Trouble: Feminism and the Subversion of Identity*. London: Routledge.
Butler, Judith. (2015a). *Notes towards a Performative Theory of Assembly*. Cambridge: Harvard University Press.
Butler, Judith. (2015b). *Precariousness and Grievability: When is Life Grievable*. London: Verso.
Carlson, Marvin. (2003). *The Haunted Stage: The Theatre as Memory Machine*. Michigan: University of Michigan Press.
Cassin, Barbara. Ed. (2014). *Dictionary of Untranslatables*. Princeton: Princeton University Press.
Choonara, Joseph. (2017). *Unravelling Capitalism*. London: Bookmarks Publication.
Christophers, Brett. (2018). *The New Enclosure: The Appropriation of Public Land in Neoliberal Britain*. London: Verso.
Cohen, Anthony. (1989). *The Symbolic Construction of Community*. London: Routledge.
Cohen-Cruz, Jan. (2005). *Local Acts: Community-Based Performance in the United States*. New Brunswick: Rutgers University Press.

314 Bibliography

Coleman, Nick. (2012). *The Train in the Night: A Story of Music and Loss.* London: Jonathan Cape.
Colomina, Beatriz. (1994). *Privacy and Publicity: Modern Architecture as Mass Media.* Cambridge: MIT Press.
Conquergood, Dwight. (2007). 'Performing as a Moral Act: Ethical Dimensions of the Ethnography of Performance', in Eds. Petra Kuppers and Gwen Roberston. *The Community Performance Reader.* Abingdon: Routledge, pp. 57–70.
Corbin, Alain. (1999). *Village Bells: Sound and Meaning in the Nineteenth-Century French Countryside.* Trans. Martin Thom. London: Papermac.
de Certeau, Michel. (1983). *The Practice of Everyday Life.* Trans. Steven Rendall. Berkeley: University of California Press.
de Certeau, Michel. (1988). *The Writing of History.* Trans. Tom Conley. New York: Columbia University Press
de Sousa Santos, Bonaventura. (2018). *The End of the Cognitive Empire: The Coming of Age of Epistemologies of the South.* Durham: Duke University Press.
Dead Centre. (2016). *Chekhov's First Play.* London: Oberon Books.
Dean, Jodi. (2017). *Crowds and Party.* London: Verso.
Deleuze, Gilles and Guattari, Féliz. (2004). *A Thousand Plateaus: Capitalism and Schizophrenia.* Trans. Brian Massumi. London: Continuum
Deleuze, Gilles. (1981). *Cinema 1: The Movement Image.* Trans Hugh Tomlinson. London: Athlone.
Deleuze, Gilles and Guattari, Félix. (2009). *Anti-Oedipus: Capitalism and Schizophrenia.* Trans. Robert Hurley. London: Penguin.
Delgado, Maria and Rebellato, Dan. (2010). *Contemporary European Theatre Directors.* London: Routledge.
Derrida, Jacques. (1991). *Cinders.* Trans. Ned Lukacher. Lincoln: University of Nebraska Press.
Derrida, Jacques. (1992). *The Other Heading: Reflections on Today's Europe.* Bloomington: Indiana University Press.
Dolan, Jill. (2005). *Utopia in Performance: Finding Hope at the Theater.* Michigan: University of Michigan Press.
Edgerton, David. (2018). *The Rise and Fall of the British Nation: A Twentieth-Century History.* London: Penguin.
Elliot, Jane. (2018). *The Microeconomic Mode: Political Subjectivity in Contemporary Popular Aesthetics.* New York: Columbia University Press.
Dean, Jodie. (2018). *Crowds and Party.* London: Verso.
Epskamp, K. (1989). *Theatre in Search of Social Change.* The Hague: Centre for the Study of Education in Developing Countries.
Erven, Eugene van. (2001). *Community Theatre: Global Perspectives.* London: Routledge.
Federici, Sylvia. (2012). *Revolution at Point Zero.* Oakland: PM Press.
Federici, Sylvia. (2019). *Re-Enchanting the World: Feminism and the Politics of the Commons.* Oakland: PM Press.
Fisher, Mark. (2009). *Capitalist Realism.* London: Zero Books.
Fisher, Mark. (2015). *The Weird and the Eerie.* London: Repeater Books.
Fisher, Mark. (2018). *K-PUNK.* Ed. Darren Ambrose. London: Repeater Books.
Frank, Claudine. Ed. (2003). *The Edge of Surrealism: A Roger Caillois Reader.* Durham: Duke University Press.
Franklin, Seb. (2015). *Control: Digitality as Cultural Logic.* Cambridge: MIT Press.
Freud, Sigmund. (1997). *The Diary of Sigmund Freud. 1929–1939.* Trans. M. Molar. London: Hogarth Press.

Friel, Brian. (1995). *Translations*. London: Faber.
Graeber, David. (2014). *Debt: The First 5000 Years*. New York: Melville House.
Gramsci, Antonio. (1930). *The Prison Notebooks*, Notebook Number 3, accessible at: https://isreview.org/issue/108/morbid-symptoms (accessed on 24 August 2019).
Gramsci, Antonio. (1917/2012). 'Avanti!', in *Selections from Cultural Writings*. Eds. D. Forgacs and G. Nowell-Smith. London: Lawrence and Wishart.
Groves, Rebecca. (2017). 'On Performance and the Dramaturgy of Caring', in Eds. Anna Street, Julien Alliot and Magnolia Pauker. *Inter Views in Performance Philosophy*. Houndmills: Palgrave, pp. 309–318.
Guattari, Féliz. (2000). *The Three Ecologies*. Trans. Ian Pindar and Paul Sutton. London: Athlone.
Guéry, François and Deleule, Didier. (2014/1972). *The Productive Body*. Trans. Philip Barnard and Stephen Shapiro. London: Zero Books.
Gucbilmez, Beliz. (2007). 'An Uncanny Theatricality: The Representation of the Offstage' (May 2007), *New Theatre Quarterly*, vol. 23, no. 2, pp. 152–160.
Haedicke, S. and Nellhaus, T. Eds. (2001). *Performing Democracy: International Perspectives on Community-Based Performance*. Ann-Arbour: University of Michigan Press.
Hammond, Simon. (2019). 'K-Punk at Large', *New Left Review*, No. 118, July/August 2019.
Han, Byung-Chul. (2017). *Psycho-Politics: Neoliberalism and New Technologies of Power*. Trans. Erik Butler. London: Verso.
Han, Byung-Chul. (2018). *Topology of Violence*. Trans. Amanda Demarco. Cambridge: MIT Press.
Harman, Graham. (2018). *Object-Oriented Ontology*. London: Penguin.
Hartman, Saidiya. (2008). 'Venus in Two Acts', *Small Axe*, vol. 12, no. 2 (June 2008), pp. 1–14.
Hartman, Saidiya. (2019). *Wayward Lives: Beautiful Experiments*. London: Serpent's Tail.
Harvie, Jen. (2013). *Fair Play: Art, Performance and Neoliberalism*. Houndmills: Palgrave.
Heller Roazen, Daniel. (2009). *The Enemy of All: Piracy and the Law of Nations*. New York: Zone Books.
Hermassi, Karen. (1977). *Polity and Theatre in Historical Perspective*. Berkeley: University of California Press.
Hirsch, Afua. (2018). *Brit(ish): On Race, Identity and Belonging*. London: Vintage.
Hlavajova, Maria and Hoskote, Ranjit. Eds. (2015). *Future Publics: (The Rest Can and Should be Done by the People)*. Utrecht: BAK.
Hollinghurst, Alan. (2004). *The Line of Beauty*. London: Picador.
Hulton, Peter. Ed. (1977–2016). *Theatre Papers* and *Arts Archives*. Exeter: www.arts-archives.org (accessed on 12 October 2019).
Hutton, Margaret-Anne. (2018). *The Contemporary Condition*. Berlin: Sternberg Press.
Jackson, Shannon. (2011). *Social Works: Performing Arts, Supporting Publics*. London: Routledge.
Jacobs, Jane. (1961). *The Death and Life of Great American Cities*. New York: Vintage Books.
Jameson, Fredric. (1984a). 'Postmodernism: Or The Cultural Logic of Late Capitalism', *New Left Review*, 1/146, July/August 1984.
Jameson, Fredric. (1984b). 'The Politics of Theory: Ideological Positions in the Postmodern Debate', *New German Critique*, No. 33, Modernity and Postmodernity (Autumn 1984), pp. 53–65.
Joseph, Miranda. (2002). *Against the Romance of Community*. Minneapolis: University of Minnesota Press.

Joseph, Miranda. (2012). *The Romance of Community*. Minneapolis: University of Minnesota Press.
Kartsaki, Eirini. (2016). *On Repetition*. Chicago: University of Chicago Press.
Katz, Marc. (1998). 'Rendezvous in Berlin: Benjamin and Kierkegaard on the Architecture of Repetition', *The German Quarterly*, vol. 71, no. 1 (Winter 1998).
Kear, Adrian. (2013). *Theatre and Event: Staging the European Century*. Houndmills: Palgrave.
Kear, Adrian and Steinberg, Deborah Lynn. Eds. (1999). *Mourning Diana: Nation, Culture and the Performance of Grief*. London: Routledge.
Kelleher, Joe. (2015). *The Illuminated Theatre: Studies on the Suffering of Images*. Abingdon: Palgrave.
Kennedy, Joe. (2018). *Authentocrats: Culture, Politics and the New Seriousness*. London: Repeater Books.
Kennedy, A. L. (2019). *A Point of View: Cookery Shows ... and Hungry People*. BBC Radio 4, Sunday 24 February 2019.
Kershaw, Baz. (1992). *The Politics of Performance: Radical Theatre as Cultural Intervention*. London: Routledge.
Kershaw, Baz. (2009). *Theatre Ecology: Environments and Performance Events*. Cambridge: Cambridge University Press.
Kester, Grant. (2004). *Conversation Pieces: Community and Communication in Modern Art*. Berkeley: University of California Press.
Kierkegaard, Søren. (1983). *Fear and Trembling* and *Repetition*. Trans. and Eds. Howard V. Hong and Edna H. Hong. Princeton: Princeton University Press.
Kirkkopelto, Esa. (2014). 'The Most Mimetic Animal: An Attempt to Deconstruct the Actor's Body' in *Encounters in Performance Philosophy*, Eds. Laura Cull Ó Maoilearca and Alice Lagaay. Houndmills: Palgrave, pp. 121–143.
Kirshenblatt-Gimblett, Barbara. (1998). *Destination Culture: Tourism, Museums and Heritage*. Berkeley: University of California Press.
Klossowski, Pierre. (2017). *Living Currency*. Trans and Ed. Daniel W. Smith, with Vernon W. Cisney and Nicolae Morar. London: Bloomsbury.
Klossowski, Pierre. (2000) *Nietzsche & the Vicious Circle*. Trans. Daniel W. Smith. London: Athlone.
Korsch, Karl. (1970). *Marxism and Philosophy*. London: New Left Books.
Kott, Jan. (1964). *Shakespeare Our Contemporary*. London: Methuen.
Krikorian, Gaelle and Kapczynski, Amy. (2010). *Access to Knowledge: In the Age of Intellectual Property*. New York: Zone Books.
Kuftinek, Sonja. (2003). *Staging America: Cornerstone and Community Based Theatre*. Carbondale: University of Illinois Press.
Kunkel, Benjamin. (2017). 'The Capitalocene', in *London Review of Books*, Vol. 39, no. 5, 2 March 2017, pp. 22–28.
Kunst, Bojana. (2015). *Artist at Work: Proximity of Art and Capitalism*. London: Zero Books.
Kuppers, Petra. (2007). *Community Performance: An Introduction*. Abingdon: Routledge.
Kwon, Miwon. (2004). *One Piece after Another: Site Specific Art and Locational Identity*. Cambridge: MIT Press.
Lacan, Jacques. (1988). *The Seminar of Jacques Lacan: Book 1, Freud's Papers on Technique 1953–1954*. Ed. Jacques-Allain Miller. Trans. John Forrester. New York: Norton.
Laruelle, François. (1993). *The Concept of an Ordinary Ethics or Ethics Founded in Man*. Trans. Taylor Adkins, accessible at: www.scribd.com/document/233744571/Laruelle-The-Concept-of-an-Ordinary-Ethics-or-Ethics-Founded-in-Man (accessed on 28 August 2019).

Latour, Bruno and Weibel, Peter. Eds. (2005). *Making Things Public: Atmospheres of Democracy*. Cambridge: MIT Press.
Latour, Bruno. (1993). *We Have Never Been Modern*. Trans. Catherine Porter. Cambridge: Harvard University Press.
Lauzon, Claudette. (2016). *The Unmaking of Home in Contemporary Art*. Toronto: University of Toronto Press.
Lazzarato, Maurizio. (2012). *The Making of Indebted Man: An Essay on the Neo-Liberal Condition*. Trans. Joshua David Gordon. Cambridge: MIT Press.
Lazzarato, Maurizio. (1996). 'Immaterial Labor', in Eds. Paolo Virno, and Michael Hardt. *Radical Thought in Italy: A Potential Politics*. Minneapolis: University of Minnesota Press, pp. 142–157.
Levin, Laura and Schweitzer, Marlis. Eds. (2011). 'Performing Publics', *Performance Research*, Vol. 16, No 2, June 2011.
Lewis, Paul (2018). 'Revealed One in Four Europeans Vote Populist', the *Guardian*, Tuesday 20 November 2018.
Liedman, Sven Eric. (2018). *A World to Win: The Life and Works of Karl Marx*. Trans. Jeffrey N. Skinner. London: Verso.
Little, Adrian. (2002). *The Politics of Community: Theory and Practice*. Edinburgh: Edinburgh University Press.
Lorrey, Isabel. (2015). *State of Insecurity, Government of the Precarious*. Trans. Aileen Derieg. London: Verso.
Lovink, Geert. (2007). 'The Politics of Organised Networks: The Art of Collective Coordination' in *New Media, Old Media: A History and Theory Reader*. New York, NY: Routledge.
Lyotard, Jean-François. (1993). *Political Writings*. Trans. Bill Readings, with Kevin Paul Geiman. London: UCL Press, p. 97.
Maitlis, Emily. (2019). *Airhead: The Imperfect Art of Making News*. London: Penguin.
Mann, Thomas. (1999). *Dr Faustus*. Trans. John E. Woods. New York: Vintage International.
Marder, Michael. (2013). *Plant-Thinking: A Philosophy of Vegetal Life*. New York: Columbia University Press.
Marder, Michael. (2015). *Pyropolitics: When the World is Ablaze*. London: Rowman and Littlefiled.
Marder, Michael. (2019). *Political Categories: Thinking Beyond Concepts*. New York: Columbia University Press.
Marranca, Bonnie. (1996). *Ecologies of Theatre*. New York: PAJ Publications.
Martin, Randy. (2015). *Knowledge Ltd: Toward a Social Logic of the Derivative*. Philadelphia: Temple University Press.
Martin, Randy. (1994). *Socialist Ensembles: Theater and State in Cuba and Nicaragua*. Minneapolis: University of Minnesota Press.
Martin, Randy. (2002). *Financialisation of Daily Life*. Philadelphia: Temple University Press.
Marx, Karl. (1933). *A Critique of the Gotha Program*, London: Martin Lawrence.
Marx, Karl. (1990). *Capital Volume 1: A Critique of Political Economy*. Trans. Ben Fowkes. London: Penguin.
Massey, Doreen. (1994). *Space, Place and Gender*. London: Polity Press.
Massey, Doreen (2003). 'Some Times of Space', in *Olafur Eliasson: The Weather Project*. Ed. Susan May. London: Tate Publishing, accessible at: www.f-i-e-l-d.co.uk/writings-violence_files/Some_times_of_space.pdf (accessed on 1 March 2019).
Matynia, Ezbieta. (2009). *Performative Democracy*. Boulder: Paradigm Publishers.
McKenzie, Jon. (2001). *Perform or Else!: From Discipline to Performance*. London: Routledge.

McManus, Clare. (2002). *Women on the Renaissance Stage: Anna of Denmark and Female Masquing in the Stuart Court (1590–1619)*. Manchester: Manchester University Press.
Mei, Todd. (2017). *Land and the Given Economy*. Evanston: Northwestern University Press.
Mondzain, Marie José. (2007). *Homo Spectator*. Paris: Boyard.
Moore, Jason. (2015). *Capitalism in the Web of Life*. London: Verso.
Mouffe, Chantal. Ed. (1992). *Dimensions of Radical Democracy: Pluralism, Citizenship, Community*. London: Verso.
Mouffe, Chantal. (2000). *The Democratic Paradox*. London: Verso.
Mouffe, Chantal. (2019). *For a Left Populism*, London: Verso
Nancy, Jean-Luc. (1991). *The Inoperative Community*. Ed. Peter Connor. Trans. Peter Connor. Minneapolis: University of Minnesota Press.
Nancy, Jean-Luc. (2008). *Philosophical Chronicles*. Trans. Franson Manjali. New York: Minneapolis: University of Minnesota Press.
Nancy, Jean-Luc. (2016). *The Disavowed Community*. Trans. Philip Armstrong. New York: Fordham University Press.
Nicholson, Helen. (2005). *Applied Drama: The Gift of Theatre*. Houndmills: Palgrave.
Nicholson, Helen, Nadine Holdsworth and Jane Milling. Eds. (2018). *The Ecologies of Amateur Theatre*. Houndmills: Palgrave.
Norris, Pippa. (1999). *Critical Citizens: Global Support for Democratic Government*. Oxford: Oxford University Press.
O'Hagan, Andrew. (2018). 'The Tower' in *London Review of Books*, vol. 40, no. 11, 7 June 2018, pp. 3–43.
O'Hagan, Andrew (2019). *The Living Rooms*, accessible at: www.artangel.org.uk/die-familie-schneider/the-living-rooms/ (accessed on 19 August 2019).
Ophir, Adi. (2005). *The Order of Evils: Toward an Ontology of Morals*. New York: Zone Books.
Orr, Deborah. (2014). *Guardian*, 24 January 2014, accessible at: www.theguardian.com/commentisfree/2014/jan/24/benefits-street-caused-controversy-worthwhile-legacy (accessed on 24 August 2019).
Perry, Gill. (2013). *Playing at Home: The House in Contemporary Art*. London: Reaktion.
Phelan, Peggy. (1993). *Unmarked: The Politics of Performance*. London: Routledge.
Pollan, Michael .(2002). *The Botany of Desire*. London: Bloomsbury.
Raban, Jonathan. (1971). *Soft City*. London: Picador.
Racz, Imogen. (2015). *Art and the Home: Comfort, Alienation and the Everyday*. London: I. B. Tauris.
Rae, Paul. (2018). *Real Theatre*. Cambridge: Cambridge University Press.
Raban. Jonathan. (1971). *Soft City*. London: Picador.
Rancière, Jacques. (2003). *Short Voyages to the Land of the People*. Trans. James B. Swenson. Stanford: Stanford University Press.
Rancière, Jacques. (2009). *The Emancipated Spectator*. Trans. Gregory Elliott. London: Verso.
Rancière, Jacques. (2012). *Proletarian Nights: The Workers' Dream in Nineteenth Century France*. Trans. John Drury. London: Verso.
Rancière, Jacques and Panagia, Davide. (2000). 'Dissenting Words: A Conversation with Jacques Rancière'. *Diacritics*. Vol. 30, no. 2, (Summer), pp. 113–126.
Rancière, Jacques. (2011). *Staging the People: The Proletarian and His Double*. Trans. David Fernbach. London: Verso.
Rancière, Jacques, (2019). *Ten Theses on Politics*, accessible at: www.scribd.com/document/34219878/Jacques-Ranciere-Ten-Theses-on-Politics (accessed on 1 March 2019).

Ratto, Matt and Boler, Megan. Eds. (2014). *DIY Citizenship: Critical Making and Social Media*. Cambridge: MIT Press.
Read, Alan. (1984). 'The Shadow of Theatre', *Theatre Papers*, Dartington College of Arts, Series 4, No. 7.
Read, Alan. (1993). *Theatre & Everyday Life: An Ethics of Performance*. London: Routledge.
Read, Alan. Ed. (1996). *The Fact of Blackness: Frantz Fanon and Visual Representation*. Seattle: Bay Press.
Read, Alan. Ed. (2000). *Architecturally Speaking: Art, Architecture and the Everyday*. London: Routledge.
Read, Alan, Ed. (2000). 'On Animals', *Performance Research*, vol. 5, no. 2.
Read, Alan. (2007). *Theatre, Intimacy and Engagement: The Last Human Venue*. Houndmills: Palgrave.
Read, Alan. (2013). *Theatre in the Expanded Field: Seven Approaches to Performance*. London: Bloomsbury.
Read, Alan. (2016). *Theatre & Law*. Houndmills: Palgrave.
Reinelt, Janelle (2019). *What I came to Say*, accessible at: www.researchgate.net/publication/283882145_%27What_I_Came_to_Say%27_Raymond_Williams_the_Sociology_of_Culture_and_the_Politics_of_Performance_Scholarship (accessed on 24 August 2019).
Ridout, Nicholas. (2013). *Passionate Amateurs: Theatre, Communism and Love*. Ann Arbor: University of Michigan Press.
Rogoff, Irit. (2000). *Terra Infirma: Geography's Visual Culture*. London: Routledge.
Rose, Gillian. (1992). *The Broken Middle: Out of Our Ancient Society*. Oxford: Blackwell.
Santner, Erik. (2011). *The Royal Remains: The People's Two Bodies and the Endgame of Sovereignty*. Chicago: University of Chicago Press.
Sassen, Saskia. (2014). *Expulsions: Brutality and Complexity in the Global Economy*. Cambridge: Harvard University Press.
Said, Edward. (2003). *Freud and the Non-European*. London: Verso.
Said, Edward (2019). *Philosophical Papers*, accessible at: https://philpapers.org/rec/SAIOAC (accessed on 15 December 2018).
Schechner, Richard. (1985). *Between Theatre and Anthropology*. Philadelphia: University of Philadelphia Press.
Schneider, Rebecca. (1997). *The Explicit Body in Performance*. Abingdon: Routledge.
Shakespeare, William. (1997). *King Lear*. Ed. R. A. Foakes. London: Thomson.
Shukman, Harry and Flanagan, Jane. (2019). *The Times*, London edition, 3 July 2019, p. 15.
Sofer, Andrew. (2013). *Dark Matter: Invisibility in Drama, Theater and Performance*. Michigan: University of Michigan Press.
Steenbergen, B van. Ed. (1994). *The Condition of Citizenship*. London: Sage Publications.
Stengers, Isabelle. (2010). *Cosmopolitics*. Trans. Robert Bononno. Minneapolis: University of Minnesota Press.
Steyerl, Hito. (2012). 'In Defense of the Poor Image' in *The Wretched of the Screen*. London: Sternberg Press.
Stiegler, Bernard. (2010). *Taking Care of Youth and the Generations*. Trans. Stephen Barker. Stanford: Stanford University Press.
Sweeney, Mark (2012). *Guardian*, Friday 30 November 2012, accessible at: www.theguardian.com/media/2012/nov/30/piers-morgan-phone-hacking-leveson-inquiry (accessed on 24 August 2019).
Taine, H. A. (1878). *The Revolution*, 'Les origins de la France contemporaine', vol. 1, Trans. John Durand, London: Daldy, Isbister & Co.

Taussig, Michael. (1999). *Defacement: Public Secrecy and the Labor of the Negative*. Stanford: Stanford University Press.
Thompson, James. (2003). *Applied Theatre: Bewilderment and Beyond*. Oxford: Peter Lang.
Thompson, James. (2005). *Digging up Stories: Applied Theatre, Performance and War*. Manchester: Manchester University Press.
Thoreau, Henry David. (1916). *The Maine Woods*. Boston: Houghton Mifflin.
Valencia, Sayak. (2017). *Gore Capitalism*. Cambridge: MIT Press.
Vidler, Anthony. (1994). *The Architectural Uncanny: Essays in the Modern Unhomely*. Cambridge: MIT Press.
Virno, Paolo. (2004). *A Grammar of the Multitude*. Trans. Isabella Bertoletti, James Cascaito, Andrea Casson. New York: Semiotexte.
Virno, Paolo. (2015). *Déjà Vu and the End of History*. Trans. David Broder. London: Verso.
Virno, Paolo and Hardt, Michael. Eds. (2008). *Radical Thought in Italy: A Potential Politics*. University of Minnesota Press.
Wallerstein, Immanuel. (1983/2011). *Historical Capitalism*. London: Verso.
Wark, McKenzie (2019). *Capital is Dead. Is this Something Worse?* London: Verso.
Watkinson, Philip. (2018). 'Staging Money: Theatre and Immateriality following the 2008 Financial Crisis', *Theatre Journal*, vol. 70 (2018), pp. 195–208.
Weber, Max. (2001). *The Protestant Ethic and the Spirit of Capitalism*. Trans. Talcott Parsons. London: Routledge.
Weibel, Peter. Ed. (2013). *Global Activism: Art and Conflict in the 20th Century*. Cambridge: ZKM/MIT.
Wickstrom, Maurya. (2012). *Performance in the Blockades of Neoliberalism*. Houndmills: Palgrave.
Wickstrom, Maurya. (2018). *Fiery Temporalities in Theatre and Performance: The Initiation of History*. London: Bloomsbury.
Williams, Raymond. (1980). *Problems in Materialism and Culture*. London: Verso.
Wills, David. (2008). *Dorsality: Thinking Back through Technology and Politics*. Minneapolis: University of Minnesota Press.
Yates, Richard. (2006). *Revolutionary Road*. London: Faber.
Ypi, Lea (2014). *Global Justice and Avant Garde Political Agency*. Oxford: Oxford University Press.
Zuboff, Shoshana. (2016). *The Age of Surveillance Capitalism: The Fight for a Human Future at the New Frontier of Power*. London: Profile.

INDEX

absentee landlords 287
abuses 1, 75, 79, 132, 161, 174, 245; human 173; interpretive 211; systemic 45
ACME 11, 109
'acoustic shock' 227, 230–1, 239, 241–3, 247, 249, 252, 256–7, 266
action groups 273, 279, 282–4, 286, 304
activists 283–4, 288
actors 153, 155, 165–6, 189–90, 193; and claims of simulation 180; and language 191; and performances 165, 189; 'with talent for controlling the diaphragm in ways others cannot' 191
Agamben, Giorgio 23, 51, 189, 192
agencies 10, 38, 40, 76, 110, 191, 230, 279, 281, 290; human 207; internet 95; political 39–40, 52
Airhead: The Imperfect Art of Making News 268–9, 271
'Alice in Candyland' 50
allotments 208, 215, 217, 221
Alston, Philip 74–5
'Alternative fur Deutschland' 89
Althusser, Louis 30, 206–7, 220–1
An American Family 68–9
ancestors 144–5
anthropocene 35–7, 207, 213
anti-theatrical prejudice 34, 206, 297
apartments 10, 42, 50–1, 114–15, 132, 134–8, 141, 145, 294; effected 134–5; expensive 45; glasshouse 129; luxury 41, 140; modern 143
aquaculture, sustainable 86

Aquinas, Thomas 211
archaeological work 220
architecture 62, 128, 143–4, 146–7, 316, 319; critics 295; domestic 144; modernist 146; role played through post-Corbusier modern history 143
Arendt, Hannah 205, 235
armies 30, 34, 202
Arnell, James 137–9
art galleries 133–4
Artangel (arts organisation) 121–3, 302
artists 27–8, 38, 40, 91, 96, 119–20, 122, 124, 178, 180, 182, 214, 216, 229–31, 304; artisanal 18; Beryl Robinson 148, 301, 305; big-ticket 39; distressed 13; favourite theatre 110; Gregor Schneider 122–3, 127, 129, 135, 172; Josef Beuys 178, 180; Khadija Saye 296
arts 35, 38, 84, 86, 143–4, 230, 233, 236, 246, 254, 258, 295, 297, 312, 315–20; financial 163; government-funded 5; institutions 258; live 84, 96, 259; visual 164
Arts Council of England 201
ashes 1, 53, 268, 273–4, 278, 289, 305
Assange, Julian 126, 270
assembly 183, 199, 202–9, 211–12, 214, 219–20, 224, 313; domestic 208; political 209; riots 23; unpredictable 205
Attenborough, David 200
audience 27–8, 60–3, 65–7, 69, 85–7, 89–95, 160–1, 171–2, 174–5, 202–3, 230, 235, 241, 260–1, 304; assembled 160; consumption 176;

audience *continued*
  enfranchised 120; eruption of 10, 62, 70, 88, 94, 98; global 64; members 115, 160, 162, 165, 261
Auslander, Philip 84, 249
Avignon 89, 171, 173, 176–7, 180, 185

Bachelard, Gaston 12, 127
Back Streets of Bermondsey 6
backdrops 12, 84, 103
Baker, Bobby 109–10, 112, 118–19, 124, 141, 231, 302
Baker vs. Quantum Clothing Group Ltd 2011 (Nottingham textile workers) 231
Bankside power station 137
Barbican Theatre 61, 160
Bataille, Georges 183, 303
Battersea Arts Centre 20, 260–2, 267, 272–3, 289, 303–4
Baudrillard, Jean 70, 206
BBC 68, 85, 147, 269, 297
Belarus Free Theatre 154
Belfort, Jordan 160–2
Benjamin, Walter 2, 12, 34, 84, 118, 145, 205, 220, 289
Berlin 53, 89, 110, 112–13, 115, 128, 145, 177, 315–16
Berlin Opera House 118
Berlioz, Hector 185–6
Bermondsey 6, 22, 31–2, 159, 290
Beswick, Katie 200, 302
Beuys, Josef 178, 180
Big Brother 63, 66–8, 77, 88
Bird, Jon 13, 155
Bishop, Claire 37, 122
Blair, Tony 72, 286
Blake, Daniel 75–6
Bloch, Ernst 96, 129
bodies 18, 30, 32, 71, 73, 91, 154–5, 165–6, 168, 185, 187, 190, 204–5, 207, 240; 'black bag' 127; female 167; human 207; lab-coated 109; laboring 207; masculine 117; political 207; prostrate 190; vulnerable 207
botanists 208, 210
bourgeois 99, 114–15, 129, 133, 141; beliefs 98; fear 128; freestanding 132; historic 142
bourgeois stage-setting 120
Bradbury, Ray 67, 103, 145
Brett Bailey, Christopher 227–30, 255, 261–2, 267, 290–3; 303
Brexit negotiations 75
Britain 63, 67, 72, 85, 130, 258, 286, 290, 313; estate agencies 43; people of 208; twenty-first-century 77; values of 75

Broughton, John 293, 295
Brown, Gordon 47
Brussels 53, 175, 185–6, 192
Brussels Opera House 184, 187, 191
buildings 42–4, 131–4, 137, 140, 160–1, 172, 248, 270, 272, 277, 280, 283, 285, 287, 289; costs of 13, 241; empty 285; green 86; private bank 137; public house 294; regulations 285; residential 50, 286
business 2, 7, 22, 44–5, 47–8, 119, 132, 223, 245, 250; daily court 47; model of show-business 242, 259; real-estate 46
Butler, Erik 204–8
Butler, Judith 4, 205–8, 221

caesura 189, 205, 218
Caillois, Roger 116–17, 129, 194
Cambridge Analytica 94
cameras 66, 145, 147, 187–8, 192
Cameron, David 282
camps 13–14, 22–3, 37, 50, 203, 221, 245
Canary Wharf 11, 16
Candy, Chris 43, 45, 49, 130, 242
Candy, Nick 43–4, 46–8, 51, 130
canonical work 113, 241
capacity 16, 40, 54, 73, 111, 164, 181, 189, 212, 220, 250, 252, 254–5; defensive 116; human 191, 251; infrastructural 204; special 17
capital 2–3, 11–12, 14–16, 20, 22, 36, 63, 71, 75, 99, 101–2, 111, 115, 123–4, 312; accumulation 15, 37; critical 163; global 154, 288; inflows 29
capitalism 7, 15–16, 26, 30, 35–6, 65–6, 79–80, 99, 101–3, 123, 129, 138, 155, 161, 163; competitive 52; contemporary 165; global 14; historical 15, 36; late 315; surveillance 51, 64, 70–1, 94–6, 143, 204, 302
capitalist 16, 65, 78, 111, 292; accumulation 71, 138; culture-class 49; development 209; enterprise 16, 238, 258; expansionism 209, 223; instability 66; markets 7, 251; modes of production 3, 157, 271; society 137, 236
Capitalist Realism 24, 77
'capitalocene' 3, 7, 14–15, 26–7, 29, 35, 37, 44–5, 48, 51–3, 62, 155, 163, 199, 207
Castellucci, Romeo 166–8, 171–2, 174–8, 180, 182, 184–5, 187–9, 194, 227, 232, 303
Cathy Come Home 68
Chaplin, Charlie 32
Chauvet caves 179, 183

Chekhov, Anton 20–1, 162
children 25, 35, 70, 76, 87, 134–5, 141, 147, 174, 185, 215, 247, 259, 275; 'adulterised labouring' (Dickens) 259; starving 200; unborn 48, 50; and work 70, 147; young 73, 141
Churchill, Caryl 159, 161, 200
Cinders 273–5, 280, 289, 305, 314
claimants 49, 51, 132, 234, 238–43, 247, 251–4, 257, 260; and the Appeal Court 257; and compensation 247; and the disappearance of hearing 249; and the law 132, 231, 257; and the Royal Opera House 245
claims 5–6, 19–20, 45, 83, 99, 133, 140, 236–7, 239–41, 247, 249, 252, 256–7, 278, 281; common 251; compensatory 253; contentious 279; ethical 275; insurance 256; legal 223, 239; orchestral 252; political 239
classes 51, 60, 71, 128, 131, 161, 227; and the 'culture-class' 61; and identity 52; and the performatariat 77; political 275
classrooms 220, 275–6
clients 13, 24, 37, 43, 45, 133, 139, 254, 296
climate change 36, 207, 209
coercive powers 80
Coleman, Nick 247
Coles, Melanie 275–7, 282
colleges 41, 270, 292
Colomina, Beatriz 143–4, 146
Come Dine With Me 63, 66–7
commitments 11, 26, 38, 41, 50, 52, 93, 100, 113, 140, 201, 222, 227, 302; cultural 11, 42; lifetime 22; theatrical 35, 54
Common Law 132–3, 252
communism 81
community 30, 34, 40, 63, 66, 74–5, 92, 96, 98–103, 130–1, 182–3, 215, 281–2, 291, 296; academic 303; dockland 11, 293; gated 203; interventions 121; local 25, 39, 137; mining 64; northern 75; political 100; post-industrial 18; post-working-class 40
community arts 37, 70
community theatre 29, 53
compensation 1–3, 7, 246–8, 253, 257, 301
concentration camps 245
Condell, Henry 155
Constantius, Constantine 110, 112–19, 124, 128–9, 145–6
contracts 21, 44, 48, 96, 168, 266; economic 13; and property 21; and the theatre 265

controversy 232, 269
Coogan, Steve 90
Costello, Elvis 240
costs 7, 43, 61, 81, 114, 116, 130, 137, 157, 162–3, 165, 214, 220, 248, 256; building 13, 241; personal 72, 249; real-estate 162; transitionary 81
council 35, 51, 132–3, 223, 232, 241, 270, 277, 281–8, 294–5; accommodation 13; housing 284, 287, 290, 293–4, 313; local 39, 41, 270, 275, 281, 283, 286, 293–4; power 286; representatives 284, 286; workers 285, 288
councilors 284, 288
court system 252
courtrooms 45, 47–9, 52, 129, 132–4, 136, 143, 231, 247, 254
courts of law 44–6, 48–51, 120, 129–34, 136, 139–41, 144, 147, 231, 234–8, 240–2, 244, 246–7, 249–53, 256–7
Covent Garden 241, 248, 258, 266, 292
Covid-19 (Coronavirus) *see* 'The Loss Adjustor' for collateral damage wrought by the Capitalocene 1–8
Cowell, Simon 91
Creed, Martin 134
crime scenes 50–1, 53, 74, 83, 121, 145, 147
Critcher, Teresa 304
Critical Inquiry 205
critiques 20, 65, 78–80, 99–100, 110, 188, 233, 317; cultural 45; Marx 99; partisan 82
Crouch, Tim 230
cruelties 5, 61, 245, 248, 254, 256, 271, 278; *see also* cultural cruelty
cultural artefacts 39, 193
cultural conventions 66
cultural cruelty 5, 227, 229, 231, 233, 235, 237, 239, 241–3, 245–51, 253–7, 259, 261, 269, 272
cultural expressions 62, 77
cultural theory 18, 27, 64
culture 9, 19, 29, 48, 61, 66, 75, 82, 85, 95, 198, 201, 203, 245, 254; capitalist 65; destination 61, 316; inclusive 199; museum 143–4; political 190; subordinate 13
culture-class 60–2, 77, 87, 139, 199, 243
The Culture Industry 66

Daffarn, Edward 283
damages 1–2, 232, 236–7, 239, 241–2, 244–8, 250–3, 255–7, 260; cerebral 185; claiming of 244; collateral 1, 12, 54, 97; intermittent bomb 30; payment of 247

Dante Alighieri 171–3, 176, 185–6, 193
Dark Theatre 3, 5–6, 9, 11, 13, 41, 43, 49–51, 53–4, 89–90, 94–5, 129–30, 163–4, 198, 210–12; bankrupted 90; expulsion 15, 53; performances 29, 50; poor 50; and social media 142
Davies, Justice Nicola 234, 236, 242–3, 253, 256
de Balzac, Honore 159
de Certeau, Michel 42, 86, 266–7, 271, 289, 314
de Sade, Marquis 164, 167, 254
Dean, Jodi 97–8, 314
death 23, 43, 121, 155, 186, 193–4, 200, 212, 216, 221, 229, 259, 265–6, 268–9, 273; human 212; living 192; moment of 212; unexpected 47
The Death and Life of Great American Cities 12
death camps 187
debt 16, 18, 29, 31, 39, 49, 68, 102, 118, 155, 162–3, 165–6, 192, 301–2, 304; collectors 49; consumer 18; creation 49; institutes 29; logic of 49; political 28; special 36
decapitation 176
defence 132, 134, 144, 232, 236, 239, 241, 243, 246–7, 252, 254, 256, 266, 276, 281; altruistic 37; capability 116; claimant's 241; council 240–1; first 99; lawyers 141; mechanism 116; portfolio 132; teams 240, 248, 253, 304
Defoe, Daniel 75
Degas, Edgar 110, 118, 153–7
Deleuze, Gilles 66, 164, 166, 314
Delgado, Maria 303
Derrida, Jacques 102, 206, 273–5, 277, 280–1, 289, 305
developers 13, 16, 24, 50, 135, 137–8, 145, 217, 291, 295; Grosvenor Estates 34; housing 290; real-estate 43
Dickens, Charles 133, 259
dictatorship 60, 62–3, 70, 72, 74, 77–84, 95, 99, 101–3, 219, 233, 302; 'of choice' 66; historical 81; proletarian 79; revolutionary 78, 94
Diderot, Denis 190–1
Die Familie Schneider 122, 124–5, 128–9, 145, 173, 302
Die Walküre 234–5, 237–8, 241, 254
'Digital Welfare State' 76
directors 21, 131, 171–3, 175–7, 194, 215, 261
disempowerment 15, 18, 52, 66, 292; gratuitous 15; local 18; pervasive 52

displacement 16, 19, 23, 84, 119, 216; economic 24; performance 191
docklands 12, 14, 18, 22–3, 25, 27, 61, 64, 83, 89–90, 100, 271–2, 287, 290–1, 295; area 10, 21; brown-field 290; capitalised 21; community 19, 21, 36, 293; historic 21; land wars 23; landscape 16, 43; local 291; neighbourhood 27, 65; theatre 60; urban heritage 13; wharf buildings 198
docks 16, 29, 34–6, 51, 291
Dolan, Jill 79, 81, 96
Dragset, Ingar 118–20, 144
Dunn, Peter 11–12
dynamics 36, 49, 53, 79, 86, 99, 159; and the contestation between competitive capitalism and socialism 52; political-theological 71; populist 97

East London 2, 63, 109, 121–2
economics 5, 19, 76, 164, 265; concentrated 99; depression 121; stability 291; uber-accelerated 51
economy 5, 13, 38, 50, 52, 111, 114, 116, 124–5, 156, 163–5, 250, 253, 284, 288; capitalist 15; communist 16; domestic 120; of exchange 254–5; financial 165; monetary 165; of performance 52, 116, 182; and the post-OPEC oil-crisis 32
Église des Célestins 176
El-Enany, Nadine 267–8, 271
employees 34, 85, 241, 243
employers 29, 34, 139, 165, 242, 244
employment 29–30, 38, 67, 75–6, 93
empowerment 53, 91, 313
An Enemy of the People 159
Engels, Friedrich 79–81
"English Garden" effect 214–15, 304
English law 44, 133
environment 19, 35, 53, 62, 115, 117–20, 166, 198, 217, 219, 254; activists 201; economic 293; natural 14
eruption 60–1, 63, 67–9, 71, 73, 75, 77, 79, 81, 83, 85, 87, 89, 91, 93; analogue 65; of the audience 10, 62, 70, 88, 94, 98; eclectic 64
essays 92, 123, 164, 202, 204, 219, 254, 285, 294, 302
estate 5, 11, 14, 21, 34, 37, 43–6, 48, 130, 138, 159, 162, 286–7, 292, 294–5; agents 11; and council housing 287, 292–3; inland 11; public-housing 130
Estates Gazette 46, 48
Europe 15, 72, 75, 87, 89, 175, 210, 245; banking elite 75; colonialism 268; continental 183; touring 161; twentieth

century arts work 69; *see also* Western Europe
evidence 23, 28, 48, 50, 76, 132, 135–6, 144, 183, 258, 272, 279–80, 282, 284, 288–9; admissible 46; claimant's 236; collateral 51; concrete 80; email 45; expert 279
exchanges 46–8, 90, 135, 139, 141, 165–6, 193, 246, 254–5; bitter 46; complaint 284; corporeal human 166; economic 253; online 25; reciprocal 166
experience 61, 63, 113, 116, 153–4, 156, 174, 176, 181–2, 219–20, 230–1, 241, 247, 249, 255; abstract 246; childhood 126, 228; common 179; domestic 116; historical 179; neoliberal 290; psycho-political 109; shared 219
expulsion 11, 14, 19–20, 22, 29–30, 38, 49, 52–3, 61, 74, 199, 259, 271–2, 292–3; aesthetic 28; anxiety of 122; local housing 19; logic of 9, 14, 18–19, 54, 80, 83, 246; neighbourhood resisting 27; radical 14, 52
Extinction Rebellion 26, 63, 201, 220

factories 29–30, 32, 34, 38–9, 60, 110, 233
Faith Hope and Charity 160
false memory syndrome 61, 180
fantasy 79, 85, 97, 99, 169, 207, 278
Farocki, Harun 34, 39
Fearn, Claire 141–2
Federici, Silvia 111, 123, 137, 208–10, 219–20, 223
female residents 130, 147
female workers 165, 231
First World War 2, 5, 30
Fisher, Mark 3, 16, 27, 65–6, 69, 77, 126, 302
For a Left Populism 81–2, 90
Foucault, Michel 70, 164
Frean, George 29–30
Friel, Brian 24–5
Fry Law Solicitors 231, 304

The Game 159
ghosting 28, 42, 192, 250
Gibbons, Scott 173, 175–7
Gilroy, Paul 271, 304
global capital 154, 288
global markets 17, 21, 51
Gluck, Christoph Willibald 185–6
Goldscheider, Chris 231, 234–44, 246–61, 304
Gramsci, Antonio 70–1, 123, 205, 233

Grenfell Tower 40, 53, 74–5, 251, 265, 268–9, 271, 273–7, 280, 282–3, 285–6, 288–9, 293–7, 304
Grenfell Tower Inquiry 139, 269–72, 274–5, 278–83, 286, 288–9, 292–7, 313
Guattari, Félix 203, 211

Han, Byung-Chul 33, 62, 65, 70, 101–2, 315
Hardt, Michael 311, 317
Harraway, Donna 198, 207
health 22, 127, 153, 236, 242–3, 245, 256–7, 261, 272, 284; mental 23, 85, 110, 273; public 71; regulations 239; risks 293; statutory 243
Herzog and de Meuron (Swiss architects) 39, 130–1, 139
High Court, London 134, 143, 159, 228, 230, 236–8, 240, 246, 256–7, 302
historians 124, 266, 291; cultural 3; poor 267; of science 209
history 5, 7, 11, 15–16, 42–3, 45, 69, 181, 183–4, 219–20, 266–8, 289, 292, 301, 304; analogue 63; barbarous 74, 244; colonial 268; cultural 272; intervening 79; legal 143; local 25; modern 143; natural 35, 250; political 47; social 44
Hitchcock, Alfred 126, 145
Hobbes, Thomas 22
Hoffman, Dustin 255
Holyoake, Mark 43–6, 48–9, 51, 159, 254
Home Office 75, 272
hospitals 49, 66, 147, 179, 185–7, 190, 194
'household performance' 118
households 68, 114, 116, 120–1; conflict-ridden 120; private 114; working-class 68
houses 21, 60, 77, 94, 116, 120–2, 125–9, 142, 144–6, 174–5, 208, 216, 259, 277; dilapidated 130; domestic 119; guest 128; inhabited 127; private 144; terraced 121, 141
housework 111, 123
housing 22, 39, 86, 138, 293; estates 286; social 14, 287–8, 293–4
Hugo, Victor 72
Huizinga, Johan 182
The Human Condition 205
human rights 27, 74–5, 88, 93, 142, 258, 311
human slavery 184, 268
human venue 154, 159, 164, 168, 182, 187, 192–4, 199, 202, 215, 249, 303
humanists 36, 116, 183, 208, 211, 213
humanity 36, 51, 183, 296, 312

humans 16, 23, 116–17, 125, 128, 165, 179, 183–4, 190, 213, 217–18, 223, 240, 247, 249–50; productive 255; and society 222; stewardship 213; talented 139

Ibsen, Henrik 159
identity 51–3, 90, 98–9, 116, 132, 143, 157, 167, 171, 183, 205, 216, 221, 289, 291; and classes 52; existential 145; integrated 212; legitimate 245; pluralistic 100; political 19, 89, 97–8
Ideological State Apparatuses of the 1970s 220
images 29, 31, 73, 91, 133, 138, 142–4, 147, 180, 183, 187, 200, 273, 278, 280; digital 87; engineering 155; fake 92; Instagram 133; pictorial 143; plagiarised 91; projected 297; stolen 144; sublime panoramic 148; televisual 85; video 186
imaginary, economic 156
'Immersive Capitalism' 163
impulses 166–8, 184, 188, 230; communitarian 67; contradictory 103; political pragmatic 17
Industrial Buildings Preservation Trust 42
industrial production 165
Inferno 171–6, 180, 280
injuries 2, 147–8, 232, 234, 237, 241, 243, 245, 247, 252–3, 256, 258, 284
injustice 5, 7, 51, 72, 80, 163, 216, 223, 248, 251, 272, 282, 289
Instagram images 133
Institute of Contemporary Arts, London 61, 122, 131, 136, 166, 202, 303, 305
institutional racism 256
institutions 39, 83, 85, 133–4, 136, 140, 143, 223, 230, 232, 236–7, 243–6, 249–50, 258, 260; arts 258; cultural 141, 245, 256; financial 290; freedom-restoring 80; neighbourhood 10; platformed 222; public 146; social 258
insurance claims 256
iPhone 87, 142–3

Jameson, Fredric 16, 64–5, 302
Johnson, Boris 82, 201
Joint Docklands Action Group 11
Jones, Inigo 71–2
Joseph, Miranda 96, 99–102, 206
journalism 270, 278
Jubb, David 261, 267
judges 87, 133–6, 139–41, 240, 248, 252, 255, 257, 270; Justice Mann 39, 131, 143; Justice Nicola Davies 234, 236, 242–3, 253, 256; Justice Nugee 43, 45–6

justice 43–4, 48, 52, 79, 86, 223–4, 231, 235–6, 244, 246–7, 250–1, 258–60; and courtrooms 247; interests of 3, 269; and the Royal Courts of Justice 43–4, 231, 235–6, 247, 250–1, 258–60; social 38

Katz, Marc 112–15, 316
Keays, Sarah 24–5
Kelleher, Joe 20, 167, 186, 303
Kelly, Mary 38–9
Kennedy, Joe 5, 14
Kensington and Chelsea Council 288
Kensington and Chelsea Tenant Management Organisation 277
Keynesian economics 90
Kierkegaard, Søren 110, 112, 114–16, 118, 128–9, 145, 184, 260, 316
King Lear 4, 153–7, 164, 319
Klossowski, Pierre 131, 164–8, 254, 303
knowledge 17, 52, 95, 115, 126, 181, 210, 230–1, 272, 280; long-lost 199; new 94
Konigstadter Theatre 110, 113–15, 118, 125, 146

La Faillite 159
la Ramblas (Barcelona) 60–1
labour 20, 38–9, 111, 123–4, 184, 188, 201, 203–4, 207–8, 215, 217, 232–3, 236, 250, 254; cheap 258; concealed 111; corporeal 31, 38; human 124; immaterial 233, 236, 244; markets 233; productive 236; unions 54, 63; values 30, 235; wages 236
Lacan, Jacques 115, 146, 316
land 19–22, 27, 35–6, 90, 131, 138, 186, 199, 216–18, 220, 223, 271, 287, 290–3, 303; accessible 290; grabbing 19, 53; local 292; plots of 53, 209; privatisation 90, 291; public 289–90, 293, 313; reclaimed 24; shared 292
land-hoarding, private-sector 290
landlords 152, 283, 287
landscape 29, 35, 37, 109, 198–9, 215–17, 289, 291, 293, 295, 304; brackish 218; cosmopolitan 75; dockland 36; fiscal 152; permeable 119; threatened 218
Landy, John 121
Landy, Michael 124
language 5, 91, 136, 180, 191, 193, 200, 209, 212, 217–18, 228, 235, 237, 244, 257; arresting 217–18; common 233; everyday 155; expansionist 218; lyrical 33; natural 155; theory 209; universal 155
Latour, Bruno 27, 141

Lauzon, Claudette 119, 122
law 45–6, 48–9, 130–3, 142, 147, 176, 212, 219, 231–3, 237, 240–2, 244, 251–4, 256–7, 261; and claimants 231, 257; new 21; ordinary 22–3; and responsibility 243, 253, 257
lay community 38, 66, 103
lay theatres 9, 28, 62, 64–5, 74, 87, 94, 97
'Lazarus Affect' 188–9
Le Corbusier 142, 144–5
Leeson, Lorraine 11–12
legal 19, 23, 46, 48, 51, 129–30, 132–4, 136–7, 141–3, 217–18, 230–1, 234, 253–4, 257–9, 274; claims 223, 239; process 239; teams 46, 48, 234, 240; transparency 48
Lenin, Vladimir 79, 99, 123
Les Misérables 71–2
liberal democracy 82
libraries 61, 76, 118, 219–20, 250
listeners 178, 236–7
litigation 130, 237
'living currency' 18, 71, 131, 163–6, 168, 173, 184, 186, 303
Loach, Kenneth 68, 76
loans 14, 47, 49–50
London 11, 18–21, 38–9, 49–50, 60–1, 135, 201–2, 205, 209–10, 258, 266–8, 280–1, 287–8, 291, 302–4; hospitals 147; housing crisis 295; transforming of 291; workplaces 136
London Development Corporation 42
London Docklands 6, 61, 291
London Docklands Development Corporation 11, 24, 37, 53, 290–1
London Eye 131, 137
London International Festival of Theatre 109
London Metropolitan Police 280
London Review of Books 274, 279, 282, 287–8
London Underground Network 212
Loos, Adolf 145–6
Lost Gardens 214–15, 217–18, 303–4
Love Island 63, 67
LRB see *London Review of Books*
luxury residences 41, 50, 140
Lyotard, Jean-François 119, 164, 166

Maitlis, Emily 271, 274, 285, 295
Mann, Justice 39, 131, 143
Mann, Thomas 260
Marder, Michael 211–14, 222, 271, 273, 303
markets 7, 17–19, 53, 85, 157, 216, 251, 292; capitalist 7, 251; free 90; global 17, 21, 51; labour 233; television 64
Martin, Randy 17–19, 29, 65, 163, 311
Marx, Karl 20, 63, 77–81, 110–12, 128, 157, 163, 165, 182, 203, 235–7, 271
Marxism and Philosophy 78
Massey, Doreen 17, 119
Massumi, Brian 202, 314
Matta-Clark, Gordon 121
McKellen, Ian 181
media 10, 35, 71, 86–8, 91, 96–8, 100, 142–6, 188, 207; communications 85; conflicts 84; dystopians 85; international 63; mainstream 297; modern 144
memories 24, 41, 115, 120, 126, 166, 180, 184, 228, 251, 276, 312; conflicted 6; earliest 228; faculties of 179
mental health 23, 85, 110, 273
Merkel, Angela 89
miners 64–5, 292
Minton, Anna 287–8
Mobile Homestead 121
model 23, 37, 39, 42, 82, 114, 144, 166, 203, 205, 284, 291; agricultural 21; anarchist 81; business 242, 259; Quantum machinic 232
Modern Architecture 142, 144, 314
Modern Times 32
modes 7, 23, 25, 36, 77, 79, 95, 115, 179, 201, 209, 219, 224, 244, 259; activist 40; capitalist 3, 157, 271; energy-saving 94; microeconomic 66, 291; transitionary 79
Mondzain, Marie-José 182
money 16, 36, 45, 49, 126, 134, 159, 162, 165, 241, 250, 256, 287, 291, 296
mono-culturalism 89
Moore, Jason 15, 27, 36–7
Moore, Thomas 81
Moore-Bick, Sir Martin 281
morals 244, 246
Morgan, Piers 90–2
Morris, Frances 39, 130, 138–41, 302
Mouffe, Chantal 81–3, 89–90, 206, 284
mourning 1–4
Museum of Modern Art, New York 136–7, 144–5
museums 39, 145, 250, 253; contemporary 143; as a function of modern media 144
music 60, 177, 185–6, 191, 202, 216, 228, 232, 239, 241, 254, 314; brass 240; industry 242; orchestral 245, 250, 255; venues 241
musicians 186, 231, 236–8, 241–3, 245, 248, 250, 252; human 240; orchestral 234; second-string 239

Musicians' Union 237, 239

Nancy, Jean-Luc 183
National Art Library, London 90
National Health Service 88
National Theatre, London 28, 41, 77, 95, 160
Native Land Development Company 133, 137–8
naturalism 67, 120, 173–4, 177
nature 9, 11, 20–1, 35–6, 38, 115, 133, 183, 189–90, 198, 203–4, 208, 210, 219, 235; altruistic 222; changing 218; cheap 29, 35–6, 51, 199, 223; decentred 213; exterminist 50; extra-human 36; global 265; historical 36; public 274; scientific 190
neighbourhood 2, 13–14, 16–17, 29–30, 37–8, 40–1, 43, 267, 269, 272, 284, 286, 290, 292, 294; declining docklands 29; gentrifying 131; institutions 10; local 22, 43, 140; participants 40; proud 12; white working-class 61
neighbours 13, 37, 85, 95, 137, 139–40, 166, 215, 218, 270, 275, 279, 290, 297, 304; anonymous 279; good 140; new 134; recitative-inclined 61; repetitive 121
Neo Bankside residents 49, 129–33, 137–8, 140–2, 144–7, 175
neoliberalism 37, 49, 62, 70, 78, 89, 291, 315, 320
Nestroy, Johann 112–13
New Left Review 64
New York 125, 203, 205
New Yorker 270
newspapers 91, 94
Niquet, Hervé 186–7
nudity 91, 93
Nugee, Justice 43, 45–6

O'Hagan, Andrew 126, 136, 269–70, 274–89, 294, 297, 304; leans on the scholarship of Anna Minton 287; prose 286; works of 288
oikonomia 111, 114–15, 119
oikos 112, 116, 119–20, 128
O'Mara, John 130, 138–9
online responsiveness 82, 84, 92, 94, 276
ontology 118, 192, 205, 244, 246, 248, 318; of the event 241; of performance 235
opera 185–8, 192, 232–3, 240, 248
opera houses 185, 187, 190, 234, 240, 242, 248, 253, 258; Berlin Opera House 118;
Brussels Opera House 184, 187, 191; closures of 241; opulence of 245; Royal Opera House 231–2, 234–43, 245–8, 250, 252–4, 256–61; Sydney Opera House 248; Vienna Opera House 88
Ophir, Adi 7, 193–4, 199–200, 202, 244–6, 248–52, 255, 301
orchestra pit 242, 244, 248, 253
orchestral music 245, 250, 255
orchestral players 235, 238–40
orchestras 114, 119, 186–7, 192, 234, 238, 240–2, 244–5, 254
Orpheus and Eurydice 168, 184–7, 190–1
Oval House, London 227–30, 234, 245, 262

paintings 118–19, 143–4, 202, 296
Palace Theatre 267
Palais des Papes 171–2, 174, 193
paradise 173, 176–7, 214
Parc des Expositions (Chateaublanc) 173, 175
Parker, Cornelia 122, 241, 247, 252
Parkinson, Cecil 24–5
party politics 24
pathologies 14, 26, 75, 116, 179, 252; borderline 63; male 116; of performance 122; of services 116
Pech Merle caves 179
Peek Frean Factory 13, 30–4, 38
penthouses 49, 137–8
people 77–8, 82–3, 87, 93–4, 175–6, 213, 215, 217, 236, 275–7, 280, 284–5, 287–8, 292, 296; business 130; impaired 260; like-minded 134; professional 242; racialised 267, 271; young 96, 156
'People's Armada' 12
performance 2–4, 16–20, 24–9, 50–4, 81–4, 112–16, 120–2, 165–6, 179–80, 182–5, 188–9, 191–3, 205–9, 211–14, 314–20; abstract 192; art 237, 255; capacities 216; compensations of 171; contemporary 81; ethics of 244, 260, 319; histories 206; humanist 6; linguistic-communicative 237; loss-making 3; participatory 64, 131; partisan 82; peak 82; politics of 3, 54, 193; practices 206; research outcomes 73; staged 167
Performance Foundation (Somerset House) 72, 209, 304
performatariat 62, 70–4, 77, 82–9, 91, 94–8, 103, 119, 144, 219, 233; consciousness 94; cultural 90; mediatised 86; parallels 96; stars 94; transitions 83

phantasmic states 167, 175
'phantasms' 83, 166–8, 173, 175
Phelan, Peggy 2–3, 84, 118, 205, 235, 248–9, 260
philosophers 22, 164, 167, 188, 199, 209, 212; mental state of 167; twentieth-century arrondissement 206
philosophy 89, 211
'phyto-performance' 207–9, 304
Plato 182–3, 206, 211, 297
Platt, David 241–2, 247
The Player's Passion 190–1
Playground Theatre 295
The Poetics of Space 12
poetry 67–8, 177, 202
political action 205, 233, 235, 238
political claims 239
political economy 19, 164, 291, 317
political philosophy 27
political scientists 28, 79
politicians 40, 139, 156, 211, 272; female 28; improvised 95; local 288; right-wing devout Christian 97
politics 5–6, 10, 16, 19, 23, 27–8, 77, 79, 81–2, 88, 98–9, 164, 207, 268, 291–2; civic 96; cultural 51; feminist 209; neoliberal 49; partisan 82; party 24; socialist 15, 64; statist 40
'poor history' 7, 267–9, 274, 278–9, 281, 289, 292
populism 64, 87–8, 90, 94, 97
populist forces 87, 89
populists 82, 88, 144
post-pandemic/pre-pandemic: *see* The Dark Theatre as symptomatic of inter-pandemic writing 1–320
poverty 34, 75–7
power 25–6, 29, 70, 94, 96, 143–4, 181, 205, 209–10, 212, 219–22, 284, 286, 290, 292; administrative 5; allied (of state and church) 210; cultural 276; entrenched 82; local authority 293; monarchical 72; nationalist 5; pre-emptive 210; primordial 174
practices 14, 16, 37–8, 40, 69–70, 83, 85, 98–100, 139–40, 204, 206, 208–10, 222, 267–8, 271; abandoned 38, 167, 199, 204, 208–9; communitarian 37; excised arts 193; institutionalised 271; plant 222; theatrical 10, 83, 165, 228; vegetal 210
prejudices 33, 115, 267; anti-theatrical 34, 206, 297; writing of 267
presumptions 10, 23, 26–7, 35, 73, 90, 95, 109, 125, 176, 180, 186, 205, 208, 210;

collaborative 244; common 245; political 130; separatist 28; state-sanctioned 271
privacy 95, 103, 116, 128–9, 131–4, 136, 141–2, 184, 258, 297, 314; increasing 137; laws 130; and publicity 141–2, 314; traditional sense of 143
private partnerships 294–5
private-sector land-hoarding 290
privatisation 18, 131, 286, 290–1, 294
privilege 9, 72, 117, 141, 191, 193, 252, 276, 278
processes 15–16, 18, 34, 36, 70–1, 73, 111–12, 117, 119, 124, 138, 209–10, 212–13, 217–18, 290–1; appeals 257; applications 76; democratic 288; historiographical 267; improper performative 217; industrial 32, 232; legal 143, 253, 258, 272; political 288; productive 237; refurbishment 283
production 28, 30–1, 77–8, 87, 175, 177–8, 180–1, 184, 186–8, 190, 231–3, 235, 244–5, 248, 250; cultural 193; global 265; intellectual 233; lines 31–2, 39; operatic 233; processes 32; valedictory 184
programmes 78, 132, 143, 172, 177, 184, 186, 202, 230, 267; house-building 295; land privatisation 291; political 210
projects 10, 33, 38, 64–5, 71, 96, 99, 120, 122, 208, 210, 213, 217, 293, 301; Artangel 121; artist-led 11; long-term workshop 19; Umpfenbach 215
proletariat 63, 70–1, 77–80, 89, 99, 101, 233, 302
protests 25, 190, 205, 218, 238
psycho-politics 23, 62, 65, 70, 78, 315
public housing 13, 67, 90, 271, 280, 286, 289, 293
public inquiries 276, 278, 280
public land ownership 290
publicity 130, 132, 141–4, 314; human 147; machine 72; profiles 273

Queen Mary University of London 201
Queen's Theatre, London 72

race 52, 62, 101, 111, 268, 272, 315
racism 210, 256
Rancière, Jacques 27, 81, 120, 166, 190, 206, 239
real-estate development 11, 14, 44
Reality TV 66–7
refurbishment 277, 280, 294
Rendall, Steven 313–14

repetition 10, 110, 112, 114, 116, 120, 128–30, 146, 167, 173, 180, 316; conference 302; domestic 118; habitual everyday 112; historical 201; therapy 113

representations 2, 39, 73, 77, 82–3, 87, 143, 164, 167, 180, 182–3, 218–19, 249, 255, 260; cultural 70, 88; democratic 95; knowledgeable 245; local 283; political 83, 224; struggle for 13

residents 11, 13, 22, 25, 35, 131, 134–6, 139, 141–3, 145–6, 277–8, 280–1, 284–6, 289–90, 293–4; embattled 29; female 130, 147; Grenfell 269, 272; Neo Bankside 49, 129–33, 137–8, 140–2, 144–7, 175; student 284

response 5, 65, 71, 75, 91, 200–1, 230, 234, 238, 268, 271, 275–6, 282, 285, 313; affective 213; complex 200; critical 304; cultural 5; historical 292; imaginative 278; reasoned 93; sympathetic 136

responsibility 1, 5, 24, 50, 67, 233, 240, 242–3, 252–3, 257–8, 261, 268, 279, 282, 284–6; direct 288; fraught 200; palpable 256; shared 258; social 258

Ride of the Valkyries 232, 234, 239

Ridout, Nicholas 20, 114, 244, 303

risk 18, 45, 129, 207, 228, 234, 242, 249, 265–6, 274, 284, 291–2, 297, 304, 311; exposing 242; health 293; managing 19; potential 123

Roach, Joseph 190–1

Robinson, Beryl 148, 301, 305

Rogers, Richard 45, 147

ROH *see* Royal Opera House

Rotherhithe Theatre Workshop 24–5, 27, 42, 60, 62, 64, 70, 99, 109, 138, 140, 290, 292, 295, 301

Royal Courts of Justice 43–4, 231, 235–6, 247, 250–1, 258–60

Royal Opera House 231–2, 234–50, 252–4, 256–61

Sassen, Saskia 14, 16, 21, 80, 119

Savoy Theatre 266, 289

Schneider, Gregor 122–3, 127, 129, 135, 172

Schneider, Rebecca 118, 249

sculptural work 135

The Sea & Poison 208

seating arrangements 116, 202–4, 240–1

Second World War 5, 30, 89

securities 23, 44, 50–1, 101, 109, 111–12, 133, 139, 169, 224

Sehgal, Tino 137, 147

self-knowledge 183

Serious Money 159, 161

Serota, Nicholas 131, 147

sex work 123, 254

Shakespeare, Steven 304

Shakespeare, William 118, 152–7, 258

Simon, Taryn 1, 3–4

Slater, David 6, 27, 35, 301

slavery 123, 165, 184, 268

social housing 14, 287–8, 293–4

social media 60, 62–3, 67–8, 84, 88, 103, 130, 135, 141–2, 144, 160, 277, 279, 297, 302

social reproduction 67, 110–12, 115, 117–18, 120, 122, 127, 130–1, 137, 142, 209, 219, 244

Socìetas Raffaello Sanzio 171, 173, 194, 227, 303

Soft City 12, 26, 318

South Bank, London 129, 138

South East London 9–10, 16–17, 64, 90

Southwark Council 39, 42–3, 293, 295

sovereignty 71, 73–4, 176

SRS *see* Socìetas Raffaello Sanzio

St Paul's Cathedral 137–8

staging 20–1, 49, 82, 91, 120, 145, 199, 203, 227, 240, 316, 318

stairs 126–7, 161

stalls 156, 160, 236

Stengers, Isabelle 27, 209–10

Strand, London 236, 258–60, 304

subjects 69, 71, 117, 121, 143, 146, 167–8, 180, 183, 191–2, 207–9, 217, 220–1, 274, 277; collective political 82; controversial historical 79; emerging bourgeois-urban 112; modern 129; subjugated 33; unmanageable 191; viewing 114, 146

suffering 41, 116, 167, 207, 229, 237, 242, 244–6, 254–8, 316

Surrey Docks 24–5, 27

surveillance capitalism 51, 64, 70–1, 94–6, 143, 204, 302

sustainable aquaculture 86

Sydney Opera House 248

symmetry 91, 135, 144, 219, 249, 269; homeopathic 172; self-help 273; small 20; uncanny 33

system 3, 15, 19, 34, 45, 75–6, 95, 111, 154, 232–3, 246, 251–2; capitalist 15, 251; economic 3, 7, 35; historical 15; natural 15

The Talisman 112–13

Tate Modern 38–9, 129–47, 152, 175, 222, 302; administration 147; architects 138; collection 135; core mission 140; defence team 132; original building 131; Director Frances Morris 39, 130, 138–9, 141, 302; Director Nicholas Serota 135

Thatcher, Margaret 13, 16, 24, 203–4, 286, 293

theatre 2–7, 9, 13–14, 16–20, 27–9, 40–3, 83–4, 95–6, 112–20, 167–9, 192–4, 198–9, 205–6, 265–8, 311–20; auditorium 116–17; bankruptcies 41; bourgeois 117; box 113, 145–6; classical Athenian 202; 'epochal' 194, 199; mainstream 35; musical 232; political 38, 53, 201, 217, 312; practices 16, 166, 206; representational 153; social 29; workshop 6, 34, 38, 41, 50, 61, 131, 289

Theatre & Everyday Life 9–11, 14, 17, 20, 26–9, 60, 62, 64, 66, 69, 83–7, 110, 193, 198, 265–8

Théâtre de la Monnaie 184–5, 193

Theatre Intimacy & Engagement 190

theatrical 41, 52–4, 82–3, 85–6, 119–20, 159–61, 163–9, 171–2, 176, 180–3, 185–7, 189–90, 193–4, 205–6, 228–9; acts 85, 229; audiences 53; commitments 35, 54; deploying 11; endeavours 83, 168; events 31, 39, 182; performances 190; representations 72, 163

The Three Ecologies 202–3

tourist guides 113–14

transactions 22, 49–50, 254, 290

translations 24–5, 71, 95, 164, 176, 202, 315

translators 165

Truinas (Commune of) 21, 89, 125

Trump, Donald 67, 88, 91, 102, 203–4, 211

tweets 91–3, 102, 201

Twitter 91, 94, 135, 200–1

UK 3–4, 10, 25–6, 63, 66–9, 74–7, 84–5, 88–9, 92–3, 96–7, 121, 258–9, 271–2, 288–90, 293–4; building sites 234; economics 33; Labour politician Tony Blair 47; theatre 28

Umpfenbach, Christine 215, 303

United Kingdom *see* UK

universities 85, 219–20, 233, 292

University College London 292

Urquart, Lindsay 135, 141, 146

value 30, 51, 101, 111, 136, 140, 235–6, 244, 246, 248, 252–3, 283, 287, 312; aesthetic 100; artistic 243; design 11; high land 294; new social 111, 143

Verbatim Theatre 86

vertigo 152–4, 157, 164, 191, 283

victims 4, 50, 242, 244, 285–6; artistic 244; innocent 69; unexceptional 244, 246; young 148

Victoria and Albert Museum, London 118

Vienna Opera House 88

viewing platform 39, 131–5, 137, 139–41, 143–8; episode 143; opening hours 137; public 131–2, 137, 152; vista 136

Virno, Paolo 179, 235, 237–8

virtuosos 235–7

visitors 31, 121–3, 125, 131–2, 134, 139, 147, 214, 260; experiences of 137, 139; gallery 178; new 123; regular 139; unannounced 120

vocabularies 19, 166, 193, 244, 252, 257; non-political 26; political 25

voices 87, 97, 187, 237–8, 274–7, 280, 282, 289, 304; dissenting 282; loud 284; quiet 237; soft 203; working-class 66

Wagner, Richard 232, 238, 240, 254, 258

Wall Street 159–62, 164–6, 168

Wallerstein, Emmanuel 15, 36

warehouses 10, 38, 41, 44, 65; dilapidated 13; disused tobacco 159; industrial 245, 248; riverside 9–10, 64; theatre 30, 40, 64, 162

Warhol, Andy 69, 71, 180

Wark, McKenzie 14, 70, 100–2, 206–7

wealth 15, 38, 60, 75, 111, 136, 157, 238; cultural 130; of people 135–6, 162; private 130; relative 294

West London community 22, 53–4, 98, 229, 265, 267, 270, 272, 285, 294

Western Europe 3, 37, 63–4, 84, 90, 96, 121, 265

Whiteread, Rachel 120–1

Williams, Raymond 35, 211

Wills, David 124–5

witness statements 234

witnesses 1, 10, 22, 44–6, 48, 113, 141, 161, 174, 184, 188, 200–1, 235–7, 266–7, 280–1

witnessing 179, 223, 231, 246, 251

women 29, 31, 35, 38, 48, 67, 76, 92, 111, 232, 318

work 9–10, 26–9, 34–6, 38–41, 51–4, 100–2, 109–13, 121–6, 164–7, 185–93, 202–4, 213–23, 233–8, 292–6, 302–4; compositional 227; curatorial 301; musician's 237

'The Work of Art in the Age of Mechanical Reproduction' 254
workers 111, 123, 229, 232–3, 235, 241–3, 245, 247, 254–6; artist 230; council 285, 288; female 165, 231; low-income 14; male 165; orchestra 243; unemployed ex-dock 14
working classes 63, 131, 185

writers 15, 46, 60, 214, 230, 278–9, 281–2
The Writing of History 42

Yates, Richard 193, 297
Ypi, Lea 40, 79, 81, 302

Zeldin, Alexander 160